REGNUM EDINBURGH 2010 SERIES

Mission and Postmodernities

REGNUM EDINBURGH 2010 SERIES

The Centenary of the World Missionary Conference of 1910, held in Edinburgh, was a crucial moment for many people seeking direction for Christian mission in the twenty-first century. Several different constituencies within world Christianity held significant events around 2010. From 2005, an international group worked collaboratively to develop an intercontinental and multi-denominational project, known as Edinburgh 2010, based at New College, University of Edinburgh. This initiative brought together representatives of twenty different global Christian bodies, representing all major Christian denominations and confessions, and many different strands of mission and church life, to mark the Centenary.

Essential to the work of the Edinburgh 1910 Conference, and of abiding value, were the findings of the eight think-tanks or 'commissions'. These inspired the idea of a new round of collaborative reflections on Christian mission – but now focused on nine themes identified as being key to mission in the twenty-first century. The study process was polycentric, open-ended, and as inclusive as possible of the different genders, regions of the world, and theological and confessional perspectives in today's church. It was overseen by the Study Process Monitoring Group: Miss Maria Aranzazu Aguado (Spain, The Vatican), Dr. Daryl Balia (South Africa, Edinburgh 2010), Mrs. Rosemary Dowsett (UK, World Evangelical Alliance), Dr. Knud Jørgensen (Norway, Areopagos), Rev. John Kafwanka (Zambia, Anglican Communion), Rev. Dr. Jooseop Keum (Korea, World Council of Churches), Dr. Wonsuk Ma (Korea, Oxford Centre for Mission Studies), Rev. Dr. Kenneth R. Ross (UK, Church of Scotland), Dr. Petros Vassiliadis (Greece, Aristotle University of Thessalonikki), and co-ordinated by Dr. Kirsteen Kim (UK, Edinburgh 2010).

These publications reflect the ethos of Edinburgh 2010 and will make a significant contribution to ongoing studies in mission. It should be clear that material published in this series will inevitably reflect a diverse range of views and positions. These will not necessarily represent those of the series' editors or of the Edinburgh 2010 General Council, but in publishing them, the leadership of Edinburgh 2010 hopes to encourage conversation between Christians and collaboration in mission. All the series' volumes are commended for study and reflection in both the church and the academy.

Series Editors

REGNUM EDINBURGH 2010 SERIES

Mission and Postmodernities

Edited by
Rolv Olsen
with Kajsa Ahlstrand, J. Andrew Kirk, Tania Petrova,
Teresa Francesca Rossi, and J. Jayakiran Sebastian

First published 2011 by Regnum Books International

Regnum is an imprint of the Oxford Centre for Mission Studies
St. Philip and St. James Church
Woodstock Road
Oxford OX2 6HR, UK
www.ocms.ac.uk/regnum

09 08 07 06 05 04 03 7 6 5 4 3 2 1

British Library Cataloguing in Publication Data
A catalogue record for this book is available from the British Library

ISBN: 978-1-506476-66-7

Typeset by Words by Design

The photo on the cover shows particpants of the Edinburgh 2010 conference in front of the statue of John Knox at New College, Edinburgh.

This volume has been sponsored by the
Areopagos Foundation in Norway and Denmark

Distributed by 1517 Media in the US and Canada

CONTENTS

FOREWORD

Knud Jørgensen

'Mission and Postmodernities' was one of the study themes for the Edinburgh 2010 centenary celebration. Work under this theme was to concern issues raised by the new phenomena of postmodernity in its various forms in North and South and its significance for mission. This was expected to involve an investigation of 21st century thought structures, religious beliefs and practices as well as ethical principles in a world of information technology. It would also require consideration of the influence of post-colonialism, economic structures, internationalism and engagement (or disengagement) with institutions and particularly with institutional religion. People involved in this study were expected to discern commonalities and particularities in postmodern developments in different regions of the world. The first outcome of this study process was an extensive report from the work of a multi-national study group.[1] The second outcome is this comprehensive presentation of a multi-faceted and complex theme.

Looking at Western history in the rear-view mirror, we know that sharp transformations have occurred every few hundred years. Sometimes we call these occurrences 'paradigm shifts'. In popular language it means that we cross a 'divide'. Following the crossing of the divide, culture and society work hard to rearrange themselves, including basic values, world view, social structures, arts, and institutions. After some decades there is a 'new world', and the people born in the new world cannot imagine the world of their grandparents and ancestors. I think that we are living through such a transformation today. We have left the former paradigm, but have not arrived fully at a new paradigm. This period in 'the desert' is a period of liminality;[2] the very term 'postmodern' indicates this 'in-betweenness'. The present volume expresses the same by admitting that there is no one way to understand postmodernities. The plural form of 'postmodernity' is not a misspelling, but to be taken seriously.

Postmodernities imply a supposed break with modernism, just as modernism broke with tradition. Modernism was 'a manifesto of human

[1] Daryl Balia & Kirsteen Kim (eds.) *Witnessing to Christ Today* (Oxford: Regnum Books International, 2010), 61-85.

[2] Allan Roxburgh, *The Missionary Congregation. Leadership and Liminality* (Valley Forge: Trinity Press International, 1997).

self-confidence and self-congratulation; postmodernism is a confession of modesty, if not despair'.[3] Some will claim that there is no truth, only truths. Principles are replaced by preferences. Instead of grand reason, we have only reasons. There is no privileged civilization or culture or belief, only a multiplicity of cultures and beliefs. The grand narrative of human progress of modernity has been transformed into the numerous small stories of peoples and cultures. The sense of universal knowledge and objectivity that my generation grew up with is under heavy critique. People like me and my generation who grew up under the last decades of modernity, are in many ways left with a feeling of confusion and uncertainty. We are in a *terra incognita*, a world we have not lived in before. We have been shipwrecked, cast onto a shoreline for which we have had no preparation. Now we sit on a new desert island under such strange trees as multiplication of endless choices, loss of a shared experience and a fragmentation of meaning, decentring of the self so that many feel adrift, without identity, life lived around surfaces and images, and anger and resentment that the dominant story has been replaced or compromised.[4]

It is here, under these trees on my desert island that this volume takes on meaning because its authors honestly struggle with and debate how we should relate to postmodernities. Should our response be accommodating, relativising or counter-cultural? How do we strike a balance between listening and understanding, and at the same time exploring how postmodernities influence the interpretation and application of the Bible as the normative story of God's mission in the world?

Some may consider 'postmodernities' a Western dilemma. The contributions from some writers in the Global South (China, India and Korea) unfold a larger canvas and explore the implications for Christian mission. This focus on 'mission' is central: this is not just a book about the many facets and trends of postmodernities. It is a book about the implications for mission, for what it means to live as Christians and as churches in a *terra incognita*, in a world where we have not been before.

We know how postmodernities influence the understanding of the gospel, and how it/they may make Christianity merely one local story among many. We have seen how 'truth' has become a plural word and how we are left with 'personal preferences'. But we are not losing hope. Here is a volume to be studied under the trees, on how to understand, how to wrestle with and how to confront these challenges in a constructive way, on various levels and in various parts of the world.

Let me, therefore, congratulate editors and conveners of study theme

[3] Os Guinness, *Fit Bodies, Fat Minds: Why Evangelicals Don't Think, and What to Do about It* (Grand Rapids: Baker, 1994), 103–105.

[4] Darrell L. Guder, *Missional Church. A Vision for the Sending of the Church in North America* (Grand Rapids: Eerdmans, 1998), 36 ff.; Allan Roxburgh, *Leading through Transition. Leadership in a Time of Change* (unpublished manuscript, 1999).

three for bringing together such a wide spectrum of contributors and laying the stones for a useful and stimulating discussion of what it implies to witness to Christ in a postmodern world.

Knud Jørgensen, Ph.D.
Adjunct Professor of Mission at MF Norwegian School of Theology and the Lutheran Theological Seminary, Hong Kong

PREFACE

Rolv Olsen

The many-faceted phenomenon of postmodernities and its significance for Christian mission represents a pressing challenge to the church as it considers how to be a credible witness in today's society. Preparing for the Edinburgh 1910 Centennial, the Nordic Institute for Missiological and Ecumenical Research (NIME) agreed to take responsibility for the work on the theme of 'Mission and Postmodernities'. The first stage of the study process is published in Swedish Missionary Themes, Vol. 95, No. 4, 2007, and is available online at www.missionsresearch.org. The Egede Institute, Oslo, Norway, was given the administrative responsibility for the further process, with its director Rolv Olsen (Lutheran) appointed co-ordinator. A Core Group was formed, with the task of inviting scholars to send in their written contributions and to explore the theme further on the basis of the received material. This Core Group consisted of J. Andrew Kirk (Anglican, UK), convenor, Kajsa Ahlstrand (Lutheran, Sweden), co-convenor, Tania Petrova (Pentecostal, Bulgaria), Teresa Francesca Rossi (Roman Catholic, Italy) and J. Jayakiran Sebastian (Church of South India, India), with the co-ordinator as secretary of the group.

The Core Group looked for contributions from people who share different perspectives on the subject: those attracted by postmodernity, those critical of it and those who may not believe that it exists at all; those who believe that it is relevant to mission, and those who do not; those who think it offers a positive environment for mission and those who believe it undermines mission. Participants to the process were at liberty to interpret the theme as they wished, on the grounds that there is no one way of understanding it. The group was interested in postmodernity's putative effect on mission spirituality, mission action and church life in all its dimensions and on how it may shape an understanding of mission and the nature of the Christian community. There is a particular interest in how postmodernities may influence the interpretation and application of the Bible as the normative story of God's mission in the world.

The intention was to solicit contributions that reflected different styles of writing: reflective essays that seek to grapple with theoretical constructs from an historical, philosophical, theological or human sciences perspective; presentations in the form of case-studies; reports of action groups, conversations about contemporary modes of liturgical life, and others that emphasize the place and influence of the arts in relation to the theme. The emphasis desired, after the analysis and critique of postmodernities had been achieved, was that of creative engagement. Hence, the letter of invitation asked the recipients to bear in mind that the intended outcome of all the study-groups was to provide rich material for thought and action, not so much for the academy as for grass-roots' Christian communities in their mission calling. For this reason, the language and structure of the essays should reflect the need to communicate with non-specialised audiences. The overall objective was to call for a renewed understanding of mission and renewed ways of being in mission that address in concrete ways the urgent issues of concrete situations.

The Core Group met for initial deliberations during the 2008 International Association of Mission Studies (IAMS) Conference in Balatonfüred, Hungary, and convened in Prague from June 22-26, 2009 to assess the contributions received so far and to prepare the statement of the group. Kirk Sandvig (Lutheran, USA), the Edinburgh 2010 Youth Coordinator, also participated in the Prague conference. Sadly, due to visa problems, Sebastian was prevented from attending. The Core Group Statement is submitted in the volume *Edinburgh 2010 Volume II: Witnessing to Christ Today*, as a part of the preparatory material for the Edinburgh 2010 Delegates.[1]

This volume is simply given the title *Mission and Postmodernities*, and its content is divided into four main parts: a dialogical introduction; elaborations on the theme, roughly divided into two groups as an attempt at creating a counterpoint, and finally, a chorus of voices from the Edinburgh Conference.

The two articles forming the *Introductory Dialogue* are distinguished by representing the only direct discussion between two viewpoints within this volume. *Jan-Olav Henriksen* reflects on postmodern challenges to churches in the Northern Hemisphere, proposing an accommodationist rather than a confrontational approach in mission. Although he writes with a special interest in the Scandinavian context, his analysis and reasoning is readily translatable to other contexts. In his reply, *Andrew Kirk* argues that it is part of the study of mission to take note in any and every situation of the counter-cultural force of the Gospel. The latter has its own criteria for deciding the nature and extent of its contextual relevance; passing cultural trends or fashions should never determine its ultimate validity and cogency.

In *Witness to a Post-Christendom Era*, the focus is on challenges encountered through the demise of Christendom in Europe and the implications for Christian mission. *Michael Herbst,* analysing the ultra-secular condition of the 'post-*Volkskirche*' situation[2] in East Germany, suggests that, although people may 'have forgotten that they have forgotten

[1] Balia, Daryl and Kirsteen Kim (ed.) *Edinburgh 2010 Volume II: Witnessing to Christ Today.* Oxford: Regnum Books International (2010) 61-85.

[2] *Vokskirche,* literal translation "folk church", a German and Scandinavian equivalent of English *Christendom.*

God', search for a wider reality and re-enchantment of the world may be taking place and connections with the transcendent cherished. Starting in a similar context, *Friedemann Walldorf* introduces three possible missiological models for Europe, and maintains that Europeans have not abandoned the search for truth for the experience of relationships, but rather that they seek relationships *and* a truth with which to carry these. *Veli-Matti Kärkkäinen* analyses Lesslie Newbigin's critique of modernity with the purpose of exploring fruitful strategies for the church in its encounter with contemporary society. From a Roman Catholic perspective, *Marco Fibbi* explores the faith of young people in a post-Christendom world.

The scope of *Mission in a Postmodern World* is wider, not limited to the particular European context. The late *David Kettle* gives an original, interdisciplinary approach to the question of hope, giving much food for thought, arguing that one major shortcoming of postmodernity is its lack of hope. For the church to communicate the gospel of hope meaningfully in a narcissistic culture, it needs to be characterized by authentic spirituality, hospitality, participation, and prophecy. *John Hitchen* considers challenges particular to mission to primal religious groups, and discusses biblical models for mission among adherents to primal religions in a postmodern context. Speaking from a Chinese perspective, *Jieren Li* points out that postmodernity, though rooted in Western post-industrial society, might still be relevant for the Third World, and discusses the implications for mission in postmodern China, analysing the strengths and weaknesses of various approaches. *Olga Zaprometova* gives a creative response to the question of emotions and their potential to bring union between Christians, from a Russian perspective. She explores ways of enhancing mutual understanding and co-operation, insisting that no Christian tradition is sufficient by itself. *Jayakiran Sebastian* reflects on challenges to churches on the Indian subcontinent and, exploring the understanding of *missio Dei*, advocates reinterpreting it as mission 'to' God, opening up new and fresh ways of thinking, belief, and praxis.

Finally, in the *Responses from the Edinburgh 2010 Conference,* a collection of initial reactions to the theme and the Core Group Report are given, representing the transversal themes as well as the various confessional and regional conferences. *Sebastian C.H. Kim*, expressing a viewpoint representative of the International Peace and Reconciliation Conferences, reflects on aspects of healing and reconciliation, with an emphasis on Korean experiences of despair and hope, through stories, poetry and visual images. *Ernst M. Conradie*, reflecting the Christian Faith and the Earth Symposium, voices ecological perspectives on mission. He argues for the crucial need to proclaim boldly and embody a vision of a renewed earth in which God is coming to dwell. *Claudia Währisch-Oblau*, echoing some of the findings of the 2009 United Evangelical Mission's Theological Consultation on Mission, suggests that mission today is first and foremost trying to live as the body of Christ, a community which overcomes racial, social, economic and cultural barriers and boundaries in an increasingly fragmented world. *Gianni Colzani*, of the Pontifical Urbaniana University, Rome, analyses the dual challenges of reducing knowledge to scientific knowledge and of the separation between politics and religion, arguing for an *agapeic-kenotic* view of Christian revelation and a theology capable of developing the prophetic role of the Church as a school of humanity. A Pentecostal perspective was given by *Harold D. Hunter*, in which he criticized the Core Group's Report for what he considered its acquiescence in relativizing Christian truth claims in a postmodern context and in affirming a ubiquitous salvific presence in all religions.

Our intention was that the contributors should be representative of the worldwide church, in age, gender, ethnic background, denominational affiliation and geographical spread. In this, we did not entirely succeed. European nations are over-represented. We acknowledge this as a shortcoming. Two things, however, may be said to mitigate this unwanted imbalance. Firstly, the problem is not so much that there are too many Western contributions, but rather that there are too few voices from the Global South. Secondly, although it may be that the challenges represented by postmodernities are as relevant in the South as in the North, it is also possible that they are perceived by people in the Western world as more urgent than by those living in societies where the impact of modernity has been less thorough. Nevertheless, it cannot be denied that the imbalance in the Core Group membership, as well as in the sample of contributions received, constitutes a deficiency. It is to be hoped that, in spite of this partiality, the content may inspire and provoke the reader[3] to further reflections and continued conversation.

[3] Or, as P.G. Wodehouse once expressed it: 'Or rather, to be optimistic, the *readers*'.

Introductory Dialogue

MULTIFACETED CHRISTIANITY AND THE POSTMODERN CONDITION: REFLECTIONS ON ITS CHALLENGES TO CHURCHES IN THE NORTHERN HEMISPHERE

Jan-Olav Henriksen

Introduction

This year (2009) it has been 30 years since Jean-Francois Lyotard published his much quoted and highly acclaimed report *The Postmodern Condition*,[1] in which he deals with – among other issues –what and how knowledge appears under the present cultural and social circumstances. By making the American continent his starting point, he was able to detect and describe features of the postmodern condition that we have later been able to recognize elsewhere in the Western world, and especially in the more affluent parts of Europe. It is from my own position in such a society that the present article takes its point of departure.

Lyotard's report still recommends itself for anyone interested in understanding what goes on in postmodernity. In the present context, I am not so interested in giving an account of his insights per se, as I aim to reflect on how some of the issues he addresses provide us with the means for understanding the *religious* scene of postmodernity. It is not hard to argue that we cannot understand the religious dimension of postmodernity without paying attention to the present cultural and social conditions on which the church exists in this part of the world.[2] So, how do Lyotard's thoughts matter for theology – and for the church? To pose this question is especially apt as, given that we assume Lyotard is right, quite a substantial part of the time-span of the 100 years since Edinburgh 1910 has been postmodern, although one could also argue (which I will not do here) that

---

[1] Lyotard, Jean-Francois, *The Post-Modern Condition: A Report on Knowledge*, (Theory and History of Literature, 10: Mineapolis: University of Minneapolis Press, 1984, French original, 1979). Cf. L. Boeve, *Interrupting Tradition: An Essay on Christian Faith in a Postmodern Context*, Louvain Theological & Pastoral Monographs ; 30 (Louvain ; Dudley, MA: Peeters Press, 2003).

[2] The last sentence should be read as taking into account that the church does not necessarily exist on postmodern cultural conditions everywhere – cf. my references to Inglehart's analysis of different cultures below.

what took place at that time was a manifestation of a distinctively modern approach to the church and its mission, due to its universal scope.

Firstly, we should consider that the notion 'postmodernity' may not function well as a notion depicting a clearly defined stage in history. Lyotard teaches us that modernity and postmodernity are notions that are better used in order to depict certain cultural and intellectual trends in the development of a given society. Thereby, these notions help us to identify some main elements of that society, and point out what gives society its shape under certain conditions. We could say that postmodernity as well as modernity are the conceptual lenses through which we can look at our own culture, and since the lenses are shaped differently, they help us to see different things that occur in the picture at the same time.

On this basis, the very notion of postmodernity helps us to get hold of important traits in the cultural and societal sphere. We can, e.g., see a more aesthetically oriented, self-reliant and experience-oriented approach to life-fulfilment instead of collective, institution-based and socially conditioned approach to life. Moreover, we find a stronger emphasis on contextual and local features than on what is universal or common to all, corresponding to what Lyotard calls the postmodern incredulity of meta-narratives. Such scepticism toward meta-narratives also suggests that the Western, secularized and techno-based way of understanding society and culture may not be the only way to approach what is going on and may be of interest to people in the present. There are other ways of seeing and understanding the world, based on relationships, local traditions and institutions that are not part of the Western grand narrative about the progress of secularization, detraditionalization and rationalization.[3] Hence, another description of postmodernity that seems relevant for the present context that this article is dealing with would be the following:

> Postmodern thought understands that interpretations of text, history, society and oneself must go on within the cultural context of vastly plural interpretative and disciplinary schemas, cultural perspectives, and historical narratives. Postmodern analysts speak of the self as "decentred", no longer the confident, autonomous self employing language as an instrument to express one's depths and to name and thus control reality. The self can no longer claim full "self-presence" because it is inextricably shaped by multiple narratives, histories, and languages which each limit and distort even as they disclose.[4]

For those of us familiar with what emerged as contextual theology, this focus on the "vastly plural" may seem like old news and, in one sense, it is. On the other hand, analysis of postmodern culture may tell us how much the development of theology is conditioned by the cultural context. Moreover, the above quote also points us toward an important element

---

[3] This narrative is powerfully argued in Inglehart 2003.

[4] W.C. French / R.A. Di Vito "The Self in context: The issues" in McCarthy, J. (ed. 1997) *The Whole and Divided Self. The Bible and Theological Anthropology*, p., 34.

where other cultures than the modern Western seem to have "got it" better: in the recognition of how the subject is dependent upon conditions and relations to others in ways that question the ability to understand oneself solely from one's own point of view. I will return to how this may impact theology and the mission of the church below.

Multiple Descriptions of the World as a Challenge for Communication

A valid insight that postmodern thinkers often promote, is that there is no neutral, commonly valid or acceptable description of the world. If we describe the culture we live in as postmodern, we make a certain judgement, and the very words we are using are related to what we perceive and want to emphasize from our given point of view. It is Ludwig Wittgenstein who has most thoroughly argued that all use of language is rooted in a context, and that contexts must be seen as pragmatic conditions for understanding and communication. This is followed up by the German philosopher Karl-Otto Apel, who points to how the meaning of expressions is rooted in the *communicative use of language*.[5] When we use language, and talk about something, our understanding of what we are talking about is constituted by the notions we are offered by our participation in a community of communication. These notions help us to identify the very phenomena we are talking about. But as there is no neutral language, and no generic language accessible to all, we have to consider what this means when we proclaim a message that is rooted in a specific historical context, and builds on pragmatic and cultural conditions that not all of us share. To speak of a Gospel is thus not only a question about "finding the right words", it is also about making accessible a different way of looking at and engaging with the common world we may share with those we interact with. Hence, one of the main questions for a church existing in a postmodern context is: How can the church help people to remain faithful to the Gospel about Jesus Christ in a context where the conditions for communication and understanding are no longer the same for everyone, and where a common understanding cannot be taken for granted as something given, and something kept together for all in a grand narrative?

This may not be such a new challenge to Christianity and the church as it may appear at first sight. St. Paul was aware of the importance of being a Jew for Jews, a Roman for the Romans etc. But the understanding that Lyotard, Wittgenstein, Apel and others provide for us, means that different languages are not only different languages, but rooted in different contexts. Accordingly, as the contexts are different, we also get different understandings and expressions of understanding when we discuss the same topic. The insistence on the difference in understanding, and the need

---

[5] Apel, *Transformation der Philosophie* (Frankfurt 1978).

for understanding topics from many different points of view, has been a growing one over the last 100 years, given the development of the Ecumenical movement and the mission of the church in the 20th century. However, do we understand these differences in a sufficiently radical way? Postmodern theory suggests that this is not necessarily the case.

Different Types of Difference: or Difference and Plurality

There is a difference between difference and difference – or, there are different modes of difference. Recognizing and accepting cultural and ecclesial differences leads to a recognition of plurality. At this point, I think the German philosopher, Wolfgang Welsch, is right when he states that *plurality is the key issue in postmodernity*. We cannot understand postmodernity at all if we do not recognize this. Welsch states this clearly in the following quotation that I suggest we label *the thesis of plurality*:[6]

> Plurality is the key notion of postmodernity. All known postmodern topics – the end of meta-narratives, the dissolution of the subject, the decentring of meaning, the simultaneity of the not simultaneous, the lack of possibilities for synthesising the manifold life-forms and patterns of rationality – become understandable in the light of plurality.[7]

Welsch includes several reflections in this statement that are important in order to get hold of the implications of the postmodern condition he describes. On the one hand, he holds that there is a difference between what he calls plurality on the surface, *and* the deeper, more fundamental plurality, which is rooted in what he calls *basic differences*. The phenomenon this distinction helps us to identify is how that which seems to be pluriform at first glance, turns out to be a variation on the same theme when we are looking closer. I think there are good examples of this in Christian churches. Looking closer, many of them are not really exhibiting a deep and basic difference, but are based on the same patterns. Therefore, at least in the Christian churches, we also participate in the struggle for Christian unity. However, we do not struggle for a *similar* unity with Jews, Moslems or atheists. Facing them, we recognise a deeper and more basic difference that makes unity harder, if at all possible, to achieve. This is what Welsch calls real or fundamental difference, which is of a different kind. In this type of difference, we have to realize that we face *the Other*.[8]

The basic differences, those that go beyond the surface, give rise to what Welsch calls *hard pluralism*. That is the pluralism that has no hope of being reconciled, a pluralism that, if you try to overcome it, will imply the

---

[6] I have developed this and the following thesis more extensively in "Postmodernitet som kulturfenomen", *Svensk Teologisk Kvartalsskrift* (1998/3).

[7] W. Welsch *Unsere postmoderne Moderne* (Darmstadt 1991³) XV. My translation.

[8] I return to the importance of this figure of thought more extensively in a section later.

violation of the identity of that which you try to reconcile. Using the example of religions again, you offend both Jews and Christians if you say that they are basically the one and the same religion. There are many reasons for this. One is that you then ignore, perhaps even disrespect, the local and contextual differences that constitute the phenomena of the respective Christian or Jewish communities. Another is that you thereby also ignore how one of these religions (Christianity) is in fact constituted by its difference to the other. Hence, what Welsch reminds us about with his insistence on how postmodernity is constituted by differences, is that we do not understand anything at all about the complexity of the cultural condition if we neglect taking into account how differences both constitute identity and is the precondition for unity.

This insistence on difference is a serious challenge for anyone who would promote a message of universal importance or relevance. How can the church back such a message if the cultural situations to which it relates seem to be deeply sceptical toward such universally significant messages? Does the church under postmodern conditions run the risk of becoming just one more "cultural tribe" which seeks to increase its influence and dominion? How can it avoid becoming perceived as such? In the present global situation, especially given the way the US has over the last years been acting as a kind of empire in other parts of the world, the aspiration of Christianity to be of universal significance has become increasingly complicated, given the way some of its political right-wing followers appear as eager allies with the military power of this empire. As I will conclude below, the only way to overcome some of these problems is if we can revitalize the emphasis on the powerlessness of the church and the more pacifist strands of its tradition, without letting go of the call to proclaim the Gospel for all peoples.

Christian Self-Criticism Emerging for the Recognition of Plurality

Among the important ethical consequences of the thesis of plurality, as formulated by Welsch, is one that also exhibits postmodernity as a phenomenon dependent upon the ideals of Enlightenment modernity. Since there are unlimited possibilities of understanding phenomena in different ways, one should not stick to one mode of understanding, but constantly try to overcome, criticize, make more complete and transcend what is a finalized and given position. The past and the already given cannot have any inherent and final normativity, nothing that *secures* its authority in the contemporary cultural situation. While this may seem like a natural consequence of Enlightenment critiques of religious traditions and authority, it may also be possible to see the acknowledgement of the imperfect in any position not-to-be-taken-for-granted-as-religious-authority as a late fruit of the Christian understanding of creation and sin: Creation, insofar as what is human is always limited and marked by finitude, and hence in need of being criticized for not saying it all or covering all kinds of contexts and situations. Sin, insofar as sin consists in absolutizing your own position as the privileged starting point and the point from which to assess everything else, thereby ignoring that you are not God and are not able to have an authority based on a "God's eye view" of the world. Against the background of these insights, the authority of the church in a postmodern context is not first and foremost threatened by a culture of relativism, but by one in which one is not able to have a serious discourse with all relevant positions in order to clarify what can count as reliable. Such a discourse is important in order for the church to self-critically scrutinize some of its past positions and practices, in order to identify what stalled or petrified positions it is called to overcome or leave behind, because they are no longer adequate in the present context. The recognition of the church as itself being shaped by the conditions of creation and sin suggests that it needs to engage with the world's understanding of it, if it is to serve its mission well.

The charge of relativism, so often directed against the postmodern cultural condition, is not as relevant against this backdrop as the fact that we, by using this charge as a cover-up for no positive engagement with the culture in question, run the risk of ignoring the basic differences as important starting-points for discussing how to understand the Gospel in our own contexts. Hence, more important that the relativism that tends to ignore the Other, is the realization that the postmodern cultural contexts challenge the church to face the Other in a manner that allows for a self-critical stance and a scrutiny of the practises and ways of preaching the Gospel.

Constructing an Understanding of the World: The Prescriptive Dimension of a Christian Worldview

We could remain with Welsch's definition of postmodernity. But I do not think Welsch says all that there is to say if we are to understand postmodernity as a challenge to the mission of the churches in our contemporary cultural context. Hence, I have formulated an additional thesis that is meant to identify another side of the plurality of postmodernity. I suggest we call the following the *thesis of construction*:

> *All cultural expressions contribute to the articulation – and thereby the construction – of those parts of reality that only exist due to our understanding, i.e. the cultural sphere. Hence, the articulation of culture (in the wide sense of the word) constitutes the reality that is articulated.* The cultural reality thereby appears as a construction made by humans.

Even when we affirm that our faith is the result of God's revelation, the above implies that we are also well advised to see Christian faith as a cultural construct, always articulating itself in different places on the basis of the cultural resources with which it interacts. Several implications follow: First, any such articulation is to some extent contingent and could have been made otherwise. Second, since the construction is exactly that, i.e., a *contingent construction*, it is also possible to *deconstruct* it. Third, the construction is thus one of many possibilities for articulating a certain phenomenon against the background of the interests of a specific group (communicative community). Consequently, cultural constructions are pragmatic: they serve as tools for understanding reality, communicating about it, making it normative in some sense, and organizing it. It is my contention that we should acknowledge this as an important element in understanding what theology is like in a postmodern context, because this means that theology and preaching the Gospel are not only about describing the world and given realities, but is also, to a certain degree, a *prescriptive* enterprise that informs us about how to understand others and the world and interact with them.

In postmodernity, the insight into how many human phenomena are made accessible to us by the constructive means of language or symbols is thus taken to its logical conclusion. Moreover, construction and contingency are elements that fit well with the insistence on plurality that Welsch gives testimony to. The thesis of construction underpins the understanding that none of our expressions of self-understanding needs to be what they are, and that they could be different. Hence, it also opens for a deeper understanding of *why radical plurality can appear as a central option in the present cultural condition.* As long as we can construct otherwise, we will have plurality.

Consequences so far

Let me now very briefly spell out how we may interpret many of the well-known key words of postmodernity on the basis of the above. The background they offer us, gives a possibility for reconstructing quickly the following postmodern topics as a rather coherent pattern.

The insistence on the absence of a common human rationality in postmodernity becomes understandable: It is due to the insight into the fact that we reconstruct different or plural forms of rationality according to specific interests, needs and concerns. We cannot transcend, in any radical way, the fact that we live in and are conditioned by a certain context that has its special patterns of understanding, rationality and communication. But, contrary to those that see this as a reason for 'sticking to his/her own', I would argue that this calls for a more dedicated communicative engagement with different and differing positions. The result would be a witness to the universality of the Christian message, as well as to the fact that we take every culture and every person equally seriously.

That contextual reason implies *perspectivism* is, according to the above, a call to acknowledge the necessity of dialogue with different cultural contexts, in order to provide the fullest possible articulation of what

Christian faith may imply in different contexts. The fact that different cultures have different ways of seeing the world, concerns, interests etc., informs us about the necessity of constantly re-articulating the Christian message in new ways. This is not a new feature when we compare the postmodern condition to previous times, but it is all the more pressing now.

Given that there is no universal and unifying reason, we have to accept plurality, even when it comes to conflicting, disturbing and contradicting positions. This follows from the insight that all constructions could be otherwise, and that they then do not cover everything, but need to be supplemented by other constructions. It implies, as a radical consequence, a more open acknowledgment and acceptance of the fact that what Christianity is may appear differently within different cultural contexts.

Finally, to recognize the constructive character of cultural resources for the articulation of Christianity gives us the possibility to reconstruct patterns, constructions, and rationalities in the light of other insights. This not only contributes to the multiplicity of constructions, but also amplifies the experience of plurality and contingency. A multifaceted Christianity is far better than having one cultural expression of it that tends to hijack and monopolize the way people's opinion of it is shaped. Christianity is rich enough to make visible patterns of design that are to be found beyond any cultural construction, but which are not always recognized, and which are important for the fulfilment of human life everywhere.

Theology on the Conditions of Postmodernity? The Other

To some, the reconstruction of the cultural conditions and the challenges following it, that I have sketched so far, may seem to imply a destabilisation of not only culture in general, but also of the ground for theological work more specifically. However, tacit in the postmodern insistence on plurality and construction, there is hidden a topic, in addition to the mentioned communicative engagement, that could counter this impression. This topic is also important because it points to central issues in theology. For the lack of any better name for it, I call this topic or figure *the Other*.

Philosophically, *the Other* can be identified as an ontological as well as an epistemological figure: If we think of the Other as a concrete person, the other is both someone who is not ourselves, and s/he is also an opportunity for learning something more about the world. Hence, the Other is always someone who widens my world, or opens it up to new dimensions I have not yet perceived. Postmodernity, as a more theoretical way of understanding cultures, explores forms of thought that work from a basically pluralistic perspective, and, in this regard, we can see how the churches over the last 100 years have learned a lot of lessons on how to approach and understand otherness and the Other. The Other is not someone determined and perceived solely from my own privileged point of view, but someone who offers me another point of view, from which I can see both her and myself. The deconstruction in the wake of post-colonialism and the emergence of third world theologies of different kinds may be seen as manifestations of how Otherness presents itself differently now from what it did 100 years ago.

Taking Welsch' notion of pluralism as a point of departure for exploring the *contribution of otherness to theology*, any kind of epistemological recognition of such pluralism implies that there is something different from my own, presently known position which may challenge my already given position. The Other is, epistemologically speaking, that which is not possible to integrate into the presently given framework of understanding, that which cannot be reduced categorically to the already established patterns of thought. Hence, the Other is, as an epistemological category, both a witness to pluralism and a challenge to the already present forms of understanding.

Theology should not be surprised if it finds the Other as a category implicit in postmodern forms of thought and knowledge. The well-known expression, *Deus semper major,* contains the insight that God always transcends our notions and ideas of what God is. The category of the Other, that which cannot be reduced to the known, is especially fitting for theology. In all forms of postmodernism that insist on the existence of deep pluralism, we find the possibility for taking care of this theological concern. Basically, it means that we have more to learn and to understand from this world in which God has placed us with God's mission.

Moreover, there is another theologically relevant element here – an element that can be identified on the anthropological level. The recognition of Otherness as a constitutive element in the establishment of human knowledge and reason, also points to the common insight that Christian theology safeguards, namely that not all there is, is due to human effort, action, or insight. There is more to reality than what we can produce. Anthropologically speaking, this makes us as humans responsive, responsible and existing in a relation to that which we know. If we do not acknowledge this *constitutive relationship with the Other*, we run the danger of turning ourselves into gods, epistemologically speaking, because then everything in our reason and knowledge has its source in us. I think it is obvious from experience that this is not the case, but my point here is that this is also a theologically valid insight. It indicates that we, as humans, are related to something other than ourselves – to something *given*.

The theological position that is primarily associated with the notion of the Other, is *Karl Barth's*. His emphasis on God as the «wholly other» was designed not only to develop a theology that made God more than the mere reflection of what was the moral and religious needs of liberal Protestantism (Kulturprotestantismus). However, in doing this, Barth came very close to suggesting that there is no possibility for experiencing God, or traces of God, in common human experience, or outside faith. And this is the point where I part from Barth's concern: Although he is right in insisting that God must be seen as the Other, this does not mean that there are no possibilities of experiencing otherness in the world, including otherness that bears witness to who and what God is.

At this point, we are talking ontologically, and as an ontological category, we can call the Other *the given*. This category fits well as an expression in what has been a major concern in Scandinavian theology in the last century, namely the doctrine on creation. With leanings towards both Barthian Christocentrism, Neo-Kantian cultural Protestantism and the positivistic German theology of Orders in the thirties (Ordnungstheologie), several Scandinavian theologians (e.g., K.E. Løgstrup and G. Wingren) have worked out a way of understanding the doctrine of creation that expresses the following concerns:

- It stresses how God is active in all of creation, also outside the spheres of faith and church
- It has emphasis on how God's work is prior to any human activity
- It points out how God's work in creation is also a positive framework and an important supposition for his redemptive work in Christ
- It points to phenomena in human experience that are signposts for a qualitative dimension in our world. This dimension shows itself in phenomena that are not dependent upon our decisions, our mental efforts or our active participation. Examples are trust, mercy and similar phenomena that occur spontaneously, and that need a human effort, a decision or an active distortion in order to *not* appear.

Hence, we see how the doctrine of creation can provide a framework for interpreting the experience of the given in this world. However, these given phenomena, or these patterns in reality, are not something completely outside of human experience, and the otherness they express, is not unmediated with our actual life-fulfilment. What they do is to indicate that there are elements in our lives that are outside our control, but still determine our lives. Let my try to elaborate this through an example that will also show more clearly how this is important when we try to appropriate postmodern modes of reflection and understanding:

We live as a body. The body is given. It is not something we decide to have, or not have. We are our bodies. The body is also our relation to the world. By senses, perception, drives and needs that are there before we are able to say or think «I» or «me», the givenness of the body shapes our actual lives. Hence, not everything in the world is constructed – something is there before the construction that takes place in human reason through understanding and reflection. In other words, what is given is also given as material for constructions. The given suggest boundaries for our constructions, as well. This implies that a total relativism is impossible, simply because we cannot construct the body or the world in any way we like. The construction is always a construction of the given, although the given itself is only accessible through a certain cultural shape (construction).

Theologically speaking, this means several things: Our constructions are dependent upon the given character of God's creation. Hence, they are already initially determined by what God has already done. However, this does not imply a total determination of any shape and content of our lives. The basic point is that before we are able to do or think or sense anything, God is by and with us and acting with us and for us. But this is not all there is to say. God is also working in and by means of our cultural constructions: He works for the sustaining of his creation, e.g., by informing us by experience and inspiring us through his Word. This means that God's Word can have an impact upon how we develop the constructions of our culture, and on our understanding of and ordering of the world. Here we are at the core of the task for the church when engaging with a postmodern culture.

However, as God continues to create, this also means that his creative work is present *in, with and under* our cultural constructions. But as our constructions are always facing new challenges, problems, and experience, they need to alter and adapt. Hence, the recognition of the given as something basic and unavoidable, must be supplied with an openness for the possibility of changing our constructions of how we take care of and relate to the given. This means that contingency as well as the possibility of deconstructing outdated or obsolete constructions of cultural forms can be seen as an integrated part of the theological enterprise. At the same time, here there is a basic linking to the given that sets up a barrier against any total relativism. Here we have the possibility for developing a theology that recognizes otherness, takes the provisional and contingent character of its own expressions into account, and still maintains an understanding of God and the world that corresponds with the shape human experience also has in a postmodern framework.

A theology built on these conditions is structurally opposed to totalitarianism. Even though theology, as an intellectual enterprise, is an effort to think the whole, theology is also founded on the insight that theology cannot think the whole to its end. It is precisely because there are elements in reality that do not fit into our immediate human understanding, that we do theology, and try to interpret the world – in spite of knowing we will never gain full insight. Theology combines the quest for a comprehensive understanding with the insight into the impossibility of this, and the openness for otherness in the wide sense of the word. This also means respect and tolerance for those not sympathetic to Christian faith and thinking. That is a consequence of accepting that we live in a postmodern culture, marked by plurality.

Re-traditionalizing Christianity

Modernity has meant increased dissolution of trust in religious authority and traditions, but in later years, there has also been an increasing engagement with institutions. Individualization implies less strong relations to institutions and to others, and thereby also to traditions that are represented by authoritative figures. However, in a postmodern context where elements from different historical and cultural contexts may live side by side, we can also see traits of a new and different approach to the resources of religious and cultural traditions that should not surprise us. These approaches lead to what I, for lack of better words, call re-traditionalization (as opposed to detraditionalization, the process that leads to an increasingly less tradition-shaped culture and society). I will look a little more into this phenomenon in order to provide a concrete example of some of the features I have described above.

A significant sample of such processes is the renewal of pilgrimages. These have largely been associated with practices of the pre-Reformation era, and even more so with a typical Roman-Catholic form of piety. Now, however, churches all over Europe are experiencing how people desire something new, possibly something other than what is given with their everyday life routines. It is also a sign of ecumenism or post-confessionalism as what used to be a Roman-Catholic practice is now recognized as something in which also people of other confessions can take part without restriction. Plurality in terms of an ecumenical attitude is recognized. The impact of differences between the confessions is tuned down. With postmodernity, emphasis is not on doctrine, but on *religious culture as providing means of self-expression.*

Let me spell this out more extensively: The above understanding of the postmodern scene makes it possible to see how institutionally based religion is no longer the defining *point of departure* for religious life and religious expression. The defining point of departure is *the secularized individual* and his or her need for finding a more comprehensive pattern of meaning and understanding in his / her life. However, this approach also offers us an understanding of re-traditionalization as a consequence of pluralism and globalization: Because globalization makes world-views more relative, and recognizes the equality of different forms of socio-cultural formation and simultaneously celebrates heterogeneity and variation, questions related to "identity, tradition and the demand for indigenisation" become more important.[9]

The concept of re-traditionalization is thus meant to identify elements of a postmodern culture that counters the effects of secularization and differentiation, be it in forms of morality, community shaping, narratives, aesthetic expressions and /or sacred symbols. It is important to underline that it also involves processes that we would not normally count as

---

9 Cf. Voyé 1998, 10.

religious in a strict sense. Its moral aspect is related to the purpose of establishing a framework for understanding and identity where certain values can be legitimized and made accessible.

That re-traditionalization is a postmodern phenomenon, can be argued along the following lines: It is selective and / or eclectic, it is based on and made possible by a pluralistic culture, and it reflects quite strongly the active and constructive element in the *individual's* relation to the "tradition". Hence, it is different from more collective approaches to assumed traditions that attempt to reshape society in order to return society as a whole to the values of the past (e.g., in different forms of fundamentalism). On the other hand, it is not possible to see it as something that leads to the ongoing promotion of a non-reflexive and unchallenged authority. As previously said, authority in a re-traditionalization process does not lie with the tradition in question, but with the individual. Thus, when churches offer *resources for the shaping of personal identity in a culture of pluralism, they are in no way justified in assuming that their authority is something they can take for granted.* This perspective is supported in the more recent work of Ronald Inglehart and colleagues. Inglehart writes:

> This has not only opened for tradition to regain status, but created a need for a new legitimating myth. In the Postmodern worldview (sic!) tradition once again has positive value – especially non-western traditions. But the revalorization of tradition is sharply selective (Inglehart 1997, 25).

In a society with far more access to information than earlier, we also have access to far more materials from traditions than what we are able to relate to and make active use of. To speak of a tradition in this context thus presupposes that we make a choice from a wide spectrum of resources that can be called tradition, because these resources are handed over from former times and from other cultural places than the one in which we find ourselves. As indicated, *choice* is an important element in the reflexive construction of re-traditionalization.

> Even more generally, tradition is always a matter of human attribution: nothing about the materials themselves requires that designation. Even ongoing customary forms of action and belief do not constitute a tradition until they are marked as such and thereby assigned a normative status [10]

Linking this back to my initial example of pilgrimage, re-traditionalization takes place where one is challenged to reinterpret one's own tradition in the light of the presence of other religions and faiths. That is what happens when churches get involved in processes of re-traditionalization that have relevance for the shaping of their own identity. On the other hand, through the churches, *individuals* are given access to cultural resources that are *instruments* for the shaping of their own identity – although this is something that is also dependent upon participating in

10 Tanner 1997, 133.

structures of community (traditions are, as we know, never individual). Hence, the individual's appropriation of the traditional resources for identity formation, as found in the churches, indicates that the churches are perceived as relevant for the contribution of resources to this process.

Given the large membership of the mainstream Nordic churches, we are now able to develop a perspective in order to understand the factor that a majority of people maintain their membership in these churches without actively practicing religion or sharing the "official faith" or confession of these churches: We can understand this in the background that people find themselves able to make use of, in the aestheticl, moral, identity-shaping and or identity-defining elements offered in these churches (a relation that also presupposes a differentiation between different elements contained in the churches). The paradox of the mainstream Nordic churches is then perhaps possible to describe in the following way: *The churches offer resources for living and believing in a variety of different ways, because they have been able to maintain their own identity in a way that does not only make themselves agents of a specific confession and a specific confessional group. The churches but also provide or represent resources of morality, history, cultural identity etc. that is recognized by most members of society as relevant for their own shaping of identity, irrespective of their personal faith.*

This paradox, then, also indicates that in a pluralist society, we seem to become more dependent upon traditions – seen as resources or instruments for coping with pluralism. It can be argued that there is a decrease in the way traditions function as legitimizing and normative. On the other hand, traditions seem to have an increasing impact on the development of a meaningful framework for the interpretation of personal life and the changes that take place in a culture shaped more by pluralism. Traditions also seem to contribute to the experience of belonging – a need that has not disappeared in modernity.

Re-traditionalization and Post-Materialism

Given the above, the church is involved in the recent events and processes of re-traditionalization that we find traces of in postmodern cultures. Although the Nordic countries are counted among the most secularized in the world, this does not mean that the interest in religion is declining in every respect. Rather, it may be taken to indicate that, while interest in the traditional forms of church services is weakened, the churches do function as a kind of resource pool and reference point for people's different religious attitudes. How are we to understand this in a more cultural-analytic perspective?

The American sociologist, Ronald Inglehart, is perhaps the one that has studied the development and changes in lifestyles, values and attitudes towards religion most extensively in the last decades. In his studies, he also presents material that is relevant, in order to see what makes a common or unifying cultural matrix for the Nordic countries, in a way that can also take into account the increasing growth of pluralism or diversity that we can identify there.

Inglehart builds a distinction between materialist and post-materialist attitudes and societies. This distinction also impacts the understanding of the religious and cultural spheres. Materialist and traditionalist values are predominant in societies, where the struggle for survival is still an important element. He also suggests that this pattern is more common in countries where the economical development is linked with industrialization that is still growing. On the other hand, the post-materialist attitude is more closely liked with the post-industrialized countries, where affluent conditions and the rise of service and knowledge sectors are shaping peoples lives. This should not be taken as meaning that people living in the post-materialist world are not interested in material things: They are. But as of now, when their basic concerns for survival are satisfied, they can relate to the cultural sphere and to values in different ways than earlier. While the emphasis was on the survival issues earlier, they now more and more tend to be directed towards self-expression. In this dimension, personal development, life– and self-fulfilling practices, cultural orientation and more liberal values are more strongly emphasized.[11]

Inglehart thus estimates cultural and religious development from two basic dimensions: One showing itself in a development from survival values to increased emphasis on values of self-expression, and one signifying the development from a traditional society towards one shaped by rational and secular approaches to society, its institutions and its preferences. Given that he is right, the difference in cultural and societal patterns that he identifies may have huge impact on how the Christian message is understood and communicated.

The Nordic countries are more or less in the same area both in terms of their development of secularization, as well as in terms of focusing on self-expression values, and they score high for both. From the point of view of the churches, this is worth noting for several reasons:

That the secularization process has come so far means that there is little or no reason to think that the churches have a given impact on how people shape their religious life (or their morals) *per se*. Tradition, as a unifying principle of society, has no great impact. In other words, the churches, when it comes to the questions of to what extent they actually contribute to how people live their lives, can take nothing for granted. However, there is a large amount of plurality when it comes to how people relate to the church – be it as a close-bond community, as an institution for specific religious services, as a bearer of traditions and religious cultural

---

[11] R. Inglehart & W.E. Baker "Modernization, Cultural Change, and the Persistence of Traditional Values" in *American Sociological Review 65* (2000), 19-51, p.35.

expressions, as a community of common believers etc. The diversity in attitudes towards the church shows that one still counts on the church – but for a wide variety of reasons.

Secondly, what the churches in the Nordic countries probably *can* take for granted is that they will continue to have some impact on Nordic culture in the years to come as well. But as the "demands" for the church are playing on so many different strings, a probable future scenario is the following: The churches will have most impact when they can promote themselves as able to help people to live their lives and develop as humans – in a way that leads to deeper spiritual life (note how this may seem as the other side of the self-expression dimension in Inglehart). Thus, the churches will be filling the void left by a consumerist culture, that not only leads to a uniform and flat type of cultural sphere, but which is also basically unable to provide people with a sense of life's meaning and direction. This may also improve the cultural resources and conditions for participating in communal practices. In the present consumerist context, it is the present that counts, not tomorrow or yesterday. This is so even for the post-materialists that are interested in consumption, but only as far at it is a means for their own self-expression. However, once one starts to reflect past the present, religion is perhaps the strongest device for facilitating such reflections, and it provides people with what we loosely can call an experiential framework. It is, on this basis, that we can see cultural expressions like pilgrimage return to experiential modes of religiosity.

In a cultural context shaped by less weight on tradition and more on rational and utilitarian values, there is less emphasis on institutions as such and more on individual preferences and interest, which, in turn, opens up to the above suggested increasing emphasis on self-expression. The basic terms here are individualism and not institution, privatization and not community. As the institutional aspect is playing a weaker role in people's lives, this does not mean that everything that is provided by and through institutions lack importance. Professor Otto Krogseth, at the University of Oslo, has suggested that although secularization is taking place in the *social* arena – leading to individualism and privatization in religious matters, a process in the opposite direction is taking place in the *cultural* sphere: Here, religion gains importance, and religious expressions are given new attention that many of us were unable to predict 20 years ago. So, secularization in the institutional and social sphere does not rule out the basis for a re-sacralization on the cultural scene – but then this does not take place within the framework of, or is generated by, traditional institutions – but at their margins, so to say.

It is, from this perspective, that we can see both an increasing interest in pilgrimage, as well as the new constellations, under which religion functions today: in a postmodern cultural context, religion becomes more a means of self-expression and a search for meaning and continuity in life, and less an arena for dealing with life and death, guilt and recognition (although these factors are in no way totally distant). We turn to tradition, but are not traditionalists, we need religion, but not the regulations and demands of religious institutions; we need morality, but are in no way willing to let the neighbour tell us what to do. We need identity – but want to construct it ourselves, and not receive it as something pre-described. In this sense, diversity rules, although the churches still contribute to a unifying institutional framework that covers most of society in terms of membership and some kind of relation.

In this regard, the churches' cultural function in the Nordic societies, can be seen as one *providing resources for life-interpretation and a different way of engaging with reality.* The challenge of the churches is to recognize their new role in a more diversified society, without losing sight of the fact that the resources they provide in the cultural context are only possible to maintain if they are able to maintain a clear and distinct tradition, so that people know that they can find in the church what cannot be found elsewhere. After all, the churches also have something to say about living a life in which God takes part and that God helps to shape that is not offered elsewhere. Hence, we can sum up the challenge to the churches in this cultural context in the following sentence: *Openness for a diversity of approaches to religion – and a responsibility for maintaining a unifying tradition based on preaching the one Word of God to all people at the same time.*

Conclusion: The Predicament of Christianity in a Postmodern Culture

In a culture that increasingly manifests a plurality of life-views and features of multiculturalism, one easily runs the risk of developing what we can call religious illiteracy, i.e. a lack of understanding of religious practices and their meaning because there are so many and diverse religious expressions present, and one can hardly get to know them all. In such a cultural situation, the church cannot any longer take for granted that it is well known what its message is. We can no longer count on people to know what Christianity is all about. Therefore, to provide a viable and relatively stable and coherent presentation of Christianity in this context and in this age is perhaps the most important challenge the church is facing in the present. Moreover, the church will have to recognize – especially in this context – the fact that what people *may* know of the church is mostly a narrative of its infamous past. The focus on this past is not always a welcome fact in the light of the ambivalent history of the Western churches when it comes to alliances with political powers pursuing projects of colonialism, state-building efforts, and using religion to enforce national identity. This negative history is a serious challenge to a church that is no longer alone in the religious marketplace, and has to advocate its position while facing alternatives or competitors that do not have a similar history.

As indicated, one of the ways to "improve" the cultural image of the church is to wipe the dust off ideals linked to pacifism, and to dissociate as much as possible from powers that may appear as having imperial aspirations. Association with such powers, history tells us, has almost always made the gospel less visible in the world.

In addition to this, Christianity is today in a position where it needs to engage positively with different cultures, and make manifest how the Christian message provides an opportunity to interpret vital and important experiences in people's lives in a manner that makes their experiences matter religiously. The days of rejecting people's experiences as not "fitting" Christian doctrine are past. Today, we need to ask more productively how the church provides resources for interpreting the experiences people have, and how the church is able to offer a way of making sense of those experiences that will also allow for a deeper understanding of the Gospel's message. A constructive and productive engagement with people's experiences is called for in a postmodern context, where the church can no longer define on its own what counts and what does not count as having spiritual significance. This is the only way it may become culturally apparent how and why the church still has something to say, and why people should engage with it as an institution providing resources for their lives.

Hence, a world-rejecting and culture-critical church has limits when facing the postmodern religious conditions, although it is also sometimes in a place to do so. Thus, it is important that the understanding of what Christian doctrine and life mean in today's world is not hijacked by conservative or fundamentalist groups that claim monopoly on what the correct understanding is, and who also easily retreat from the present cultural climate by simply ignoring or demonizing it. A basic affirmation of this world as God's world is a pre-condition for arguing that the Gospel is good news. One of the challenges, in this regard, is that some conservative groups have developed a way of relating to modern science that may prove deeply problematic in the long run. Although there are good reasons for questioning approaches to modern science that seem to desire that it should replace religion, it is, nevertheless, important that Christianity in a postmodern context offers an affirmative approach to modern science, including the natural sciences. If not, it runs the risk of not placing itself on the side of what is needed in order to overcome some of the main challenges we are facing in the present century, especially with regard to climate change. It is conservative groups like these that critics of religion like Dawkins seem to need, in order to continue their unfair representation of contemporary religion. On the other hand, it is also people like Dawkins that provide conservative groups with a self-legitimation saying that they have a mission against positions like his.

Christianity is one thing – and many. The lessons learned from world mission, since Edinburgh, have proved this to the fullest. The present challenge of the churches, when this lesson is learned, is to see the many, culturally-shaped faces of Christianity as resources and gains, and not as problems. Only then can the Christian message be presented and proclaimed in the future as what opens up people's lives to their fullest potential.

The Postmodern Condition and the Churches' (Co)Mission

J. Andrew Kirk

This article has been prompted by the discussion of postmodernity and mission initiated by Professor Henriksen of the Norwegian School of Theology. [1] His thesis is, in my opinion, challenging, provocative, and in parts questionable. I will, therefore, set forward a different missiological response to the phenomenon of postmodernity, in so far as this latter can be grasped with some degree of accuracy. On reading Henriksen's approach to the question of postmodernity and mission, four main elements seem to stand out. I will take these as the main headings of my interaction with the issues.

Understanding Postmodernity

Although a fairly prevalent social and cultural set of circumstances, known as postmodernity, has influenced the beliefs and life-styles of many people living in Western nations in recent decades, its exact nature is not easy to pin down. It is an exaggeration, however, to say that "quite a substantial part of the time-span of the 100 years since Edinburgh 1910 has been postmodern." Most historical accounts place its incipient origins in the mid 1950s, beginning in the field of architecture, with the collapse of modernist architecture, described as:

> ...harsh, rigid skyscrapers and standardised mass housing which does away with individualized nooks and crannies, the idiosyncrasies of clutter, in the name of purity and clarity.[2]

However, a notable cultural revolt against the pretensions of modernist aspirations in other fields of endeavour did not really gather momentum

---

[1] 'Multifaceted Christianity and the Postmodern Religious Condition: Reflections on its Challenges to Churches in the Northern Hemisphere' (in the present volume). Unless indicated otherwise, the unattributed quotations in the main text are taken from this article.

[2] Quoted from Ayn Rand's novel *The Fountainhead* (1947) by Diane Morgan, 'Postmodernity and Architecture' in Stuart Sim (ed.) *The Icon Dictionary of Postmodern Thought* (Cambridge: Icon Books, 1998), 79.

until the beginning of the 1970s (at the earliest); whilst Lyotard's book,[3] first published in 1978, was a main contributory factor in the development of a postmodern consciousness. The statement that a society "has been postmodern" is also problematical. It suggests a massive shift of thought and value systems away from the cultural assumptions imbibed from a modernist or Enlightenment worldview to something substantially different. I believe that the force and influence of postmodern ideas are greatly exaggerated, not least by Christian thinkers, perhaps under the illusion that these produce a cultural environment more conducive to spiritual and religious sympathies than the rigid, secular mentality fostered by an over-rationalist modernity.

Western societies are neither modern nor postmodern in any all-pervasive sense. They shown signs of an unstable mixture of elements from both tendencies. In many areas of life, such as science, technology, economics, business, law and education (not least the requirements for higher degrees in the University sector), the rational procedures highlighted by modernity are still taken for granted. At the same time, some of the characteristics of the postmodern condition, highlighted by Henriksen, are apparent in some sectors of society. He identifies the following traits. First, there is *a scepticism towards grand narratives*. These are over-arching accounts of the reality of the universe and of men and women's place in it. They may claim to describe the direction in which history is going, as in the case of Marxist accounts of the class struggle or neo-liberal accounts of the beneficial progress of capitalism as a wealth-creating mechanism. They may subscribe to the belief that scientific discoveries will eventually explain all the mysteries of life and will ultimately produce for all freedom from the struggle for existence. They may be based on religions that proclaim a universal message of liberation from the anxieties, abuses, violence and self-centredness of human life:

> In contrast to these comprehensive and globalizing theories about human existence, postmodernity proposes a reading of history always bound by limited, context-specific, fallible, and therefore constantly revisable perspectives.[4]

Secondly, *there is doubt about the view that language accurately depicts an objective reality*. In the words of Henriksen, 'There is no neutral, commonly valid or acceptable description of the world…There is no neutral language and no generic language accessible to all.'

Language, it is said, is rooted in particular contexts, and can only ultimately be understood by those who share that context. The consequence of recognising this, according to Henriksen, is that 'We also get different

---

[3] *The Postmodern Condition: A Report on Knowledge* (Minneapolis: The University of Minnesota Press, 1984).

[4] J. Andrew Kirk, 'Postmodernity' in J. Corrie (ed.) *Dictionary of Mission Theology: Evangelical Foundations* (Nottingham: IVP, 2007), 299.

understandings and expressions of understanding when we discuss the same topic. The insistence on the difference in understanding…has been a growing one over the last 100 years.'

This could well mean that our use of concepts is so diverse, given radically different cultural assumptions that we simply fail to engage in a mutually comprehensible conversation with those of other backgrounds.

Thirdly, following on from the variations in the use of language, *we cannot assume that there is a common human rationality*. According to Henriksen:

> We construct different or plural forms of rationality according to specific interests, needs and concerns. We cannot transcend in any radical way the fact that we live in and are conditioned by a certain context that has its special patterns of understanding, rationality and communication.

Finally, and most importantly, we live in an age that celebrates a plurality of views, expressions, customs, traditions and ways of living:

> In its attitude to social existence, postmodernity delights in difference. In line with its deep suspicion of a culturally imposed, rational uniformity, it proposes the inviolable right of minority groups to deviate from the norms of the majority. [5]

To recognise plurality is to recognise the legitimacy of being different and thinking in divergent, contrasting, inconsistent and even conflicting ways. The result is that 'the Other,' (the excluded opposite) is given a chance to be listened to and is allowed to:

> unsettle the 'essences' and 'certainties' of 'normal' society, in order to rehabilitate those ideas and institutions which have been marginalized or eliminated from the mainstream of social engagement. [6]

Postmodern thought is concerned to undermine the assumption that there is only one way of thinking, reasoning, relating to the world, using language, setting goals, relating to other humans and discerning right and wrong. It wishes to subvert the view that the only future for humanity is an extrapolation of a civilisation (Western) that emphasises rational planning, creates global markets, encourages endless consumerism, considers scientific knowledge to be the only universally valid understanding of the world, exalts technology as the solution to all ills and exploits and corrupts the environment. Above all, it is troubled by the perceived threat of an imposed uniformity on social engagement and cultural expression through the enactment of ever more restrictive laws that control what may be said and what it is permitted to do.

---

[5] Kirk, 'Postmodernity', 300.
[6] Kirk, 'Postmodernity', 300.

Challenges to Christian Mission

There is, of course, much more that can be said about postmodernity. [7] This is enough, however, to realise that the postmodern condition poses serious questions to the Christian community in assessing its calling to be light in the world and the salt of the earth: what world and which earth? Henriksen spells out some of these problems. There is the case of what he calls *hard pluralism*. That is the realization that there are differences of opinion so severe that there is little or no hope of them ever being resolved. To use the language of philosophy, they are incommensurable. This fact has implications for inter-religious dialogue. It is futile to pretend that all religions, though using different languages and concepts, are all pointing to the same ultimate reality:

> You offend both Jews and Christians if you say that they are basically one and the same religion...You thereby...ignore how one of these religions (Christianity) is in fact constituted by its difference to the other.

What is true of these two religions, which share the same Scripture, is even truer of other religions which stand much further apart.

Given that there is abroad a deep scepticism towards any statement that claims to be addressed equally to all people, promoting a message of universal importance and relevance becomes problematical. Moreover, there is the danger that 'the church under postmodern conditions runs the risk of becoming just one more "cultural tribe" which seeks to increase its influence and dominion.'

In other words, it is hard to avoid the accusation that the church has concocted a message, simply in order to be able to assert and promote its own unique and privileged position within all cultures and social contexts.

Another major question has to do with notions of historical contingency and limited perspectives. If it is true that "there are unlimited possibilities of understanding phenomena in different ways" and that, therefore, "one should not stick to one mode of understanding, but constantly try to overcome, criticize, make more complete and transcend what is a finalized and given position", then "the past and the already given cannot have any inherent and final normativity". And, if it is true that no-one can claim an "authority based on "God's eye view" of the world, then it would seem logical that in order "to clarify what can count as reliable", one needs to "have a serious discourse with all relevant positions".

In other words, nothing from the past can be taken for granted (including a written text as Scripture and the formulation of basic beliefs in the ecumenical creeds) and nothing in the present is secure, unless it has been subjected to the opinions of others who may legitimately see the meaning of existence in radically different ways. This will lead the Church to "the

---

[7] My own views have been set out in some detail in my book, J. Andrew Kirk, *The Future of Reason, Science and Faith: Following Modernity and Postmodernity* (Aldershot: Ashgate Publishing, 2007), and see the bibliography there.

necessity of constantly rearticulating the Christian message in new ways". The message at all times (including presumably the time of the apostolic testimony to Jesus, the Messiah) could have been stated differently. It is basically a message set out in terms of shifting cultural resources. This being the case, there is always:

> the possibility to reconstruct patterns, constructions and rationalities in the light of other insights. This not only contributes to the multiplicity of constructions, but also amplifies the experience of plurality and contingency.

The Present Situation of Christian Faith

Prior to setting out his own vision for the mission of the church in a postmodern context, Henriksen turns his attention to two further considerations relevant to the question in hand. First, he wishes to give full sway to the notion of 'the Other:'

> The Other is not someone determined and perceived solely from my own privileged point of view, but someone who offers me another point of view…

In other words, the Other represents a disturbing presence which (who?) does not allow me to remain content with my understanding of reality, but challenges me to leave the comfort zone of my own understanding hitherto and embrace (in all likelihood) another way of looking at the world. As often cited in postmodern thinking, the Other cannot be reduced to the same. This means that I cannot simply fit different views into my own framework, thereby nullifying their critical force. Henriksen hints that the Other ultimately can be categorised as God, the one who stands over against humanity calling it to account and expanding the boundaries of what can be perceived.

Henriksen is surely right that "we have more to learn and to understand from this world in which God has placed us with God's mission." It would be arrogance of the most extreme form to pretend that we already had all the answers to the complexities of human existence in a vast universe. We do not know from what direction we may receive wisdom and knowledge that will enrich our appreciation of the full reality of existence. All this is true. However, it is not necessary to invoke the spectre of postmodernity to make this point; it should be deeply embedded in our self-understanding as the finite creatures of an infinite God. Not only is there always more to learn about God and God's world, there is a responsibility to be open to correction.

In the case of postmodernity, it is not easy to see why I should be interested in listening to and regarding as important what the Other has to say. The problem is that, in a postmodern setting, I personally am the ultimate reference-point for deciding what is worth listening to, and what is not. And, if this is so, by what criteria do I judge whether the Other is to be taken seriously? I do not believe that postmodern thinking can give a coherent answer to that question. Listening to the Other may simply give rise to more confusion. There is an incredible babble of voices in our contemporary world, many of them saying wholly contradictory things. What we need, therefore, is not simply a listening ear, but *discernment*: we need to know whether the other is talking sense. We need some kind of utterly reliable reference-point in relation to which we can have some assurance that we are not being deluded.

Henriksen points to God as this ultimate benchmark. However, he immediately invalidates his own line of reasoning by suggesting "that God always transcends our notions and ideas of what God is." Here, we have to be extremely careful that we do not fall into the postmodern trap of an endless deferment of knowledge, such that we are constantly revising our notions, never ever capturing the essential nature and meaning of anything. Such a move would be self-defeating, for we could never know that God is not like the way we know him, unless we already had reliable knowledge of how God is. In other words, we need to be able to start with a true understanding of God, even though limited, in order to be able to correct our false notions of God. Apart from this, everything we say is either pure personal preference or speculation, neither of which amounts to an Other from whom we may receive additional insights and understanding about the human condition.

So, contrary to Henriksen's assumption that the postmodern "insistence on plurality and construction" points to the figure of the Other, the Other actually vanishes in the very undifferentiated plurality that postmodernity espouses. Now, Henriksen seems to acknowledge that this may be the case when he turns to his second major consideration, the notion of *givenness*. The Other now becomes the given. This implies a robust doctrine of creation and the related ideas of natural law and natural theology. "God is active in all of creation, also outside the spheres of faith and church." "God's work is prior to any human activity." "Not everything in the world is constructed – something is there before the construction that takes place in human reasoning through understanding and reflection." "The given suggests boundaries for our constructions as well. This implies that a total relativism is impossible, simply because we cannot construct the body or the world in any way we like." "Our constructions are dependent upon the given character of God's creation. Hence, they are already initially determined by what God has done."

The burden of Henriksen's argument at this point is that there is a given reality, which remains what it is independent of our thinking about it or acting upon it. This is profoundly un-postmodern, which stipulates that the real can only be reached through our subjective perceptions and constructions. The philosopher Kant has been enormously influential in persuading generations that we cannot know how things are in themselves; "we can only know them as they appear to us through the categories of the mind." [8] Here, Henriksen seems to be somewhat equivocal, for having developed the concept of the given in ways that suggest an objectivity not compromised by our whole subjective mental apparatus, he then seems to advocate another form of philosophical idealism: 'The given itself is only accessible through a certain cultural shape (construction).'

The problem with this affirmation is that, if taken at face value, it means that we cannot get behind our constructions of the world to the ultimately given. Henriksen, however, wants to maintain that we must, so that we can deconstruct 'outdated or obsolete constructions of cultural forms' and set up 'a barrier against any total relativism.' Science, ultimately, is dependent on a realist view of the material world, for the predictive success of scientific theories demonstrates the ability of scientific method to make contact with the ultimately given. It shows that the given is not just an hypothesis but can actual be known. Science, however, does not have the ability to know everything about human life in God's given world, so we also need God's word to help us discover the fuller picture: 'God's word can have an impact upon how we develop the constructions of our culture, and on our understanding of and ordering of the world.'

Here, I think Henriksen could be more positive about the place of God's word in appreciating the nature of reality and being involved in its guardianship and supervision. Thus, for example, if "God is…working in and by means of our cultural constructions …by inspiring us through his Word", he also sometimes has to work against us when we decide to flout the workings of creation and do violence to the people he has created.[9] We also need to know whether the Word has a determining impact not just a motivating and encouraging one. The main given has to be the Word of God; creation is also a given, but needs the Word to interpret it. These are the two 'books of God' to which Francis Bacon made reference.

Henriksen's final conclusion to his discussion of the 'Other' and the 'given' is that:

> this means respect and tolerance for those not sympathetic to Christian faith and thinking. That is a consequence of accepting that we live in a postmodern culture, marked by plurality.

There are two basic problems with this statement. Firstly, respect and tolerance do not belong to the same moral categories. Respect for other human beings, whatever their beliefs and actions, is an absolute moral injunction, since they bear the very image of God. They have a value, intrinsic to their humanity, which cannot therefore be either conferred upon them by other humans or taken away. Tolerance, however, is by no means a categorical moral duty. There are many things we should not tolerate, such as withdrawing respect from others, abusing them and arbitrarily taking

[8] Kirk, *The Future of Reason*, 173 and 54-55.

[9] Although we cannot develop the thought here, post-modern reconstructions are inimical to the prophetic word of judgement against idolatry and injustice.

away their freedoms. [10] The two moral virtues may well clash; when they do, respect trumps tolerance. This is a truth often misunderstood in our ultra-liberal, postmodern societies in the West. Tolerance of difference, often in the name of multi-culturalism, can easily be the consequence of or result in indifference to various forms of ill-treatment.

Secondly, for a Christian neither respect nor an appropriate tolerance is the result of 'accepting that we live in a postmodern culture, marked by plurality.' It is, rather, the consequence of accepting the Gospel of Jesus Christ that takes both the dignity of human beings and the reality of their sin seriously. In other words, our attitude and behaviour towards others cannot be grounded in the shifting sands of an ever-changing cultural mood, but in the tried and tested eternal Word of God.

The Mission of the Church

The whole preceding discussion sets the context in which the church's engagement with contemporary Western society and culture takes place. Naturally, the nature of this engagement will depend to some degree on one's assessment of the character and importance of the postmodern condition. I have already given reasons why, at crucial points, I dissent from Henriksen's interpretation of the present context for mission in the West. It is not surprising, therefore, that I should find myself disagreeing fairly profoundly with his principal proposal that the major task of those who represent Christian faith in the West is to find appropriate ways of retraditionalising it.

The key defining point for engagement in mission is apparently no longer, as the church had long thought, the commission that comes from its resurrected Lord to proclaim and live out the reality of God's kingdom and make disciples of Jesus among all peoples, but '*the secularized individual* and his or her need for finding a more comprehensive pattern of meaning and understanding in his/her life.' The church's task, according to this way of looking at mission is to offer '*resources for the shaping of personal identity in a culture of pluralism,*' where individuals decide, according to their own sense of need, what makes their life worth living.

According to this view, in an inescapably pluralistic culture, the church simply represents one set of traditions among a plethora of options available that may or may not seem relevant to people's felt need for '*resources of morality, cultural identity etc... .irrespective of their personal faith.*' It is to be hoped that in societies like the Nordic countries, where 'a majority of people maintain their membership in these (mainstream) churches without actively practicing religion or sharing the "official faith"

---

[10] Among actions and beliefs that should not be tolerated are some that are sanctioned by religious teachings, such as the way that women are regarded and treated.

or confession of these churches,' the people may turn to the church in order to 'develop as humans – in a way that leads to deeper spiritual life.' 'Thus, the churches will be filling the void left by a consumerist culture that not only leads to a uniform and flat type of cultural sphere, but which is also basically unable to provide people with a sense of life's meaning and direction.' In this kind of context, the church's main task, according to Henriksen, is to find ways of capitalising on its long deep association with and impact on society and culture in Western secularised nations, so that people may find 'resources for life-interpretation and a different way of engaging with reality.'[11]

For a number of reasons I believe that this approach to mission in a postmodern climate is profoundly mistaken. I will try to set out the arguments that should, I believe, point to a different account of the church's mission engagement with contemporary life-forms in Western nations.

Postmodernity is itself a problem

Throughout his article, Henriksen seems to believe that postmodernity is a given reality that simply has to be accepted. He allows that a plurality of beliefs, moral values, and life-style choices are just a fact of life, and are to be welcomed because they challenge all monolithic interpretations of human existence. He resolutely refuses to admit that the main characteristic of postmodernity is that it is infused with a spirit of relativism. Humanity's great enemy, according to postmodernity, is the claim that ultimate truth can be known, for this leads inexorably to hegemony and doctrinaire authoritarianism:

> Postmodernism…means cutting ourselves adrift from solid and stable boundary markers of what is right and wrong, good and bad, correct and incorrect, true and false, real and illusory and sailing off into the unknown without benefit of map and compass. [12]

For postmodern thinking truth-claims are always relative to a particular tradition. There is no universally valid norm to measure all possible deviations. Human discourse can describe what is counted as *normal* belief and behaviour at any one time; it has no tools for measuring what is *normative*. Now Henriksen seems to go along with this way of conceiving reality, rather than seeing it as a profound difficulty for human flourishing.

---

[11] One may speculate that this approach to mission in a post-modern culture leads to the reverse of Grace Davie's famous phrase that Western populations in general 'believe without belonging' (to organised religion) (see her, *Religion in Modern Europe: a Memory Mutates* (Oxford: OUP, 2000). In Henriksen's account, at least in countries with a strong tradition of national churches, people may now "'belong' without believing."

[12] Gene Blocher, 'An Explanation of Postmodernism', in Castell (*et al.*, eds.) *An Introduction to Modern Philosophy: Examining the Human Condition* (New York: Macmillan College Publishing House, 1994).

It leads to the absolute authority of the individual "I" in deciding what is to be believed and practised:

> Authority in a retraditionalization process does not lie with the tradition in question, but with the individual.

What postmodernity recommends is that individuals keep their options open among a wide variety of interpretations of experience. Choice becomes the main factor; and for choice to be meaningful there needs to be 'a wide spectrum of resources that can be called tradition.' It is amazing that, given Henriksen's subsequent criticism of some forms of Christianity (most notably those that associate themselves with 'powers that may appear as having imperial aspirations'), he should recommend a process that can and does lead to people choosing the exotic and the unfamiliar – the whole gamut of new age fantasies, alternative medicine and therapies and any crackpot invention that can be touted for profit – or an authoritarian creed, where the individual submits blindly to the programme of a cult figure. The problem is that postmodernity dismisses truth-claims as discriminatory and, therefore, oppressive; for, if there are true statements about reality, there are also false ones. However, in his account of the plurality of traditions, Henriksen does not seem to acknowledge the very real possibility that some may be erroneous and destructive. With the emphasis on the authority and choice of the individual and the entirely pragmatic advantages of opting for one tradition over against another, what might hinder a person choosing to follow a tradition (perhaps unwittingly) that is thoroughly harmful to human life?:

> It is a strange irony of the postmodern stance that the apparently radical idea of ridding thought of the notion of correspondence actually encourages the determination of 'truth' by means of arbitrary power and authority. Unless there is an independent point of reference, truth equates with subjective reckonings and issues are settled by either superior force or persuasive power. [13]

To take the postmodern condition at face value without apparently submitting it to critical scrutiny is to expose people to the very real possibility of deceptive, noxious and fantastical beliefs and practices.

The Christian faith is not just one option among many

Henriksen certainly gives the impression that in a postmodern climate it would be arrogant and futile to distinguish too readily between different kinds of religious traditions and spiritual experiences. Thus he says, for example,

> With postmodernity, emphasis is not on doctrine, but on religious culture as providing means of self-expression…Globalization makes world-views more

[13] Kirk, *The Future of Reason*, 169.

> relative, and recognizes the equality of different forms of socio-cultural formation and simultaneously celebrates heterogeneity and variation.

It is true that Henriksen is here describing the way in which postmodern consciousness shapes the attitude of the contemporary generation in their attitude towards religion and experiences of the spiritual dimension of life. He is not necessarily giving his own view. Nevertheless, in the final section of his article, he appears to endorse the legitimacy of plurality in people's approaches to the spiritual:

> The days of rejecting people's experiences as not 'fitting' Christian doctrine are past…A constructive and productive engagement with people's experiences is called for in a postmodern context where the church can no longer define on its own what counts and what does not as having spiritual significance.

Taken at face value, these affirmations seem to be saying that every experience that people have of a reality beyond the mundane should be affirmed by the Christian community. If this is not the case, how may one discriminate between valid and invalid experiences, if Christian doctrine is not a reliable guide?

The church as it contemplates its calling within a postmodern climate is caught in a dilemma. On the one hand, and quite rightly, it no longer commands any particularly privileged position within the populace. It cannot any longer take for granted that people will listen to its message as having authority and a normative value just because it comes from the church. In this sense, Western nations are decidedly post-Christian:

> The church cannot any longer take for granted that it is well known what its message is. We can no longer count on people to know what Christianity is all about.

On the contrary, what often filters through to the general population as constituting the belief of Christians is a highly distorted version, fabricated by the media. One can almost guarantee that many professional commentators on matters religious, including the religious correspondents of newspapers and the broadcast media, not to mention the opinions of the 'new atheists' (Dawkins, Grayling, Harris and many others), will seriously misrepresent mainstream Christian belief. Therefore, there is no alternative but to begin where people are 'spiritually' in their postmodern habitat.

On the other hand, as Henriksen recognises, there is a givenness to the shape of the world and human existence within it, which is objectively real, whatever people may think or experience. Moreover, the church has been entrusted with '*a responsibility for maintaining a unifying tradition based on preaching the one Word of God to all people at the same time.*' In other words, God's revealed Word is applicable to all people. It is contemporary. It is one, in the sense that it is not open to many, varying and even contradictory interpretations. Henriksen sums up this aspect of the Church's calling, by saying that 'a basic affirmation of this world as God's world is a precondition for arguing that the Gospel is good news.'

However, this strand in Henriksen's perception of the mission task of the church is not developed. Nowhere does he equate God's Word with Jesus Christ as interpreted by the first witnesses of his life, death and resurrection. Nowhere does he set forth what he understands by the good news of the Gospel; that, for example, the Gospel is good news because it proclaims what God has done and is doing to rescue humanity from all kinds of idolatry (including religious idolatry) and injustices that are destroying God's good creation.

Whatever Henriksen's ultimate intention, he gives the impression of promoting what one might call an ultra-accommodationist approach to culture. It appears to begin from the old presupposition (strongly represented in the 1960s) that 'the world sets the agenda.' His diagnosis of the mood of contemporary Western, secular cultures, is perceptive. However, he does not really begin to explore the negative effects of pluralism and relativism. Though he speaks about Christian tradition, he does not identify it. Does it have an irreplaceable core that is not modifiable according to the shifting sands of time and place? His argument about difference would seem to show that he is equivocal at this point. If it does not have this recognizable and non-negotiable core self-understanding, from where does the identity of the Christian community come? How do we recognise one another across history and cultures as belonging to the same one body of Christ? The Christian faith (tradition) can only offer resources, if it is true to its founding message; otherwise, it can easily be remade in the image of culture, and lose its distinctiveness and its savour.

It is symptomatic of Henriksen's approach to contemporary postmodern culture that he finishes his article by reaffirming, in the vaguest of terms, that 'the Christian message also (is to) be presented and proclaimed in the future as what *opens up people's lives to the fullest.*'[14] This is a significant statement for it is precisely the kind of attitude that Charles Taylor in his massive study of the rise of what he calls 'exclusive humanism' diagnoses as one of the main causes of secularism. It is the belief that has crystallised over the last three and a half centuries in the West that human beings can flourish without recourse to the transforming power of God's grace. The problem with many attempts to analyse the postmodern condition is that they presuppose a deep rupture with the convictions of modernity. This, however, is far from being true. There is an enormous amount of continuity between the two, and not least in their common assumption that our age is defined by its secularity. Without a thorough grasp of the all-pervading notion of the secular mind-set, people have misinterpreted postmodernity as a rediscovery of the spiritual, a re-enchantment of the world.

Taylor's analysis of contemporary western, secular culture is more profound than that which pretends that postmodern thinking represents a radical break with the world-view of modernity. Already in the late 19th

[14] Emphasis has been added.

century, he recounts how some people who had firmly rejected Christian faith nevertheless returned to the assumed spiritual capacity within human experience "but within the bounds of an impersonal framework."[15] In other words, it is still viable to speak the language of the spiritual, but only within an imminent world order:

> Religion is afraid to face the fact that we are alone in the universe, and without cosmic support. As children, we do indeed, find this hard to face, but growing up is becoming ready to look reality in the face.[16]

I suspect that the postmodern generation, whom Henriksen wishes to address, considers itself to be adult in this sense, and yet at the same time is willing, indeed feels a strong need, to explore a 'spiritual' dimension to life. Many of them are the people (dare I say it?) who have been confirmed within the Nordic Lutheran churches as adolescents and who have, subsequently, interpreted their experience as the culminating-point of their relationship with orthodox Christianity, from which they have graduated into a kind of indifferent agnosticism. The only novelty that postmodernity has brought into the situation is to give a kind of cultural permission to explore spirituality, without having to accept all the baggage that comes with formal religion. As Taylor says, I believe correctly, 'a spiritual-but-not-Christian (or Jewish or Muslim) position, adopted on something like these grounds, has remained a very widespread option in our culture.'[17]

If this is a more comprehensive explanation of the majority view of religion in contemporary Western societies than that given by those who confine themselves to reflecting on postmodernity, then Henriksen's proposal for engagement with the present generation may well fall wide of the mark. Of course, the Christian message has to be related to the present context. It is not enough to assume that language familiar to the church community will have any direct resonance with those outside. The word of God must be in the language of the people. Mission is about communication (not only with words, but also deeds), and communication is about translation. The language of many of our contemporaries is devoid of any reference to anything beyond the mundane. The principal point of contact between the Gospel message and a so-called postmodern generation is not so much postmodernity, as a view of the world, as the experience of being human. What is at stake is what it means to be human. I believe that the notion of human flourishing is a place where Christian faith can engage with contemporary culture with a starting-point that both sides can agree is significant.

However, unlike, what I take to be Henriksen's approach, the mission of the church is not to offer resources that will help people articulate better for

---

[15] Charles Taylor, *A Secular Age* (Cambridge, MA: Harvard University Press, 2007), 364.

[16] Taylor, *A Secular Age*, 364.

[17] Taylor, *A Secular Age*, 364.

themselves their own sense of meaning and direction, but to *persuade* people first that genuine human flourishing or fulfilment is impossible within a secular view of life, and secondly that it can be accomplished *only* by allowing one's life to be transformed by the real presence of Jesus Christ in every aspect of existence. Mission in the Western world has to be engaged in advocacy, partly to correct all the false pictures that people may have of the true nature of faith and spirituality, but more importantly as witness to the ways in which God, who created us as human beings, wishes to restore to us the fullness of our humanity.

Witness to a Post-Christendom Era

Plural Mission and Missionary Plural in a Post-Socialist Context: Using the Example of a Post-'Volkskirche', East German Region

Michael Herbst

Introduction

Two dialogues are not entirely atypical for the sociological context discussed in this article[1].

The first one: This happened during a school conference in the city of Greifswald. There was a parent representative on the school council who was completely unchurched, and he was interested in the cathedral of Greifswald. He knew the church from various visits and now asked me the very telling question: 'Do worship services still take place here, occasionally?' The question was telling because, on the one hand, it expressed the assumption that religious life in this city had perished long ago; on the other hand, the question signals that, although the religious life of this church has not perished, it happens in the corner of those who are faithful to the church anyway, and it does not really become public. Is this still 'publice docere', if the public does not know about the teaching anymore?

The second one: In a diaconical institution, a young unchurched man is doing an internship. In a staff meeting, the difficult situation in the institution is discussed. At one point during the discussion, the intern comes forward and recommends to the leader: 'Couldn't you now tell again the fairy tale of the enlarged barns?' What he meant was: the Parable of the Rich Fool in Luke 12. Again, the impression is ambivalent: On the one hand, for this young man, the parable is on the same level as the fairy tale of Hansel and Gretel, on the other hand, he has taken it in with fresh

---

[1] I owe many thanks to my colleagues Matthias Clausen, Ulf Harder and Martin Reppenhagen for the translation of this paper. It has been originally presented to the European Church Leadership Consultation of the Lutheran World Federation held in Greifswald from 11-16 September 2008. The presentation was held on September 13th at a churchplant in a town district of the city of Bergen (Bergen-Rotensee) on the island Rugia in northeastern Germany. Typical East German architecture and a very low percentage of church members among the inhabitants characterize this particular district.

curiosity, as an exciting story, and now he can apparently offer it as a powerful intervention.[2]

Plural Mission in East Germany often takes place at zero point situations like this, where church and unchurched people encounter one another. The repository of tradition has been used up. Knowledge of tradition is not even rudimentary. But if contact is successfully made, then trust grows, and the freshness of the encounter makes the gospel resonate anew.

I would like to place this ambivalence at the beginning of my talk, in order to provide a first insight into our missionary context, and also in order to prevent me and us from seeing mission in East Germany as all-too easy or as all-too hard. A zero point situation means: Beware of old and easy recipes, they might not be up to this situation. But a zero point situation also means: Beware of self-imposed depression and hopelessness. They could overlook what surprises God already has in store in this situation.

Thus my thesis is almost formulated: *In the East German context, the missionary challenge of the church presents itself anew. I am convinced that we can only be faithful to our calling as a Lutheran church in this context if we live and work in a way that is at once sober and hopeful, inspired by mission and competent in dealing with plurality.*

I want to develop this thesis in three ways. I will begin with a fresh encounter of the term mission and its relevance for the church. Afterwards I will describe the sociological context of Dechristianization in East Germany and its impact on churchlife to present a closer view on the chances and challenges. Lastly the Protestant Church in Pomerania serves as an example to illustrate characteristics of a plural mission in a mainly unchurched context.

Missional Church: Rehabilitating an 'Un-Word'

A 'diseased word'

I do not have to comment at length on the fact that mission evokes complicated reactions: For some, it is enthusiasm, for others, it is skepticism and rejection. For some it is the key commission of any Christian and of the whole church, for others it smells of the overpowering of people, of a know-it-all attitude and of intolerance. This is the case already within the church, and more so outside the walls of the church. There, the word mission is a 'burnt up' word.

For instance, the young East German writer Juli Zeh, in her novel with the title "Schilf" ('Reed'), describes a nun entering the compartment of a train. There she meets the novel's protagonist, Maike. 'The nun is pestering

[2] Told by Rev. Christine Rösch who ministers in the Protestant church of Central Germany (Evangelische Kirche in Mitteldeutschland).

every passenger walking past with the attempt to start a conversation, as if to prove to the poor Lord Jesus that people still do not want to be left alone after all. Love your neighbour, or whoever happens to sit on your neighbouring seat. Maike shivers.' [3] Is this mission: making people shiver, talking without connecting to them, pestering whoever is sitting next to you, ignoring people who are not interested? Apparently, at least we do not automatically earn the right to talk to people about our innermost faith.

Rehabilitation of mission within the church

In the perspective of the church, however, a lot has happened. We have rediscovered that mission belongs to the very nature of the church. In the Evangelical Church in Germany, this is connected, for example, to the statement of the General Synod in Leipzig in 1999: 'Coming from this Synod, the signal is: For the Protestant church, the issue of faith and the missionary commission is its first priority.' [4] In the understanding of the synod, mission is the mission of God, into which the church is taken up, but which does not happen for the sake of the church. The synod maintains: 'Our commission is to open people's eyes to the truth and beauty of the Christian message. We want to win them for freely binding themselves to Christ and to keep to the church as the community of believers.' [5]

Since then, mission has been on the agenda of the church in Germany. Our Research Institute for Evangelism and Church Development in Greifswald is situated within that context. For the first time, there is an academic institution that is able to concentrate, in research and teaching, on questions of mission in our context. It is financed by charitable foundations and by churches, and supported especially by the Pomeranian church and its Bishop. [6]

The process of reform that the Evangelical Church in Germany has started to implement with the thesis paper "Kirche der Freiheit" (Church of Freedom) in 2006 is also unthinkable without the affirmation of mission. Mission – and there is an ecumenical consensus on this – is not what we do by sending out missionaries to others. Mission is what we need ourselves. Thus it is said in the thesis paper:

> Part of what is encouraging today is that in all streams and groupings of the church, a missionary reorientation of the church is welcomed. When talking of "mission", people do not only think of partnerships with churches on other continents; and a missionary orientation is not only equated with evangelistic

---

[3] Juli Zeh, *Schilf* (Frankfurt/M. 2007) 194.

[4] Kirchenamt der EKD (ed.) *Reden von Gott in der Welt. Der missionarische Auftrag der Kirche an der Schwelle zum 3. Jahrtausend* (Frankfurt/M. 2001) 41.

[5] Kirchenamt der EKD, *Reden von Gott in der Welt*, 38.

[6] Cf. Michael Herbst, Johannes Zimmermann und Jörg Ohlemacher (ed.) *Missionarische Perspektiven für eine Kirche der Zukunft* (beg 1: Neukirchen-Vluyn, 2005).

> forms of proclamation. Rather, mission is recognized as the task of the whole church to address people in our own society in a way that awakens their faith, a task that must show and be emphasized in all areas of church work.[7]

In the implementation of the process of reform, the missionary venture is one of three main focuses. [8] This is also reflected in the foundation of a 'Centre for Mission in the Region', which will be situated in Dortmund, Stuttgart, and Greifswald from 2009.

In the Lutheran context, reference must also be made to the Lund declaration of the Lutheran World Federation: Here, the office of the bishop is interpreted in the context of the apostolicity of the church.[9] In paragraph 28, the connection of the bishop's office and apostolicity is interpreted in terms of the theology of mission. Reminding of the sending (or mission) of the Easter witnesses at the empty tomb (Mt 28:10) and of the disciples on the mountain (Mt 28:16-20), it is said: 'The mission to which the apostles were called remains the mission of the whole church throughout history. As this mission shapes the church, so the church is rightly called apostolic.' [10]

By the way, in the English-speaking world, it is becoming more common to speak of a 'missional church' rather than a 'missionary church', in order to break away from an outdated understanding of mission. Thus, mission is the holistic ministry of the church, which is understood as the 'hermeneutics' (the interpreter) of the gospel, and which witnesses to God's love in word and deed, embodies this love and makes it tangible, and invites people to faith.[11]

I cannot develop a full-blooded theology of mission here, but I want to make one more statement on the nature of mission.

A statement on the nature of mission: crossing boundaries

How can mission correspond to rather than contradict the original missionary, Jesus himself? What does the mission of Jesus of Nazareth look like, who declares: 'As the Father has sent me, I am sending you'

---

[7] Kirchenamt der EKD (ed.) *Kirche der Freiheit. Perspektiven für die evangelische Kirche im 21. Jahrhundert. Ein Impulspapier des Rates der EKD* (Hannover, 2006) 18.

[8] Next to 'Worship and Sermon' and 'Spiritual Leadership in Church'.

[9] Lutheran World Federation, *Episcopal Ministry within the Apostolicity of the Church. The Lund*

Statement by the Lutheran World Federation – A Communion of Churches (Lund, 2007).

[10] Lutheran World Federation, *Episcopal Ministry*, 6.

[11] Cf. e.g. Darrell L. Guder *Missional Church: A Vision for the Sending of the Church in North America. The People of God Sent on a Mission* (Gospel & Our Culture: Grand Rapids, 1998); Lesslie Newbigin *The Gospel in a Pluralist Society* (Grand Rapids/Genf, 1989) 222ff.

(John 20:21)? My thesis is: The mission of Jesus of Nazareth was the constant crossing of boundaries for the sake of the love of God.

Allow me to explain this in more detail: In New Testament times, there was a clear code as to who was to associate with whom, and also: who was not to associate with whom. Pious people were sure that they did God a favour when they kept themselves at a distance, when they separated from others and drew fine distinctions: separating themselves from the tenants of Roman tax booths, from women from the allegedly oldest profession in the world, from leprous people and Samaritans, from women, children and certainly all kinds of Gentiles. In their eyes, holiness was about separation: profane from sacred, holy from unholy, pious from worldly, outside from inside. On this view, according to the German sociologist and prominent thinker in the sociological systems theory Niklas Luhmann, religion has an excluding effect.[12]

But what does Jesus of Nazareth do? Apparently, he is a boundary crosser by conviction. He is about inclusion rather than exclusion[13], and he draws inside the very people who are outside. Therefore, he crosses boundary after boundary. Worse still, he claims that there is rejoicing in heaven when the walls come down and when people with which God had nothing to do and who had nothing to do with God – when people like this come home to the Father (Luke 15:7). And he claims that God is by no means honoured when we build walls and keep people from entering the Father's house. From now on, to be holy means to cross boundaries, to connect with others and to welcome the very people who had previously been "outside the door". In the eyes of Jesus of Nazareth, the greatest sin is not to be connected to those who the Father loves, on whose misery he has compassion, and to whom he wants to grant access to his presence. With his whole being and work, Jesus radiates the message: There is a lot of space next to me, come here, 'in my Father's house are many rooms' (John 14:2).

The companions whom Jesus had called to him saw this in their master. They experienced it in their circle. They were amazed: The person who in their eyes was the holiest person on earth was also the one who was the least exclusive and the most decidedly inclusive. Thus, the mission of Jesus of Nazareth also became their mission, and crossing boundaries became their passion. Jesus sent them to all, to the entire world, to all nations and peoples. He did not draw any distinctions anymore; becoming a disciple should be the privilege of all people.

This can be seen, for example, in the Apostle Paul. He is infected by the vision of Jesus, and so he is ready to radically deny himself. He is ready to put his own good completely on hold as the task is to reach people with the

---

[12] Cf. Niklas Luhmann: *Inklusion und Exklusion* (Soziologische Aufklärung. Bd.6, Opladen 1995, 237-264) 262.

[13] Cf. Miroslav Volf, *Exclusion and Embrace. A Theological Exploration of Identity, Otherness and Reconciliation* (Nashville, 1996).

message of the gospel. He does not want to ask any longer: What is dear and holy to me, what is my tradition of living in the community of faith, what is my style of worshipping God? He wants to do everything that connects people to the gospel, and he wants to leave everything what could keep them away from the gospel, as long as it is really the message of Christ. He wants to become all things to all people so that by all possible means he might save some (1Cor 9:19-23).

So I can only participate in the gospel when I join in with its dynamic movement towards people who have never heard of Jesus and still live their entire lives without connection to him. If I refuse to join in with this inclusive effort of the gospel, then I exclude myself from it. A church should be a community on the move, crossing boundaries and making inclusion possible.

So God has a mission, which he has never cancelled. He is determined to look for and find people. And when he meets with people, then he does what is necessary. And apparently he does have those who are privileged and favoured: those who seem to us to be furthest away. And apparently various things can happen when God comes close to somebody: The sick get healthy, the hungry get fed, the crushed are lifted up, and children are blessed. Word and deed, diaconical service and evangelism belong together; they are like the two legs of the dance of mission.

In theological language, I could say it like this: There is no mission without incarnation, at least, when this is about God's mission. There is no mission without incarnation, that means: As the word became flesh and dwelt among us (John 1:14), so the mission of the church of Jesus must become 'flesh' and go where people are, overcome social and cultural boundaries and immigrate into every social environment.

Mission Impossible? The Situation in East Germany

Mission happens never without its context: God's mission will take its own shape in every context and will substantiate the more abstract statements of the first chapter. Thus we have to look at the East German context in particular. And it is in West- and East-Europe – maybe together with the Czech Republic as a special case of high-grade Dechristianization.[14]

We could speak about statistics for a long time

For the mission of the church, one of the main challenges is certainly the stable situation of unchurched people in Germany:

> By this we mean people who have not belonged to any church for three or four decades and "who have forgotten that they have forgotten God." In the

[14] Karl Gabriel e.a., *Religion und Kirchen in Ost(Mittel)Europa: Deutschland-Ost* (Gott nach dem Kommunismus: Ostfildern, 2003).

East of Germany, they make up 70-75% of the population, which is about 10-12 million people, in the West, they make up 25-30%, which is about 15 million people.[15]

Of course, numbers are always likely to be impressive. In 1959, the Pomeranian Church still had 700.000 members, whereas now only around 100.000 people belong to the Protestant Church, which is about 20% of the population. The Catholic Church is traditionally very small in the North East, while free churches and other groups do not play a major role. They even have more difficulties with mission, because any given Pomeranian will prefer to get involved with the traditional Church, if ever he wants to have a go at religion, rather than getting involved with any of these groups which to him look obscure. We can also talk about the average age in the Pomeranian Church and find out that the average age is even higher than in the ageing society in general. It is close to 60 years or older, whereas the percentage of children and young people is low. The numbers show a small church with the status of a minority. By the way, it is a church which still is shrinking, although it does not shrink so much because its membership is declining but because of migration to the West and because its membership is getting older. It has been like this for at least one generation: Many leave, and mainly those who are gifted. We speak about the 'brain drain', the loss of the elites. It is a small church in a minority situation. If the "Volkskirchen" are characterized by the fact that it is normal for most people to belong to the church – to whatever degree – then our church is surely no longer a "Volkskirche". We could speak about statistics for a long time, but we would only scratch the surface of the problems.

We could speak about history for a long time

No doubt, this is crucial, too. However, in thinking about history, we should not start with the German Democratic Republic.[16] We need to go further back to follow the roots of the meagre situation in the North East in the past 200 years.

In a small research study in 1893, Pastor Wittenberg from the small village of Swantow, on the island of Rugia, in Northeastern Germany, came to the conclusion[17] that the average Pomeranian is not only cumbersome and sceptical of everything new[18], but is also 'largely indifferent' towards

---

[15] Hartmut Bärend, *Kirche mit Zukunft. Impulse für eine missionarische Volkskirche* (Gießen, 2006) 43.

[16] To the deep historical roots points Helmut Geller, Karl Gabriel e.a. in their paper: 'Die Kirchen in der DDR vor und nach der Wende', Karl Gabriel e.a.., *Religion und Kirchen in Ost(Mittel)Europa: Deutschland-Ost.*, (P.M. Zulehner e.a. (ed.): Gott nach dem Kommunismus: Ostfildern, 2003) 325-336.

[17] H. Wittenberg, *Die Lage der ländlichen Arbeiter in Neuvorpommern und auf Rügen* (Leipzig, 1894).

[18] H. Wittenberg, *Die Lage der ländlichen Arbeiter*, 47.

the Christian faith.[19] Church attendance is around 3% rather than around 6%,[20] and it is more about adhering to church rituals, which are deemed unavoidable, like attending infant baptisms, weddings, and funerals.[21] The catechumenate of the children is almost completely missing.[22] Pomerania is – according to Wittenberg in A.D. 1893 – a 'spiritual grave yard'.[23]

Our part of Pomerania has never been a flourishing spiritual landscape. Revivals only happened locally. After World War II, there was not very much left of the country and the church in Pomerania. What was spiritually inspiring was mainly the immigration from East Pomerania. These immigrants played a major role within the local churches.

The success of the propaganda of the GDR fell on a ground, which was well prepared by religious indifference and abstinence from church life. However, what was new was that atheism was now anchored above the level of the individual: Not only individual people are unchurched, but most parts of public culture, the educational system, civic places are unchurched as well.[24]

The marginalization of Christians by the regime of the Socialist Party also belongs to history. The politics of the reigning party was hostile towards the church and attacked it mainly where it hurt most: in education and lifetime support. In education, this happened with the fight against religious education and youth work. Education also meant to gradually establish an atheist picture of the world, which then functioned as a scientific world view, and to plant this into the minds and hearts of children and young people. This crop flourished and for many people, it is still part of their deepest beliefs today. And as for lifetime support, the socialist state created its own rites: The church lost its interpretive authority with regard to the major turning points in life, and the authority to support and counsel people from the cradle to the grave, because now the state was able to dedicate names, to turn young people into grown up socialists and to comfort people, more or less, in their last hour. Education and lifetime support were taken away from the church, and people were weaned from Christianity generation by generation. In addition, there was pressure, discrimination, and social disadvantages. It became expensive to remain a Christian. Socialist cities emerged, and church steeples should not disturb their appearance. Some steeples in old cities had to give way, some blown

---

[19] H. Wittenberg, *Die Lage der ländlichen Arbeiter*, 67.

[20] H. Wittenberg, *Die Lage der ländlichen Arbeiter*, 59.

[21] H. Wittenberg, *Die Lage der ländlichen Arbeiter*, 70.

[22] H. Wittenberg, *Die Lage der ländlichen Arbeiter*, 67.

[23] H. Wittenberg, *Die Lage der ländlichen Arbeiter*, 70ff.: 'Where ever one goes in the religious field, everywhere indifference, and it is the most evil of all. Is it not possible to find means to abolish it, New Pommerania and Rugia remains for ever what they are, a spiritual grave yard.'

[24] Cf. e.g. Ehrhart Neubert "Konfessionslose in Ostdeutschland. Folgen verinnerlichter Unterdrückung", *PTh* 87 (1998), 368-379.

up like the church of the University of Leipzig. When rural life was industrialized, the agricultural culture shaped by the church was finally replaced by socialist production co-operatives.

History – it ought to be told as family history: of the grandfather who had still been confirmed but then withdrew, the father who was never baptized, and the child for whom it is now normal not to belong to any church. The loss of the language of faith should not be underestimated. The grandfather still knew the Christian ABC, but did not pass it on to the father. However, some subversive grandmothers did it anyway. But most of the fathers did not have anything left to pass on. Children did not learn the language with which they could have learned to believe.

The "Wende" in 1989 did not bring any change. The revival and revitalization that had been hoped for failed to appear. People did not return in crowds, on the contrary, the church continued to shrink. Do people not become more and more spiritual, do we not talk of the return of religion and the re-spiritualization of humankind? Yes, but not here.

Fact is: the majority of people are far from faith

It is not for nothing that bishop Noack from the East German city Magdeburg says again and again: 'Don't fool yourselves. We "Ossis" (people from East Germany) are immune against religion.' Despite all hopes, the East German variety of being unchurched is deeply anchored in the biography of many East Germans. 'East Germany is as a-religious as Bavaria is catholic', Eberhard Tiefensee, philosopher at Erfurt University in East Germany, formulates.[25] What he describes is religious immunity: 'East Germans don't go to the Dalai Lama either.'[26]

Within 50 years, a new normality has cropped up.[27] Before that, it was more or less normal to belong to a church. Now the opposite is normal, unquestioned, the model of the majority, with which the people in the East are brought up and live. These unchurched people come along with an atheism, which is deep but not necessarily aggressive. This atheism comes with a far-reaching indifference for the whole religious interpretation of life, including the offers of the church. They are known, but are of no interest whatsoever to the average East German.[28] 'You know, I am not

---

[25] Eberhard Tiefensee, "Chancen und Grenzen von "Mission" – im Hinblick auf die konfessionelle Situation in den neuen Bundesländern", M. Bartels und M. Reppenhagen (eds.) *Gemeindepflanzung – ein Modell für die Kirche der Zukunft?* (BEG 4: Neukirchen-Vluyn, 2006) 68-85, 69.

[26] Tiefensee, "Chancen und Grenzen", 70.

[27] Cf. Wolfgang Pittkowski,"Konfessionslose in Deutschland", W. Huber e.a. (eds.) *Kirche in der Vielfalt der Lebensbezüge. Die vierte EKD-Erhebung über Kirchenmitgliedschaft* (Gütersloh, 2006 89-110) 89.

[28] Eberhard Tiefensee "Chancen und Grenzen von "Mission" – im Hinblick auf die konfessionelle Situation in den neuen Bundesländern", M. Bartels und M.

religious,' a train conductor said when she was asked about church related issues. That is common. Focussing on these unchurched fellow human beings, e.g. in the prefabricated slab-construction buildings of our cities or in the underdeveloped rural areas, Roman Catholic bishop Wanke of the diocese Erfurt, in the Southeastern state of Thuringia, says: 'To lead an unchurched Thuringian to Christ seems to me to be more significant, at least more difficult, than to baptize an animist African.'[29]

Compared to this, the situation of the congregations is diffuse. Some are involved in missionary attempts at crossing boundaries, and they realize how difficult it is. This is because even the linguistic constructions of reality are different. Others are sceptical against opening up to the outside world. 'We understand ourselves as a confessing community', a pastor who rejected mission told me. A confessing community: These are those who paid the price for keeping the faith already in the past, who suffered in many ways. Do we really wish to have the former secretary of the socialist party sitting next to us in the pew, and the teacher of the grammar school, and the spying neighbour? Whoever thinks they have an easy answer to this underestimate the hurts of the time of dictatorship. Nevertheless my question is: 'Are church members open for new people to be won? Are you ready to welcome strangers and to make space for them? Are the congregations ready to question liturgical traditions which may have been tested over long times and are deeply familiar – in order to reach those who simply cannot do anything with highly sophisticated offers like this?'[30]

We have to add here the enfeeblement of the congregations who are out of puff. Reforms of the structures are exhausting, because they usually mean it will become more difficult as the numbers decline and neither money nor power will suffice. The grappling with church fusions and the threatening end of their church in the village bind energies and mellow people. The focus is more on maintaining what is there than on reaching out to those who are outsiders.

The North German Broadcast Station (NDR) broadcasted a report recently about a young pastor close to the border with Poland: 'The Lord of 13 steeples'.[31] For many, this is normal: small and tiny church services, mainly elderly people, here and there a few children, rarely men, rarely men and women between 30 and 60. But all the more church buildings where services have to be celebrated: 'The Lord of 13 steeples'. Moreover,

---

Reppenhagen (ed.) *Gemeindepflanzung – ein Modell für die Kirche der Zukunft?* (BEG 4: Neukirchen-Vluyn, 2006) 79.

[29] Joachim Wanke, "Missionarische Herausforderungen im gesellschaftlichen Kontext Deutschlands – Perspektive Ostdeutschland", EMW e.a. (ed.) *Aufbruch zu einer missionarischen Ökumene* (Hamburg, 1999) 138.

[30] Hartmut Bärend, *Kirche mit Zukunft. Impulse für eine missionarische Volkskirche* (Gießen, 2006) 50.

[31] NDR-Nordreportage *Herr der 13 Türme – Der Landpfarrer vom Randowtal.* 25th Februar 2008, 18.15h North German Broadcast Station (NDR).

he is also a solo entertainer who has to do everything alone. In one person he is liturgist and preacher, choir leader, organ -player, youth worker, master builder, counsellor, administration manager and teacher. He has a few funerals, but rarely baptisms and weddings. It is a poor region, there in the geographical region named Uckermark. Whoever can leave will leave, whoever stays does so because they have to.

So a little courage is needed to travel to the border with Poland, to look into the face of the parochial church council and of the young pastor and to say: It is about mission, outreach, and growth! Courage is needed, or the humour of faith, like the bishop of Magdeburg Noack: 'We must gladly decline and yet wish to grow.' For what that means is: We still have to accept the decline of congregations and cope with it, to mourn together and to assent to the dying of what is familiar. But at the same time we shall set out, venture for new things and not give up wishing to grow.

But how can we imagine that this missionary challenge is easy, fast, or could be accomplished with only few resources?

- How do we reach the ageing people, those who withdrew from the church in the past?
- How do we reach the people of the middle generation brought up in the GDR?
- And how do we reach the young people who grew up in a kind of ideological and religious nowhere land?
- How do we get public attention again so that we are seen and recognized as respectable?

It should not be denied or denigrated what good approaches can be seen. To do otherwise would be like a self-ordered depression. Without doubt there are smaller and bigger stories of success. We can at least guess what chances there are for the future. The regular ministry in our local churches can have missionary effects – as long as it is fostered by Christians with the heart of a missionary. It is a chance to found Protestant schools, to show a new presence in the educational sector and to earn trust. Furthermore: If people in a village get involved with maintaining a church building, this can lead them to identify at least with the building where faith is expressed. It can also make people think when they get in touch with a Protestant care facility like a hospice and experience it as somewhere different. These are important approaches.

There might be even more chances, if diaconical and educational institutions, those caring for evangelism and those interested in church ceremonies, understand themselves as a confessing community, focusing on winning unchurched people for Christ. As the East German theologian Ehrhart Neubert puts the critical question: 'It should be researched whether most of the church staff in the East has a background that makes it difficult for them to see the mission to the unchurched as a major challenge.'[32] Here we have a major problem: In some places, not only are we not able, but also we do not want it.

To add to the complexity, we also need much more missionary imagination to develop plural missionary models for unchurched contexts, for the ageing former church members, for adults brought up in the GDR, for young people brought up in an ideologic and religious nowhere, for poor educated rural youngsters, for the faithful atheist elites and so on. There is a lot of homework to do.

Interlude: Hebrews 10:35f

When this article was written, I did it in parallel to preparing a sermon for the 16th Sunday after the Feast of the Trinity. The given text from Hebrews 10:35-39 helped me to ward off the dark thoughts about the situation of the church, which jumped around like wild dogs: *'So do not throw away your confidence; it will be richly rewarded. You need to persevere so that when you have done the will of God, you will receive what he has promised.'* In this passage, faith appears in the two forms of confidence and perseverance. Both are needed when we think about the mission of the church in the East:

- Confidence that God's mission to us has never been cancelled. He himself is at work in people. Confidence that we have to go new ways, By new missionary paths, even new forms of congregations, starting from near zero.
- And perseverance: perseverance for going the extra mile. Perseverance means: remaining in it and not running away.

Confidence and perseverance have God's promise: He won't forsake us. We shall receive the promised. To this also belongs the experience that people become followers of Christ, being baptized and taught in the Gospel.

Mission in Pomerania: Main Features of Plural Mission

The Pomeranian Bischop Abromeit in Northeastern Germany surely hit the point on the head: 'We live in a situation that challenges us in a missionary way.'[33] Mission in Pomerania has already begun long ago. It happens in various congregations that seek to get in touch with people next door. They strive to gain public attention. They open their church doors and seek to get in touch with their dechurched and unchurched neighbours. Plurality is not a problem as long as it remains oriented towards the common mission. In

---

[32] Ehrhart Neubert, "Konfessionslose in Ostdeutschland. Folgen verinnerlichter Unterdrückung", *PTh* 87 (1998), 377.

[33] Hans-Jürgen Abromeit, "Wahrnehmungen aus dem Bischofsamt in Ostdeutschland", *LVK-Forum* 3/2002, 26-30, p. 27.

such a case, it is not a problem but a strength, and even a necessity, to reach as many as possible. In other words: Because there is not just one single kind of the typical unchurched person, a plural approach is indispensable.

For example, let us look at children's and youth work. The number of children and young people who attend religious education in school is far higher than the number of church members of the same age. A seeker service project in Greifswald reaches about 200 teenagers each month. Many of them grew up without the church. A youth church in "Grünhufe", a typical former socialist housing district in the nearby city Stralsund, is active in a mixture of social and evangelistic projects among young people. Many young people in other church districts of Pomerania become involved with the church by Christian camps that pool the hours of confirmation classes.

Special missional activities make an impact as well. It is just not true that activities that were in practice in Western Germany for a long time cannot be effective in the East. The project "Neu anfangen" ('starting anew') succeeded exceptionally well in reaching unchurched people in a Pomeranian city (Loitz). Every household in this region with a published phone number was called and offered a small booklet with testimonies from the region. A volunteer would personally bring the booklet to their front door if they accepted the offer on the telephone. They would then be invited to a series of evening discussions. A different approach: Twice a year, about 200 women meet in the cafeteria of Greifswald university for "Frühstückstreffen für Frauen" ('breakfast meeting for women'). Many of them are unchurched. They have breakfast together and listen to a talk on a contemporary issue from a Christian perspective. In several places, there are 'Seeker services' which entice people to come to church – new forms of services with a short piece of drama, modern music, and a sermon with a thematic focus. Not least, several congregations make very positive experiences with missionary nurture courses. In a short-run project lasting 6-7 weeks, interested people get to learn the tenets of the Christian faith and to discuss them with Christians. As you have probably seen by now, most of these activities seek to offer easy access with a low threshold and most of them are short-term offers. They tie in with themes that query modern vital issues from a Christian perspective. Attendees neither need to be especially educated nor pious. They normally take place in a hospitable setting, allow first and fresh experiences of church, and invite to seek for more. A few people are reached by public relations work. But most are reached by personal relationships. The local pastor can invite people when he is known as trustworthy. Even more so, church members can invite other people, when there are connections with a bit more depth, and unchurched people do not have to suspect that the invitation is more about missionary success than about themselves. If all works well, then activities like this build bridges to the rest of the life of a church. Very often though, this turns out to be a problem as well, since many congregations are not very much accustomed to hosting formerly unchurched newcomers. More steps need to be taken. It is a long journey to faith!

In some places, the start has to be from scratch. We see entire areas that are hard to reach. It is part of socialism's aftermath that its intention to create 'cities without God' proved to be very effective in some places. This is especially true for the city-districts containing the typical East German architecture with large grey concrete housing blocks. On average, the number of church members is here below 10% of all inhabitants in the district. Even worse, in Bergen-Rotensee,[34] we experience that those who are still officially church members have turned their back on the church and conversely the congregation does not know them either. Congregational fellowship vanished from Rotensee. Not to mention missionary endeavours. There has to be a completely fresh start here. The Church of England taught us a lot about 'Church Planting' and how to root missionary congregations in formerly unreached regions. That was and still is our intention here in Bergen-Rotensee. A new congregation shall grow with the help of a young minister who sets up contacts to local institutions of welfare services, to schools, clubs, and, most of all, to individual people living in Rotensee. He himself lives next door to those he seeks to reach with the gospel. Diaconical work and evangelistic outreach have to go hand in hand. It is also important for us that worship services are taking place in Rotensee. We expect a lot from word and sacrament, from prayer and worship, even if people do not at first recognize it.

That sheds a little more light on the idea of a plural Mission. Let us move on a little further though.

The "Pommersche Perspektivplan" (2005) ('Pomeranian Prospect Plan') also needs to be mentioned in this context. It was established by a task group led by Bischop Abromeit[35] and focuses on the missionary calling. It is striking how mission and social context are connected with one another in this document. People shall be addressed at weddings and during difficult times in their lives, and they are to sense: the church and its message help me to get along with my life. And then they can also discover: the gospel is much more. It unlocks a whole new world shaped by the love of God. I believe we need to follow up on such questions much more intensely. Let me name just three examples: (1) Facing high unemployment rates in our region, the "Pommersche Perspektivplan" prompts us to think about the meaning of human work and to offer meaningful assignments to people. (2) The "Pommersche Perspektivplan" identifies the assets of our region for tourism and well-being. How do we, as a missionary church, reach those who visit our region for well-being and relaxation? (3) The "Pommersche Perspektivplan" apprehends the various

---

[34] Cf. footnote no. 1 above.

[35] Cf. Pommersche Evangelische Kirche, *Leben in Gottes Gegenwart. Perspektiven für die Pommersche Evangelische Kirche. Ergebnisse des Leitbildprozesses von 2002 bis 2005* (Greifswald, 2005).

turns in the history of Pomerania as the old or new home. It encourages us to look at the often painful history of the 20th century, to tell this story and to seek for reconciliation in various ways. Work, health and glances at history are such possible point of contact in our region, for a mission, which crosses boundaries.

By now, plural mission in a post-socialist context might appear like an assortment of different stand alone activities, which is a little too colourful and confusing. What is necessary for plural mission in a post-socialist context to succeed? I see five main necessities.

First: We need people who enjoy the Christian faith and who love to share it. Methods and activities lead nowhere if a joyful faith is not continually renewed and refreshed from within the church. The innermost and hidden basis of a renewed mission are fellowship, celebrating in worship, laughing and weeping together, prayer and finding words to share the faith. The preaching of the gospel needs, therefore, to be heard by us as well. Mission is not just directed from the inside to the outside, as if it was just us sharing something with others. We ourselves remain addressees of God's mission. He cares for us and longs to win us over to his love. This should encourage us to realize that our faith is not a run-down model or should be kept secret. Spiritual renewal begins with ourselves.

Second: We are not so much concerned with certain models, projects or activities. Individual activities will fail if they are not rooted within a renewed culture of church life.[36] Therefore, we desperately need a culture of church life that is hospitable, welcoming, and that opens up to others. It is about our sense of 'who we are'. Who are we? How do we interact with one another and with strangers? How do we celebrate? What is important and dear to us? The culture of a church is a reflection of its character. So it is possible to say that 'we are open to others', but the life of the church tells a different story. We insist on being welcoming and hospitable, but no visitor would understand our liturgies or could even find a liturgical order for directions. At coffee break after the service, the unexpected visitor stands alone in a corner. It is very cold in church. Children are sent away to be stored somewhere with outdated toys. I am exaggerating to make this clear. It must become our innermost conviction that as a church, we want to become a guesthouse. Only then does it make sense to have missionary activities. Otherwise, all newcomers will sense that this is unreal and will be disappointed. A guest can 'feel' a culture, often upon entering our rooms! But changing culture is much more difficult than changing a structure or organization. What some learned, during the years of the socialist regime as suitable survival skills, has sometimes to be unlearned now. I am speaking about the withdrawal into a niche, and about the inner separation of those outside from us inside. We need to be sensitive for the

[36] Cf. Peter Böhlemann, *Wie die Kirche wachsen kann und was sie davon abhält* (Neukirchen-Vluyn, 2006).

secret languages that we speak to one another. We need to learn to look at our church buildings with the eyes of potential visitors. And there is much more that could be listed here. We need a hospitable culture in our congregations. Only if we achieve this can we hope that the widespread feeling of a loss of good companionship and cohesion, a feeling that many East Germans mourn about, can become an open door to the church and to faith.[37]

Third: We need missional hermeneutics for preaching and witnessing. We have not yet thought through theologically the post-socialist context. Our theological education is indeed more interested in parts of culture that are still soaked with Christian or religious ideas. But it has not roused enough interest for a culture that has forgotten all Christian elements and considers religion to be dispensable. It is not adept enough to address the life questions of our post-socialist contemporaries, or relate them to our message in a fresh way. What do people believe who believe nothing? Which prejudices need to be critically worked upon? Which aspects of faith might interest our post-socialist contemporaries? We should not only train our future ministers to foster existing congregations, but need to help them to become missionaries, at least to become leaders, who care for a missional culture in church.

Fourth: We need a missional hermeneutics in the church and congregation. An example, for such hermeneutics, comes from the Lutheran context of the United States. Pat Keifert, Professor of Systematic Theology in St. Paul (Minnesota), developed the 'Partnership for Missional Church'.[38] In a 'Partnership for Missional Church' about 12-15 congregations in a region work together for three years. They are accompanied by the 'Church Innovation Institute'. Together, they learn much better than on their own to find out where God is already at work in their specific context. Thus it is evident: This is not about patent remedies. Mission has to be plural because God already has his own particular story with every city or village and every congregation. The goal is to find out what kind of story this is. How? Well, above all else, the churches are trained to do two things. They should share time reading bible passages that speak about the church's missionary calling. And they should also become active to learn more about their social context, especially the context of those who join the same congregation and those on the outside who live nearby. They study the Bible, pray, read the life stories of those living nearby, and talk with many. Combining these two ways of reading should help in learning more. Where do we dare to do something new? What needs

---

[37] Maren Rinn, *Die religiöse und kirchliche Ansprechbarkeit von Konfessionslosen in Ostdeutschland. Eine Analyse auf Grundlage empirischer Untersuchungen in der Evangelisch-Lutherischen Landeskirche Mecklenburgs und Evangelischen Landeskirche Anhalts* (Hannover, 2006) 50-52. Found at www.ekd.de/si-download/SI-Konfessionsloe_Ostdeutschland-korr2.pdf on Feb 20th, 2007).

[38] Cf. Patrick Keifert, *We are here now* (Idaho: Eagle, Idaho, 2006).

to be done in our town to join God's mission? You are probably not surprised to hear that once again diaconical or social welfare work and evangelistic witness are closely linked to one another. A missionary hermeneutic will initiate spiritual processes, will renew the eagerness to read the Bible, will help to focus upwards while being grounded in a real congregational setting with a well known social context, so that finally suitable plural missional strategies will develop.

Fifth: We need a renewal of the baptismal catechumenate. What I mean is: Opportunities to get to know the Christian faith, which also take up the pastoral component from the catechumenate of the early church by connecting life and faith and encourage us to take the first steps of faith on the way to baptism and church membership. As the normal biographies become consciously chosen biographies, it is just not enough anymore to offer standardized assistance from infant baptism to the funeral. We need a new adult catechumenate. Nurture courses should be part of a congregation's normal curriculum, just like confirmation classes. This is just the necessary way to go. The 'EMMAUS-Walk of faith' is a wonderful example for a nurture course that finally guides us to baptism.[39] It leads through vital Christian issues and shows how to begin in the Christian faith. It assists seekers with Christians, who accompany them. It does not offer long lectures but short inputs and much space to explore the Christian faith through discussions and personal Bible reading. We desperately need such a catechumenate, because in a post -socialist context absolutely nothing can be taken for granted for a Christian mission to build upon. A professor from Western Germany suggested 'Oh well, no need to worry that is just a temporary state. It will soon be very normal again to belong to church. Just sing with the people the well known hymn "Großer Gott wir loben dich" (God we praise thee). Everybody knows that.' No, they do not know it. Nor do they know the Lord's Prayer. They have never heard of Jesus and how much he longs to be close to them. That is why we need a renewal of the baptismal catechumenate.

Let me close by reminding us of Hebrews 10. We are not the first and last missionaries. It is not our duty to preserve church and Christianity. Otherwise, we would have to think of the church in a post-socialist context *etsi deus non daretur*, as if there were no God to be seen. We should not throw away our confidence and perseverance. What the German and English Bible translations render as "confidence" in Greek is called *parrhesia*, 'frankness' or 'freedom of speech'. So what comes first is: We have access to the Father and the freedom of speech in his presence, in order to ask him to put forth his mission in the post-socialist context.

[39] Cf. Michael Herbst (ed.), *Emmaus – Auf dem Weg des Glaubens. Handbuch* (Neukirchen-Vluyn ^{2}2006; Matthias Clausen, Ulf Harder and Michael Herbst: Emmaus – Auf dem Weg des Glaubens. Basiskurs 2.0. Neukirchen-Vluyn 2008).

Consequently we have the freedom of speech to joyfully share our faith wherever we find open doors.

Searching for the Soul of Europe: Missiological Models in the Ecumenical Debate on Mission in Postmodern Europe

Friedemann Walldorf

At the World Missionary Conference, in Edinburgh in 1910, Europe was classified as '"Christian" territory' and thus excluded as a field and context for mission.[1] Today a plurality of religious, cultural and commercial missions is competing for the soul(s) of postmodern Europe. In the course of the 20th century the Christian churches in Europe had to learn to overcome their Eurocentric perspective and to view their continent through the hermeneutical lens of the *missio Dei* and the eyes of their sister churches in the non-Western world. This essay examines the last thirty years of the ecumenical missiological quest for a deeper understanding and a spiritual renewal of European culture(s) on the background of economic, political and religious changes. The developments are described in two historical phases and interpreted in three contextual missiological models, which in the second phase seem to have moved from distance to dialogue and from controversy to conversation – with significant crosscurrents.

The Debate on the New Evangelisation of Europe 1979-1992

The vision for a New Evangelisation developed in the last period of the cold-war division of Europe, when the first signs of communist breakdown already appeared. In Western Europe the European Communion rapidly moved towards a single market and a single currency.[2] While Francois Lyotard, in 1979, had diagnosed Western (and European) society with a 'postmodern condition' and 'incredulity' towards the 'metanarratives' of secular modernity,[3] the ecumenical missiological debate was more concerned with the issues of secularism, atheism and nominal Christianity.

---

[1] cf. B. Stanley, 'Defining the Boundaries of Christendom: The Two Worlds of the World Missionary Conference, 1910', *IBMR* 30 (4/2006), 171-176: 171.

[2] cf. F. Walldorf, *Die Neuevangelisierung Europas. Missionstheologien im europäischen Kontext* (Systematisch-theologische Monographien 8: Gießen/Basel: Brunnen TVG, 2002).

[3] cf. Jean-François Lyotard, *La Condition Postmoderne: Rapport sur le Savoir* (Les Editions de Minuit, 1979).

The issue of postmodernity did not come into full view before the 1990s. In respect to mission theology, the debate took up the challenge for contextual theologizing that had been coming from the Catholic bishops in Latin America (Puebla 1979) and Third-World theologians in the Evangelical Lausanne Movement and the World Council of Churches.

In 1979, the Polish Pope John Paul II initiated his tenure with the formulation of a new vision: the *New Evangelisation of Europe*. In the Holy-Cross-Church in Mogila, Poland, he explained: 'We received a sign that the gospel will enter anew at the threshold of a new millennium. A New Evangelisation has begun, as if it was some kind of second evangelisation even if in reality it is always only one evangelisation.'[4] The Pope unfolds this vision as a mystical, spiritual and cultural renewal of the church and society in Europe. One year later, in 1980, the Polish workers′ union *Solidarnosh*, supported by the Catholic Church, caused the first cracks in monolithic communist Eastern Europe and brought with it winds of political renewal. New Evangelisation turned into a central topic at the symposia of the Catholic Council of European Bishops (CCEE) between 1979 and 1989, leading up to the *Special Synod of Bishops on Europe* in Rome 1991 with the theme 'That we may be witnesses of Christ who has set us free

In 1984, the evangelical *Lausanne Movement* initiated a European branch, the *European Lausanne Committee* (ELC). Rolf Scheffbuch, the Lutheran pastor from Germany, became the first president of the committee and wrote: 'A new chapter has been opened. ... It has become clear that Europe is in need of re-evangelisation ...We do not believe in the pope and his authority, but we agree in the truth of that need'.[5] The ELC, as a consequence, convened two major study and leadership conferences on the contextual missiological challenges of Europe, the *European Leadership Conference on World Evangelization* 1988 in Stuttgart and the *European Leadership Consultation on Evangelization* in Bad Boll, Germany, which was held in partnership with the European Evangelical Alliance (EEA) and led to the start of the network *Hope for Europe*.

In 1984, Emilio Castro, the Uruguayan theologian and director of the WCC-Commission for World Mission and Evangelism, challenged the *Conference of European Churches* (CEC), the forum of Protestant and Eastern Orthodox churches in Europe, to concentrate on mission in Europe. At a common conference of the CEC and the Council of the Catholic bishops of Europe at Lake Garda in Italy, Castro maintained that, in the face of rising unbelief in Europe, it was not inter-church-relations, but common missionary witness that should be of paramount concern to Christians.[6] The CEC took up this challenge from a representative of the

[4] Walldorf, *Neuevangelisierung*, 47.
[5] Walldorf, *Neuevangelisierung*, 203.
[6] Walldorf, *Neuevangelisierung*, 110.

churches of the non-Western world and in 1986 the full assembly of the CEC in Sterling/Scotland resolved to give top priority to 'the mission of the Churches in a secularised Europe [...] The European churches owe it to the churches on other continents which they once evangelised to now focus on mission on their own continent.'[7] Different aspects of this mission were studied in succeeding consultations on 'Secularisation' (Les Geneveys, Switzerland, 1987), 'Bible and Mission' (Sigtuna, Sweden 1988) and 'Practical Aspects' (Kolymari, Krete, 1993).

The missiological extract of these developments can be described in three models, which are derived from a basic triangular model, which interrelates three components of contextual mission theology: (1) the *Bible* as the classic and basic *text of mission*, (2) the *churches* and Christian fellowships in Europe as the *community of mission* and (3) European *culture* and society as the *context of mission*.[8] Each of the following three models integrates all three factors, but emphasizes them differently.

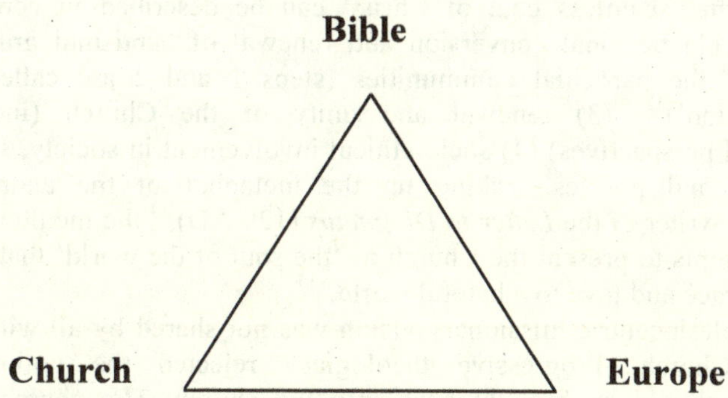

The church as the soul of Europe – the inculturational model

'Europe cannot give up Christianity as a travelling companion, who has become a stranger, just like a human being cannot give up his or her reasons for life and hope without bringing disaster to him- or herself.'[9] The centre of John Paul II's vision for the New Evangelisation is the

[7] Encounter at Sterling. Report of the Xth Full Assembly of the CEC, cit. Walldorf, Neuevangelisierung, 111.

[8] cf. e.g. D. Bosch, *Transforming Mission*, Maryknoll, 1991, 497; C. van Engen, 'Specialization and Integration in Mission Education', J.D. Woddberry et al. (eds.) *Missiological Education for the 21st Century: The Book, the Circle and the Sandals* (Maryknoll: Orbis, 1996), 208-228; D. Bosch, *Transforming Mission* (Maryknoll, 1991), 497.

[9] John Paul II at the 5th Symposion of the European Bishops 1982, cit. Walldorf, *Neuevangelisierung*, 50-51.

inculturation of the gospel in present-day Europe on the basis of its Catholic-Christian past. His goal is a new creative synthesis between the Church and postmodern European culture. The Pope's vision for Europe is inspired by his conviction that Europe is intrinsically Christian, since its Catholic baptism in the early medieval times.[10] Thereby, he personifies European culture and history and treats it according to sacramental doctrine. Europe continues 'under the sacramental sign of its covenant with God.'[11] European unity is pictured mystically as the "seamless coat of Christ" (cf. John 19:23), which needs to be re-captured by overcoming the historical and theological rifts that were caused by the break with the Eastern Orthodox Church, the Protestant Reformation churches and by secularist atheism.[12]

The basic missiological structure of the New Evangelisation is a combination of cultural-theological analysis and spiritual renewal from an ecclesiological centre, in expectation and realisation of the eschatological reign of God. The missiological outward-movement with the goal to recapture the 'seamless coat of Christ' can be described in concentric circles as: (1) personal conversion and renewal of baptismal grace, (2) renewal of the parochial communities (steps 1 and 2 are called 'self evangelisation')[13], (3) renewal and unity of the Church (including ecumenical perspectives) (4) socio-ethical involvement in society, science, economics and politics. Taking up the metaphor of the anonymous missionary writer of the *Letter to Diognetus* (129 AD),[14] the inculturational model attempts to present the Church as 'the soul of the world' that brings 'vitality, grace and love to a hateful world.'[15]

This ecclesiocentric missionary vision was not shared by all within the Catholic Church. Progressive theologians rejected the notion that Europeans should be brought back into the church. The church rather should meet people where they are and encourage them in their own spiritual journey. The German Catholic theologian, Otmar Fuchs, criticises: 'The concept of New Evangelisation (Re-Evangelisation) presupposes a relationship between Church and Society which should have been left behind at least since Vatican II. The talk of Re-Evangelisation falsely suggests an already evangelised Church leading a desperately secularised

---

[10] John Paul II at the 5th Symposion of the European Bishops 1982, cit. Walldorf, *Neuevangelisierung*, 51.

[11] John Paul II at the 5th Symposion of the Council of European Bishops 1982, cit. Walldorf, *Neuevangelisierung*, 53.

[12] John Paul II at the 6th symposion of the Council of European Bishops in 1986, cit. Walldorf, *Neuevangelisierung*, 66-67.

[13] John Paul II, Sermon at the 4th Symposion of the Council of European Bishops 1979, cit. Walldorf, *Neuevangelisierung*, 49-50.

[14] "What the soul is in the body, that Christians are in the world." cit. N. Thomas, *Classic Texts in Mission and World Christianit*,(Maryknoll: Orbis, 1996), 5.

[15] Thomas, *Classic texts*, 5.

Europe back to the right faith. The Church is supposed to have what Europe lacks.'[16] Fuchs suggests that evangelisation should not so much expect that 'the unchurched will return into the ecclesastical institutions, but that they will be met and encouraged right where they are and probably will stay within their own intrinsic capability for hope and humanity'.[17]

Discovering God in Europe – the dialogical model

A view similar to progressive Catholics was presented by the Protestant and Orthodox theologians of the *Conference of European Churches.* This model represents an almost complete reversal of the Catholic concept. Here,it is not the church that is pictured as the soul of Europe, but the 'incognito-presence of Christ through the Holy Spirit in every creature within and outside of the Church'[18] Christ's incognito-presence is understood as expressing itself in the pluriform *missio Dei*, which is taking place in European society at large. The basic theological structure of this model is a combination of Orthodox *theosis*-theology and ecumenical *kosmos*-Christology with Paul Tillich's interpretation of the *justificatio* in the modern European context. Tillich maintained that God, the transcendent and indefinable ground of all being, is not only justifying the sinner, but modern European doubt and despair as such.[19] In this way, modern European religious and secular experience themselves as becoming holy ground and a sacrament, where God and human beings meet. The Enlightenment is interpreted as a soteriological event in European history, which liberated society from monolithic ecclesiastico-political inculturations. Mission in Europe, according to the CEC, should therefore not fall back into an ecclesiocentric paradigm and propagate an institutional church, but should move churches into dialogue with the Holy Spirit's immediate work in modern European society – in order to discover God's presence there. At the CEC-Consultation in Les Geneveys 1987, the Scottish theologian, Elisabeth Templeton, proposed: 'Every interpretation of the mission of the churches in Europe has to liberate itself from the factual claim that the churches are the bearers of the gospel. Maybe we have to accept that the gospel is being brought to us ... partly from within our own secular culture, partly from churches in Eastern Europe that together with their Marxist partners have started to explore the human condition'.[20]

---

[16] Walldorf, *Neuevangelisierung*, 46.

[17] O. Fuchs, "Was ist Neuevangelisierung?", *Stimmen der Zeit* 210 (1992), 465-47:, 471.

[18] Report on Section 3 of the CEC-study consultation at Les Geneveys 1982, cit. Walldorf, *Neuevangelisierung*, 137.

[19] Heinz Zahrnt, *Die Sache mit Gott* (München, 1980), 376.

[20] Walldorf, *Neuevangelisierung*, 129.

Not everyone in the CEC agreed. The Rumanian Orthodox theologian, Dimitru Popescu, suggested a New Testament based Christology 'from above' as a basis of a truly liberating mission in Europe.[21] Raymond Fung, former Secretary of Evangelism at the WCC, emphasised the missionary *koinonia* in the fellowship of the Triune God as the adequate European sons to experience the love of the Father as well as the active running towards them in the crossing of frontiers.[22]

Sharing the gospel of Christ with Europeans – the translational model

Close to these latter views, we find the model of the *European Lausanne Committee* (ELC). The basic structure of this model can be understood in the categories that have been provided by Lamin Sanneh´s interpretation of mission as translation on the basis of the 'translatability' of the gospel. [23] The model can be described as a holistic and dynamic-equivalent[24] (re-) translation of the biblical witness of Jesus Christ into the lives of modern Europeans – in the power of the Holy Spirit and through the missionary witness of Christian churches and fellowships. John Stott highlighted the Christological centre, 'The only way to be delivered from Europessimism is to catch a fresh vision of Christ!'[25], as well as the missiological process: 'identification with loss of identity'. [26]

European history, culture, churches and politics are interpreted in the tension between judgment and grace as bridges and barriers to the gospel.[27] Contrasting the inculturational and the dialogical model, the translational model tries to clearly distinguish the gospel from societal developments and ecclesiastical institutions. According to this perspective, the *missio Dei* can neither be discovered directly in European history, nor be identified with European ecclesiastical interpretations. Ulrich Parzany, the Lutheran pastor and former president of the YMCA in Germany, stated his

---

[21] Popescu in Sigtuna, cit. Walldorf, *Neuevangelisierung*, 143.

[22] Fung in a Bible study on John 13:34-35 in Sigtuna, cit. Walldorf, *Neuevangelisierung*, 167-170.

[23] Lamin Sanneh, *Translating the Message: The Missionary Impact on Culture* (Maryknoll: Orbis Books, 1989).

[24] The dynamic-equivalence model has been developed in translation theory and was used as a model for missionary contextualisation at the Willowbank Consultation of the Lausanne Movement in 1978, cf. J. Stott, *Making Christ Known Historic Documents of the Lausanne Movement* (Carlisle: Paternoster, 1996), 99-100.

[25] John R. Stott in his plenary speech "Christ and Mission" at Stuttgart 1988, cit. Walldorf, *Neuevangelisierung*, 210.

[26] J. Stott at the Stuttgart conference in 1988, cit. Walldorf, *Neuevangelisierung*, 209.

[27] cf. the contribution of the *London Institute of Contemporary Christianity*, 'Barriers and Bridges to the Gospel in Europe and how to exploit them, in Stuttgart 1988, Walldorf, *Neuevangelisierung*, 234-239.

conviction that 'Europe's mainline churches have a mission. But it is not a matter of methodology whether the churches will fulfil their mission or not. Above all it depends on whether or not they will regain a clear biblical understanding of the gospel. The most paralyzing blocks which prevent us from effectively implementing our mission exist within the churches not outside.'[28]

According to ELC, the scope of contextualised mission in Europe has to be holistic and includes cultural and political transformation on the basis of the gospel. This is underlined when Peter Kuzmic, the Croatian Baptist theologian, interpreted the breakdown of Communism: 'Followers of Christ all across Eastern Europe are aware that this is the work of the Lord of history who has seen their suffering and longing for freedom, answered their prayers and provided them with a special *kairos* period to call their nations back to God and to the spiritual foundations for a free and truly new society.'[29]

This missionary call is understood as 'the *proclamation* and the *demonstration* of the love of God in Jesus Christ.'[30] It is to be realized through a pluriform network of local churches crossing cultural and religious bridges and barriers in the neighbourhoods of Europe. The local church, interpreted as 'all believers in that place', is seen as the premier agent of missional witness: 'we will give ourselves in a servant spirit to meet material, spiritual ... and cultural needs of as many people as possible in our neighbourhoods.' While not everyone in the ELC agreed that Orthodox and Catholic churches should be viewed as part of this broad evangelical coalition of churches and mission organisations in Europe,[31] the ELC affirmed ecclesiological plurality within the unity of mission in Europe.[32]

Towards a Common and Complex Model

The first period of the missiological debate had reached a high point with the downfall of the Berlin Wall in 1989 and the dismantling of the Soviet Union in 1991. At the same time, it seems to have come to a halt with the beginning of the Balkan wars in 1991/1992, which disillusioned any kind of missiological or political Euro-euphoria. In the course of these and

[28] U. Parzany at the Stuttgart conference in 1988, cit. Walldorf, *Neuevangelisierung*, 217.

[29] At the Bad Boll consultation 1992, cit. Walldorf, *Neuevangelisierung*, 267. Similar perspectives were offered by the Norwegian Presidentr Kjell Magne Bondevik at Bad Boll 1992, Walldorf, *Neuevangelisierung*, 268.

[30] The Bad Boll Commitment (BBC) 1992, cit.Walldorf, *Neuevangelisierung*, 303-305: 303.

[31] cf. Walldorf, *Neuevangelisierung*, 276.

[32] Scheffbuch in a post-conference report 'Time to restore Relationships' in 1993, cit. Walldorf, *Neuevangelisierung*, 287.

coming events, the missiological debate of the churches took some new turns.

Under the auspices of Jacques Delors[33] as President of the European Commission, the Treaty of Maastricht was signed in February 1992 and entered into force in November 1993. It turned the European Community (EC) into the European Union (EU) and finally led to the creation of the euro as a common currency.[34] At that point of the process, Delors highlighted the need to 'give a soul to Europe'. The famous phrase can be traced in the notes of a conversation with church representatives in February 1992:

> Believe me, we won't succeed with Europe solely on the basis of legal expertise or economic know-how. It is impossible to put the potential of Maastricht into practice without a breath of air. If in the next ten years we haven't managed to give a soul to Europe, to give a spirituality and meaning, the game will be up. ... This is why I want to revive the intellectual and spiritual debate on Europe. I invite the Churches to participate actively in it. We don't want to control it; it is a democratic discussion, not to be monopolised by technocrats. I would like to create a meeting place, a space for free discussion open to men and women of spirituality, to believers and non-believers, scientists and artists. We are working on the idea already. We must find a way of involving the Churches.[35]

Delors obviously picked up and varied a theme that had been inherent and even prominent in the preceding missiological discussion on Europe, especially in the vision of John Paul II. In response to Delors' plans, in 1994, the EU created the 'A Soul for Europe'- budget line A-3024 to financially support projects that foster reflection on the ethical and spiritual foundations of Europe.[36] Beginning in 2004, a series of Berlin Conferences became a major expression of the project and brought together members and officials of the EU 'with representatives of civil, business and artistic society.'[37] By now, the Soul-project had taken a more cultural turn into 'a process for placing sustainable cultural growth at the heart of the European project.'[38]

One of the reasons why Delors introduced the 'Soul of Europe'- motif may have been the intention to strengthen European unity in view of the new challenge of the integration of Western and Eastern Europe.[39] While

---

[33] Jacques Delors was President of the European Commission from 1985 to 1995.
[34] The Euro entered circulation on 1 January 2002.
[35] Hans-Jürgen Luibl, "A-3024: Auf der Suche nach Europas Seele", *Hermeneutische Blätter* 1-2/2005, www.leuenberg.net (7 pages), called up: 17.8.2009.
[36] Luibl, A-3024, 1.
[37] 'The Berlin Conference 2004', www.asoulforeurope.eu/what/berlin-conference/2004 , 18.8.2009.
[38] 'The Berlin Conference 2004', www.asoulforeurope.eu/what/berlin-conference/2004, 18.8.2009.
[39] cf. Luibl, A-3024, 3.

Delors' concern probably majored on the economic challenges of the Eastward expansion of the EU, the developments in post-Communist Eastern Europe also raised missiological questions. Communism as a thorny context for mission had given way to national, ethnic and religious searches and struggles for identity and orientation. Optimistic visions for the evangelisation and transformation of Eastern European societies were put to a hard test by the horrors of the Balkan wars, which exploded between 1991 and 1995. The wars mocked the hopes of religious renewal and dialogue, as it instrumentalized religion to deepen ethnical divides.

In a similar way, the Islamist terrorist attacks in New York in 2001, in Madrid in 2004 and in London in 2005, impacted the context for the missiological debate on Europe. In this background, the debate itself started to change and keeps changing into the present. The different models did not disappear, but they seem to have moved closer towards a more integrated and at the same time more complex view. In the following, I will outline some exemplary developments and features of the debate and offer some conclusions.

Reconciled diversity

In 1995, representatives of the European Lausanne Committee (ELC) and the Conference of European Churches (CEC) came together for a consultation in Dorfweil, Germany, and issued the declaration 'Aspects of Mission and Evangelization in Europe Today: Towards a Common Mission'.[40] The declaration acknowledges 'common contents of faith and a common obligation for mission', while 'radical differences in the concepts of evangelisation' are admitted. Especially, views on missionary work among secularized nominal Christians were differing. While some allowed for the evangelisation of secularized members of another denomination, others thought it generally wrong to judge the faith of other believers.[41] As a possible model for common mission it was suggested to enter into 'a partnership..., in which both partners respect the faith and tradition of the other and at the same time are invited to challenge each other in love.'[42]

Although the CEC had so far taken a more critical stance towards Catholic visions of Christianity as the soul for Europe, it convoked the European Ecumenical Forum on Gospel and Culture 1996 in Hamburg, in co-operation with the 'A soul for Europe'-programme of the European Union to find 'new ways of inculturation.'[43] The reception of these concepts in the CEC shows the level of cross-fertilization that, by then, had

[40] The declaration was published in German: "Aspekte der Mission und Evangelisation im heutigen Europa. Auf dem Weg zu einer gemeinsamen Mission", *Ökumenisches Forum* 18 (1995), 327-331.

[41] Aspekte, 329.

[42] Aspekte. 330.

[43] Vgl. Ionita, 539.

been reached in the missiological debate on Europe. This kind of mutual recognition is further illustrated by an assessment of the Evangelical movement by Walter Kasper, Cardinal and President of the Pontifical Council for Promoting Christian Unity in Rome. He maintained that 'today it is the "Evangelical movement" which – in difference to the large churches – keeps the missionary idea alive; while the traditional Protestant churches are declining worldwide, Evangelicals are experiencing rapid growth.'[44] In 2002, the CEC started a research project on mission in Europe. Darrell Jackson, a responsible researcher, came to the conclusion that the differences between ecumenical and evangelical persuasions were less deep than formerly believed and should be accommodated in reconciled unity in order 'to win Europe for Christ' together.[45]

A further significant expression of the intentions towards reconciled diversity can be found at the World Missionary Conference in Athens, in 2005. In the concluding 'Letter from Athens,' the Conference committee highlighted:

> For the first time the meeting included a significant number of fully participating delegates from non WCC member churches, that is the Roman Catholic Church and some Pentecostal and Evangelical churches and networks. 'We', therefore, are a diverse group [...]. In these days, we have journeyed together, although we have not always agreed. We are in mission, all of us, because we participate in the mission of God who has sent us into a fragmented and broken world. We are united in the belief that we are 'called together in Christ to be reconciling and healing communities'. We have prayed together. We have been particularly helped by readings of Scripture as we struggled, together, to discern where the reconciling, healing Spirit is leading us, in our own contexts, two thousand years after St Paul arrived on these shores carrying the good news of the gospel of Jesus Christ.[46]

Regionalisation

In the 1990s, pan-European missiological visions somewhat receded and made way for regional and confessional perspectives. Paradoxically, at the same time, mission theological perspectives became less contextual and

[44] W. Kasper on the 'New Evangelisation of Europe', 4 June 2007 at the 175th anniversary of the Missionswissenschaftliches Institut Missio e.V. in Aachen. www.mwi-aachen.org

[45] Darrell Jackson, "Von Lausanne nach Athen: Europäische Mission in ökumenisch-evangelikaler Begegnung", *Europa: Christen, Kirchen und Missionen, Jahrbuch Mission 2006* (Hamburg: Missionshilfe, 2006), 253-65:p. 55.

[46] Conference on World Mission and Evangelism, A Letter from Athens to the Churches, networks and communities, 2005, www2.wcc-coe.org/pressreleasesen.nsf/index/pu-05-16.html.

more universal, emphasizing the constants.[47] By the mid-1990s, it had become evident that Europe was more complex and that cultural and religious differences were greater than some missiological plans had suggested. The maintenance of European structures was stretching some churches and initiatives too far. The Euro-visions of the 1980s needed to be translated into empirically grounded, locally anchored and feasible approaches. While the European and ecumenical horizon was not lost sight of, missionary projects and reflections became more regionally and confessionally oriented.[48] Developments in Germany are an example of this.[49] In 1998, the Association of Christian Churches in Germany (ACK) 'initiated a process of reflection and action ... with regard to mission in ecumenical cooperation in Germany.'[50] In 1999, the Evangelical Church in Germany (EKD) dedicated its Leipzig Synod to the topic of 'mission and evangelism.' It reinforced its support of missionary projects[51] and critically engaged with the aspect of 'self-secularization' in its own recent history, a term coined by EKD-bishop Wolfgang Huber.[52]

Klaus Schäfer identifies three 'features in this reappearance of a new interest in mission' in the churches in Germany: (1) 'Mission is clearly perceived as mission in the local context.' (2) 'There is a clear emphasis on mission as the conversation about faith issues and the invitation to a living faith in Jesus Christ. ... an evangelistic dimension of mission.' (3) The attempt to place mission 'centre stage in the agenda of all the churches' and not to leave it to 'only one particular tradition in our church.'[53] One exemplary result of the new orientation was the foundation of a research institute for evangelism and church development at the University of Greifswald on the Baltic Sea.[54] These regional and confessional

---

[47] cf. Robert J. Schreiter, *The New Catholicity: Theology Between the Global and the Local* (Maryknoll: Orbis, 1997). S. Bevans /R. Schroeder, *Constants in Context: A Theology of Mission for Today* (Maryknoll: Orbis, 2004).

[48] For a Reformed confessional perspective on mission in Europe see: Christine Lienemann-Perrin, Hendrik Vroom, Michael Weinrich (ed.) *Contextuality in Reformed Europe: The Mission of the Church in the Transformation of European Culture* (Amsterdam, 2004).

[49] For the larger picture see: F. Walldorf, "Missionarische Bemühungen im Kontext gesellschaftlicher Veränderungen in Deutschland von 1945 bis 2000, *Evangelikale Missiologie* (1- 2/2007), 2-15.38-53.

[50] Klaus Schäfer, 'Mission in Secular and Postmodern Societies: The Example of Germany', *International Review of Mission* XCII No. 364 (2003), 40-44: 40.

[51] cf. the programmatic EKD-Text 68: *Das Evangelium unter die Leute bringen. Zum missionarischen Dienst der Kirche in unserem Land (*Hannover, 2000).

[52] W. Huber, "Auf dem Weg zu einer missionarischen Kirche", A. Feldtkeller, T. Sundermeier (ed.) *Mission in pluralistischer Gesellschaft*, (Frankfurt: Lembeck, 1999), 107-135,108. Cf. Schäfer, *Mission*, 41.

[53] Schäfer, Mission, 41.

[54] cf. M. Herbst, "Ach, Sie sind also der Missionar!? Kontext, Enstehungsgeschichte und Aufgaben des Greifswalder Instituts", Herbst, M., Ohlemacher, J.,

developments did not lack trans-European and ecumenical links as they were partly inspired by the Anglican Decade of Evangelism (1990-2000) in Britain and its experiences with church planting in the Church of England. Catholic impulses came from the Austrian pastoral theologian, Paul Zulehner,[55] just to mention a few examples.

Critical postmodernism

Since Friedrich Nietzsche had called *truth* 'illusions about which one has forgotten that this is what they are; metaphors which are worn out and without sensuous power'[56], Western (and European) mentality and life was moving towards a 'postmodern condition' that Jean-Francois Lyotard described as 'incredulity towards metanarratives'.[57] Many Europeans became disillusioned with the enlightenment ideals of positivist science and technological, economic and social progress. Disappointed by the promises of modernity, they turned to a mindset and lifestyle characterised by individualism, consumerism and the mass media, but also by growing sensitivity for aesthetics, ecology, the rights of minorities and the importance of communication and relationships. Since the 1980s, postmodern theories like those of Thomas Kuhn (paradigm theory), Michel Foucault (discourse analysis), Jacques Derrida (deconstruction), Richard Rorty (neo-pragmatism) and others tried to uncover the historical and cultural relativity of knowledge, the hidden agendas of power behind scientific discourses and tried to replace metaphysics and ontology with linguistics and constructivism.

The missiological debate on Europe turned to the topic as late as the 1990s. At the Lausanne *Consultation on Faith and Modernity* in Uppsala in 1993,[58] a thorough overview of the 'rise of postmodernism' was given,[59] as well as an analysis of the New Age as a 'synthesis of premodern, modern and postmodern'.[60] The question if postmodernity was a new epoch in the history of culture (as Lyotard had asserted) or 'another twist' of late

---

Zimmermann, J. (ed.), *Missionarische Perspektiven für die Kirche der Zukunft.*(Beiträge zur Evangelisation und Gemeindeentwicklung 1, Neukirchen: Neukirchener Verlagsgesellschaft, 2005), 30-46.

[55] cf. e.g. Paul M. Zulehner, "Aufbrechen oder untergehen. Wie können unsere Gemeinden zukunftsfähig werden?", Herbst/ *Missionarische Perspektiven,* 17-29.

[56] T.R. Philipps/ D.L. Okholm, *Christian Apologetics in the Postmodern World* (Downers Grove: InterVarsity, 1995), 102.

[57] Cf. Jean-François Lyotard, *La Condition Postmoderne: Rapport sur le Savoir* (Les Editions de Minuit, 1979).

[58] cf. Sampson, V. Samuel, C. Sugden (eds.), *Faith and Modernity* (Oxford: Regnum, 1994).

[59] cf. P. Sampson, 'The Rise of Postmodernity', *Faith and Modernity,* 2-7.

[60] Lars Johansson, 'New Age – a synthesis of premodern, modern and postmodern", *Faith and Modernity,* 208-251.

modernity (as Anthony Giddens and Zygmunt Bauman had suggested) was left open. While some challenged the churches to 'question its allegiance to modernity',[61] others warned them not to 'uncritically ... join the assault on a dying modernity, only to find ourselves as but one story among many, unintentionally reinforcing the irrationalism of postmodernity'.[62] All in all, the conference took a more apologetic stance and criticised postmodernity as an 'anything goes'-philosophy[63] without the possibility of critical interaction on the basis of reason and reality, thus leaving the European seeker without reasons for hope.[64]

A more affirming perspective came from the South African missiologist, David Bosch, whose thinking also influenced European missiology.[65] While some question 'whether Bosch's missiological approach can be described as truly postmodern,' since he did not integrate the perspectives of feminism, ecology and non-Christian indigenous spiritualities,[66] it can hardly be doubted that he mediated a positive, though not uncritical view of postmodern epistemology to Protestant and, especially, Evangelical readers, and spelled out some of its consequences for missiology. He saw postmodernity as a healthy challenge to reductive enlightenment thinking, thus creating 'room for ... "communicative" reason, experience, spirituality and aesthetics in the scientific process.'[67] In the same vein of thinking, the British missiologist, Lesslie Newbigin, had already developed a missiology for the Western context as a comprehensive post-enlightenment critique. He proposed a hermeneutically reflected christocentric mission in the West as the spontaneous overflow of a doxological community into the grey wasteland of a secularized and disillusioned world.[68] Bosch's and Newbigin's perspectives became instrumental for the rise of postmodern missiological concepts such as 'missional church',[69] 'mission-shaped-Church'[70] or 'emerging church.'[71] In 2004, the Lausanne Forum in Pattaya

---

[61] Johansson, 'New Age', 240.

[62] Sampson, 'Rise', 49-50.

[63] A famous slogan used by postmodern philosopher Paul Feyerabend in *Against Method: Outline of an anarchistic Theory of Knowledge* (London: Verso, 1975).

[64] Sampson, 'Rise', 40.

[65] cf. D. Bosch, *Believing in the Future: Toward a Missiology of Western Culture* (Christian Mission and Modern Culture, Valley Forge: Trinity Press International, 1995); Bosch, *Transforming Mission*, 349-362.

[66] cf. K. Kim, 'Post-Modern Mission: A Paradigm Shift in David Bosch's Theology of Mission?', *IRM* 89 No. 353 (1999) 172-179: p- 173.

[67] Bosch, *Transforming Mission*, p-.351.

[68] cf. *Foolishness to the Greeks: The Gospel and Western Culture*, Grand Rapids, 1986, 148-149.

[69] cf. D. Guder (ed.) *Missional church: a vision for the sending of the church in North America* (The Gospel and our culture series: Grand Rapids: Eerdmans, 1998).

[70] cf. Rowan Williams, *Mission-shaped church: church planting and fresh expressions of church in a changing context* (Church House Publishing, 2004).

pointed to the positive implications of postmodern deconstruction as 'stripping a story of its ideology.'[72] While 'postmodernism' was seen as a challenge for academic apologetics, a number of case studies showed how 'postmodernity,' as a broad life orientation, could be interpreted as a bridge for missional encounters. Similar perspectives and case studies were explored at the WCC-consultation 'Believing without belonging? In search of new paradigms of church and mission in secularised and postmodern contexts,' that was held near Hamburg, Germany, in 2002.[73]

The discussion on postmodernity has become a distinctive feature of the missiological debate on Europe. It proves difficult to reach an agreement on the definition and implications of postmodernity. Some criticise postmodernity as arbitrary and as 'the cultural offspring of the consumer culture of late capitalism: freedom of choice in the marketplace is the supreme value and tolerance of other people´s lifestyle choices is the social equivalent'.[74] Others affirm its epistemological and cultural openness for new perspectives, religious orientations and relational reality. Yet some basic lines, so far, have become visible. It seems helpful to distinguish between postmodern cultural attitudes and postmodern philosophies (not all of which would call themselves postmodern). While both offer bridges for mission in Europe,[75] 'postmodern theology runs the grave risk of opening up the way to an anti-realist view of religion, in which the only reference point for belief is the language of a particular community.'[76] Postmodernist extremes, such as the total incommensurability of cultural paradigms, contradict missiological convictions of the intercultural translatability of the gospel. Postmodern rejections of truth-claims can be criticised as self-destructive, as they presuppose the truth of their own statements.

The missiological dialogue with postmodernity thus needs to develop as a *critical postmodernism*. Critical postmodernism appreciates the perspectivity and creativity of human knowledge and communication, while admitting a universally meaningful expression of empirical reality

---

71 cf. Eddie Gibbs/ Bolger, Ryan, *Emerging Churches: Creating Christian Community in postmodern cultures* (Grand Rapids: Baker, 2005). For the reception e.g. in Germany see: "Was will eigentlich die Emerging Church?" ('What does the Emerging Church want?'), *Idea-Spektrum* 46, November 12, 2008, 15-18.

72 'Lausanne Occasional Paper 45: Religious and non-religious Spirituality in a Postmodern [Western] World', David Clayton (ed.) *A New Vision, A new Heart, A Renewed Call: Lausanne Occasional Papers from the 2004 Forum of World Evangelization in Pattaya, Thailand* (Pasadena: Carey, 2005. Vol.2, 171-242), 187.

73 Documented in *International Review of Mission* Vol. XCII, No. 364 and 365 (Jan and Apr 2003).

74 J.A. Kirk, 'Postmodernity', J. Corrie (ed.) *Dictionary of Mission Theology: Evangelical Foundations* (Nottingham: IVP, 2007, 298-303), 301.

75 For examples see: *Lausanne Occasional Paper* 45, 209-231 (Case studies); More case studies in: *IRM* No. 364 (Jan. 200') 18-28.

76 Kirk, 'Postmodernity', 302.

and theological truth.[77] On the level of practical missionary dialogue, James Sire, the author and campus lecturer for Inter-Varsity Christian fellowship, suggested, that everyone rests his knowledge and actions on axioms of belief, which he assumes and hopes to be *true*, because 'the heart will not long rejoice in what the mind knows is not true.'[78]

Exegesis and ecclesiocentrism: Pope Benedict XVI

On April, 19, 2005 Cardinal Joseph Ratzinger, Prefect of the Congregation for the Doctrine of Faith, succeeded Pope John Paul II and became Benedict XVI. While he certainly shares the vision of his predecessor of the New Evangelisation of Europe, his interpretation of contemporary Europe seems to be more down-to-earth and empirical. In 2001, he asked how one could speak of a Christian society if 'in a city like Magdeburg, Christians are only eight percent of the total population, including all Christian denominations.'[79] While for John Paul II, New Evangelisation stood in-between 'real' Mission and pastoral care,[80] for Benedict it is mission in its full sense. In 1996, he emphasized: 'Above all, we should be missionaries [...] missionary responsibility means, precisely, to really attempt a new evangelisation. We cannot calmly accept the rest of humanity falling back again into paganism. We must find the way to take the gospel, also, to nonbelievers. The Church must tap all her creativity so that the living force of the gospel will not be extinguished.'[81]

An example of how Benedict understands his contribution to mission can be seen in his book *Jesus of Nazareth,*[82] where he introduces postmodern readers to the biblical person of Jesus Christ. He begins by carefully deconstructing some historical reconstructions of Jesus, which have 'distanced the person of Jesus from us'[83]. He follows a canonical approach in his exegesis of the gospels in order to overcome the modern separation between history and faith.[84] In all of this he wants to leave his

---

[77] cf. Paul Hiebert, *Missiological Implications of Epistemological Shifts: Affirming Truth in a Modern/Postmodern World* (Harrisburg: Trinity, 1999); Bosch, *Transforming, Mission*, 360.

[78] James W. Sire, 'Why should anyone believe anything at all', in D.A. Carson (ed.) *Telling the Truth: Evangelizing Postmoderns* (Grand Rapids: Baker), 93-101.

[79] Jenkins, *Godless Europe*, 116.

[80] cf. *Redemptoris Missio* 33.

[81] Joseph Ratzinger, *Salz der Erde: Christentum und katholische Kirche im neuen Jahrtausend .Ein Gespräch mit Peter Seewald* (Stuttgart: DVA, 1996), www.ewtn.com/vnews/getstory.asp?number=19347, called up: 17.8.2009.

[82] London: Bloomsbury, 2007. Quotes translated by FW from the German edition: Joseph Ratzinger/ Benedikt XVI, *Jesus von Nazareth. Erster Teil: Von der Taufe im Jordan bis zur Verklärun*(Freiburg: Herder, 2007).

[83] Ratzinger, Jesus, 11.

[84] cf. Ulrich Luz, 'Canonical Exegesis and Hermeneutics of "effective history"', *Studies in Matthew* (Grand Rapids: Eerdmans, 2005), 333-348.

papal authority out of the picture. He does not want the readers to understand his book as an official doctrinal statement, but as a personal journey and search 'for the countenance of the Lord'. [85] So the book turns into a postmodern pilgrimage toward Christ, an inculturational endeavour to 'take the gospel, also, to nonbelievers'.

While Benedict, on his exegetical mission, moves close to the evangelical translational model, at the same time, he sharpens the profile of the exclusive centrality of the Catholic Church. In the declaration *Dominus Iesus* (2000), which was drafted by the Doctrinal Congregation under his supervision, 'The Church of Christ' is seen to 'exist fully only in the Catholic Church' (DI 16). All other churches ,that do not acknowledge the apostolic succession, are 'are not Churches in the proper sense' (DI 17). Although these affirmations are not new and mostly represent quotations from Vatican II, they clearly serve the purpose to highlight the distinctiveness of the Catholic Church in the confusing postmodern plurality and in the background of the approximation of the three missiological models. Benedict's views on mission in Europe, in some respects, do come closer to evangelical and Protestant perspectives than those of his predecessor. But they are certainly not less ecclesiocentric and keep stressing Catholic uniqueness. Yet, the official view is not necessarily the opinion of all Catholic groups engaged in a common mission in Europe (see 2.7).

Crosscurrents: dialogue and deconstructed Christology

The Birmingham mission theologian, Werner Ustorf, also intends to approximate the person of Jesus Christ to postmodern Europeans. But his attempt proves rather different from Benedict's. He suggests the deconstruction of traditional biblical Christology, in order to discover a missiologically more relevant post-Christian European Christ.[86] In traditional biblical Christology, according to Ustorf, Jesus is 'depicted as an essentially admirable and innocent man leading a life showing no trace of personal negativity.'[87] Postmodern Europeans, so Ustorf thinks, cannot relate to this picture of Jesus, who 'in his perfection, is mythological and not one of us': a perfect Christ has no 'mediating powers.' In contrast, as postmodern Europeans 'we have a shadow side ... Our potential for good,

---

[85] Ratzinger, Jesus, 22. cf. Christoph Cardinal Schönborn, "Der Papst auf der Agora. Über einen Anspruch, den allein Gott stellen kann", *"Jesus von Nazareth" kontrovers: Rückfragen an Joseph Ratzinger* (Theologie aktuell 1: Berlin-Hamburg-Münster: LIT, 2007, 9-17): 9.

[86] Werner Ustorf, 'The Emerging Christ of Post-Christian Europe', T. Foust et al. (ed.) *A Scandalous Prophet: The Way of Mission after Newbigin* (Grand Rapids: Eerdmans, 128-144). Ustorf's perspectives are inspired by a paper by Stephen Pattison, "The Shadow Side of Jesus", *Studies in Christian Ethics* 8 (2/1995), 54-67.

[87] Ustorf, 'Emerging Christ', 137.

for creation and love, cannot be truly liberated if our 'shadow', hatred and evil, is ignored or repressed.'[88]

A revisionist European Christology, according to Ustorf, should overcome the 'scandal of restricted access' (John Hick) and be able to admit the shadow sides in Jesus Christ. Ustorf detects these shadow sides in Jesus′ 'ethical radicalism ... expressed in the Beatitudes' which goes along with his suppression of negative thoughts and emotions in his disciples, thus keeping them from coming 'to terms with themselves (and mature)', offering them 'a secondhand identity' Through his message ‚Jesus 'introduced additional conflict, division, and violence into society. [...] In other words, Jesus′ violent death was perhaps caused by the considerable aggression he himself had helped to arouse.'[89] Ustorf concludes: 'Jesus was not special [...] The profile of this man is that of a spirit-filled, charismatic figure; chaotic and creative, integrative and disintegrative, powerful and confused, loving and guilty.'[90] According to Ustorf, this "'Christ' is missiologically relevant since he will help Christians and non-Christians to become mature human beings that accept that 'the work of salvation has to be done by ourselves' and that failure and forgiveness both belong to that endeavour.[91] Ustorf concludes:

> It seems that the disestablishment of Jesus Christ is generating ... new space ... to overcome the heritage of anxiety and aggressiveness. This would alter very much the format and structure of Christian mission ... Christianity once disestablished, is not about itself and not about Christianizing the world. It is about sharing the fullness of life on this earth, about love and reconciliation, community and peace, justice and service. ... To risk a dangerous formulation: a disestablished Christian spirituality would have failed if it were to lead us to ‚God'; ....This missionary spirituality would lead us to our fellow human beings.[92]

Not all of Ustorf's perspectives seem to represent the consensus in missiological thinking in the European churches, but they indicate a significant crosscurrent of the discussion. In Germany, a similar crosscurrent emerged after the mission-oriented Leipzig Synod of the EKD in 1999 (see 2.2). Various theologians were criticizing the new emphasis on the evangelistic dimension of mission and feared for a growing evangelical monopolization in the EKD. They pleaded for a different understanding of mission, as an open dialogue without intentions of persuasion and conversion.[93] These crosscurrents continue the somewhat more radical

---

[88] Ustorf, 'Emerging Christ', 139.
[89] Ustorf, 'Emerging Christ', 140.
[90] Ustorf, 'Emerging Christ', 138;141.
[91] Ustorf, 'Emerging Christ', 143.
[92] Ustorf, 'Emerging Christ', 144.
[93] cf. J. Hermelink, R. Kähler, B. Weyel, "In der Vielfalt liegt die Stärke. Konsequente Mission oder interessierte Kommunikation – wie soll sich die Kirche orientieren?", *Zeitzeichen* 1 (2001), 38-40; G. Kretzschmar, "Wahrnehmung statt

emphases of the dialogical model. Although they are contrary to Benedict's ecclesiocentrism in content, they seem to fulfil the same function as a reaction against a growing consensus between the different models. Within the contemporary discussion, these crosscurrents can be seen as important contributions that remind all participants that differences, and even contrary positions, are necessary to keep the dialogue alive and attentive to the complex reality of European souls.

The Pentecostal turn

In the postmodern context, a new interest in a holistic experience and a spiritual reading of the bible has developed. For some time, both have been reflected in the missionary praxis and perspectives of world-wide Pentecostal and charismatic churches, which recently have been discovered by the ecumenical missiological mainstream.[94] This development could be described as the 'Pentecostal turn' in missiological reflexion. This turn was exemplified, not only by the special interest and openness of the World Missionary Conference in Athens 2005 towards Pentecostals (see 2.1), but also by the Third European Conference of the International Association for Mission Studies (IAMS) in Paris, in August 2006. After the conference, Jacques Matthey mused that at future meetings 'the followers of the charismatic movement' might be the ones giving the main speeches with only the 'counterpoints given by missiologists with links to Protestantism or Catholicism.'[95]

At the conference, Alan Anderson, Professor of Global Pentecostal Studies at the University of Birmingham, explored the missiological relevance of Pentecostalism in Europe.[96] He showed that Pentecostals saw the decline of the traditional European Churches as self-induced, because they lacked renewal through the Holy Spirit and faith in 'the simple and central truths of the Bible.'[97] Similar to postmodernism, Pentecostalism is

Mission. Alternative Sichtweisen zum EKD-Papier ‚Das Evangelium unter die Leute bringen'", *PTh* 91 (2002), 328-343.

[94] One of the reasons for this discovery is the numerical growth of Pentecostal and charismatic traditions in the global church. It was mainly this growth which has shifted the centre of gravity of Christianity from the Western to the Nonwestern World. Walter Hollenweger's and Donald McGavran's research and academic porgrammes with young Pentecostal theologians in Birmingham/UK and Pasadena/USA beginning in the 1970s were early pioneering efforts in recognizing these developments. Cf. M. Bergunder, "Mission und Pfingstbewegung", in: Dahling-Sander (ed.) *Leitfaden Ökumenische Misisonstheologie* (Gütersloh: Kaiser), 214.

[95] 'Introduction to the Programme of the Conference', *IRM* 95 (July/October 2006) 232-235: 233.

[96] A. Anderson, 'Pentecostalism, the Enlightenment and Christian Mission in Europe', *International Review of Mission* 95 July/October (2006): 276-281.

[97] Anderson, 'Pentecostalism', 278.

interpreted as 'a distinct reaction to the rationalism of the Enlightenment. For Pentecostals, a rationalistic intellectualism has destroyed the soul of Christianity.'[98] While postmodernism, by deconstructing the subject, ultimately 'proved the urgency of the subject,'[99] Pentecostalism affirmed the human subject and her dignity by providing 'a sense of belonging to those who have been marginalized by society.'[100] Anderson points to some lessons the churches can learn from Pentecostals for mission in Europe: [101] (1) Pentecostals engage in enthusiastic, experiential and participatory worship. Anderson thinks that this 'experience of the power of the Spirit can be a unifying factor in a global society which is still deeply divided.' (2) Charismatic mission is characterised by a radical felt-needs orientation. Anderson quotes a Nigerian pastor: 'We live in rather difficult times; dreams are constantly dashed against the rocks of adversity. People desperately need to know that things will get better. ... We preach that miracles still happen! God still fixes shattered lives... A Church that preaches a message that gives hope, encouragement and healing will never lack for attendance.'[102] (3) Pentecostal churches have a strong sense of calling by God and are dedicated to reach their contemporaries in up-to-date cultural language in music, film and television. In that respect, they are truly contextual in their use of mass media which, according to Thomas Halik, is the 'common language' of postmodern society.[103]

In conclusion, one could say that the Pentecostal turn is a turn to holistic spiritual identity, expressive community and contemporary contextuality as essential ingredients for a missiological model in Europe. The Pentecostal and charismatic traditions seem to offer all these, as they have a strong sense of the church as a 'separate', yet 'a caring, therapeutic community', 'whose primary purpose is to promote their cause to those outside the church.'[104] Yet one should not overestimate the Pentecostal potential for mission in Europe, since its very strengths can, at the same time, be weaknesses. Combined with paternalistic leadership, the strong emphasis on community can easily develop into a restricted social ecclesiocentrism that is not attractive to those Europeans, who are looking for a kind of Christian commitment in 'places where there is no obligation to opt in or to

---

[98] Anderson, 'Pentecostalism', 278.

[99] Knut Wenzel, "Radical Subjectivity", *International Review of Mission* 95 July/October (2006), 259-264:
pp. 261/262.

[100] Anderson, 'Pentecostalism', 278.

[101] Anderson, 'Pentecostalism', 278-281.

[102] Anderson, 'Pentecostalism', 280.

[103] cf. Tomás Halík sees 'religion' and 'science' as the common languages of pre-modern and modern society, while '"mass media" plays the social role of religion' in postmodern society, 'The Soul of Europe: An Altar to the Unknown God', *International Review of Mission* 95 July/October (2006), 265-270:p. 267.

[104] Anderson, 'Pentecostalism', 281.

participate in communal activities beyond the service itself.'[105] The radical felt-needs orientation sometimes crosses the line into unhealthy and unsound 'health and wealth' promises that are bound to disappoint and leave bitter feelings. Radical contemporality may prove counterproductive, in the light of a returning appreciation of traditional aesthetic and cultural expressions of Christianity like cathedrals, liturgies, classical music and pilgrimages.

Spirituality, plurality and politics

The religiously inspired Islamist terrorist attacks in New York 2001, Madrid 2004 and London 2005 caused haunting questions on the religious base for peaceful plurality in Europe.[106] Not only Catholic and evangelical Protestant theologians, but liberal thinkers like the Frankfurt school philosopher ‚Jürgen Habermas, emphasized that the *Christian* faith was foundational for freedom and democracy in European civilization.[107] Lamin Sanneh maintained that 'two major forces are contending today for Europe´s soul – radical Islam and the new Christianity.' [108] Less provocatively, the German chancellor, Angela Merkel, in a speech at the European Parliament in Strasbourg, in 2007, emphasized, 'as a Christian I expressly acknowledge my allegiance to Europe's Christian principles', adding: 'the most beautiful part of the play [Lessing's famous ring parable, Nathan the Wise] is what the Sultan asks of Nathan. Bridging all the divisions of faith, the Muslim requests the Jew to "Be my friend". Yes, ladies and gentlemen, that is what we seek and for which we strive – harmony among nations.'[109] The theological and missiological question no longer seems to be marginal to politics in postmodern and pluralist Europe.

A missionary expression of the spiritual basis of European plurality was given at the conferences of the *Together for Europe*-movement. The movement brings together Catholic, Lutheran, Anglican and Orthodox spiritual and missionary groups and initiatives like the Focolare, Cursillo, Sant´Egidio, Geistliche Gemeinde-Erneuerung [GGE], ProChrist, Alpha-

---

[105] Grace Davie, 'Is Europe an exceptional case?' *International Review of Mission* 95 July/October (2006): 247-58:p. 253.

[106] cf. Kippenberg, Hans/ Tilman Seidensticker (ed.), *The 9/11 Handbook: Annotated Translation and Interpretation of the Attackers´ Spiritual Manual* (London/Oakville: Equinox, 2006).

[107] J. Habermas, *Time of Transitions* (New York: Polity Press, 2006), cit. Jenkins, *Godless Europe*, 120.

[108] 'Can Europe be saved? A Review Essay', *International Bulletin of Missionary Research* 31 (3/2007): 121-125:p. 124.

[109] Speech by Angela Merkel, Chancellor of the Federal Republic of Germany, to the European Parliament in Strasbourg on Wednesday, 17 January 2007, www.eu2007.de/en/News/Speeches_Interviews/January/Rede_Bundeskanzlerin2.html

Courses. In 2004 and 2007, the movement convened large meetings in Stuttgart with about 9000 Christians from different European nations to represent a 'Europe of the Spirit'. The Spirit of the gospel, it is maintained, creates a culture of togetherness 'through which different peoples and individuals can welcome each other, get to know each other, be reconciled and learn to respect and support each other.'[110]

The first conference took place about the time when the Constitution of the EU was to be ratified and the discussion on the mention of God and the Christian tradition of Europe in the preamble was in full swing. The comments that a number of well-known speakers gave on this issue, at the conference, show how the connection between spirituality and politics was viewed. The Lutheran Pastor and 'Pro-Christ'-evangelist, Ulrich Parzany, pointed out that European democracy 'depends on conditions that democracy itself cannot bring about'. He saw a mention of God and Christianity in the EU constitution 'as a useful reminder' to this, but clarified that 'the destiny of Europe does not depend on whether God is named in the constitution', the destiny of Europe 'hinges on the witness of people rather than texts.'[111] Another speaker, the Italian historian, Andrea Riccardi, emphasized the complex historical significance of a reference to Christianity in the EU constitution, qualifying that it should be understood '"in a non-monopolistic fashion" – along with a reference to Auschwitz. The charter, he said, should contain a reminder of the darkness, from which the EU was founded to escape.' Romano Prodi, the President of the European Commission, reminded that the 'the fathers of the EU', the Frenchman, Robert Schuman (1886-1963), the Italian, Alcide de Gasperi, (1881-1954) and the German, Konrad Adenauer (1876-1967), 'were committed Christians, unafraid to seek guidance from their faith. [...] Christians now [must] be the leaven of the new Europe, nurturing – together with other faiths – the soul of the European project.' [112]

Similar perspectives had been expressed at the Budapest-conference of the evangelical network 'Hope for Europe' in 2002: 'We reaffirm our lifelong commitment to love God and our neighbour, European and non-European, as ourselves. We will humbly seek to do this through being a community of praying, worshipping, welcoming, culturally relevant, outward looking people who know the Bible well and are united in multiplying, inclusive, evangelising local churches. We will work for peace, justice and reconciliation and will value as equals those seen as inferior by our societies.'[113]

---

[110] Movements and Christian Communities 'Together for Europe', www.miteinander-wie-sonst.de/_en/home.html

[111] Austen Ivereigh, 'Europe of the Heart', *The Tablet*, 13.05.2004, www.thetablet.co.uk/articles/2469

[112] Austen Ivereigh, 'Europe of the Heart', *The Tablet*, 13.05.2004, www.thetablet.co.uk/articles/2469

[113] *Budapest Perspectives: Towards an Agenda of Hope for Europe*. www.hfe.org.

In an exemplary way, these perspectives express some of the political emphases of the recent missiological discussion. They do not focus on ecclesiastical politics or political Christianity, but affirm political and religious plurality on the basis of the truth of the gospel.[114] The gospel of Jesus Christ is not seen as a European religion, but as the unique revelation of God for all human beings that creates and sustains a space of grace: respect for others, meaningful communication, honesty towards failure and humility to receive and to grant forgiveness. Mission in Europe as a form of *christocentric pluralism* is seen to overcome the inverted ethics of multiple 'primary groups'[115] and enable constructive community and dialogue in Europe, even on highly controversial religious, ethical and political issues.

Searching for the Soul(s) of Europe: Some Conclusions from an Evangelical Perspective

In the preceding, I have tried to show how the missiological debate in the European churches has changed over the last thirty years. The three models that characterised the first phase are still recognizable in the second phase. It seems obvious that each of the three models contributes essential insights towards a contextual missiology for Europe. The ecclesiocentric *inculturational* model helps to understand the importance of a visible Christian community rooted in history and relevant to European culture and identity. The cosmocentric *dialogical* model reminds us that God´s mission is broader than the Church´s mission and is at work in every society, culture and religion. It rightly challenges Christians to carefully listen to and learn from secular and religious people in Europe and build a many-coloured European house together. The bibliocentric *translational* model points to the normative and creative biblical *constants* in context and challenges contextual mission thinking not to fade into some form of pluralistic or culturalistic European religion, but to be clearly centred on the unique biblical and universal witness of Jesus Christ.[116]

---

[114] For a missiological critique of pluralist theologies of religion see e.g. A. Kirk, 'Religious pluralism as an epiphenomenon of Postmodern Perspecitivism', V. Mortensen (ed) *Theology and the Religions: A Dialogue* (Grand Rapids: Eerdmans, 2003), 430-442; A. Feldtkeller, "Verlangt der gesellschaftliche Pluralismus nach einer ‚pluralistischen Religionstheologie?" *EvTheol* 58 (6/1998), 445-460.

[115] J. Bouman has pointed to the self-centred dynamics of *primary-groups* in multicultural societies:'"People are mainly interested in their immediate rational and emotional neighbourhood-family-friends-political party-ethnic group... The more distance grows between groups in respect to time, space, affections or identities, the less interest and concern for other people will be there.' J. Bouman, "Ethik und Kultur in einer multikulturellen Gesellschaft", *European Journal of Theology* 4 (1): 79-87: 86/87.

[116] cf. Stephen Bevans/ Richard Schroeder, *Constants in Context: A Theology of Mission for Today* (Maryknoll: Orbis, 2004), 33.

Still, the models have not stayed static. They have changed, interrelated and moved towards a more integrated, yet more complex and sometimes diffuse emerging model – with significant crosscurrents. This seems to correspond with postmodern times that value relationship more than reason (or at least as 'being right') and understand the relativity of perspectives. This allows for the concurrence of differing and contrary views, while (hopefully) not giving up on community. On the other hand, critical mission theological evaluation of the various perspectives still seems appropriate and possible on the basis of the 'epistemological priority' of the 'classical text, the Scriptures.'[117] From that perspective, I will take a concluding look at three essential dimensions of missiological thinking in Europe.

The context: understanding the European soul

Even though the concern of Jacques Delors to develop not only the economic, but also the affective dimension of Europe must be appreciated, it does not seem to be the task of mission to 'give a soul to Europe'. Europe is not soulless, but has a most complex and dynamic soul.[118] The task of mission would be to meet, to listen to and to try to understand the soul(s) of Europe. Here are some conclusions: (1) While *Europe and the European Union* are not identical, the economic and political partnership of the 27 countries of the European Union is an essential and almost defining element for a contemporary understanding of European reality. This partnership started after the Second World War, in 1950, with the plan of the French politician, Robert Schuman, to overcome violence and hunger and to foster peace, reconciliation and prosperity through economic interrelations in Europe. It is initself an important element of the European soul. (2) Europe can be viewed as a *post-Christian culture*. This implies the acknowledgement of the significant influence that the Christian faith in its various historical inculturations (Orthodox, Catholic, Protestant, Pietist-evangelical etc.) has had and, in many ways, still has on European history and culture. On the other hand, it includes the realization of the growing distance of many Europeans from the Christian metanarrative. (3) In a similar way, Europe can be described as a *postmodern culture*. This implies the acknowledgement of the formative role of the enlightenment and modernity for Europe, and their ongoing influence in some areas of science and technology. On the other hand, it means to understand the 'incredulity' of postmodern Europeans towards all preceding metanarratives, while, in their various turns towards aesthetics, relationships, communication, ecology and minority rights, they arbitrarily pick and choose from the rich banquet of these historical metanarratives. An example: While France is

[117] Bosch, *Transforming Mission*, 187.
[118] cf. Halik, *The soul*, 266.

diagnosed as the most secular country in Europe, 'the most esteemed figure in the nation is Abbé Pierre ..., the Catholic priest whose Emmaus movement has since 1949 helped the homeless and destitute.' (4) Only on the basis of these developments in cultural history (Christian, modern and postmodern), the countries of Europe have become a pluralist culture, which places high value on the freedom of conscience, belief, speech, science and lifestyle a basis for a multiethnic, multicultural and multireligious society, an open forum and space for the *convivencia*, dialogue and witness. I agree with Luibl:

> The history of the peoples and people of Europe is the place of the Soul of Europe. Exactly here we would find, that Europe has not one but many souls: a Romanic, a Germanic and a Slavic soul, a Catholic, a Protestant and an Orthodox Soul; a Christian, a Jewish and a Muslim soul; we would find an enlightened and a pious soul; many national souls and as many souls that are minorities and live as refugees or exiles. Only such soul-stories ..., stories of the scars in the souls, maybe there, in a history of mentality, one could discover a 'soul of Europe', put together from thousands of European souls, a patchwork-soul.[119]

Though, listening to the European soul(s) is a formidable and sometimes the most important task, it is not enough. From a mission theological perspective, hope for Europe does not originate from the 'soul' of Europe. The bible describes the human soul (hebr. *nefesh*) as completely dependent on the creative, sustaining and redemptive word and breath of God (Gen. 2,7). 'My soul thirsts for God, for the living God. When can I go and meet with God?' (Ps. 42,2).

The text: European religion or missio Dei in Europe?

It is essential for mission in Europe that it includes the invitation to Europeans, in the churches and in society, to listen and let the breath of God fill their lives. Contextual mission theology in Europe constantly needs to ask if mission in Europe is a genuine expression of the biblical *missio Dei,* or if it is moving towards an ecclesiastic or culturalist *missio Europae*, moving from an inculturational towards an ecclesiocentric or syncretistic orientation. Although the distinction between syncretism and inculturation is not an easy one and always needs to be open for revision,[120] it remains decisive to ask if the identity of the gospel is retained or alienated in the process.[121] It remains essential to clarify 'the proximity to

---

[119] Luibl, *A-3024*, 5, transl. FW.

[120] T. Sundermeier, *Was ist Religion? Religionswissenschaft im theologischen Kontext. Ein Studienbuch* (Gütersloh, 1999), 162-179.

[121] H. Wrogemann, "Theologie und Wissenschaft der Mission", C. Dahling-Sander et al. (ed.) *Leitfaden Ökumenische Missionstheologie*. (Gütersloh: Kaiser, 2003), 17-31.

or distance from the centre, Jesus Christ.'[122] Peter Stuhlmacher, the New Testament scholar in Tübingen, tried to summarize the core identity of the gospel as follows:

> The content and the status of the gospel have been given to us in the gospels and the Pauline letters. The gospel message, authorised by the one God and Father of Jesus Christ, affirms that the messianic redeemer who was announced by the prophets to Israel and the nations has appeared in Jesus, who as to his human nature was a descendant of David, and who through the Spirit of holiness was declared with power to be the Son of God by his resurrection from the dead (Romans 1: 3-4 NIV). On Calvary he was 'delivered over to death for our sins' and on Eastern morning God ,raised [him] to life for our justification'(Romans 4: 25 NIV). All Gentiles and Jews who believe in the crucified and risen Christ and confess him as Saviour and Lord will be saved (Romans 19: 9-13 NIV).[123]

Of course, any historical or present attempt to reformulate the gospel as the core of mission, on the basis of the biblical texts, needs to be open to revision. Postmodernism has rightly shaken the self-confidence of positivist epistemology and pointed to the cultural perspectivity of all hermeneutics and theology. Yet, there is more than just perspectives. Global intercultural communication in commerce and science is constantly creating 'shared spaces', that prove that not all is lost in translation, but that reality exists and can be distinguished from perception. While constant effort is needed, basic observations of nature and human behaviour are regularly translated and understood transculturally.[124] In a similar way, the reality of God's revelation in Jesus Christ that is expressed in the biblical texts is – through the power of the Holy Spirit – creating 'shared spaces' across historical and cultural divides. The growing world-wide community of Christians and churches – though with necessarily different emphases – is constantly affirming the reality, power and meaning of the gospel as the text of mission.

Mission in Europe, therefore, means to share the biblical story of the Living God, Father, Son and Holy Spirit, with Europeans in a holistic way as an invitation to life and truth. Since European media culture is filled with moving, but imaginary stories, it is decisive that the biblical story be true ,as well as life-transforming. In this respect, Ustorf's suggestion of a post-Christian European Christology does not seem to be helpful. While Europeans might be able to identify with a deconstructed European Christ, this Christ neither corresponds with the biblical records, nor is capable of giving Europeans reason and hope for *change* in their lives.

---

[122] C. Van Engen,, 'Theology of Mission', A.S. Moreau et al. (ed.) *Evangelical Dictionary of World Mission* (Grand Rapids: Baker, 949-951), 949.

[123] Peter Stuhlmacher, *Biblische Theologie und Evangelium. Gesammelte Aufsätze* (WUNT 146: Tübingen: Mohr-Siebeck, 2002), 282, transl. Walldorf.

[124] cf. H. Netland, *Encountering Religious Pluralism* (Downer Grove: IVP, 2001), 289.

The community of mission in Europe

While I can not quite agree with the notion that the Church *is* the soul of Europe, Christian churches certainly are *part* of the European culture and are called to be 'salt' and 'light' within it (Mt. 5, 13-14). The church as the eschatological community of the reign of God is called to participate in God´s mission and in his redemptive search for the soul(s) of Europe. Mission in Europe, therefore, means for the churches to let themselves be constantly renewed by the text of mission and to live it out in their context, among their fellow-Europeans.

Even if it is a myth that many Europeans are no longer interested in truth, it seems to be true that the search for truth is hidden within the search for identity, personal meaning and community. Europeans are looking for real relationships *and* for truth that can carry these relationships.[125] As the hermeneutical bridge between the biblical text and the European context has broken down to a large extent, the *communio sanctorum* is the plausibility structure (Peter L. Berger) for mission and a network of hope in the geographies, cultures, religions and denominations of Europe. It is a community that is as diverse and dynamic as European society. It is composed of national, ethnic, cultural, sub-cultural and denominational groups, traditional folk and free churches, emerging church movements, Christian fellowships and communities, migrant churches, international churches, student movements and missionary societies. This network of ethically alternative and missionary expressive Christian communities is woven into the plural web of European cultural and religious communities and, as a visible *semeion* (Greek: sign, symbol), points to the gospel of Jesus Christ.

At the World Missionary Conference in Edinburgh 1910, Europe was seen as a Christian territory and thus excluded as a field and context for mission. In the 21st century, mission in Europe has become a complex challenge for a world-wide community of Christians from many regional, cultural and religious backgrounds. Christians from Africa, Asia and Latin America, together with Europeans, already have been praying and working together in that challenge, for some time.[126]

---

[125] J. Long, 'Generating Hope: A Strategy for Reaching the Postmodern Generation', D.A. Carson (ed.) *Telling the Truth: Evangelizing Postmoderns* (Grand Rapids: Baker, 2000, 322-335), 334.

[126] J. Reimer, ‚They come with a message: The gospel of missionaries from the Two-Thirds World in old Europe', *Missionalia* 35 (2/2007) 3-17; F. Walldorf, "Mission in Partnerschaft: Zum Aufbruch der evangelikalen Missionsbewegung in Afrika, Asien und Lateinamerika", H. Kasdorf/ F. Walldorf (ed.) *Werdet meine Zeugen: Weltmission im Horizont von Theologie und Geschichte*, Neuhausen: Hänssler, 1996, 221-248.

THE CHURCH IN THE POST-CHRISTIAN SOCIETY BETWEEN MODERNITY AND LATE MODERNITY: L. NEWBIGIN'S POST-CRITICAL MISSIONAL ECCLESIOLOGY

Veli-Matti Kärkkäinen

Introduction: Setting Newbigin in the Context of Postmodernism

Similarly to the Bishop of Hippo, whom he greatly admired, the Bishop of South India felt like he was living in between the times, in a transitional era. Whereas, for St. Augustine, the transition had to do with the falling apart of the worldwide political empire of Rome, for Newbigin, the transformation had to do with the dismantling of the foundations of the worldwide intellectual empire, the Enlightenment. Newbigin often expressed this dynamic and anguish in the words of the Chinese Christian thinker Carver Yu, who claimed that the contemporary culture of the West lives in the dynamic of 'technological optimism and literary pessimism.'[1] Again, similarly to the early-fifth-century critic of Ancient Rome, the late-twentieth-century critic of the Modern West, did not live long enough to see the new empire that replaced the old one and what the implications of that shift were for the life and mission of the *City of God* on earth.

It has been noted, recently, that it was only during the last decade of his productive life that Newbigin intentionally and explicitly started addressing the challenge of postmodernism. Paul Weston, in his important essay on Newbigin's relation to postmodernism, mentions that all references to that concept occur after 1991, when he was already 82 years old.[2] Had he lived longer, Newbigin's engagement with postmodernism would have loomed large in the horizon of his cultural critique. At the same time – and this is the key to my own investigation – as Weston rightly notes, 'Newbigin can be shown to have developed a missiological approach that effectively anticipates many of the questions raised by contemporary postmodern

[1] Lesslie Newbigin, *The Gospel in a Pluralist Society* (Grand Rapids, Mich.: Eerdmans, 1989/Geneva: WCC Publications, 1989) 232; Lesslie Newbigin, *Truth to Tell: The Gospel as Public Truth* (Grand Rapids, Mich.: Eerdmans, 1991), 19, 30.

[2] Paul Weston, 'Lesslie Newbigin: A Postmodern Missiologist?' *Mission Studies* 21, no. 2 (2004), 229.

perspectives.'[3] I attempt to show in this essay that the English bishop's engagement with postmodernism goes way beyond the year 1991. Indeed, I set forth an argument, according to which Newbigin's cultural critique of Modernity offers a fruitful and a fresh way of considering the church's relation to the postmodern condition. However, what is ironic about this contribution is that the bishop himself neither attempted a response to postmodernism, nor was he, by and large, conscious of it.

I hesitate regarding the judgment of those who consider the bishop 'A "Postmodern" before Postmodernity Arrived.'[4] Rather than considering him a 'crypto-Postmodernist', I argue that a careful analysis of his writings, over a longer period of time, reveals that while he saw in some features of postmodernism orientations that helped clarify the critique of Modernity, by and large, he was extremely critical of key features of what he thought makes postmodernism. At no point did Newbigin consider the programme of postmodernism as a whole an ally to his own pursuit of 'the gospel as public truth.' I fear that one of the titles the bishop would absolutely eschew having attached to his legacy is 'postmodern.' The reason for this assessment is simply the fact that, in the bishop's understanding, postmodernism represented to him everything destructive, almost as much as his arch-enemy, Modernity.

My approach, in this investigation, is based on the methodological conviction – or at least, a hypothesis – according to which Newbigin's thinking reveals a remarkable integrity and consistency throughout the period of his mature life, beginning from the late seventies or early eighties, when he began focusing on the critique of the church's mistaken 'contextualization' strategy inWestern (European-American) culture. This is not to say that his thinking was systematic or always even tightly ordered. It was not, as he was no scholar, but rather a preacher and independent thinker – and he himself was often the first one to acknowledge it.[5] It is simply to say that upon his return from India, in a

[3] Weston, 'A Postmodern Missiologist?' 230.

[4] Weston, 'A Postmodern Missiologist?' 243.

[5] As a preacher rather than an academic scholar, Newbigin often used ideas and movements as heuristic "talking points" and examples rather than as showcases of detailed academic analysis. His writing style was occasional rather than systematic. To take up obvious examples: his tracing of the pre-history and development of Modernity from antiquity (in terms of the two narratives of Christian faith and Hellenistic philosophy) or his treatment and contrasting of Augustine and Aquinas, in its details hardly stands the scrutiny of rigorous academic investigation. Similarly, his preference for 'good guys' in history such as Athanasius and Augustine and disdain for 'bad guys' such as Aquinas and Descartes reflect much more their role in the unfolding intentionally biased reading of history than anything else. While for the purposes of academic scholarship the acknowledgment of those kinds of biases should not go unnoticed, in my opinion, they should not blur the significance of Newbigin's critique and constructive proposal. In many ways, it can

relatively short period of time, the key theses of a missionally driven post-critical thinking emerged. Therefore, methodologically, the best way to determine his relation and contribution to postmodernism is to look broadly at the writings of the whole of his mature career. Indeed, my reading of his writings has assured me, against my own initial suspicions that his critique – as well as the occasional affirmation – of postmodernism is, to a large extent, unspoken and tacit in the texture of the cultural critique, where the main target was Modernity.[6] Consequently, I fear, those who critique Newbigin for the lack of a nuanced understanding of postmodernism,[7] not only miss the point but expect of him something he never set out to do.

One of the reasons why I think along those lines is that, as I will have an opportunity to explain in the following, for Newbigin, postmodernism was parasitic on Modernity. Postmodernism, in his judgment, had no independent existence but was rather an offshoot from Modernity. He did not see postmodernism as a 'saviour' of the church, but rather another challenger along with Modernity – even when, occasionally, he affirmed some elements of this new epistemological approach.

My discussion is composed of two main parts. In part one, I will attempt a diagnostic assessment of Newbigin's view of postmodernism. Rather than trying to judge whether Newbigin's vision of postmodernism was correct or even balanced, my task is simply to analyze the bishop's view. Part two then attempts to determine what would be the key aspects of Newbigin's constructive proposal, with regard to the church's mission under the postmodern condition. Not surprisingly, in light of my methodological remarks above, I contend that Newbigin's response to postmodernism is not radically different from his response to Modernism. To both Modernists and postmodernists, he offered, as an alternative, the view of the gospel as public truth.

I repeat myself: My aim is neither to try to make the bishop postmodern nor even try to align his thinking with postmodern orientations. Rather, my ultimate goal is to use his cultural critique of Modernity as a way to help the church in the beginning of the third millennium to reappraise her mission and existence in the world.

Needless to say, all of the essay is necessarily reconstructive from the author's point of view, particularly in view of my stated purpose above:

---

be said that his innovative and bold proposal can stand on its own feet even if it can shown – unfortunately – that not all the historical and philosophical judgments do.

[6] One of the many contributions of Weston's 'A Postmodern Missiologist?' essay is that it outlines the key aspects of Newbigin's indebtedness to Michael Polanyi, the philosopher of science from whom the bishop borrowed well-known ideas such as 'universal intention', testimonies 'from within the tradition', and so forth. These are concepts that helped the mature Newbigin to construct his cultural critique and point the way towards his view of 'the gospel as public truth.'

[7] Elaine Graham and Walton Heather, 'Walk on the Wild Side: A Critique of *The Gospel and Our Culture*', *Modern Churchman* 33, no. 1 (1991), 5-7.

rather than searching for the term *postmodern* in his writings or even trying to determine veiled references to postmodernism, I reconstruct the bishop's viewpoint on the basis of his overall missional thinking and epistemology.[8]

Newbigin's View of Postmodernity

Rather than first attempting a generic description of postmodernism – if there is such a generic concept about an intellectual movement, which intentionally opposes any generalizations – my approach is 'from below.' What I mean is this: I will do my best to discern, from Newbigin's own writings, the way he discerned the effects and implications of the transition underway in the cultures of the West as the Enlightenment was slowly giving way to a new way of thinking and being. The term 'transition,' in the subheading below, is intentional and important: it seems to me that the best way – and to a large extent, the only way – to determine what Newbigin opined about postmodernism appears in the contexts, in which he is discussing the move away, or transition, from Modernity to postmodernism. Thus, seeking for and counting terms, such as 'postmodernism' is to miss the point. Without often naming what this 'post-' or 'late-' was, he focused his reflections on the implications of the transition away from Modernism to the church's mission.

The epistemological challenge of the transition from modernity to late modernity

I will divide Newbigin's diagnosis of postmodernism into two interrelated themes: epistemology and lifestyle. The first one gets the lion's share in this discussion, and is further divided into two segments. While epistemology and lifestyle are interrelated, they can also be distinguished for the sake of clarity of analysis.

The key to properly understanding Newbigin's diagnosis of postmodernism is to acknowledge its parasitic nature. As mentioned above, for Newbigin, postmodernism had no independent existence; rather it was an extension of and offshoot from Modernity. This may also help explain

---

[8] In my investigation of many aspects of Newbigin's thinking I am indebted to the published doctoral dissertation submitted to the Faculty of Theology at the University of Helsinki by Jukka Keskitalo. That careful study is the most comprehensive theological analysis of Newbigin's thinking. Unfortunately, it is written in Finnish and has only a brief English summary. Therefore, I do not give references to it unless there is a direct citation or otherwise important reason in terms of academic integrity. Jukka Keskitalo, *Kristillinen usko ja moderni kulttuuri: Lesslie Newbigin käsitys kirkon missiosta modernissa länsimaisessa kulttuurissa* [The Christian Faith and Modern Culture: Lesslie Newbigin's View of the Church's Mission in Modern Western Culture] (Suomalaisen Teologisen Kirjallisuusseuran Julkaisuja 218. Helsinki: Suomalainen Teologinen Kirjallisuusseura, 1999).

the lack of a sustained analysis of postmodernity.[9] It only came to the fore as the bishop was reflecting on the transition away from Modernity. This state of affairs is reflected in his choice of terminology. A number of terms appear in his writings, such as 'postmodern culture' or 'postmodernity',[10] 'the postmodern development of modernism',[11] as well as 'postmodern reaction.'[12] I believe the term '*late* modern' might best characterize Newbigin's view, which builds on the idea of continuity.[13] In the following, while I continue using the term 'postmodern(ism)' as the general nomenclature, I will at times use the term 'late modern' to highlight Newbigin's take on the topic. In keeping with his idea of the parasitic nature of postmodernism, one of the key observations of the bishop was that the advent of postmodernism, if such has already happened, does not mean a complete shift in terms of replacement of the old for new, but rather a co-habitation of a sort. This co-habitation includes both intellectual and lifestyle issues, as the discussion will show.

There are a number of internal dynamics, even contradictions, in postmodernism in Newbigin's analysis. On the one hand, there are many who have grown very suspicious of the project of the Enlightenment with its search for Cartesian indubitable certainty. On the other hand, this is only one side of contemporary Western intellectual culture. Among the ordinary folks – and in many ways among the educated as well – there is still a firm trust in the facts of science and Modernity. This confidence in the project of Modernity is greatly aided by the economic and scientific-technological globalization process.[14]

Over and against this continuing confidence in the Enlightenment, there is a definite shift that, for the bishop, signals the transition away from Modernity: for 'an increasing number of people ... there is no longer any confidence in the alleged "eternal truths of reason" of ... Lessing.'[15] The following 'working definition' of postmodernism by Newbigin is as illustrative of his perception of that movement as any:

> Its main feature is the abandonment of any claim to know the truth in an absolute sense. Ultimate reality is not single but diverse and chaotic. Truth-

[9] Keskitalo, *Kristillinen usko*, 214 notes that Colin Gunton's view of postmodernity is similarly parasitic.

[10] Among others, Lesslie Newbigin, *Proper Confidence: Faith, Doubt & Certainty in Christian Discipleship* (Grand Rapids, Mich.: Eerdmans, 1995), 27, 51; Lesslie Newbigin, *Truth and Authority in Modernity,* Christian Mission and Modern Culture Series (Valley Forge, Penn.: Trinity Press International, 1996), 82.

[11] Among others, Newbigin, *Proper Confidence*, 83.

[12] Among others, Newbigin, *Truth and Authority*, 7.

[13] So also Keskitalo, *Kristillinen usko*, 214.

[14] Lesslie Newbigin, 'Modernity in Context', in *Postmodern and Christians*, ed. John Reid, Lesslie Newbigin, and David Pullinger (Carberry: Handsell Press, 1996), 8.

[15] Newbigin, *Truth and Authority*, 77.

> claims are really concealed claims to power, and this applies as much to the claims of science as to those of religion. The father of this whole movement is the German philosopher F.W. Nietzsche. Nietzsche was the one who foresaw, in the closing years of the 19th century, that the methods of the Enlightenment must in the end lead to total scepticism and nihilism.[16]

At the heart of Newbigin's analysis of postmodernity is, thus, the loss of confidence in any kind of universal truth of reason a.k.a. the Enlightenment,[17] a feature he also calls 'the sickness of our culture.'[18] In Newbigin's mind, the 'foundationalism' of the Enlightenment with its belief in grandiose truths has been replaced in postmodern culture with the idea of 'regimes of truth', which stand next to each other in a pluralist society:

> In the last decades of this century, the intellectual leadership of Europe has begun to turn its back on modernity. We are in the age of postmodernity. The mark of this is a suspicion of all claims to universal truth. Such claims have to be deconstructed. The 'metanarratives' told by societies to validate their claim to global power are to be rejected. There are no privileged cultures and no privileged histories. All human cultures are equally entitled to respect. There are only different 'regimes of truth' (Michael Foucault) which succeed one another.... There are no overarching criteria by which these regimes can be judged.[19]

In order to properly understand the parasitic nature of postmodernity, one needs to acknowledge the bridge from Descartes via Friedrich Nietzsche – the 'spiritual father' of all postmodernists – to contemporary elimination of the original Enlightenment dream of the certainty of knowledge.[20] Ironically the method of doubt – which was made the main way of achieving indubitable certainty – was changed in the hands of Nietzsche into the main weapon against Modernity which, in turn, paved the way for the total loss of confidence manifested in postmodernity. 'The Cartesian invitation to make doubt the primary tool in search for knowledge was bound to lead to the triumph of skepticism and eventually of nihilism, as Nietzsche foresaw.'[21] Nietzsche replaced rational argument as the means

---

16 Lesslie Newbigin, 'Religious Pluralism: A Missiological Approach', *Studia Missionalia* 42 (1993), 231.

17 See Newbigin, *Truth and Authority*, 77 cited above.

18 Lesslie Newbigin, 'Religious Pluralism and the Uniqueness of Jesus Christ', *International Bulletin of Missionary Research* 13, no. 2 (1989) 50. Newbigin refers several times to the well-known ideas of the Jewish-American philosopher Alan Bloom, who in his influential work *The Closing of the American Mind* (New York: Simon & Schuster, 1987) sees a total relativism as the dominant feature of Western culture; see, e.g., Lesslie Newbigin, *A Word in Season: Perspectives on Christian World Mission*, ed. Eleanor Jackson (Grand Rapid, Mich.: Eerdmans/Edinburgh: Saint Andrews Press, 1994), 105-6.

19 Newbigin, *Proper Confidence*, 27.

20 See Newbigin, *Proper Confidence*, 26-27.

21 Newbigin, *Truth and Authority*, 8.

of arbitrating between competing truth-claims with the 'will to power.'[22] Terms such as 'true' and 'untrue' have simply lost their meaning,[23] what remains is simply different 'narratives', themselves historically conditioned.[24] Even science – believed by the Enlightenment pioneers to be the source of indisputable truths – becomes yet another expression of the will to power.[25]

Not surprisingly, Newbigin did not tire himself with highlighting this built-in irony of the line of development from the dream of indubitable certainty coupled with the method of doubt from Descartes to Nietzsche's rejection and replacement of all such 'uncritical' attitudes for historization of all knowledge, which finally led to the total loss of confidence of postmodernity. 'It is deeply ironic that this method has led us directly into the programme of skepticism of the postmodern world.'[26] Ultimately, the fact that postmodern culture does not allow us to know which God really is the 'true' God is for Newbigin a sign of a 'dying culture.'[27]

A pluralist society

A virtual synonym, for Newbigin, for postmodern culture, is 'pluralist culture.' While pluralism ,as such, is nothing new to Christian faith, which was born in a religiously pluralistic environment, what is new is the form of contemporary pluralism: 'The kind of Western thought which has described itself as "modern" is rapidly sinking into a kind of pluralism which is indistinguishable from nihilism – a pluralism which denies the possibility of making any universally justifiable truth-claims on any matter, whether religious or otherwise.'[28]

An important aid to Newbigin, in his analysis of the nature and effects of the late Modern pluralism, is offered by Peter Berger's *Heretical Imperative*,[29] with which he interacted extensively in several writings.[30] Berger's well-known thesis is that, whereas in pre-Modern societies heretical views were discouraged at the expense of communal and cultural

---

[22] Newbigin, *Truth and Authority*, 8.
[23] Newbigin, *Proper Confidence*, 26.
[24] Newbigin, *Proper Confidence*, 73-74.
[25] Newbigin, *Proper Confidence*, 27.
[26] Newbigin, *Proper Confidence*, 27; see also 36, 105; and Newbigin, *Truth and Authority*, 9.
[27] Newbigin, "Religious Pluralism and the Uniqueness of Jesus," 52.
[28] Newbigin, 'Religious Pluralism', 227-28 (227).
[29] Peter Berger, *Heretical Imperative: Contemporary Possibilities of Religious Affirmation* (London: Collins, 1980).
[30] Lesslie Newbigin, 'Can the West be Converted?' *International Bulletin of Missionary Research* 11, no. 1 (1987) 2-7; Newbigin, *The Gospel in a Pluralist Society*, 39-40, 53.

uniformity, in contemporary[31] Western culture there is no 'plausibility structure', acceptance of which is taken for granted without argument, and dissent from which is considered heresy. Plausibility structure simply means both ideas and practices in a given culture help determine whether a belief is plausible or not. To doubt these given beliefs and believe differently makes a heresy. Understandably, the number of those in pre-Modern society, who wanted to be labeled as heretics, was small, whereas in the contemporary culture formulating one's own views – apart from given plausibility structures or even in defiance of them – has become an imperative. Consequently, all are heretics! The corollary thesis of Berger is that, in this situation, Christian affirmations can be negotiated in three different ways: either in terms of choosing one's belief from a pool of many views, or making a distinction between beliefs that are still viable and ones that are not in light of current knowledge, or finally, building one's beliefs on a universal religious experience (as in Schleiermacher's vision), which precedes any rational affirmation.[32] Berger himself opts for the last one.

While Newbigin appreciates Berger's analysis and affirms its basic idea concerning the radically widening array of choices in late Modern culture,[33] he also critiques it for a lack of nuance. First, Newbigin complains that the pluralism of Berger's scheme is selective and it does not include all areas of culture:

> The principle of pluralism is not universally accepted in our culture. It is one of the key features of our culture … that we make a sharp distinction between … 'values' and … 'facts.' In the former world we are pluralists; values are a matter of personal choice. In the latter we are not; facts are facts, whether you like them or not.… About 'beliefs' we agree to differ. Pluralism reigns. About what are called 'facts' everyone is expected to agree.[34]

This takes us to another main dilemma of late Modern culture of the West, which – ironically – is also the malaise of the whole culture of the Enlightenment, as repeatedly lamented by Newbigin.[35] This irony could not be more pointed, and I think highlighting its significance takes us to the heart of the highly dynamic and tension-filled nature of postmodernism in the bishop's thinking. Briefly put: the fatal distinction between values and

---

[31] Berger uses the term "modern" when speaking of contemporary Western culture. I have changed it to "contemporary" to avoid confusion: obviously, what Berger is describing is the culture of postmodernity which encourages each individual to have his or her own beliefs.

[32] Berger has named these three options deductive (Karl Barth as an example), reductive (Bultmann's demythologization program as a paradigm), and inductive (Schleiermacher, as mentioned, as the showcase).

[33] See Lesslie Newbigin, *Foolishness to the Greeks: The Gospel and Western Culture* (Grand Rapids, Mich.: Eerdmans, 1986), 13.

[34] Newbigin, *The Gospel in a Pluralist Society*, 14-15.

[35] ch. 2, "Roots of Pluralism," in Newbigin, *The Gospel in a Pluralist Society*.

facts – as Newbigin believes – is not only the undergirding weakness of the culture of Modernity; this very same obscurity characterizes also late Modern culture. Consequently, the culture of Modernity would not be cured by the transition to postmodernism (any more than postmodern culture with the shift to the Modernity). Both are plagued by the distinction, which makes any talk about the gospel as public truth meaningless!

The second complaint against Berger's analysis of contemporary culture is Newbigin's incisive observation that, while 'the traditional plausibility structures are dissolved by contact with this modern world-view, and while ... the prevalence and power of this world-view gives no ground for believing it to be true, he [Berger] does not seem to allow for the fact that it is itself a plausibility structure and functions as such.'[36] In other words, the pluralist postmodern culture has not done away with plausibility structures, but, instead, has replaced the traditional for another one, namely, the presupposition that individual choices only apply to certain aspects of reality: values but not to facts. This is a selective heretical imperative. The person, who sets himself or herself against this plausibility structure – in other words, attempts to be a heretic in relation to established 'facts' – is called just that, the *heretic*. Here Newbigin sides with Alasdair MacIntyre, who argued that '"facts" is in modern culture a folk-concept with an aristocratic ancestry', 'aristocratic' referring to the Enlightenment philosopher Bacon's admonition to seek for 'facts' instead of 'speculations.'[37] In one word, for Newbigin Modernity and postmodernism do not represent two different species but rather both represent the Enlightenment project.[38]

The effects on lifestyle of the transition to late modernity

So far we have been looking at Newbigin's analysis of the intellectual climate in the culture, which is in transition from Modernity to Late Modernity. With regard to lifestyle and cultural ethos, the transition to late Modernity is causing 'nihilism and hopelessness.'[39] Along with the loss of confidence in truth, postmodern society has also lost hope and the optimism of progress, so typical of Modernity.[40] This loss of confidence, not only in

---

[36] Newbigin, *Foolishness to the Greeks*, 13-14.

[37] Alasdair MacIntyre, *After Virtue: A Study in Moral Theory* (London: Duckworth, 1981), 79. For references to this phrase, see Newbigin, *Foolishness to the Greeks*, 76-77; Newbigin, *Proper Confidence*, 55.

[38] Keskitalo, *Kristillinen usko*, 230.

[39] Newbigin, *Proper Confidence*, 47 (again, in reference to Yu's phrase, cited above).

[40] Lesslie Newbigin, *The Other Side of 1986: Questions to the Churches* (Geneva: WCC Publications, 1984), 1-2, 6; Newbigin, *The Gospel in a Pluralist Society*, 112; Newbigin, *Proper Confidence*, 46-47.

reason but also in the future, can be discerned both in the lives of individuals and the society as a whole:

> In the closing decades of this century it is difficult to find Europeans who have any belief in a significant future which is worth working for and investing in. A society which believes in a worthwhile future saves in the present so as to invest in the future. Contemporary Western society spends in the present and piles up debts for the future, ravages the environment, and leaves its grandchildren to cope with the results as best they can.[41]

Newbigin painfully found that out, as he was returning to his homeland after a considerable period of missionary work in Asia. When asked what might have been the greatest difficulty in his homecoming, his response was the 'disappearance of hope'[42] and the increase of 'pessimism.'[43] All this, in turn, has led particularly the young generation to the culture of 'instant gratification.' Whereas in the past people invested in the future, contemporary people in the West just live for today and do not see it meaningful to think of the future.[44]

While this kind of perception can be – and has been – critiqued[45] as a function of reverse culture shock, there is no denying the fact that these negative effects of postmodernity play a significant role in Newbigin's cultural analysis. The main point ,I want to make here, is that in Newbigin's cultural analysis, there is a direct link between the transition away from Modernity with its loss of confidence in reason and the lifestyle of people living under those transitional forces. The implications for the church's mission are, of course, obvious: Should the church attempt a proper response, which would entail both epistemological and lifestyle-driving reorientation of thinking and practices?

Missional Response to the Culture in Transition between Modernity and Late Modernity

Having looked at Newbigin's diagnosis of postmodernism, through the lens of the effects of the transition away from Modernity, the second part of this essay attempts to discern the main responses of the bishop. To repeat

[41] Newbigin, *The Gospel in a Pluralist Society*, 90-91.

[42] Newbigin, *The Other Side of 1986*, 1.

[43] Lesslie Newbigin, 'The Secular Myth', in *Faith and Power: Christianity and Islam in 'Secular' Britain*, eds. Lesslie Newbigin, Lamin Sanneh, and Jenny Taylor (London: SPCK, 1998), 13.

[44] Newbigin, *The Gospel in a Pluralist Society*, 90-91; see also 111-12.

[45] Werner Ustorf, *Christianized Africa – De-Christianized Europe? Missionary Inquiries into the Polycentric Epoch of Christian History: Perspektiven der Weltmimssion,* Wissenschaftliche Beiträge Band 14. Herausgegeben von der Missionsakademie an der Universität Hamburg (Ammersbek bei Hamburg: Lottbeck Jensen, 1992), 108-10; for Newbigin's response, see 'The Secular Myth', 6, 13.

myself: rather than focusing on themes related to postmodernism, I will continue gleaning widely from Newbigin's writings, in order to show that his response to late Modernity can only be reconstructed from his response to Modernity.

In order to bring to light the dynamic nature of Newbigin's thinking, I wish to reconstruct his response to late Modernity along the lines of several polarities. Clearly, the bishop envisioned the mission of the church in this transitional period being faced with a number of dynamic tensions. While the notion of a safe middle ground hardly does justice to his radical programme, in many ways, I hear him calling the church to locate herself at the midpoint of various polarities, such as the following ones:

- Calling the church to be "relevant," while declining from explaining the gospel in terms of late Modernism
- Adopting fallibilistic epistemology, while resisting the nihilism of postmodernism
- Standing on a particular tradition, while rejecting subjectivism
- Holding on to the gospel as public truth, while critiquing the "timeless statements" of Modernity
- Affirming "Committed Pluralism," while Condemning "Agnostic Pluralism"
- Trusting the power of persuasion ,while abandoning any notion of the will to power

Calling the church to be 'relevant' while declining from explaining the gospel in terms of late modernism

For the church to fulfil her mission in any culture, Newbigin argues, she has to be relevant, on the one hand, and to confront the culture, on the other hand.[46] One of the recurring complaints of the bishop against the church of Modern Western culture is her unapologetic and uncritical desire to be only relevant. This is the crux of the mistaken contextualization strategy of the church vis-à-vis Modernity: the church has completely accommodated herself to the culture of Modernity. At the heart of this mistaken strategy is the apologetic defence of the rationality of Christianity to the Enlightenment mind. The only way that this strategy of 'tactical retreat' may wish to defend the "reasonable" nature of Christian faith is to stick with the standards of rationality of Modernity.[47] But those standards are, of course, not in keeping with the 'Christian worldview.' Among other deviations from the Christian view, those standards operate with the fatal split between values and facts, as explained above.

---

[46] See Newbigin, *The Other Side of 1986*, 55.

[47] Newbigin, *The Gospel in a Pluralist Society*, 3; Newbigin, *Proper Confidence*, 139-166, 193.

The reason the church of Modernity attempts to accommodate herself to the strictures of the Enlightenment is the need to be 'relevant.' The church, that is being pushed into the margins of the society, to cater for 'values' while science, politics, and the rest of the public arena takes care of facts, feels she needs to be acknowledged. Consequently, the church purports to influence choices in the private area alone and shies away from any attempt to present the gospel as any kind of 'universal truth.'[48] In Modern theology, this move away from the idea of the gospel as public truth to catering for personal values was aided and guided by Liberal Theology, under the tutelage of Friedrich Schleiermacher and others, which finally led to the 'anthropologization' of theology.[49] When the statements of theology are non-cognitive descriptions of religious 'feelings,' rather than 'personal knowledge' with 'universal intention' – to use Newbigin's key phrases borrowed from Polanyi – an attitude of 'timidity' follows.[50]

Now, someone may ask why I am rehearsing this familiar Newbigin critique, the target of which is Modernity rather than postmodernism, the topic under discussion. The reason is what I argued above, namely, that because, in Newbigin's diagnosis, postmodernism is but an offshoot from Modernity, the church's response to postmodernism can only be reconstructed from the initial reaction to Modernity.

Similar to the culture of Modernity, I argue on behalf of Newbigin, the culture of postmodernity is willing to tolerate the church, as long as she 'behaves' according to the rules. As shown above, with all their differences, both cultures operate with the same distinction between values and facts. The differences is this: while the culture of Modernity really believed that there are facts – and thus indubitable certainty – to be distinguished from personal, non-cognitive values, postmodernism regards both 'facts' and 'values' as personal opinions.

The end result, with regard to the church's mission, however, is the same: In this transitional period of time the church is tolerated only if she suffices to be 'relevant' under the rules now of late Modernity with its idea of 'regimes of truths', none of which is better or worse off and none of which has any right whatsoever to consider other 'truths' as less valuable or less 'true.' For the church now to succumb to the temptation of being silent about the gospel as public truth would, in Newbigin's opinion, just repeat the same old mistake of the church of Modernity.

As an alternative – again following Newbigin's programme for the church that wants to recover from the Babylonian Captivity of Modernity – there has to be a new initiative to question the basic beliefs of postmodern

[48] Newbigin, *Foolishness to the Greeks*, 19; Newbigin, *The Gospel in a Pluralist Society*, 2.

[49] Newbigin, *Foolishness to the Greeks*, 40-41, 45.

[50] Newbigin, *Truth and Authority*, 81.

culture.[51] This means a shift from explaining the gospel in terms of the postmodern worldview with its denial of any kind of 'universal truth,' to explaining the postmodern worldview in terms of the gospel.[52] This bold initiative means nothing less than confronting the 'revolution of expectations' in the postmodern world.[53] Similar to the call to the church facing the forces of Modernity, the bishop would call the church of this transitional period to the 'conversion of the mind,' not only of the 'soul.' The reason is simply that there is a radical discontinuity between the gospel and the beliefs of both Modernity and late Modernity.[54]

Interestingly enough, Newbigin compares his own view of the Bible and revelation to that of the Liberation theologies. The basic purpose of Liberationists is not to explain the text but rather to understand the world in light of the Bible. Liberationists resist the idea of the Bible student being a neutral, non-committed outsider.[55] Newbigin's theological hero, St. Augustine, is also commended in this regard. Augustine was the first 'post-critical' theologian and philosopher, who subjected the prevailing culture, Greek rationalism, which was falling apart, to biblical critique. Rather than living in nostalgia, the Christian church should learn from Augustine a bold and unabashed approach to culture, by taking the biblical message as an alternative worldview.[56]

Only this kind of bold initiative would help the church balance the dual need to be relevant and to be faithful. How that may happen is the focus of the continuing discussion here.

Adopting fallibilistic epistemology while resisting the nihilism of postmodernism

A tempting way for the church to question late Modernity's lack of confidence in knowledge would be simply to adopt an opposite standpoint of affirming the Modernist program meof indubitable certainty. This is not the way the bishop wants the church to perceive her role, in this transitional period. Rather, in a surprising move, he seems to be echoing some of the key concerns of postmodern epistemology by affirming a fallibilistic epistemology. Indeed, says the bishop: 'We have to abandon the idea that there is available to us or any other human beings the sort of certitude that Descartes wanted to provide and that the scientific part of our culture has

---

[51] cf. Newbigin, *The Other Side of 1986*, 55 (which of course speaks of an initiative in relation to the culture of Modernity).

[52]cf. Newbigin, *Foolishness to the Greeks*, 22; Newbigin, *The Gospel in a Pluralist Society*, 222 (which, again, speaks of the Church in relation to Modernity).

[53] cf. Newbigin, *The Other Side of 1986*, 55.

[54] cf. Newbigin, *The Gospel in a Pluralist Society*, 9-10.

[55] Newbigin, The Gospel in a Pluralist Society, 97-99; Newbigin, A Word in Season, 111.

[56] Newbigin, *The Other Side of 1986*, 24.

sometimes claimed to offer.'[57] Here there is a link with postmodern orientations, and the bishop is happy to acknowledge it:

> We accept the postmodernist position that all human reasoning is socially, culturally, historically embodied. We have left behind the illusion that there is available some kind of neutral stand-point from which one can judge the different stories and decide which is true. The 'Age of Reason' supposed that there is available to human beings a kind of indubitable knowledge, capable of being grasped by all human beings which was more reliable than any alleged revelation, and which could therefore provide the criteria by which any alleged divine revelation could be assessed. This immensely powerful hang-over from the "modernist" position still haunts many discussions of religious pluralism.... But in a postmodernist context all this is swept away.[58]

Part of the situatedness of knowledge is to acknowledge – in the British bishop's case – its Euro-centric nature: 'My proposal will, I know, be criticised as Euro-centric, but this must be rejected. We cannot disown our responsibility as Europeans within the whole evangelical fellowship. It is simply a fact that it is ideas and practices developed in Europe over the past three centuries which now dominate the world, for good and for ill.'[59] That said, the bishop, of course, also calls himself and other Europeans to take another look at how that legacy has been passed on with regard to other cultures; the acknowledgment of the situatedness of knowledge and preaching the gospel does not save Europeans from helping their 'brothers and sisters in the 'Third World' [in] the task of recovering the gospel in its integrity from its false entanglement with European culture, and so seek together to find the true path of inculturation.'[60]

Because of the socially and locationally conditioned nature of human knowledge, Newbigin condemns any form of fundamentalism, a mistaken approach to revelation and the Bible, in its search for an indubitable certainty by appealing to 'evidence' to prove the Bible.[61]

---

[57] Newbigin, *The Gospel in a Pluralist Society*, 35.

[58] Newbigin, "Religious Pluralism," 233.

[59] Lesslie Newbigin, "Gospel and Culture," audio recording of an address given to a conference organized by Danish Missions Council and the Danish Churches Ecumenical Council in Denmark on 3 November 1995 (www.newbigin.net), 8.

[60] Newbigin, "Gospel and Culture."

[61] Newbigin finds many faults in the Fundamentalistic Bible interpretation: (1) "It is difficult to maintain without a kind of split personality if one is going to live an active life in the modern world." (2) "Those who hold this position are themselves part of the modern world; consequently, when they say that the Bible is factually accurate, they are working with a whole context of meaning, within a concept of factuality that is foreign to the Bible." (3) In the final analysis, to "prove" the Bible, Fundamentalists must appeal to experience, the experience of the Church concerning the Bible; if so, then Fundamentalists have succumbed to the same trap as Liberalism, their archenemy. Newbigin, *Foolishness to the Greeks*, 46; see also Newbigin, *The Gospel in a Pluralist Society*, 42-43, 49; Newbigin, *Proper Confidence*, 85-86.

If the Scylla of Modernity is the illusion of indubitable certainty, the Charybdis of postmodernism is the lack of confidence in anything certain. As implied above, the way from the search of indubitable certainty to virtual epistemological nihilism goes via the way of doubt. The built-in self-contradiction of the Cartesian programme is the necessity of doubt as the way to certainty. This 'hermeneutics of suspicion', when taken to its logical end, of course, leads to the doubting of everything, in other words, the dismantling of all certainty. At the end of this road, as explained above, there is the Nietzschean nihilism. This would close all doors to affirming the gospel as public truth.

Differently from both Modernity and postmodernism, the bishop – in keeping with Augustine's dictum *credo ut intelligem* – considers belief as the beginning of knowledge. Both Descartes and Nietzsche would disagree. Belief as the beginning of knowledge does not mean leaving behind critique and doubt. Rather, it means that doubt and critique are put in perspective.[62] Even doubt entails some assumptions, the doubter begins with something else, a 'tradition', an idea Newbigin borrows from Alasdair MacIntyre.[63] 'But the questioning, if it is to be rational, has to rely on other fundamental assumptions, which can in turn be questioned'[64] Briefly put: certainty unrelated to faith is simply an impossible and unwarranted goal.[65] Newbigin makes the delightful remark that both faith and doubt can be either honest or blind; it is not always the case that faith is blind while doubt is honest. One can also envision honest faith and blind doubt.[66]

While the Christian tradition represents confidence and 'fullness of truth' promised by Jesus, the Christian concept of truth is not an 'illusion' that 'imagine[s] that there can be available to us a kind of certainty that does not involve … personal commitment', for the simple reason that the 'supreme reality is a personal God.' Thus, those, who 'claim infallible certainty about God in their own right, on the strength of their rational powers,' are mistaken. Bishop Newbigin reminds us that, in interpersonal relationships, we would never claim that![67]

As an alternative and cure for both the Modernist illusion of indubitable certainty and the postmodern lapse into nihilism, the bishop presents his own view of human knowledge as 'personal knowledge.' It is borrowed from Polanyi, who negotiated between Cartesian certainty and pure subjectivism. 'Personal knowledge:'

> is neither subjective nor objective. In so far as the personal submits to requirements acknowledged by itself as independent of itself, it is not subjective; but in so far as it is an action guided by individual passion, it is

[62] Newbigin, *The Gospel in a Pluralist Society*, 19.
[63] Newbigin, *The Gospel in a Pluralist Society*, 82.
[64] Newbigin, *Proper Confidence*, 50.
[65] Newbigin, *The Gospel in a Pluralist Society*, 28; see also 4-5.
[66]Newbigin, *Proper Confidence*, 24; Newbigin, *Truth and Authority*, 7.
[67] Newbigin, *Proper Confidence*, 67.

not objective either. It transcends the disjunction between subjective and objective.[68]

Polanyi's concept of personal knowledge serves the bishop well in that it fits in with his view of reality as personal, as mentioned above. The 'object' of Christian knowledge is not a 'thing,' but rather 'who', a person, the incarnated Lord.[69] Being 'personal' means that this kind of knowledge entails a risk, it is 'risky business.'[70] It is 'subjective in that it is I who know, or seek to know, and that the enterprise of knowing is one which requires my personal commitment.... And it is subjective in that, in the end, I have to take personal responsibility for my beliefs.'[71] Yet, this kind of knowledge is not subjectivistic because, again borrowing from Polanyi, it has a 'universal intention.' It is meant to be shared, critiqued, tested, and perhaps even corrected. It engages and does not remain only my own insight. It is not only 'true for me.'[72] Thus, to repeat what was mentioned above: doubt and critique should not be abandoned, rather they should be put in perspective, by seeing them as secondary to faith.[73] Only this kind of epistemology might offer the church, that lives under the under the forces of Modernity and postmodernism, an opportunity to attain *Proper Confidence*.

Standing on a particular tradition while rejecting subjectivism

While half of contemporary Western culture still lives under the illusion of the possibility of indubitable certainty, the other half, the late Modern one, 'has lapsed into subjectivism,' which is the 'tragic legacy of Descartes' proposal' and, even more ironically, the half into which theology usually falls.[74] Modernity, on the one hand, denies the whole concept of tradition in its alleged 'neutral' standpoint. The Cartesian method mistakenly believes itself to be tradition-free. Postmodernism enthusiastically affirms traditions, 'regimes of truth', happily existing side-by-side. No one tradition is better or worse, and no one tradition has the right to impose its own rationality upon the others.[75] The implications for the church's mission are obvious. For the Modern hearer of the gospel, any appeal to a particular tradition is an anathema and a step away from the alleged neutral, tradition-free search

---

[68] Michael Polanyi, *Personal Knowledge: Towards a Post-Critical Philosophy* (Chicago: University of Chicago Press, 1958), 300; see Newbigin, *The Gospel in a Pluralist Society*, 51-52, 54-55.
[69] Newbigin, *Proper Confidence*, 67.
[70] Newbigin, *The Gospel in a Pluralist Society*, 35.
[71] Newbigin, *The Gospel in a Pluralist Society*, 23.
[72] Newbigin, *The Gospel in a Pluralist Society*, 33.
[73] Newbigin, *Proper Confidence*, 48, 105; Newbigin, *The Other Side of 1986*, 20; Newbigin, *The Gospel in a Pluralist Society*, 20.
[74] Newbigin, *The Gospel in a Pluralist Society*, 35.
[75] See Newbigin, *A Word in Season*, 187.

for certainty. For the postmodern hearer, the gospel is *a* good-news but not *the* good news.

The way out of this dilemma for the bishop is to take a lesson from both Polanyi and the ethicist-philosopher Alasdair MacIntyre[76] and speak robustly of the need to stand on a particular tradition. The necessity of acknowledging the tradition-laden nature of all human knowledge is based on the shared postmodern conviction, nurtured by contemporary sociology of knowledge, according to which all knowledge is socially and thus 'contextually' shaped. 'There is no rationality except a socially embodied rationality.'[77] Any knowledge is rooted in and emerges out of a particular context, location, and situation. The bishop boldly accepts that all truth is socially and historically embodied and thus aligns himself with a leading postmodern idea. Another ally here is, as mentioned, Alasdair MacIntyre:

> As Alasdair MacIntyre so brilliantly documents in his book Whose Justice, What Rationality? the idea that there can be a kind of reason that is supra-cultural and that would enable us to view all the culturally conditioned traditions of rationality from a standpoint above them all is one of the illusions of our contemporary culture. All rationality is socially embodied, developed in human tradition and using some human language. The fact that biblical thought shares this with all other forms of human thought in no way disqualifies it from providing the needed center.[78]

The 'situational' nature of human knowledge means that knowing can only happen from within tradition: This state of affairs, however, does not mean that, therefore, no one can claim to speak truth. Indeed, to 'pretend to *possess* the truth in its fullness is arrogance', whereas, the 'claim to have been given the decisive clue for the human search after truth is not arrogant; it is the exercise of our responsibility as part of the human family.'[79] This seeking after the truth happens first and foremost in the Christian community. Whereas Modernity focuses on the individual person's knowledge, Christian rationality – in this regard, aligning with the ethos of postmodernism – believes in a communally received knowledge, even when the act of knowing is personal, as explained above. 'It would contradict the whole message of the Bible itself if one were to speak of the

[76] Newbigin also refers at times to the well-known philosopher of science, Thomas Kuhn (*The Structure of Scientific Revolutions* (Chicago: University of Chicago Press, 1970)), who spoke of dramatic turning points in the development of science when new paradigms emerge and transform not only the methods and results but also the whole way of thinking scientifically; see Newbigin, *A Word in Season*, 91-92.

[77] Newbigin, *The Gospel in a Pluralist Society*, 87.

[78] Newbigin, 'Religious Pluralism and the Uniqueness of Jesus Christ', 50; so also 52; the reference is to A. MacIntyre, *Whose Justice, What Rationality?* (London: Duckworth, 1988).

[79] Newbigin, 'Religious Pluralism and the Uniqueness of Jesus Christ', 54.

book apart from the church, the community shaped by the story that the book tells.'[80]

For Newbigin, the church is a truth-seeking community that seeks to understand reality from its own vantage point. Again, learning from Polanyi, Newbigin claims that there is a certain kind of correspondence between the Christian and scientific community, as both build on 'tradition' and 'authority.' Even new investigations happen on the basis of and in critical dialogue with accumulated tradition, represented by scholars who are regarded as authoritative. For the Christian church, this tradition is the narrative, story of the gospel confessed by all Christians:

> The Christian community, the universal Church, embracing more and more fully all the cultural traditions of humankind, is called to be that community in which tradition of rational discourse is developed which leads to a true understanding of reality; because it takes as its starting point and as its permanent criterion of truth the self-revelation of God in Jesus Christ. It is necessarily a particular community, among all the human communities.... But it has a universal mission, for it is the community chosen and sent by God for this purpose. This particularity, however scandalous it may seem to a certain kind of cosmopolitan mind, is inescapable.[81]

There is always the danger of domestication of the tradition or, as in postmodernism, its reduction into *a* story among other equal stories – that, in Newbigin's mind, would lead to pluralism and a denial of the particularity of the gospel. The gospel can be protected from this kind of domestication, he believes. 'The truth is that the gospel escapes domestication, retains its proper strangeness, its power to question us, only when we are faithful to its universal, supranational, supracultural nature.'[82] By making universal truth claims, Christian faith co-exists with other traditions and their claims to truth.[83] Out of the framework of the gospel narrative, Christian tradition, the church seeks to understand reality – rather than vice versa.[84]

As mentioned before, rather than explaining the gospel through the lens of postmodern culture – or Modern culture for that matter – this missional ecclesiology seeks to explain the world through the lens of the gospel. Here, there is, of course, a link with the thinking of George Lindbeck and post-liberal thought. Dissatisfied with both the fundamentalistic 'Propositional Model' of revelation and the liberal 'Experiential Model,' Lindbeck suggests an alternative that he calls the 'Cultural Linguistic Model.' That model sees Christian claims and doctrines as 'rules' that

---

[80] Newbigin, *Proper Confidence*, 53.

[81] Newbigin, *The Gospel in a Pluralist Society*, 87-88.

[82] Lesslie Newbigin, "The Enduring Validity of Cross-Cultural Mission," *International Bulletin of Missionary Research* 12 (1988), 50.

[83] Newbigin, *The Gospel in a Pluralist Society*, 64; Newbigin, *Truth and Authority*, 52.

[84] Newbigin, *The Gospel in a Pluralist Society*, 53.

govern our way of speaking of not only faith but also the world. While sympathetic to post-liberalism's insight,[85] Newbigin's thinking also differs from Lindbeck's, in that Newbigin still considers Christian doctrines, based as they are on the dynamic narrative of the Bible, as historically factual and, thus, in some sense ,'propositional.' For Newbigin, the crux of the matter is to raise the question 'Which is the *real* story?'[86]

The insistence on the factual, not only 'linguistic' basis of Christian narrative is essential to Newbigin, as he willingly admits the 'confessional' nature of his starting point. This confessional standpoint, however, in his opinion, is no affirmation of fideism or subjectivism a.k.a. postmodernism:

> I am, of course, aware that this position will be challenged. It will be seen as arbitrary and irrational. It may be dismissed as 'fideism', or as a blind 'leap of faith'. But these charges have to be thrown back at those who make them. Every claim to show grounds for believing the gospel which lie outside the gospel itself can be shown to rest ultimately on faith-commitments which can be questioned. There is, indeed, a very proper exercise of reason in showing the coherence which is found in the whole of human experience when it is illuminated by the gospel, but this is to be distinguished from the supposition that there are grounds for ultimate confidence more reliable than those furnished in God's revelation of himself in Jesus Christ, grounds on which, therefore, one may affirm the reliability of Christian belief. The final authority for the Christian faith is the self-revelation of God in Jesus Christ.[87]

This clinging to the historical event of Jesus Christ takes us to the heart of his desire to defend the gospel as public truth.

Holding on to the gospel as public truth while critiquing the 'timeless statements' of modernity

The church and her mission, in this transitional period, finds herself faced with a two-fold challenge: on the one hand, there is the Modernist search for indubitable certainty, and on the other hand, the nihilism of postmodernism. At least, this is the way the bishop paints the picture.

In order to continue reconstructing the proper response to such a transitional era, a brief summary of our findings so far is in order. First, while the church seeks to be relevant, it has to resist the temptation to accommodate herself to the strictures of the existing culture. Second, this can be done best on the basis of committed, personal knowledge, which avoids the trap of the nihilism of postmodernism and the illusion of Modernity. It is knowledge with the aim to be shared with the rest of creation. Third, this kind of committed, 'proper confidence' can only be had from within a particular tradition. This tradition-driven knowledge is an

---

[85] See Newbigin, *The Gospel in a Pluralist Society*, 24-25; Newbigin, *A Word in Season*, 83-84.

[86] Newbigin, *A Word in Season*, 85 (emphasis mine).

[87] Newbigin, "Religious Pluralism," 236.

alternative to the alleged neutral standpoint of Modernity and the subjectivistic, non-committed 'regimes of truth'–driven view of postmodernism. Christian tradition avoids the dangers of domestication because it is a tradition shared and tested by an international community and it is based on a universally oriented 'true' story of the gospel. Now, this all leads to the affirmation of the gospel as public truth, while resisting any notion of the timeless truths of Modernity.

Where Modernity fails is that it does not acknowledge the social nature of its knowledge. Where postmodernism fails is in its one-sided focus on the socially embodied nature of human knowledge, to the point where there is no overarching story, framework, or criterion. All stories just exist side by side and everyone is free to choose.

The affirmation of the gospel as public truth is based on the 'foundation' of the unique authority of Christian tradition, based on God's self-revelation. That self-revelation happens in secular history,[88] to which Christ is the clue.[89] The peculiar nature of the Christian story, with regard to its truth-claims, is the 'Total Fact of Christ.'[90] The *factum*-nature (from Latin [*factum est*]: 'it's done') of Christian claims to truth in Christ has to do with history.[91] While the Christ-event is part of salvific history, it is also an event in universal history. Therefore, the subjectivistic interpretation of Existentialism according to which the events of salvation history, such as the resurrection, only 'happened to me,' is a totally mistaken view. The Christian gospel is a story, a narrative, but it is more than that: "Christian doctrine is a form of rational discourse.[92] Happening in secular history, its claims are subject to historical scrutiny. The historicity of the Christian story, then, is the reason why 'its starting point [is] is not any alleged self-evident truth. Its starting point is events, in which God made himself known to men and women in particular circumstances…'. In a sense, the argument is, of course, circular: the church interprets God's actions in history as God's actions, yet regards them as happening in history. But, says the bishop, the same principle applies to science, too, which is, in this sense, circular in its reasoning.[93]

---

[88] ch. 8 in Newbigin, *The Gospel in a Pluralist Society* is entitled "The Bible as Universal History." This view of course resonates with Wolfhart Pannenberg's view of revelation as history. For some reason, Newbigin does not engage this Lutheran theologian's ideas even though many of them, including the historicity of the resurrection or the importance of eschatology, are obvious common points.

[89] ch. 9 in Newbigin, *The Gospel in a Pluralist Society* is titled 'Christ, the Clue to History.'

[90] Newbigin, *The Gospel in a Pluralist Society*, 5.

[91] Newbigin, *The Open Secret: An Introduction to the Theology of Mission*, rev. ed. (Grand Rapids, Mich.: Eerdmans, 1995, orig. 1978), 50-52.

[92] Newbigin, *Truth and Authority*, 52.

[93] Newbigin, *The Gospel in a Pluralist Society*, 63.

If the historical nature of the Christian tradition is the safeguard against the charge of the Modernist self-evidence of truth, the historical and, thus, factual nature also marks it off from the postmodern view with no interest in the historical basis. Christian rationality, necessarily, has to raise the question of its 'objective' basis:

> The central question is not 'How shall I be saved?' but 'How shall I glorify God by understanding, loving, and doing God's will – here and now in this earthly life?' To answer that question I must insistently ask: 'How and where is God's purpose for the whole of creation and the human family made visible and credible?' That is the question about the truth – objective truth – which is true whether or not it coincides with my 'values.' And I know of no place in the public history of the world where the dark mystery of human life is illuminated, and the dark power of all that denies human well-being is met and measured and mastered, except in those events that have their focus in what happened 'under Pontius Pilate.'[94]

In other words, with all his insistence on the socially embodied nature of human knowledge and its tradition-driven nature, the bishop is not willing to succumb to the postmodern temptation of leaving behind the 'facts.' True, against the Modernists, Newbigin claims the risky, 'personal' nature of human knowledge but at the same time, against postmodernists, he sets forth the argument for the historical and factual nature of key Christian claims. This is no easy middle way but rather a radical middle!

Affirming 'committed pluralism' while condemning 'agnostic pluralism'

In light of the fact that, for Newbigin, 'pluralism' is a virtual synonym for late Modernity – as observed above – it is surprising that he is not willing to abandon the concept altogether. Rather, to paraphrase MacIntyre, he is raising the all-important question: Whose pluralism? Which pluralism? The bishop is against that kind of pluralistic ethos of contemporary Western society, in which no truth can be considered truth, an ideology of parallel and equal 'regimes of truth,' without any criteria or parameters. In his opinion, this kind of pluralism is based on the fatal distinction between facts and values. Whereas in the area of values no criteria exist, in the domain of facts, mutually assumed criteria can still be applied quite similarly to the ethos of Modernity. In other words: while, say, a scientist as a private person may have no right to argue for the supremacy of his personal values, as a *scientist*, however, she is supposed to stick with the rules of the game. In medicine, physics, and chemistry there is no 'Wild West' of pluralism, some claims and results are considered to be true, while others false. 'No society is totally pluralist.'[95] As mentioned above, this 'heretical imperative' is highly selective.

[94] Newbigin, 'Religious Pluralism and the Uniqueness of Jesus Christ', 54.
[95] Newbigin, *A Word in Season*, 158.

A significant contribution to the discussion comes from the bishop's distinction between two kinds of pluralism, one desired, the other rejected, namely, 'agnostic pluralism' and 'committed pluralism.' He defines agnostic – sometimes also called anarchic – pluralism in this way:

> ... [I]t is assumed that ultimate truth is unknowable and that there are therefore no criteria by which different beliefs and different patterns of behavior may be judged. In this situation one belief is as good as another and one lifestyle is as good as another. No judgments are to be made, for there are no given criteria, no truth by which error could be recognized. There is to be no discrimination between better and worse.[96]

In other words, this is the pluralism stemming from the failure of the Modernist programme in delivering its main product, indubitable certainty. The latter type of pluralism, committed pluralism, is an alternative to the former. The best way to illustrate its nature is again to refer to the way the scientific community functions. That community is 'pluralist in the sense that is it not controlled or directed from one center. Scientists are free to pursue their own investigations and to develop their own lines of research.' This type of pluralism is committed to the search of the truth, following mutually established guidelines and operating 'from within the tradition.' It takes into consideration the authority of tradition, while maintaining the freedom to pursue new ways of understanding the reality and truth.[97] In order for the church to come to such a place, she has to appreciate her tradition in a way similar to the scientific community.[98]

In a pluralist society of late Modernity, says the bishop, 'There are only stories, and the Christian story is one among them.'[99] The attitude of committed pluralism drives the church to dialogue with other traditions and modes of rationalities. If the church believes it is a witness to – if not the possessor of – the gospel as public truth, the 'Logic of Mission'[100] pushes the church out of her comfort zone to share the gospel. While the gospel truth does not arise out of the dialogue, it calls for a dialogue with a specific goal in mind, namely to present the gospel faithfully and authentically:

> ... [T]he message of Christianity is essentially a story, report of things which have happened. At its heart is the statement that 'the word was made flesh.' This is a statement of a fact of history which the original evangelists are careful to locate exactly within the continuum of recorded human history. A fact of history does not arise out dialogue; it has to be unilaterally reported by those who, as witnesses, can truly report of things which have happened. Of course there will then be dialogue about the way in which what has happened

---

[96] Newbigin, *A Word in Season*, 168.
[97] Newbigin, *A Word in Season*, 168-69.
[98] Newbigin, *A Word in Season*, 1p. 70.
[99] Newbigin, 'Religious Pluralism', 233.
[100] Newbigin, *The Gospel in a Pluralist Society*, ch. 10 is entitled 'Logic of Mission.'

> is to be understood, how it is to be related to other things which we know, or think that we know. The story itself does not arise out of dialogue; it simply has to be told.[101]

This Christian view of dialogue, thus, differs radically from the understanding of dialogue under the influence of agnostic pluralism. For that mindset, 'Dialogue is seen not as a means of coming nearer to the truth, but as a way of life in which different truth-claims no longer conflict with one another but seek friendly co-existence.' That kind of model of dialogue bluntly rejects any kind of 'instrumental' view of dialogue as a means to try to persuade. It only speaks of 'the dialogue of cultures and of dialogue as a celebration of the rich variety of human life. Religious communities are not regarded as bearers of truth-claims. There is no talk about evangelization and conversion.'[102]

Since, for the Christian church, dialogue is not an alternative to evangelization, one has to think carefully of how the attempt to persuade with the power of the gospel may best happen in late Modernity.

Trusting the power of persuasion while abandoning any notion of the will to power

In late Modernity, any hint of the old Christendom way of resorting to political power, as a means of furthering a religious cause, is a red flag. Bishop Newbigin was the first one to condemn any such attempt on the church's part: 'I have argued that a claim that the Christian faith must be affirmed as a public truth does not mean a demand for a return to "Christendom" or to some kind of theocracy. It does not mean that the coercive power of the state and its institutions should be at the service of the Church.'[103]

The suspicion of the 'will to power' in late Modernity, however, is deeper and more subtle than the fear of the church's political power. The postmodern suspicion has to do with the church's desire to confront epistemology that has lost all criteria in negotiating between true and false. Therefore, postmodernists argue, 'There is to be no discrimination between better and worse. All beliefs and lifestyles are to be equally respected. To make judgments is, on this view, *an exercise of power* and is therefore oppressive and demeaning to human dignity. The "normal" replaces the "normative."'[104] It is here, where the church, rather than succumbing to the

---

[101] Newbigin, 'Religious Pluralism', 233.

[102] Newbigin, 'Religious Pluralism', 240.

[103] Newbigin, *A Word in Season*, 170. Newbigin notes in another context how ironic it is that the introduction by the West of ideas, science, technology, and such products of "development" were for the most part not considered as the 'will to powe'" in the Third World. Rather, they were welcomed and embraced. Newbigin, *A Word in Season*, 122-23.

[104] Newbigin, *A Word in Season*, 168.

mindset of agnostic pluralism, should confront the people of late Modernity with the offer of the gospel as public truth. While there is no way for the church, if faithful to her mission, to avoid this confrontation, the church should also do everything in her power to cast off any sign of the will to power.

In Newbigin's vision, the church is a Pilgrim People, on the way, and thus, does not claim the fullness of truth on this side of the *eschaton*, it only testifies to it and seeks to understand it more appropriately.[105] Even the Christian witness waits for the final eschatological verification of the truth of the gospel.[106] Such a witness does not resort to any earthly power rather he or she only trusts the power of the persuasion of the truth.

Consequently, time after time, the bishop recommends to the church an attitude of humility and respect for others. While they are witnesses, Christians are also 'learners.'[107] The church does not possess the truth, but rather testifies to it, carries it on as a truth-seeking community and tradition.[108]

The refusal of the 'will to power' goes even deeper than that of the cultivation of a humble and respectful attitude towards others. It grows from the centre of the gospel truth as it is based on the cross of the Saviour:

> What is unique in the Christian story is that the cross and resurrection of Jesus are at its heart. Taken together (as they must always be) they are the public affirmation of the fact that God rules, but that his rule is (in this age) hidden; that the ultimate union of truth with power lies beyond history, but can yet be declared and portrayed within history. The fact that the crucifixion of the Incarnate Lord stands at the centre of the Christian story ought to have made it forever impossible that the Christian story should have been made into a validation of imperial power. Any exposition of a missionary approach to religious pluralism must include the penitent acknowledgement that the Church has been guilty of contradicting its own gospel by using it as an instrument of imperial power.[109]

In other words, any attempt to usurp power means nothing less than a perversion of the message of the gospel.

In Lieu of Conclusion: Seedthought for Further Reflections

It seems to me, that it is in keeping with Lesslie Newbigin's evolving and dynamic way of thinking, that no 'closing chapter' will be offered to the

[105] Newbigin at times calls the witnesses 'seekers of the truth' and commends the apophatic tradition of Christian theology for its acknowledgment that 'no human image or concept can grasp the reality of God.' Newbigin, *The Gospel in a Pluralist Society*, 12.

[106] Newbigin, *The Gospel in a Pluralist Society*, 53-54.

[107] Newbigin, *The Gospel in a Pluralist Society*, 34-35.

[108] Newbigin, *The Gospel in a Pluralist Society*, 12.

[109] Newbigin, 'Religious Pluralism', 234.

reflections on the mission and life of the church in the transitional era between Modernity and postmodernism. More helpful, I think, is to reflect on some tasks and questions for the future and map out some remaining areas of interest.

Let me first return to my methodological musings at the beginning of the essay. Again, in this context, I am not concerned about methodology primarily for the sake of academic competence; rather, my interest in it has everything to do with the material presentation of Newbigin's missional ecclesiology and epistemology. I argued that, rather than tabulating references to postmodernism in the bishop's writings, and even looking primarily at those passages, which may have a more or less direct reference to postmodernism, a more helpful way of proceeding would be to take lessons from his response to Modernity, particularly with regard to the transitional period, when the church lives under two modes of rationalities. This kind of methodology seemed to be viable in light of Newbigin's conviction that postmodernism is parasitic on Modernity. If my methodology is appropriate and does justice to Newbigin's own approach, then it means that his writings on missional ecclesiology and cultural critique continue to have their relevance, even if the shift to postmodernism will intensify in the future.[110]

If my hunch is correct, then a main task for the church of the West, at this period of time, would be to pay attention to the nature of the transition. I do not believe that we live in a culture, in which Modernity has given way to postmodernism. Rather, I regard Newbigin's insight that what makes the end of the twentieth and the beginning of the twenty-first century unique culturally is the process of transition. Modernity is alive and well, not only in the West but also in the Global South. At the same time, as a result of the massive critique of and disappointment with it, there is an intensifying desire to cast off the reins of Modernity. However, that distancing from the Enlightenment heritage does not mean leaving behind its influence, rather, it is a continual re-assessment of Modernity, as we continue living under its massive influence. To repeat myself: it is the transition that makes our time unique. To that dynamic, Bishop Newbigin's thinking speaks loud and clear.

I have mentioned, in my discussion, several movements of thought and thinkers to which Newbigin either gives a direct reference, such as Lindbeck and post-liberalism or Reformed Epistemology or, say, Stanley Hauerwas with whom he clearly has some affinity. It would be a worthwhile exercise to reflect on similarities and differences between the Reformed Epistemology of Alvin Plantinga and others, who maintain that

---

[110] My own growing conviction is that, similarly to Modernity, postmodernism has such built-in contradistinctions in its texture that it may not survive for a long time. Its contribution in my opinion has been mainly deconstructive: it has helped the culture of the West to wake up from the Modernist slumber. What becomes "post" this, I am not yet sure about.

Christian faith should unabashedly adopt God as the 'foundation,' rather than trying to look somewhere else.[111] Similarly the Hauerwasian connection, with its idea of the church as a unique 'colony' and thus unique way of understanding reality, would make a helpful contribution to our thinking of missional ecclesiology. When it comes to Postliberalism, it seems to me that Newbigin's sympathies – even with some critical notes – might have been a bit misplaced. I have a hard time envisioning a *post-Liberal* advocate of the gospel as public truth!

I am not mentioning these tasks for further study primarily to advance academic inquiry, but rather in my desire to better understand the scope and location of Newbigin's missional ecclesiology, in the larger matrix of contemporary thinking. Is it the case that Newbigin's missional ecclesiology and epistemology represents a movement *sui generis,* or is it rather that – like any creative and constructive thinker – he has listened carefully to a number of contemporary voices and echoes their motifs in a fresh way?

[111] Keskitalo (*Kristillinen usko*, 167-72) offers an insightful excursus on the topic; unfortunately, it is not accessible to English readers.

A Witness from Workers in a Particularly Difficult Situation of Challenge – Youth and Social Communication: How is the Gospel Preached and Spread, the Liturgy Celebrated, the Creed Confessed Today?

Marco Fibbi

Faith in a Post-Christianity World

In the globalized Western world today, civil institutions, economic realities and education systems consider that the more distant (and uninterested) they are from any religious and confessional institution, the more advanced they are; see, for example, the recent debate on the proposal on the European constitution and the non-introduction in its proposed text of reference to the Judaic-Christian roots of Europe. In the social structure and in the individual conscience of many countries (and for this, young people are ahead of the times and anticipate dominant trends), the religious aspect has become a private and personal issue, our own choice that no longer has support in the public dimension. That which has had a strong contribution is religious pluralism in Europe, real (or presumed) forms of conflict between civilizations and/or religious worldwide, and the 'globalization' phenomenon, that is, the universal expansion of the dominant models in economics or in lifestyle imposed by multinational companies and spread by the media, always more 'concentrated' and similar to each other.

We live a true change of *paradigms* of thoughts and of *language,* which do not allow us to face life, the world, relationships with others, faith and the great values anymore, as it was in the time of 'Christianity'. This change, which has all the features considered epochal, unavoidably involves language and lifestyles. Also the usual religious practices and forms of traditional spirituality (i.e., the Penance rite and the way to receive Holy Communion) are not perceived nor understood any longer, as they were until a few decades ago.

Faith, believed exclusively as personal choice and no longer present in the social structure, leads us to a situation of 'post-Christianity', similar to the pre-Christian context, from the dawning of the Church and of the announcement, when the Gospel preached by the apostles was accepted with scepticism, or even with explicit and violent persecution or alienation of the faithful.

In the 'Christianity' stage, which existed until the end of the first half of the last century, in most European countries, and which continued in some of them, such as Italy, Spain, Ireland and Poland until the first half of the 80's, the values and criteria inspired by the Christian faith (not properly confessional statements) were widespread and accepted even at a public and social level, and in institutions, and are present in the formulization of major charters of the Western nations (such as in the Universal Declaration of Human Rights, UN 1948, or, for example, in the Italian Constitution).

As a consequence of this epochal change, we can see, at least in Italian society, a sort of *'mimicry'* of most of the faithful, who tend to hide their own religious beliefs (considered private affairs, not relevant in the public sphere). They are baptized and traditionally faithful (from a Catholic family) but their faith does not affect private behaviour at all, and only very slightly their public conduct. In this way, the difference between Christians and the non-faithful tends to become imperceptible.

This behaviour follows a sort of formation to faith, predominant in Italy in the past century, in which Christians live their own 'creed' in a 'personal' way and not in a 'community' way, through an individual relationship with the Church and without the faithful community's 'intercession'. This is paradoxical within a Christian society, which in any case helped to direct the way of expressing this personal faith, based on the direct relationship with the priest, and the individual practice of the sacraments (Eucharist and confession, spiritual direction etc.). Since the common external reference (of the Christian society) is missing, and since we live in an individualistic and relativistic 'dogmatic' culture, this individual lifestyle of faith becomes a 'homemade' faith or built *''a la carte'*, losing any chance of acknowledging oneself in common ecclesiastic, institutional or shared forms.

Youngsters between Individualism and Relativism: The Religious Aggregation

Youngsters live in this new context emphasising their inclination to make every environment and situation extremely fluid, unstable, variable and light like the perspectives for the future; to use Zygmunt Bauman's expression, they live in the context of 'liquid times', where nothing is certain and irreversible because the dominant model is the one of television, internet and video games. Time and space have a relative meaning and they adapt themselves according to the need of the person, and no one has the right to force rules or principles. This represents a problem for every institution: state, family, school, church, etc., which tends to give to its world, action and objectives a stability which go beyond the restricted limits of the temporary and spontaneous approval of a single person. This implies the need of constraints, ties to the community, emphasised and recognizable, as in most of the forms of young aggregation, even if not linked to faith: like autonomous free space/youth houses, sport and music associations, etc.

For this reason, the young faithful also recognize themselves in environments extremely diversified; from small parish groups to the large associations and movements, which are strongly characterized by specific features; their aggregative worlds lead to a strong sense of belonging, distinguishable from other similar associations (praying methods, adaptation of rites, specific songs, etc.) as in the movements and new communities present in Rome and in many countries around the world: S. Egidio, Communion and Liberation, Neochatecumens, Focolari, Charismatic. They seem to be able to give to faith space and time and they may appear similar to communities from the beginning of the church, that were small and close, and able to resist persecutions to follow their own way, even in the secret catacombs. Indeed, these groups sometimes live in a 'catacomb' situation, that is, hiding and keeping it secret, also in respect to an official ecclesiastic environment, coming out only in certain events, such as related specific meetings (Rimini meeting or conferences, conventions etc.) or large official events (WYD), in which they can demonstrate all their 'muscular strength', bringing together many people and making themselves well known to the others.

Communication: The Role of Growth and the Strengthening of this Reality

So, will these huge gatherings of single associations, congregations, movements (for example, the Rimini Meeting, Conferences, Scout Route and pilgrimages, etc.) or international events (such as WYD) be the privileged occasions for evangelization, thanks to the enormous fame that they have through the mass media? The phenomenon deserves to be analyzed thoroughly, at least from the point of view of the interpersonal communication, of the faith exchange and enrichment of the young, who are present on these occasions, and who attend these events with many different motivations and experience of faith. But what could be the contribution of media communication as evangelization? Particularly, can television take the role of diffusion, expansion, growth or distortion of reality, to cause a persuasion or even a conversion? Mass media (press, television or internet) have a 'positive' role since they confirm and reinforce the existing beliefs, but I do not believe they are able to cause a real change in people as that requires a witness and adirect interpersonal relationship. Media are, more than anything, 'mirrors' of the existing reality, sometimes with a slightly distorted result, because they basically propose what people look for or want to hear and, for commercial needs, they must simplify, as much as possible, the language, so to make the message understandable and acceptable for as many persons as possible.

Therefore, the result is rather one of a flattening and levelling of the religious message as well, to make it similar to any other form of young crowd event: the rock concert, the sports event etc. The Pope's meetings with the young (in Germany, as well as in Rome for the Jubilee) became the 'Woodstock' of faith, due to the appeal for the unique personality of John Paul II.Today's young mass events have lost their central content of faith and witness, while keeping only the commercial and fashionable aspects. The mass media are, in my opinion, inadequate to represent, in an effective and realistic way, the depth of the faith of the young..

The Announcement of Faith in this Context: The Role of the Family

It seems useful, therefore, to maintain the classical way to announce faith, through catechism and through a direct relationship, a witness of personal faith within the community of the faithful. The sacramental catechesis appears to be largely spread in parishes: still over 90 % of new-borns are baptized; 70-80 % receive First Communion, and 60 % Confirmation, while there is a real drop in teenagers, where the percentages of presence fall down to 10-20 %, and stay about the same for young university students, even with a substantial turnover. Communities are made, therefore, of a high number of elderly, together with educational activities for children and a smaller number of adults, who show a disaffection towards faith and religion. How can parents be involved at least in the Christian education of their children? An idea is to propose, parallel to the sacramental Catechism for children, a similar course for the parents. When requesting baptism for the children, whether they are a religious married couple or simply living together, they are invited to one or more meetings which, in case of the First Communion preparation, become a true parallel course to announce faith, aiming to create a relationship between families and the parish community. The proposal is of an *'educational agreement'*, which would go beyond the simple religious aspect, so that children-youngsters can grow in an environment, where values and common criteria among families and the religious communities represent a reliable confrontation for the social, cultural, scholastic and media realities. The goal is to rebuild the texture of a Christian community, in which all its components are present, adults, parents, teachers, grandparents, children, ministers of worship and lay people of the different pastoral ministers, all in an organic and complete structure, as a real model for faithful life. Young people will be able to draw their inspiration from this for a Christian lifestyle feasible for today:

> It is necessary therefore – and it is a duty for Christian families, priests, catechists, educators, youngsters themselves with their peers, for our parishes, associations, movements, finally for the entire diocesan community – that new generations could use the Church as a group of truly reliable friends, close to life in its phases, whether nice and happy or harsh and hard, a

community that will never abandon us, not even in death, because it brings in itself the promise of eternity.[1]

A community, which is adult and mature in faith, will be the result, not only of a better organization of the pastoral structure, but also receiving the gifts of Grace and the Holy Spirit for the faithful.

A Concrete Proposal for the Faith of the Young: The Experience of Voluntary Service

I cannot deny that the biggest challenge is still how to have youngsters' faith follow them through their adulthood, that is, how to reinforce and confirm it after the age of the sacramental education. What practical experiences can be given to youngsters as a reliable sign of today's Christian life's practicability and attractiveness? The 'communication' of faith, the announcement, does not come from the primary proposal of an abstract content, but from a *lifestyle* that originated from the choice to follow Christ and the choice to take His word as a promise and for self-realization. Witness will be, therefore, the primary way for a coherent and effective communication of faith, in order to produce in youngsters what we believe in and that to which we dedicate our lives.

Therefore, if the essence of the faith experience is a personal relationship, the relationship lived between Lord Jesus and its disciple, it is necessary to create an environment in favour of the birth and the growth of faith, in those exposed to continuous incentives and very frequent changes. Generating faith means making it possible for the person to have a real experience of relationship with Jesus in a direct personal and real way, through a situation of contact with the true need for salvation/redemption. For this reason, I believe that the announcement of faith to young people should suggest the experience of voluntary service given to others, using God's love for oneself and for brothers and sisters in contact with poverty, discomfort, illness, and in all the different ways in which the Church is present. The missionary experience, the witness in places where there are pain and disabilities (handicaps), can be an exercise for those, who are already solid and strong in faith and for those, who are looking for their

---

[1] *"E indispensabile quindi – ed e il cmpito affidato alle famiglie cristiane, ai sacerdoti, ai caxtechisti, agli educatori, ai giovani stessi nei confromnti dei loro coetanei, alle nostre parrocchie, associazoni e movimenti, finalmente all'intera communita diocesana – che le nuove generazioni possano farfe esperienza delle Chiesa come di una compagnia di antici davvero affidabile, vicina in tutti i momenti e le circostanze della vita, siano esse liete e gratificanti oppure ardue e oscure, una compagnia che non ci abbandonera mai nemmeno nella morte, perche porrta in se la promessa dell'eternita".* Benedict XVI, speech at the annual Rome's diocesan meeting, June 5th, 2006. Unofficial translation.

first personal experience with God, the Word and brothers and sisters of the community:.

> Youngsters can gain from the voluntary service experience, because, if well done, it can become for them a "school of life" that will help them give to their lives a higher and more valuable sense.[2]

Therefore, from the beginning, the faith experience is a witness in itself, of God's passion for each man-woman in every life context.

Finally, I think that in this journey of testimony, youngsters should be given chance to belong to a reality that is verifiable and shared within the Church in an exercise in faith, marked by experiences and steps, which explain their personal choice explicitly and confirm their motivations. If it were possible to recall an image of the first centuries of the Church's life, I would refer to a catechumenal itinerary, made of steps and rituals with the scope of confirming their introduction and reception of faith. In our 'post-Christian' or 'neo-pagan' time, it could be useful to introduce a series of experiences witnessing, in person and as a Christian community, the presence of God's love in the world.

---

[2] *"I giovani possono trarre beneficio dall'esperienza del volontariato, perche, se bene impostato, esso diventa per loro una 'scuola di vita', che li aiuta a dare alla propria esistenza un senso e un valore piu alto e fecondo"*. Benedict XVI, audience for Catholic rescue Volunteers, February 10th, 2007. Unofficial translation.

MISSION IN A POSTMODERN WORLD

The Gospel of Hope in a Postmodern Setting

David Kettle

> May God, who is the ground of hope, fill you with all joy and peace as you lead the life of faith until, by the power of the Holy Spirit, you overflow with hope. (Romans 15.13)

Hope – radical hope – is the gift of God to humankind in Jesus Christ. We are born into this hope through him (1 Peter 1.3,4); it is our calling, in which we must persevere by our way of life (Colossians 1.23; Hebrews 10.23; Romans 15.4b). This paper urges that witness to this radical hope lies at the heart of mission in and to Western culture in the early twenty-first century. This possibility both invites reflection on the gospel, and calls for cultural self-awareness nourished by the gospel. This dual enquiry is especially important for mission in the context often referred to as 'postmodern culture'.

I shall reflect, therefore, upon the gospel, on the one hand, and postmodern cultural developments on the other, as they appear in the light of this hope. I shall begin by raising the question: how do postmodern developments appear relative to the gospel of hope? Do they signify a *change* in where people look for hope, or the birth of *new* hope, or the *collapse* of hope? It is the third possibility which I shall explore in this paper. I shall point to this loss of hope in a preliminary way by noting a widespread cultural failure in a caring, respectful attentiveness towards the world. I shall then interpret this by reference to a theological understanding of hope as an attentive, faithful disposition and practice, in which we give ourselves in an unqualified way to God and to others. Seen in the light of hope thus understood, postmodern cultural developments reveal the wounds of hopelessness. I shall trace these wounds in the cultural prevalence in the West of narcissism, neediness, credulity, sentimentality, tragic spirituality and escapism. Finally, I shall suggest some implications for the task of mission in a postmodern cultural setting.

In such matters, mission challenges Western Christians to deep cultural self-awareness illumined by the gospel – to see and articulate things taken for granted, at a deep level, in their own culture. This awareness grows through deep and attentive immersion in the testimony of Christian Scripture and tradition. It is also helped by listening well to brothers and sisters in Christ, who bring non-Western Christian perspectives on Western culture.

Hope in a Changing Culture

In postmodern developments, the face of hope has changed. How shall we appraise this change? Our answer will determine greatly how we understand the task of mission in a postmodern setting.

Should we see in postmodern developments a *change of orientation in hope*? We might judge that, whereas in modernity hope was invested in certain things to be attained in certain ways, in postmodernity hope is invested in other things, to be attained in ways appropriate to them. If so, mission in a postmodern setting requires that the radical hope of the gospel be commended ,so as to engage with other hopes than those which have been to the fore in modernity.

Should we see in postmodern developments *a new hopefulness*? We might judge that, whereas in modernity hope was framed in terms of certain goals and the methods by which they might be attained,, now there is a new discovery of hope as the constraints of this vision are recognised and its hold upon our imagination is loosened. If so, mission, in a postmodern setting, requires that we recognise in postmodern developments a glimpse of that hope which the gospel brings, and a sign (when properly received) of God's promise. And we shall commend the gospel in these terms.

Should we see in postmodern developments a *loss of hopefulness*? We might judge that, whereas in modernity hope was directed in terms of a certain goal to be achieved by certain methods, now this hope has collapsed, and with it hope, as such, has collapsed. Where there was hope, now there is hopelessness. If so, mission in a postmodern setting requires that we testify to the gospel message that there is indeed hope, and that we do so in all the ways – personal, practical and theoretical – which point to the reality of hope in God.

It is vital that we are open to finding in postmodern developments all three of these elements. The task of mission requires that we be ready to discern and engage all three. However, I believe that in postmodernity we may discern especially the wounds of hopelessness.

The loss of hope in Western culture has been remarked by many. Among them was Lesslie Newbigin. In 1974, he returned to Britain from India where he and his wife had gone as missionaries in 1936. Ten years later he wrote:

> I have often been asked: "What is the greatest difficulty you face in moving from India to England?" I have always answered: "The disappearance of hope"… Even in the most squalid slums of Madras there was always the belief that things could be improved…
>
> In England, by contrast, it is hard to find any such hope… there is little sign among the citizens of this country of the sort of confidence in the future which was certainly present in the earlier years of this century.[1]

---

[1] Lesslie Newbigin, *The Other Side of 1984* (Geneva: World Council of Churches, 1983), 1.

Newbigin then noted the growing scepticism towards, and indeed threats felt to arise from, things which had previously inspired hope: things such as science and modern democracy. He also remarked on the rise of mental illnesses 'related to the collapse of meaning'.

Another telling observation was made by David Hay and Kate Hunt in their research report *Understanding the Spirituality of People who don't go to Church* (2000). They recalled George Steiner's thesis, in *The Death of Tragedy* (1961), that the tragic sense of life expressed in classical Greek tragic drama had long declined under the influence of Jewish and Christian belief in a good God. They observed:

> We are wondering whether, forty years on from Steiner's analysis, after Auschwitz and after the many other atrocities of the 20th century, we see in post-Christian society the return of a tragic sense of life... If at the deepest level there is a conviction that life at depth is pitiless and utterly meaningless, then the optimism of Christianity become incredible. The people we spoke to were well aware of this, and it is an issue that church people need to face much more directly in their dialogue with secular culture.[2]

Why is this widespread loss of hope not more directly faced and discussed in the church and beyond it? We may identify three contributing factors. Each of them carries implications for mission.

First, because this loss of hope is painful, we shy away from facing it. Melvyn Matthews writes:

> It is the pain, the actual deadening, horrifying pain of living in the modern which is at the heart of things. Most of us totally underestimate the existence and importance of this pain as a factor in our lives. It is glossed consistently. But the pain forces us to disown responsibility... The existence of this pain deadens and numbs our moral existence. Our reserves of compassion seep away, our desire for real living is undermined by the task of moving from one day to another with the minimum of disaster.[3]

What are the implications of this for mission? It suggests that to engage in mission requires that we be ready to face our own pain, and acknowledge that we are ourselves affected by the spirit of hopelessness in our culture and our age.

A second reason why the prevalence of hopelessness is not widely acknowledged is as follows. We do not recognise either hope or hopelessness for what they are because we hold narrow, false assumptions about what they are like. In particular, modern thought typically links hope with progress, projects, initiatives and achievements; it links hopelessness, on the other hand, with stagnation, inactivity and passivity. Indeed, as modern Christians, we may casually think of hope in the same terms. But this picture is skewed; it does not reckon with, for example, the hope

[2] David Hay and Kate Hunt, *Understanding the Spirituality of People who don't go to Church*, (Nottingham: Centre for the Study of Human Relations, University of Nottingham, 2000), 38.

[3] Matthews, Melvyn, *Delighting in God* (London: Collins, 1987), 99.

manifest in a stable contemplative religious order (which can seem on the surface to be a quite passive affair), or the hopelessness driving compulsive rage – or for that matter frivolity (which can seem each expressions of life). The implication for mission is that it requires that we witness to hope with an enlarged and more faithful understanding of what hope is.

A third reason lies with the practice of those, who manage our public culture – in politics, education, the mass media, and in the public marketing of goods and services. These typically deflect, for their own strategic reasons, any concerns that popular hopes may not be fulfilled. As members of the general public, we are encouraged to believe that politicians will solve every problem they have so far failed to solve; that buying a certain product will transform our lives; that we (and especially those among us who are young) can 'change the world'. The constant flow of such messages blocks our way to quietly acknowledging that a loss of hope saps our soul's vitality. By implication, to engage in mission requires that we invite a more honest appraisal of the personal spiritual condition fostered by our culture.

Together, these three factors tend to conceal hopelessness within contemporary Western culture. It is vital that we acknowledge and understand this, however, in order faithfully to bear witness to hope. In order to do so, we need to decipher certain features of our culture, which conceal a loss of hope. By way of preliminary, let us note how prominent is *distraction* in our culture, and discern its link to loss of hope.

Hope and Attentiveness

People remark not uncommonly on 'the speed of life' today. Life is more busy – alike in work and leisure – than in the past as they recall it. Why is this? Does this reflect higher levels of productivity today? The truth is much more ambiguous. A century ago, G.K. Chesterton remarked: 'It is customary to complain of the bustle and strenuousness of our epoch. But in truth the chief mark of our epoch is a profound laziness and fatigue; and the fact is that the real laziness is the cause of the apparent bustle.'[4]

For Chesterton, this laziness was connected with a characteristic modern inattentiveness – the habit of paying only superficial, fleeting or casual attention to that which confronts us. Writing in the same period, P.T. Forsyth regretted (in language now quaint to our ears) that people 'will not attend, they will not force themselves to attend, gravely to the gravest things.... they read everything in a vagrant, browsing fashion. They turn on the most serious subjects the holiday, seaside, newspaper habit of mind'.[5] Such inattentiveness has, like busy-ness, entrenched itself further in

---

[4] G.K. Chesterton, *Orthodoxy* (LonDon: John Lane, 1909), 228.

[5] P.T. Forsyth, 'A Rallying Ground for the free Churches: The Reality of Grace', *Hibbert Journal*, IV, 1906, 828.

Western culture since he wrote. Today, it is evident in the habit of 'grazing' between television channels and 'browsing' or 'surfing' the internet, in credulous views of 'alternative' therapies, and in the casual embrace of elements from quite disparate religions within a 'smorgasbord' spirituality.

The disposition of inattentiveness remarked by Chesterton and Forsyth is by no means indifferent to human well-being. Gabriel Marcel. writing in 1934 on 'the irreligion of today', noted that very often, perhaps most often, unbelief 'takes the form of inattention, of turning a deaf ear to the appeal made by an inner voice to all that is deepest in us'. 'It should be noticed', he added, 'that modern life tends to encourage this inattention, indeed almost to enforce it, by the way it dehumanises man and cuts him off from his centre... this inattention or distraction is indeed a kind of sleep'.[6]

The 'sleep' of inattention or distraction stands in contrast to awareness of our human centre. The latter finds us attentive to our creator in awe, delighted wonder and lively responsiveness. We are open to the radically new as we look expectantly towards an abundantly good God, and, in love, embrace the responsibility bestowed upon us by this God. This is personal hope at its most deep and lively.

The philosopher, John Wisdom, likens such attentiveness to that shown by a child when it sees something for the first time: 'when we, wishing to help him to understand, tell him what it is, he hardly seems to hear us... perhaps this is part of why we are told that if we wish to find the truth, we must become like little children... We need to be at once like someone who has seen much and forgotten nothing, and also like one who is seeing everything for the first time'.[7]

It is in such hopeful attentiveness towards the new that the real is revealed. Aelred Squire writes that a proper spirituality encourages us to 'allow our immediate experience constantly to break in upon our preconceived notions with such fresh news that we find ourselves suddenly where we actually are, in a world quite different from the one we supposed it to be, and with many a burning bush among what we always thought to be a waste of dry shrubbery'.[8]

Modern culture constantly works against such wondering, hopeful attention. Rather, it disperses our attention, it distracts us. The novelist, Saul Bellow, remarks that distractions surround us today as never before. Advertisers catch our eye by every possible means, sound-bites grab our fleeting attention, and information floods over us. 'Vast enterprises described as the communications industry inform, misinform, or dis-inform the public about politics, wars, and revolutions, about religious and racial conflicts, and also about education, law, medicine, books, theatre, music, cookery', he writes. 'To make such lists', he adds, 'gives a misleading

---

[6] Gabriel Marcel, 'Some Thoughts on Faith', in Marcel, *Being and Having* (London: Dacre Press, 1949), 203-216, 212.

[7] John Wisdom, *Paradox and Discovery* (Oxford: Basil Blackwell, 1965), 137.

[8] Aelred Squire, *Asking the Fathers* (London: SPCK, 1973), 4.

impression of order. The truth is that we are in an unbearable state of confusion, or distraction'.[9]

How much does this matter? A great deal. As Blaise Pascal warned three and a half centuries ago:

> Diversion prevents us thinking about ourselves and leads us imperceptibly to destruction. But for it we should be bored, and boredom would drive us to seek some more solid means of escape, but diversion passes our time and brings us imperceptibly to our death.[10]

We might hear an echo of Pascal's warning in our own generation, in the title of Neil Postman's book: *Amusing Ourselves to Death: culture in an age of show business.*[11]

By reflecting, in this way, on the prevalence of distraction in contemporary culture, we have begun probing the fortunes of hope within it. Let us now explore further what hope is theologically, properly understood. When we have done so, we shall be in a position to discern further the face of hope in modern and postmodern culture.

Hope Theologically Understood

What is hope? In common understanding, it is a subjective feeling inspired by some anticipated objective state of affairs. Such hope is itself, therefore, no part of the state of affairs in question.

However, our reflections, above, on hope and God, remind us of another kind of hope, which in integral to our very enquiry into the real. There is an original, hopeful attentiveness *out of which is born knowledge of objective reality in the first place.*

Knowledge of God always remains a matter of such hopeful attentiveness. More particularly: God, who raised Jesus Christ from death, has inaugurated a new covenant between himself and humankind, revealing himself as the whole, decisive and unqualified ground of hope. Through Christ, God's people find themselves born into a living hope – radical fullness of hope, paradigmatic and standing in special relation to every act of hope. This radical hope has the following characteristics.

(a) *In what* is radical hope placed, and what is this hope *for*? The answers to both these questions are implied in the following: radical hope is hope for the *transcendent*; it is hope for that which is fundamental; it is *comprehensive* in scope; and it is hope placed in what is *sure*. It is hope for

---

[9] Saul Bellow, 'The Distracted Public', The Romanes Lecture, Oxford University, 10 May 1990, in Bellow, *It All Adds Up: From the Dim Past to the Uncertain Future: A Non-fiction Collection* (New York: Viking, 1994), 153–69, 155-6.

[10] Blaise Pascal, No. 414, in *Pensees* (Harmondsworth: Penguin, 1966), 120. See also his more extended reflections in *Pensees,* VIII: Diversion (nos. 132-139), 37-43.

[11] Neil Postman, *Amusing Ourselves to Death: Public Discourse in the Age of Show Business* (London: Methuen, 1987).

the *transcendent:* to hope in God is to hope for unqualified blessing beyond anything we can conceive within creation or history. It is *fundamental*: it concerns hope for that without which human life is without meaning. It is *comprehensive*: it constitutes hope for ourselves, for humankind, and for all creation (Romans 8.19-24) in God's kingdom; on behalf of each human person, it is the hope of eternal life through resurrection like Jesus, and on behalf of the cosmos, the hope of a new creation. And it is *sure*: it reaches out for and takes hold of unshakable grounds for hope.

(b) Such hope in God is *paradigmatic* in its orientation: hope, which is for the transcendent and for the fundamental, which is comprehensive and for what is sure, is hope directed in a paradigmatic way.

(c) To hope in God is to reach out and apprehend God as he reveals himself. It is God himself, who awakens the disposition of wondering, receptive hope, in which we offer up ourselves and our world in an unreserved way in attention to God. 'God is our hope' is, thus, properly bivocal: God is our hope at once in an objective and a subjective sense.

(d) This unqualified activity of hopeful attention reflects God, who inspires it. Indeed, it may be said to participate, by God's grace, in God's own unqualified gift of himself in hope towards his creation. It is God, who hopes first, not we ourselves. God's own hope is at once free and faithful: in it he binds himself in covenant with his people and his creation.

(e) The act of unqualified, self-giving hope in God is a wholehearted response to God, which is at once *receptive* and *responsible* in orientation. In *receptivity* we are *open to* the inspiration of hope, beyond our reliance upon any practical mastery or grasp of creation of our own. *Responsibly,* we *maintain the practice* of unqualified hope with patience, fortitude and forbearance.

(f) This active disposition of unqualified, self-giving hope is the paradigm for each and every act of hope. By reference to it, light is shed on every act of hoping for, or investing hope in, God, ourselves and creation.

In passing, we might note that the characteristics, just described, are shared by the other theological virtues of faith (or trust) and love. These too, inspired by God's self-revelation, are a matter of unqualified self-giving in receptivity and responsibility towards what is real; these too inform our practical engagement with, and reflect God's own purposes for, the whole of creation.

Hope, however, may be said to have a certain primacy among the theological virtues. Moltmann writes: 'Faith believes God to be true, hope awaits the time when this truth shall be manifested; faith believes that he is our father, hope anticipates that he will ever show himself to be a Father towards us; faith believes that eternal life has been given to us, hope anticipates that it will some time be revealed; faith is the foundation upon which hope rests, hope nourishes and sustains faith… Thus in the Christian life faith has the priority, but hope the primacy.'[12]

Charles Peguy acclaims a more radical primacy still for hope. He ends his beautiful poem, *L'Esperance* (*Hope*), by extolling faith and love, and then concludes:

> But my hope is the bloom, and the fruit, and the leaf, and the limb,
> And the twig, and the shoot, and the seed, and the bud.
> Hope is the shoot, the bud of the bloom
> of eternity itself.[13]

Hope, Evasion, and Redemption in Christ

Given such an understanding of hope, how shall we understand hopelessness? Moltmann identifies it as sin. He writes:

> If faith thus depends on hope for its life, then the sin of unbelief is manifestly grounded in hopelessness. To be sure, it is usually said that sin in its original form is man's wanting to be as God. But that is only the one side of sin. The other side of such pride is hopelessness, resignation, inertia and melancholy.[14]

Moltmann quotes Joseph Pieper's *Uber die Hoffnung* (1949):

> hopelessness can take two forms: it can be presumption, praesumptio, and it can be despair, desperation. Both are forms of the sin against hope. Presumption is a premature, self-willed anticipation of the fulfilment of what we hope for from God. Despair is the premature, arbitrary anticipation of the non-fulfilment of that we hope for in God.... Both rebel against the patience in which hope trusts in the God of the promise.

Now this passage conveys two key insights. First, what Pieper calls 'premature anticipation' is, like despair, a form of hopelessness. It is an evasion of the demands of maintaining hope, which arise when there appear no immediate grounds for hope. It is a (self-concealed) dismissal of the requirement to live within creaturely limits, to live with the tragic, to live with human perversity, while remaining hopeful. Refusing this, we presume to exalt, as the fulfilment of hope, that which we ourselves can define and pursue with mastery. In so doing, we place ourselves (whether openly or secretly) at the centre of our own hope.

Second, Pieper recognises rebellion, not only in premature anticipation, but also in despair. We should note that he does so even though the despairing person presents the experience of despair to themselves as one of being *overwhelmed by* the world rather than *acting upon* the world. In despair, we actively collude with that which overwhelms us, although we conceal this from ourselves.

---

[12] Jürgen Moltmann, *Theology of Hope*, (London: SCM, 1967), 20.

[13] Charles Péguy, 'L'Espérance', in Peguy, *Basic Verities* (Pantheon Books, 1943), 232 –249.

[14] Moltmann, *Theology of Hope*, 22.

Let us turn to the vital question, which now arises: how does the hope which God inspires address the sin of hopelessness? After all, we find no more compelling grounds for despair over a person, than their own persistent rejection of hope. And what of ourselves, we might ask, who fail repeatedly to rise to the demands of hope? Is there hope for the hopeless?

In the crucifixion and resurrection of Jesus, the final encounter between hope and hopelessness is revealed. Unfathomable hope and the unfathomable contradiction of hope confront each other, in what may rightly be called ultimate conflict, as follows.

Jesus lived among people, who hoped for a future Messiah, who would inaugurate once and for all the rule of a righteous God. This was their ultimate hope. When Jesus himself began proclaiming the coming of God's kingdom, and restored hope to many victims, these expectations began to focus on himself.

In the context of this ultimate hope, the prospect of Jesus' rejection and barbaric execution presented the worst possible scenario. For Jesus himself, it presented the most radical temptation to despair both of *God* and of *humankind.* It urged him to despair utterly of *God*, because if God now allowed his own Messiah to be killed, this would surely mean that rather than bringing his purposes to final fulfilment, God had betrayed and abandoned his purpose. It also presented Jesus with the most radical temptation to despair of *humankind.* Jesus' hope in God involved an implicit hope that God's purpose would be fulfilled among his people, as they responded to God in faith. Faced with his own crucifixion, however, such hope for God's people must appear futile. If the Messiah himself was rejected by God's people, what possible hope could now placed in them to respond to God in faith?

If the prospect of the crucifixion of the Messiah presented *Jesus* with compelling grounds for despair, its execution forever urges the same upon us as *humankind.* In Jesus' crucifixion, we see ourselves as human beings opposing, without qualification, the very hope upon which meaningful human life depends. What conceivable hope remains for us? The temptation is extreme for us, either to turn away or be overwhelmed.

Jesus Christ, however, neither turns away nor is overwhelmed by his abandonment by God and us. Rather he addresses God, and addresses us: 'Father, forgive them, they do not know what they are doing'. He calls us to remain attentive to himself and – painfully – to what we have done to him. He calls us not to turn away, dismissive – just as he has not turned away from God or us – but rather to stand with him in trusting hope towards God. And he calls us not to be overwhelmed in despair – just as he has not despaired of God or us.

In the resurrection of Jesus, the gift of Jesus' own radical hope, enacted here in his crucifixion, is revealed as our own calling. It is the calling to face, in Christ, the demands of hope in every situation, and not to turn away or be overwhelmed by them. Jesus' crucifixion and resurrection, in their radical opposition, open us to depths of hope and hopelessness, which we cannot fully fathom, and which enlarge our souls, as we are drawn further into the mystery of divine hope.

Public Hope and Modern Culture

Earlier, I quoted a reference to 'Judaeo-Christian optimism'. It is clear from the above, however, that authentic Christian hope is very different from optimism. *Unlike optimism, it is fully open to grounds for despair; unlike pessimism, it faces them without despair.*

When we turn to hope within modern culture, however, we find its relation to optimism is more ambiguous. Let us examine this ambiguity now; it is vital that we appraise modern hope in this way before turning to postmodernity. This is because postmodernity has arisen in large part as a reaction to modernity, and so cannot be understood apart from it.

The Christendom, in which modern society was born, was nourished by a lively disposition of hope in God and his kingdom. Modern thinkers, however, focussed their hope upon social progress through the advance of science and technology and in the civilising of and general education of, an innately good and rational population. While the resulting modern society was framed publicly, without explicit reference to positive Christian beliefs, it drew, nonetheless, upon a Christian imagination, and Christian belief remained widely taken for granted.

The popular hope invested in such progress could be exultant. Consider the following response to the creation of rail transport in place of horse-drawn transport:

> Lay down your rails, ye nations near and far -
> yoke your full trains to Steam's triumphal car.
> Link town to town; unite in iron bands
> The long-estranged and oft-embattled lands.
> Peace, mild-eyed seraph – Knowledge, light divine,
> shall send their messengers by every line...
> Blessings on Science, and her handmaid Steam!
> They make Utopia only half a dream.[15]

The modern hope in progress was severely shaken in the course of the twentieth century. The century opened with, as Oliver O'Donovan describes it, a 'massive cultural certainty that united natural science, democratic politics, technology, and colonialism.' 'The four great facts of the twentieth century that broke the certainty to pieces', he writes, 'were two world wars, the reversal of European colonisation, the threat of the nuclear destruction of the human race, and, most recently, the evidence of

---

[15] Illustrated London News, quoted in Stanley L. Jaki, *The Purpose Of It All* (Washington: Regnery Gateway, 1990), 6-7.

long-term ecological crisis.'[16] Today, we have a widely felt legacy of guilt over Western exploitation of peoples and resources, an uneasy conscience about the West's current global economic and military hegemony, and apprehension over the future prospects for our planet. The confident modern hope of progress has been shaken. More radically, there is disorientation regarding 'progress' itself. 'Western society' writes O'Donovan, 'finds itself the heir of political institutions and traditions which it values without having any clear idea why, or to what extent, it values them. Faced with decisions about their future development it has no way of telling what counts as improvement and what as subversion. It cannot tell where "straight ahead" lies, let alone whether it ought to keep on going there.'

The collapse of modern hope lies behind much which has surfaced in postmodernity. However, the link between the two will be interpreted in different ways, according to how we answer these questions: *has modern hope equated fully with hope? Does the collapse of modern hope represent the collapse of hope as such?*

Accordingly, three considerations bear upon how we interpret the link between modern hope and postmodernity. We shall explore these below. First, modern hope has stood in ambiguous relation to radical, Christian hope. In its public ideology, it displays a tendency towards what Pieper calls proud, premature *anticipation* of the fulfilment of hope. Second, and in the course of this, modern hope has produced – in a displaced, private, alienated life among individuals – an underbelly of premature *despair* of the fulfilment of hope. Third, public hope has increasingly colluded with such private despair, in a perverse symbiosis. While this threefold observation grossly simplifies a complex situation, it will help us reflect on postmodernity as the setting of mission today. Let me enlarge:

(1) The developments, which in the twentieth century, have robbed the modern hope of credibility now make it impossible, as Christopher Lasch writes, 'for those who believe in progress to speak with confidence and moral authority'. They also reveal modern hope in a new light, as having been less a matter of hope than of optimism. Lash writes:

> If progressive ideologies have dwindled down to a wistful hope against hope that things will somehow work out for the best, we need to recover a more vigorous form of hope, which trusts life without denying its tragic character or attempting to explain away tragedy as 'cultural lag'. We can fully appreciate this kind of hope only now that the other kind, better described as optimism, has fully revealed itself as a higher form of wishful thinking. Progressive optimism rests, at bottom, on a denial of the natural limits on human power and freedom, and it cannot survive for very long in a world in which an awareness of those limits has become inescapable. The disposition properly described as hope, trust, or wonder, on the other hand – three names for the same state of heart and mind – asserts the goodness of life in the face

---

[16] Oliver O'Donovan, *The Ways of Judgement* (Grand Rapids: Eerdmans, 2005), xii.

of its limits. It cannot be defeated by adversity. In the troubled times to come, we will need it even more than we needed it in the past.[17]

The main problem is that in modern public life, progressive optimism has been taken as defining hope itself, and this has deformed hope both in thought and in practice. The things, in which modern hope is invested – scientific and technological advance, economic growth, education and civilisation, and the goodness and rationality of man – have been mistakenly held to define hope. We see public hope as trust placed in that which can be achieved in principle by the methods of the natural and human sciences. In so doing, we exalt the goal of human mastery into the vision, which takes hold of us in romantic idealism. However, we deceive ourselves here by ignoring the unresolved issues presented by creaturely limits and contingencies, by the tragic, and by human perversity. This vision represents a 'premature expectation of the fulfilment of hope'; it is an evasion of the full demands of hope which require us to invest hope beyond the reach of human mastery and beyond the limits and tragedy of created life.

The deformation of hope, within progressive optimism, intensifies when romantic ideology is adopted and its programmes for the rationalisation of society dogmatically pursued, whether in totalitarianism or neo-liberal economic ideology. Here, neglect of the transcendent horizons of Christian hope leads on to their programmatic suppression. Michael Polanyi describes this in his analysis of the loss of cultural self-confidence following the First World War.[18] He describes the Enlightenment as having injected liberal humanism into science, as science picked up the mantle of responsibility from medieval Christianity (I would describe this rather in terms of the continuing tacit nourishment of a secular moral imagination by humanistic Christian faith). Such humanism worked in partnership with science, qualifying its sceptical tendency in a partnership, which held popular confidence until the First World War. After this, however, a more radical scepticism gained ground, feeding the pathological 'moral perfectionism' of evolutionary secular ideology described by Polanyi and evident in both Communism and Nazism.

These political developments are a reminder to us that the subversion of progressive optimism has originated by no means simply from 'outside of' such optimism, in events contingently related to it. It also has origins within this optimism itself. For in reality this optimism is integrally related to a distinctively modern scepticism, and the hope it embodies is a distortion of authentic hope.

---

[17] Christopher Lasch, *The True and Only Heaven: Progress and Its Critics* (New York: Norton), 529-530.

[18] Michael Polanyi, 'Why did we destroy Europe?', in P. Weiss (ed.) *Knowledge in Search of Understanding: The Frensham Papers* (New York: Future Publications, 1975), 1-8.

(2) Modern public hope, then, tends towards a *premature expectation of the fulfilment of hope*. However, in private, it also secretly breeds a *premature expectation of the non-fulfilment of hope*. When hope is defined in terms of public progress, and pursued through public programmes of rationalisation, the individual's experience of non-participation in the fulfilment of such hope becomes displaced into a private realm of despair.

This dualism between public hope and private despair is noted by Chinese theologian Carver T. Yu. He finds Western culture characterised by 'technological optimism and literary despair'.[19] Much Western literature of the past century and beyond has indeed witnessed a private life alienated from any public hope. This is evident, not only in nihilistic and existentialist writings, but also in sentimental and romantic stories of fulfilment found in an intimate private life. Michael Paul Gallagher notes a turn to sentiment already in Charles Dicken's *Bleak House*, remarking that 'this privatisation of horizon is a trait of much nineteenth-century fiction'.[20] He takes this as a starting-point for theological reflection upon contemporary Western narcissism – a phenomenon we shall ourselves explore below. Jane Austen's *Mansfield Park* can be seen precisely as a lament over the turn away from the pursuit of responsible public vocation towards the individual, restless, private life of 'acting'.[21] Richard Sennett concludes *The Fall of Public Man* (a fall which he traces through the 19th and 20th centuries) with a chapter titled 'The Tyrannies of Intimacy', in which he describes a contemporary society deformed by its measurement 'in psychological terms,' or in terms of the intimacy it promises. 'The defeat which this deals to sociability', he writes, 'is... the result of a long historical process, one in which the very terms of human nature have been transformed, into that individual, unstable, and self-absorbed phenomenon we call "personality"'.[22]

Restless private disorientation has come to the fore more recently in postmodernity, but it has a history stretching back to the modern period. Its new prominence reflects developments in public institutions, described by Edward Farley (in the U.S.) as follows:

> The predominantly marketing and consumer society in which most Westerners live has transformed virtually all traditional institutions (governments, corporations, universities) and created new or transformed institutions (the media, entertainment and leisure, professional sports,

---

[19] Carver T. Yu, 'Truth and Authentic Humanity', Plenary address at The Gospel and Our Culture Consultation,Swanwick, 1992. Displayed online at www.gospel-culture.org.uk/yu.htm

[20] Michael Paul Gallagher, 'The Tone of Culture: from Prometheus to Narcissus', in Gallagher, *Struggles of Faith* (Eire: Columba Press, 1990), 84–93. Displayed online at www.gospel-culture.org.uk/Gallagher.htm.

[21] Peter J. Leithart, 'Jane Austen, Public Theologian', *First Things*, 139, January 2004, 28-38.

[22] Sennett, *The Fall of Public Man* (New York: Knopf, 1977), 338.

> communications)... Moreover, the social shift I describe has isolated certain powerful institutions (corporate, military, governmental, media, entertainment) from the influence of the co-called normative institutions such as education, religion and the arts. Indeed, the great cultural transformation of our time has changed the character of these normative institutions, drawing them into the marketplace and the world of image-making, of salesmanship and of managerial orientations. This massive shift has had a devastating effect on the once-deep cultural values that exerted their force upon most of society's institutions – values of truth, duty, discipline, reading, beauty, family, tradition, justice among many others.[23]

Meanwhile these same decades have seen a huge growth in the formulation of public norms through legislation and mass social 'programming,' which has eroded the primary, informal culture of personal life in the family and local community. Such programming has been enabled by new information and communication technology and pursued by those, who work in politics and the civil service, the mass media, education, and marketing, and by spokespersons for businesses and professions. The government has introduced regimes of accountability to shape public practice more directly, explicitly and in a more thoroughgoing way, according to its own ideological doctrines. It has done so by such means as legislation, directives and protocols, targets, and the requirement of repeated re-accreditation. Such political initiatives have extended to an attempt to 'professionalise' a range of familiar community practices (paid and voluntary, formal and informal) by requiring or promoting 'official accreditation' for those involved. Pursued today without sufficient discrimination, this bureaucratic revolution subverts morale in more informal, participatory areas of personal life.

(3) The social transformation summarised above, Edward Farley refers to as 'postmodern'. This reminds us that postmodernity is not simply about changes in our private lives, but about changes in public life, which demand private re-orientation. Indeed, in the light of the foregoing analysis, it might be said that the modern vision exploits the hopelessness it has generated in private. Modern culture turns its instrumental rationality upon 'postmodern' habits of distraction and puts them to use to its own ends (typically for private profit of one kind and another). Thus consumerism (for profit) actively inflames and manipulates personal desires. This exploitation was already described three-quarters of a century ago by G.K. Chesterton:

> the philosophy of blind buying and selling; of bullying people into purchasing what they do not want; of making it badly so that they may break it and imagine they want it again; of keeping rubbish in rapid circulation like a dust-

---

[23] Edward Farley, 'Transforming a Lukewarm Church', *The Christian Century*, August 27-Sept 3, 1997, 754-757, 757.

> storm in a desert; and pretending that you are teaching men to hope, because you do not leave them one intelligent instant in which to despair.[24]

These reflections, on the link between the collapse of modern hope and postmodernity, have introduced the topics of narcissism, consumerism and sentiment. Attention to these will provide helpful leads as we turn now to consider the marks of hopelessness in postmodernity.

Hope: Postmodern Developments

When feelings of despair are widely prevalent in a culture, their expression often takes cultural forms. In modern culture, the dichotomy between a modern public vision and the individual's private life breeds private despair and shapes its expression. It breeds, in particular, a hopeless narcissism. Many features of postmodern culture are informed by this, as we shall now see.

Let us begin by reminding ourselves that in Christ, human persons are called to live receptively and responsibly in relation to God and to fellow human beings under the conditions of creation. We are called to lively hope, embracing the demands at once of hoping in God transcendent and of living in the real world, in which God has set us as creatures. We are called to trust in a God beyond our control and yet upon whom we utterly depend, while living within the limits of creaturely contingency. Such hope in God is implicitly hope for other people, for ourselves, and for all God's good creation; entrusting ourselves to God, we find our true selves as we are affirmed and incorporated into the loving purposes of God.

Seen in this context, there is a classical myth which tells the story of one, who lives a contradiction of hope in God: the myth of Narcissus.[25] It tells of a young man, who is exceptionally beautiful in appearance. His beauty makes Narcissus the object of intense longing by others, whom he scorns. In particular, he is desired by a young nymph called Echo who, when rebuffed, pines away to a shadow. One of the gods is indignant with Narcissus and decides to punish him by causing him to suffer in the same way as he causes others to suffer. The god causes him to see his own image in a pool and to be captivated by his own beauty. His desire for intimate union with his image is overwhelming and insatiable, but such union is unattainable. As his image mocks him from the pool, he suffers for himself the anguish of unrequited longing which Echo and others had for him, until he himself is finally lost.

We may see Narcissus as scorning the demands of hope in God as they have been described above, and, thus, as scorning God, the created world and his true self – only to be overwhelmed by these demands instead. Like

---

[24] Chesterton, 1935, 'Reflections on a Rotten Apple', in Chesterton, *The Well and the Shallows* (London: Sheed & Ward, 1935). Italics mine.

[25] Ovid, *Metamorphoses*, 340-500.

the persons he has scorned, he now becomes spellbound by his image – an image in which he invests his 'self' and yet which renders this self unattainable. He is totally absorbed in gazing, in his reflected image, upon a self which he essentially lacks. The world fades into the background; in his self-absorption, he forsakes any regard for the world as distinct from himself; instead he sees the world only in relation to the reflected image, upon which he gazes. But he is mocked by the world he has dismissed – it mocks him in his unattainable self.

For psychiatrists today, 'narcissism' denotes a personality disorder illuminated by the story here told. Here, one is disoriented and defeated by the demands of hope, and turns away from the world in despair and constructs a 'self,' which becomes the focus of one's life and which reduces other people and the world into a mere extension of this self. The demands of the real world and of real other people, intractable before this self, are now experienced as oppressive. Driven by the spell of unresolvable lack and futile longing, one insatiably devours everything in the world in pursuit of this unattainable self, but never with satisfaction. Ironically, the effect of this is to entrench one's sense of lack, and further subvert the discovery of one's true self. The narcissistic figure is one of isolation and desolation.

Since the 1970s, psychiatrists in the United States have found numbers of patients presenting with a 'narcissistic' personality disorder, characterised by self-absorption and the distress of uncontrolled and unfulfilled longing for meaning and intimacy. The clinical indictors of narcissism include 'a grandiose sense of self-importance or uniqueness; preoccupation with fantasies of unlimited success, power, brilliance, beauty, or ideal love; exhibitionistic need for constant attention and admiration; feelings of rage, inferiority, or emptiness in response to criticism or defeat; lack of empathy; sense of entitlement without assuming reciprocal responsibilities'.[26]

In *The Culture of Narcissism* (1979)[27], Christopher Lasch showed that many features of Western culture, today, can be understood by reference to a wider sub-clinical prevalence of this 'borderline personality disorder' (as it has been classed). When Lasch was repeatedly misunderstood as writing about excessive self-love, he went on to write *The Minimal Self: Psychic Survival in Trouble Times* (1984).[28] The deeper origins of narcissism lie not in self-love but rather in a profound loss of sense of self. Narcissism is a defence against the pressing threat of personal disintegration.

Where lie the roots of narcissism? Heinz Kohut[29] identifies its origins in early childhood, in the experience of not having one's needs met for

[26] Peter Moore, *Disarming the Secular Gods* (New York: IVP, 1989), 82.

[27] Christopher Lasch, *The Culture of Narcissism* (New York: Norton, 1979).

[28] Christopher Lasch, *The Minimal Self: Psychic Survival in Troubled Times* (New York: Norton, 1984).

[29] Heinz Kohut, *The Analysis of the Self: A Systematic Approach to the*

personal attention and affirmation. The young child, who does not find herself 'mirrored' well enough by her mother or other significant figures, withdraws from personal, trusting, exploratory engagement with the world. Feeling worthless, she no longer trusts herself to the outside world, for fear that she will be let down again. She may deny her vulnerability by maintaining an illusion of control, or she may incline towards aimless, vagrant, promiscuous behaviour. While she may seem totally absorbed in self-love, her deeper attitude towards herself is akin rather to self-hatred. It is a defence against feelings of helpless dependency, and an evasion of what she sees as the unfaceable demands of living with hope and trust.

The impoverished parenting ,to which Kohut traces narcissism, has, in turn, been linked by Christopher Lasch to particular modern historical developments. Lasch was prompted to write *The Culture of Narcissism,* from studies 'which had led me to the conclusion that the family's importance in our society had been steadily declining over a period of more than a hundred years. Schools, peer groups, mass media, and the "helping professions" had challenged parental authority and taken over many of the family's child-rearing functions'[30] This invasion has 'created an ideal of perfect parenthood while destroying parents' confidence in their ability to perform the most elementary functions of child-rearing'.[31] Ironically, this has sponsored a measure of parental self-withdrawal from parental roles and subverted the quality of parent-child interaction, fostering narcissistic depletion in their children.

This particular historical development is, in turn, linked to the broader modern picture I painted earlier. According to this, modernity invests too much in an optimistic vision of public progress, and, in so doing, diverges from the path of personal and communal hope, scorning social structures old and new, which embody such hope and spawning a hopeless loss of self in its population.

Christopher Lasch has documented well in *The Culture of Narcissism* and *The Minimal Self,* the diverse aspects of culture, which reflect the prevalence of narcissistic personality traits. Let me now identify some such aspects of culture which (a) are recognisably linked with postmodern cultural developments, and (b) express the sense of overwhelming lack and hopelessness which drive narcissism.

Personal neediness. Narcissism constructs the fiction of life directed towards an unattainable self, pursuing self-displacing mirages of personal fulfilment, on the one hand, and fleeing inescapable, haunting spectres of personal annihilation, on the other. The consumerist marketing of goods and services routinely exploits and reinforces this fictional world, functioning as its 'plausibility structure'. 'Who would have thought that

---

Psychoanalytic Treatment of Narcissistic Personality Disorders (New York: International Universities Press, 1971).

[30] Lasch, *The Culture of Narcissism*, 238.

[31] Lasch, *The Culture of Narcissism*, 238.

someone like *me* would find great shoes like *these* in a store nearby? It's K-Mart', runs an advertisement. Participation in the 'real' is projected forever beyond the consumer, being promised through acts of consumption which fulfil a certain self-image but never fulfil this promise. 'It doesn't matter whether you win or lose', runs an advertisement: 'what matters is how you look while you play the game'. In 'needy' consumerism, the 'real' lies not in the home-made but in the mass-produced product with a brand name; not in what can be achieved in self-reliance but in the professional job; not in the exemplary practitioner to be emulated through apprenticeship, but in the celebrity to be envied; not in the community calling for responsible participation but in the soap opera to be followed unfailingly. Such consumerism is deeply complicit with an overwhelmed, needy, narcissistic evasion of the demands of hope.

Credulity and promiscuity. In place of a life open to the demands made by authentic hope, there is now a restless tasting of possibilities, without the costly personal commitment of real exploration. Caught between longing and lack of expectation, this becomes an entertaining diversion or distraction. So to speak, we cast around *for* hope in a spirit of futility, in a superficial and indeed *hopeless* way. This fosters promiscuity in relationships and elsewhere, and a life of anomie without either responsible, personal giving or receiving in any depth. It also prompts credulity towards the claims of consumer advertising and of novel therapies and new technologies. Such credulity, we must remember, masks a radical incredulity: it conceals an incredulity towards God and the world as unworthy of trust. As in the saying ascribed (problematically) to G.K. Chesterton, 'When people stop believing in God, they don't believe in nothing; they believe in anything'.

Sentiment. Loss of personal hope informs popular stories in which, in a distortion of divine grace, sentimental private solutions arise miraculously for characters, who inhabit a heartless world. Hollywood feeds film-goers with a diet of stories featuring needy figures, for whom there is an unrealistic, gratuitous and contrived happy ending. From *The Wizard of Oz* to *The Matrix* trilogy, Hollywood preaches an unattainable salvation to the needy soul: the victorious power of positive thinking and of self-originating choice in the face of a bleak deterministic world, bringing inexplicable fortune. Such sentiment simply reinforces personal anomie and demoralisation; nothing here nourishes the recovery of responsible, hopeful engagement with the real world.

Tragic Spirituality. Occasions of searing victimhood declare the world a place, where human worth and meaning are fundamentally and finally mocked, and the human soul is fated to be overwhelmed. This resonates powerfully for despairing narcissism, which now finds sacred meaning in the figure of the victim. Victims become the occasion of 'spiritual' gestures, as when the death of the Princess of Wales brought a flood of candles and flowers and impromptu monuments in Britain. A few years later, when two young English schoolgirls were murdered, over 15,000 candles were lit by visitors to Soham Parish Church, a similar number of letters were sent and flowers placed in the churchyard, and around 2,000 teddy bears were given.

We need to distinguish these gestures from traditional Christian acts of memorial, which reach out in hope. The gestures over the death of the Princess of Wales testified to a tragedy claiming the last word upon one already seen as a tragic victim. The same is true of the growing practice of placing of memorials at the site of road traffic accidents. Lying in sharp disjunction from their bleak public setting, roadside tributes at the scene of accidents speak of tragic violence done to a 'private' life. Unlike the traditional grave, clustered among others around the building where a faithful God is worshipped, such tokens – even in their seeming defiance – intimate that *violation has the last word.* They declare a tragedy not to be forgotten, rather than a life lived and now remembered as a gift from God. Gifts of teddy bears in memory of a lost child are enactments of futile giving, intimating unresolved feelings of powerlessness in face of tragedy.

In a further twist, popular gestures are, today, synthesised and cued through mass manipulation, as explored by Stjepan Meštrović.[32] While the resulting gestures, therefore, have a certain 'fake' aspect, they reflect the real pain, which drives their underlying narcissism: an unfaceable loss of hope.

Escapism: the addictive pursuit of pleasures and fantasies of control. Pleasure may be used to escape from the stress of a life deformed by hopelessness. Such enjoyment is neither a proper delight in God's blessings, nor, for that matter, the unchecked expression of human vitalitybut rather an ineffective and passing relief from pain. Dorothy Sayers saw twentieth-century pornography and promiscuity as related not to 'sheer exuberance of animal spirits' but to 'boredom and discontent'. She wrote: '... in periods of disillusionment like our own, when philosophies are bankrupt and life appears without hope – men and women may turn to lust... (they) go to bed because they have nothing better to do.'[33] Used in this way, 'feel-good' experiences are a matter of addiction. Indeed, some writers have seen addiction as a key category for understanding the dynamics of life in contemporary Western culture. Pleasures promise escape in a variety of different ways. Alcohol and drugs temporarily blank out stress; sex and violence can be used to override, with excitement, feelings of emptiness. Gambling enacts a sense of powerlessness to attain desirable goals, as the gambler entrusts himself to the mercy of fortune. The addiction of escapist pleasure helps to fuel a culture of debt, generating a vicious circle of despair and escape.

---

[32] Stjepan Meštrović, *Postemotional Society* (London: Sage, 1997).

[33] Dorothy Sayers, *Creed or Chaos: and other Essays in Popular Theology* (London: Methuen, 1947), 66.

An illusion of escape from hopelessness and powerlessness may also be found in fantasies of control; similarly, an illusion of escape from a worthless, anonymous life may be found in fantasies of personal impact or celebrity. Computer games can provide for these kinds of escapism, through an immersion in virtual worlds; television contests can do so, by inviting viewers to cast their vote for their favourite contestant. A self-obsessed pursuit of health, beauty and fitness may be driven by the pursuit of an essentially unattainable control over one's own life, and enacts narcissistic despair.

Mission: Bearing the Gospel of Hope

I have devoted much of this paper to a cultural analysis guided by theological awareness. I have done so since, without this, no amount of rhetoric about cultural mission will yield an authentically mission-shaped church. *With* such analysis, meanwhile – if it is truthful – readers will be in a position to draw implications for themselves about the proper shape of mission in a postmodern context. However, it may be helpful if I here suggest some implications, as I see them.

Fundamentally, it is the vocation of Christian mission in a postmodern context to proclaim the gospel of hope, and to pursue practices, which embody this gospel, in such a way as to reflect faithfully the reality and nature of radical hope outlined above. Such proclamation and practice requires discerning attention to the Christian scriptures and tradition, on the one hand, and to contemporary culture, on the other, in the desire to obey this hope. This exercise of discernment calls us to be at once faithful (holding fast to the hope of the gospel) and free (being open to the Spirit under whose guidance hope is embodied in unanticipated, creative ways).

Such mission will properly fulfil two requirements. First, authentic mission will rise above complicity with a cultural spirit of hopelessness, wherever this manifests itself. This needs saying because Christian religion is always at risk of domestication by culture. Christian religion must beware of merely replicating, in its own religious terms, cultural expressions of hopelessness such as needy consumerism, romance, sentiment, a tragic sense of life and escapism. The desire to engage culture, in a missionary way, can easily lead to collusion with cultural habits and assumptions, which need rather to be challenged in the name of the gospel. Nor is the danger of cultural captivity avoided by declaring a 'countercultural' stance; such a stance can easily leave the church 'of but not in the world' – and without the gospel. The true vocation of the church to be 'in but not of the world' – to act like salt or yeast – is rather to reveal both the gospel, and culture, in the light of the gospel. Here, rightly to challenge culture is precisely to engage it, while rightly to affirm it is precisely to call it to conversion.

Second, authentic mission will commend a gospel of hope for all: it will witness to a reality calling for wondering, reverent attention attention by all, and calling for a new apprehension of the whole world by all. The gospel is betrayed, when it is commended merely as a private source of hope; this involves no true embrace of hope. This means that the gospel of hope must be allowed to inform public life, as well as private life, and to heal the division between the two. The gospel reveals both public ideology and private narcissism in the light of a hope, which is at once public and personal. In so doing, on the one hand, it checks the excessive investment of hope in progressive public ideology, setting the methods and goals of its programmes (e.g. technological advance, economic rationalisation, civilisation through programmes of education and legislation) in the context of the vision of human flourishing under God. What can be achieved by these methods is of real but qualified value, and this will be acknowledged by pursuing them in the 'good-enough' form, which best serves human good without ascribing to them power of salvation. On the other hand, the Gospel affirms hope for those ,who find themselves marginalised, devalued or alienated by the implementation of public ideology – among whom, according to the foregoing analysis, a large section of the population belong in general ways.

What practices will find their place in such mission? What current practices invite special commendation? Let me make four suggestions.

Authentic spirituality. As we saw earlier, Gabriel Marcel discerns that, today, the refusal to believe takes the form commonly of inattention or distraction, which is encouraged, indeed almost enforced, by modern life. He goes on: 'the inattentive man may be awakened just by meeting someone who radiates genuine faith – which, like a light, transfigures the creature in whom it dwells. I am', he wrote, 'one of those who attach an inestimable value to personal encounters. They are a spiritual fact of the highest importance, though unrecognised by traditional philosophy.'[34]

Godly personal presence liberates hope: it breaks the spell of inattention and distraction. It frees us to attend fully with hope towards the real; it frees us to love what is real, rather than to live bound by illusions of fear and desire. It opens up a space to inhabit in this freedom, a space illumined with hope, amidst all its limitations and ambiguities of creation.

Hospitality. Such space is hosted ultimately by God. It is God's hospitality, which God's people offer, by his grace. And it is for all: God's hospitality is public hospitality. The church is called to model public space, which is open to all and rooted in, and nourished by, God. In our time, such hospitality may be experienced in a special way, through residential events and residential communities, where people find the whole of daily life framed by faith. Examples are places of pilgrimage, such as Taize and Iona; retreat events, including those which combine prayer with artistic

[34] Marcel, 'Some Thoughts on Faith', 212.

endeavour; the Cursillo movement; and large Christian festivals ranging from Greenbelt and Soul Survivor to the German Kirchentag. Such events and settings can be beacons of hope for those living in the exile of a culture, which colludes with a spirit of hopelessness – and they can be signs of a deeper and more hopeful belonging. Also, hospitality speaks eloquently of hope, when it is extended to those 'homeless,' in one way or another: those needing nursing care, the dying, the unborn child, the child unsafe at home, the refugee, the scapegoat.

Participation. Such hospitality, when it is offered in the name of God, treats people, not merely as consumers, but as dignified participants. It beckons people into liberation from the spell of narcissistic self-absorption, as they entrust themselves towards a purpose beyond themselves inviting responsible personal exploration and stable commitment in costly self-giving service. The invitation to participate in life inspired by hope in God reflects God's hope in the one invited, and itself inspires hope within that person. A special role is played here by voluntary service projects with goals such as social, health or environmental ones.

Prophecy. While commitment to routine acts of service may witness powerfully to hope in God, such witness also calls for prophecy. Faithful service points to the hope offered by a faithful God; prophetic acts point to the hope offered by God, in his sovereign freedom, in quite new ways. They liberate by opening eyes and breaking spells, awakening that wondering attention towards the new, which lies at the heart of radical hope. Prophetic acts range from small but potently disturbing counter-cultural gestures to weighty acts of self-sacrifice.

There will be many other practices than these, which will find their place in mission bearing the gospel of hope. One vital touchstone, for such mission, however, will always be a faithful theological understanding of radical hope, united with discernment towards a postmodern culture, marked with the wounds of hopelessness.

Mission to Primal Religious Groups in a Postmodern Context

John Hitchen

Introduction

This paper considers the significance of primal religious beliefs and concepts, and groups who adhere to them, within the task of mission in our postmodern context, at the beginning of the twenty-first century.

The 1910 Conference Legacy: Within the Edinburgh 1910 World Missionary Conference's overall purpose of considering 'missionary problems in relation to the non-Christian World',[1] Commission IV focussed on 'The Missionary message in Relation to Non-Christian religions'. 'Animistic Religions' were included: twenty-five of the one hundred and eighty-five responses to Commission IV's fact-finding questionnaire came from missionaries working amongst 'animistic' peoples. The 'Animistic Religions' chapter of Commission IV's Report definitively summarized the challenge of mission amongst such groups for the ensuing century.[2] The Report reflected the respondents' varying perspectives, and imposed an integrative emphasis compatible with the preferred missionary strategy recommended for other world religions, leaving ample material for continuing academic discussion and debate.[3] This debate most recently

---

[1] The title pages of the official preparatory Conference Report Volumes were headed, "World Missionary Conference, 1910 (To consider Missionary Problems in relation to the non-Christian World)"; see *Report of Commission IV, The Missionary Message in relation to Non-Christian Religions* (Edinburgh & London: Oliphant, Anderson & Ferrier, 1910), V.
Conference, 1910 (To consider Missionary Problems in relation to the non-Christian World)"; see, e.g., *Report of Commission IV, The Missionary Message in relation to Non-Christian Religions* (Edinburgh & London: Oliphant, Anderson & Ferrier, 1910), V.

[2] *Report of Commission IV*, 6-37. See summary below.

[3] See, J. Stanley Friesen, *Missionary Responses to Tribal Religions at Edinburgh, 1910* (New York: Peter Lang, 1996), who identifies five different models for approaches to primal religions in the Responses to Commission IV: a German Lutheran Continuity and Change model; a religion as Moral foundation for Society model; a Religion as foundation for Ethics model; a dialectical radical rejection and fulfilment model; and a fulfilment through affirmation of human nature model. Cf., Brian Stanley, *The World Missionary Conference, Edinburgh 1910*, (Grand Rapids,

assesses the gem-studded 1910 material from the perspective of postmodern or post-colonial discourse.[4]

Johannes Warneck, the great German mission administrator and theorist, concluded Conference discussion of Commission IV's Report, on Saturday 18 June 1910, thus:

> It is of great importance for all missionaries among the different animistic nations to observe carefully which part of the Gospel is the most needed there, and that should be emphasised first in our preaching. Therefore, we require a careful study of the heathen mind and of the effect of the Gospel on that mind. It is my conviction that Christ is not only the Saviour for all mankind, but that He has a special gift or blessing too for each nation according to its special wants and needs. And so, if we consider the effects of the Gospel on the different heathen peoples, we see with astonishment and joy that Christ grows greater and greater, and all kinds of men [sic] find in Him what they need and seek.[5]

This 1910 three-fold anticipation of what we now call 'contextualization', of 'postmodern' insights on the distinctiveness of each cultural 'Other', and of awareness that cross-cultural communication of the Gospel can expand our knowledge of Christ, sets a helpful foundation for our discussion.

Postmodernity's Gift and Challenge to Primal Religious Peoples[6]

By confronting modernity's presuppositions and priorities, postmodernity has contributed significantly to the context, within which a resurgence of primal or indigenous consciousness has been possible, in the final quarter of the twentieth century. In this sense, postmodernity has been a gift to primal societies facilitating their voice on the global stage. A resurgence of awareness amongst primal societies is incontestably evident across the African continent; amongst First Nation peoples of North America; tribal peoples in South America; in Polynesia, Melanesia, Micronesia and

---

MI: Eerdmans, 2009), 235-45, who finds Friesen's analysis "unpersuasive"(p. 240), and emphasises the ways in which the differing responses can be used to illustrate differences being espoused by different contributors to post-colonial critique of Western studies on African 'religion' during the twentieth century, while at the same time showing how the Edinburgh 1910 Responses question assumptions commonly held by post-colonial writers.

[4] Brian Stanley, *The World Missionary Conference, Edinburgh 1910*, 240-45.

[5] World Missionary Conference, 1910, *Report of Commission IV: The Missionary Message in relation to Non-Christian Religions* (Edinburgh & London: Oliphant, Anderson & Ferrier), 300-01.

[6] This paper does not attempt to give a definitive description of the nature and features of postmodernity or postmodernism. We expect other papers in this volume will do that. As a working basis we are assuming definitions such as those of Stanley Grenz, *A Primer on Postmodernism* (Grand Rapids, MI: Eerdmans, 1996), 12.

Australasia; among those Andrew Walls calls the "Himalayan-Arakan" peoples spanning the South East Asian boundaries of Nepal, India, China, Myanmar, Thailand and the Malay Peninsula;[7] and amongst the migrant and tribal peoples of Europe and mainland Asia.[8] As we shall see, how to explain this resurgence is hotly debated, but its reality as a postmodern phenomenon cannot be ignored.

Aspects of postmodernity's contribution to the resurgence of primal consciousness

At least the following features of postmodernity contributed to this new awareness of primal beliefs and values:

Postmodernity rejects the hegemony of any particular 'metanarrative' applying to all peoples and welcomes instead plurality and diversity of perspective and viewpoint.[9] Insofar as modernity's commitment to the meta-narratives of rationalism and the "Enlightenment project" muted the expression of alternative explanatory myths from a primal perspective,

---

[7] Andrew F. Walls, 'Commission One and the Church's Transforming Century,' David A. Kerr and Kenneth R. Ross (eds.) *Edinburgh 2010: Mission Then and Now* (Oxford: Regnum, 2009), 34.

[8] Descriptions of such resurgences abound: Kolig, describes the New Zealand Maori movement:

'While perhaps no more than twenty years ago it seemed as if Maori 'traditional' culture, or any resembling form of it, was inexorably sliding towards its ultimate, inevitable disappearance, it has bounced back thanks to concerted efforts by leading Maori, and perhaps also by some Pakeha [whites of European extraction]. The ceremonious congregation on the *marae* [tribal meeting ground], *iwi* (tribal) structure and leadership, language and spiritual traditions have been reinvigorated and play an increasing role in the lives of those people who wish to emphasise a Maori identity. ... Maori renaissance is tantamount to a mobilisation of indigenous culture as a 'strategic resource' in political programmes. Such programmes are aimed at achieving a number of objectives such as an economic betterment, political empowerment ... cultural prestige and recognition, strengthening of ethnic pride and cohesion so as to offer a more effective front towards the majority of Pakeha.' (Erich Kolig, 'From a "madonna in a condom" to "claiming the airwaves": The Maori cultural renaissance and biculturalism in New Zealand,' in Meijl, Toon van, and Jelle Miedema (eds.) *Shifting Images of Identity in the Pacific,* Leiden: KITLV Press, 2004),146-7.

[9] As Stanley Grenz summarizes it: 'The postmodern outlook entails the end of the appeal to any central legitimating myth whatsoever. Not only have all the reigning master narratives lost their credibility, but the idea of a grand narrative is itself no longer credible. We have not only become aware of a plurality of conflicting legitimating stories but have moved into the age of the demise of metanarrative. ... Consequently the postmodern outlook demands an attack on any claim to universality – it demands, in fact, a "war on totality"'. Grenz, *A Primer* 45, citing Jean Francois Lyotard, *The Postmodern Conditio,8* Minneapolis: MN: University of Minnesota Press, 1984), 82.

postmodernity has broken that previous hegemony and opened the arena for fresh primal input.

As a consequence of this, 'Postmodernism has been particularly important in acknowledging "the multiple forms of otherness as they emerge from differences in subjectivity, gender and sexuality, race and class, temporal… and spatial geographic locations and dislocations"'[10] The welcome for diversity in the postmodern intellectual climate invites those marginalized by modernity's criteria to now step forward, speak up and expect to be afforded the same dignity as others.

Postmodernity's re-evaluation invites fresh consideration of concepts and ideas previously relegated to the periphery, downplayed or devalued by modernity's priorities. Even beliefs and values, contradicted or apparently disposed of by modernity's ruling narratives, may now be re-considered. In each of these cases, the characteristics of a primal consciousness (as we shall see in our next section) have something fresh to bring to the discussions.

Postmodernity's focus, the concerns of a primal consciousness, of the indigenous resurgence and of Christian mission, all coalesce around the issue of cultural identity. As anthropologists, like Simon Harrison, point out, 'increasing trans-national flows of culture seem to be producing, not global homogenization, but growing assertions of heterogeneity and local distinctiveness'.[11] This, in turn, means that 'communities may often mobilize themselves by representing themselves as having clear boundaries which are *endangered* – as having essential qualities … or distinctive ways of life, which are under threat from the outside'.[12] Representations of such perceived threats, according to Harrison, can either see cultural boundaries being 'polluted' by the intrusion of foreign cultural forms; or see the threat coming from foreign misappropriation, 'piracy', of their local cultural forms.[13] The common assumption is that cultural identity can only be retained if the assumed cultural boundary is protected from erosion. This cultural identity issue has long been a factor in the response of primal religions to the Gospel. Harold Turner classified new religious movements in primal societies according to their response to the Christian Gospel by grouping them along a continuum from 'Neo-primal', to 'Synthetist', to

[10] David Harvey, *The Condition of Postmodernity: An Inquiry into the Origins of Cultural Change* (Oxford: Blackwell, 1990), 112, citing A. Huyssens, 'Mapping the Postmodern,' *New German Critique,* Vol. 33, 1984:50.

[11] Simon Harrison, 'Cultural Boundaries', *Anthropology Today*, Vol. 15(5), Oct 1999:10.

[12] Harrison, 'Cultural Boundaries': 10, citing A.P. Cohen, *The Symbolic Construction of Community* (London: Tavistock, 1985), 109. Italics in original.

[13] Harrison, 'Cultural Boundaries', 10-11.

'Hebraist', to 'Independent Church'.[14] Concerns over cultural identity 'pollution' or 'piracy' are important motives in movements at the 'Neo-primal' end of the continuum, whereas claims to a renewed, transformed or fulfilled cultural identity predominate at the 'Independent Church' end. Missiological discussion of 'bounded' and 'open' sets provides a further framework for considering these identity questions.[15] Our point is that postmodernity has significantly opened up this intellectual context for articulating the identity issues and, thereby, drawn fresh attention to primal perceptions of these concerns.

In at least these ways, then, the resurgence of primal religious consciousness and indigenous resurgence globally, in the late twentieth century, can be related to trends and drivers stimulated by Postmodernity.

Aspects of postmodernity's challenge to a primal consciousness

This positive contribution by postmodernity is counter-balanced, however, by challenges postmodern emphases bring to a primal consciousness.

Postmodernity's discourse on primal societies can easily become an idealised discussion of a romantic view divorced from the tensions many primal societies face. Using the Maori within New Zealand society as an example, the social anthropologist, Steven Webster, suggests a 'contradictory and ideological relationship between prevailing definitions of Maori culture and the realities of Maori society has developed historically… it has been brought to a head by postmodernist interests in Maori culture.' [16] Commenting from a socialist perspective, Webster warns, 'Maori culture must not be seen abstractly in the Romantic tradition as a "whole way of life" somehow unique, integral, harmonious and Other than that supposedly led by European societies [in New Zealand].' Rather, 'it must be grasped concretely as *a whole way of struggle* inextricably bound up with a particular colonial history.'[17]. Likewise, Erich Kolig speaks of the 'ideal as well as imaginary and highly fictitious scenario" that credits New Zealand with "an international reputation of tranquil, even peaceful, race relations, exemplary protection of indigenous rights, complete religious

---

[14] Harold W. Turner, 'New Religious Movements in Primal Societies', John R. Hinnells (ed.) *A New Handbook of Living Religions (*London: Penguin 1997), 581-593.

[15] See, e.g., Paul G. Hiebert, 'The Category *Christian* in the Mission Task', *Anthropological Reflections on Missiological Issues* (Grand Rapids, MI: Baker Books, 1994), 107-136; and, Michael W. Payne, 'Mission and Global Ethnic Violence', *Transformation*, Vol. 19(3), July 2002, 206-216.

[16] Steven Webster, 'Postmodernist Theory and the Sublimation of Maori Culture', *Oceania* Vol. 63 (3), 1993, 226

[17] Webster, 'Postmodernist Theory'.

freedom, and social and legal egalitarianism'.[18] Webster and Kolig both warn against the danger in postmodern discussion of idealizing a view of the indigenous reality on ideological grounds, or for the sake of a postmodern 'political correctness'. Many, if not most, of such primal ethnic groups seeking to make their mark in a globalised postmodern world, grapple with serious contradictions, both in applying their traditional cultural values in their very different Westernised settings, and in the ongoing 'way of struggle' resulting from pressures and long-standing inequities in relationships with the dominant culture, as Webster highlighted. If postmodern theorising is unable to account for and address these conflicting realities, then it is inappropriate. But with no recourse to explanatory meta-narratives to account for both evil and good in the same humans and their societies, postmodern theory can easily damn, with faint praise, the cultures they want to idealise or at least treat as equals. Postmodernity's inability to offer solid hope to answer the darker side of the primal societies' daily realities, invites an alternative missional evaluation and prognosis from those with a Gospel grounded in a biblical realism about the human predicament.

Postmodern thought presents a further threat by treating primal voices as just one more view in a diverse range, all of equal significance. Rex Ahdar illustrates this problem in his paper dealing with ways the New Zealand legal system has handled the renewed interest in Maori spirituality.[19] For Ahdar, 'New Zealanders' reactions to Maori spirituality and its official fostering and recognition have been mixed, ranging from hostility and ridicule, at one end of the spectrum, to warm acceptance at the other.' He identifies 'at least five distinctive views, three of which are critical and two that are sympathetic and supportive…'[20] Ahdar classifies these varying views as those of 'Secular Rationalists', 'Egalitarian Liberals', 'Conservative Theists', 'Liberal Theists', and 'Affirmative Action Liberals'. Ahdar points out that this renewed, albeit varied, focus on Maori culture and spirituality only came to fruition in a wider context of 'such diverse ideological streams as postmodernism, anti-colonialism, post-colonial guilt feelings and fascination with New Age values'.[21]

Our point is that such a climate is inherently contradictory: while supporting respect for resurgent Maori spirituality, the postmodern commitment to equal validity for all viewpoints provides no adequate basis

---

[18] Erich Kolig, 'From a "madonna in a condom" to "claiming the airwaves": The Maori cultural renaissance and biculturalism in New Zealand,' in Meijl, Toon van, and Jelle Miedema (eds.) *Shifting Images of Identity in the Pacific* (Leiden: KITLV Press, 2004), 135.

[19] Rex Ahdar, 'Indigenous Spiritual Concerns and the Secular State: Some New Zealand Developments,' *Oxford Journal of Legal Studies*, Vol. 23(4), 2003, 611-637.

[20] Ahdar, 'Indigenous Spiritual Concerns', 623.

[21] Ahdar, 'Indigenous Spiritual Concerns', 631.

for judging between them or resolving their contradictions. Ahdar tersely sums up, from the legal perspective, the inherent clashes of belief systems, worldviews and practical administrative difficulties encountered, when a secular state attempts to publicly recognise such a primal religious consciousness: 'It is the sort of messy, ad hoc, postmodern situation that has something in it to offend almost everyone'.[22] This is hardly the level of public support committed adherents of Maori spirituality desire, but postmodernism's presuppositions require just such a downplaying of any wholistic integration of life around a spiritual centre, despite claiming to respect and honour those views.

Probably the most serious challenge to a primal consciousness comes from postmodernism's emphasis on constructivism and the way it can be, and has been, used to explain, or explain away, the whole primal religious 'renaissance'. We shall again refer to Maori as our example. The fact of Maori cultural 'reinvigoration' is undeniable. How to understand it is controversial. In late 1989, the recognised Pacific anthropologist, Allan Hanson, published in *American Anthropologist* an article, 'The Making of the Maori: Culture Invention and its Logic'.[23] His abstract begins, ''Traditional culture'' is increasingly recognised to be more an invention constructed for contemporary purposes than a stable heritage handed on from the past. Anthropologists often participate in the creative process...' Hanson's fellow American Social Anthropologist, Steve Webster, analyses and explains the furore this article occasioned amongst New Zealand academics.[24] Webster sees Hanson's position as the natural flowering of modernist symbolic, meanings-based (semiological) anthropology into a fully fledged postmodern understanding: 'Hanson argues that the construction of cultures is not essentially different from the development of linguistic meanings, a process of (in Derrida's terms) 'sign-substitution in a play of signification.''[25] Again, Webster explains, 'Hanson addresses the dilemma of how anthropologists can be taken seriously if there are no clear criteria by which an account of culture can be assessed as more or less authentic, and if, furthermore, anthropologists are active participants in the "invention" of culture.' Hanson suggested that focusing on cultural authenticity in terms of a 'primordial culture' or 'historically fixed tradition,' in Derrida's postmodern categories, was a form of 'metaphysics of presence,' 'logocentrism' or 'nostalgia'. 'Cultural authenticity,' from this postmodern perspective, can mean no more than that the bearers of the culture claim it as their heritage.[26] Webster goes on to contrast positions

---

[22] Ahdar, 'Indigenous Spiritual Concerns', 636.

[23] A Hanson, 'The Making of the Maori: Culture Invention and its Logic,' *American Anthropologist,* Vol. 91,(1989), 890-902.

[24] S Webster, 'Postmodernist theory and the sublimation of Maori culture,' *Oceania,* Vol. 63, (3) 1993, 222-239.

[25] Webster, 'Postmodernist theory', 229.

[26] Webster, 'Postmodernist theory', 230.

taken by other New Zealand academics in response to Hanson's article, distinguishing between those retaining a concrete historical and political approach with those espousing modern 'meanings-based' or semiological views. For Webster, the latter face the same philosophical problems as Hanson's more consistently postmodern approach.[27] We need not pursue the ongoing debate.

Our point is that if, as a postmodern position suggests, there are no criteria for evaluating the validity of claims to have 'revived' or 're-invigorated' a 'traditional culture', and if pragmatic present-day political, socio-economic or prestige concerns really motivate cultural renewal or 'invention', then the so-called 'renaissance' is on shaky ground indeed. Nor is this simply a Maori cultural issue. To cite just two examples from a growing international list of materials: In his assessment of Australian Aboriginal claims to a cultural renaissance, while couching much of his argument around a questioning of the semantic validity of the word 'renaissance' for what has been happening in Australia, Kenneth Maddock comes to similar conclusions to Hanson as he evaluates 'modern constructions' amongst Aboriginals. Maddock gathers historical data for the loss of Aboriginal culture from neglected mid-twentieth century anthropologists to throw doubt on the historical continuity of cultural traditions at the heart of contemporary Aboriginal claims.[28] Or again, in his careful study of the Zulu Shaman, Credo Mutwa, David Chidester presents careful documentation to support his claims that significant 'invention' of traditional ritual and 'appropriation of authenticity' has been occurring in the shaping of at least one present-day African folk religion.[29]

Postmodernity, then, proves an ambivalent friend of the primal religious consciousness. The reality of the move beyond modernity's hegemony over intellectual discussions to a more open, respectful and welcoming public

---

[27] Webster, 'Postmodernist theory', 231-4. Webster's discussion raises the probability that Christians confronting some postmodern philosophical positions may find in continuing Marxist theorists, like Webster, if not allies, then at least co-belligerents!

[28] Kenneth Maddock, 'Revival, renaissance and the meaning of modern constructions in Australia,' in Erich Kolig and Hermann Muckler (eds.) *Politics of Indigeneity in the South Pacific: Recent Problems of Identity in the Pacific (*Novara Bd 1: Munster: Lit, 2002), 25-46. Cf., Erich Kolig's careful documentation and argumentation regarding the 'traditional validity' of testimonial evidence used in the "construction of indigeneity" in the 'women's business' aspects of the 'Hindmarsh Island Case', in his, 'Legitimising Belief: Identity Politics, Utility, Strategies of Concealment, and Rationalisation in Australian Aboriginal Religion,' *Australian Journal of Anthropology*, Vol. 14 (2), 2003, 209-228.

[29] David Chidester, 'Credo Mutwa, Zulu Shaman: The Invention and Appropriation of Indigenous Authenticity in African Folk Religion,' Chidester, David, Abdulkader Tayob and Wolfram Weisse (eds.) *Religion, Politics and Identity in a Changing South Africa* (Religion and Society in Transition, v.6: Munster: Waxmann: 2004), 69-88.

space with room for primal perspectives, is a real gift for primal societies. But the 'often unacknowledged'[30] alternative metanarrative of postmodernism, which threatens to become a new hegemony, leaves any primal viewpoint vulnerable in these new debates.

Developing Missiological Appreciation of the 'Primal Imagination'

Our next step is to clarify the leading features of the 'primal imagination' or 'primal consciousness' about which we are speaking. We look first at two snapshots: one from Edinburgh 1910, the second from the twentieth century doyen of the study of primal religious movements, Harold W. Turner.

'Animism' at Edinburgh 1910

The Edinburgh 1910 Commission IV Report's chapter on 'Animistic Religions' set a benchmark for understanding primal religions at the beginning of the twentieth century. The Report addressed the features of Animism under the headings set by the pre-Conference Questionnaire sent to missionaries.

The Report began with two definitions of animism, reflecting the best of current anthropological and missionary theorists' thinking, from Edward Burnett Tylor and Johannes Warneck respectively.[31] Under the subheading, "The Religious Value of Animism"[32] the Report summarised the nature of the sprits (souls, anima, life force) at the centre of animism as, capricious, needing to be placated, able, in the form of ancestor spirits, to either bless or punish the living, to cause sickness and possess or bewitch humans. Animism is based on traditions passed down from the ancestor and embodied in rituals, sorcery and witchcraft, which engender fear that ensnares and debilitates the living. The only consolation, Animism offers its adherents, is a sense that, if properly appeased, the spirits may have

[30] Webster, 'Postmodernist theory', 223.

[31] *Report of Commission IV,* 1910:6. Citing Edward Burnett Tylor, the recognised academic authority of the day, 'The theory of Animism divides into two great dogmas; first, concerning souls of individual creatures, capable of continued existence after the death or destruction of the body; second, concerning other spirits, upward to the rank of powerful deities', *Primitive Culture: Researches into the Development of Mythology, Philosophy, Religion, Language, Art and Custom*, 2 Vols., (London: John Murray, 1871, Vol. 1), 426; and Johannes Warneck, leading Continental missionary thinker, 'Animism is a form of paganism based on the worship of souls. Men, animals and plants are supposed to have souls; and their worship, as well as that of deceased spirits, especially ancestral spirits, is the essence of a religion which probably is a factor in all heathen religions,' *The Living Forces of the Gospel.*

[32] *Report of Commission IV,* 1910: 7-12

friendly intentions towards them. Fears and ritual observances may restrain anti-social or violent behaviour towards other kin and taboos can protect property and crops.

Under the section headed 'Points of Contact between Christianity and Animism,' [33] the Report expanded these basic ideas, referring to: the widespread belief in the existence of a Higher Power or Supreme Being – now thought of as the distant Creator; belief in an afterlife – even immortality of soul; the dead can bless or harm the living; the idea and practice of sacrifice seen as a preparation for Christian teaching; in some cases there is a rudimentary moral sense and dim consciousness of sin; and the concept and use of prayer – occasionally to the chief Spirit – were all noted as helpful points of contact.

Assessing the 'Appeal of the Gospel' to Animists, [34] the respondents' consensus listed theological insights, which appealed to the animist, such as: God as a loving, all-powerful Father, a Living God, personal and accessible; redemption by Christ, especially as deliverance from evil powers; hope of everlasting life; and the impartial justice, kindness, adherence to truth, brotherhood and works of love characteristic of Christian life. The evidence suggested different aspects of the Gospel appealed more directly amongst different peoples as effective starting points for appreciating the Good News. Some require clarification of Old Testament ideas before Christ's death is explained – others responded quickly to God's love in Christ. Occasional mention was made of dreams, answers to prayer, confessions, Christian sacraments, preaching of the sinfulness of sin, regeneration, forgiving those who sin against us, fear of the law, and the promise of deliverance from evil habits and propensities. Aspects of the Gospel arousing opposition included: high moral standards; confronting local custom regarding status of women, or individual responsibility over against tribal loyalty, etc. The idea of the resurrection of the body proved incomprehensible for some.

The Report called for missionaries working amongst Animists to cultivate three basic attitudes: '...study and get to know the native religion. ... strive to understand the native conception of things and the heathen method of thinking'; 'The whole attitude of the missionary should at all times be marked by sympathy'; 'The missionary should look for the element of good [in the animist's religion], should foster it, and build upon it, gently leading on to the full truth. ... In all his labours, however, the missionary must never attempt to combine Animism and Christianity. A syncretism is impossible.'[35]

These features of the missiological understanding and approach to animistic thought, in 1910, accurately reflect the prevailing understanding

[33] *Report of Commission IV,* 1910: 24-28.
[34] *Report of Commission IV,* 1910: 28-33.
[35] *Report of Commission IV,* 1910: 19-24.

of comparative religion and are in line with the cotemporary European academic orthodoxy on such matters.[36] In 1910, missionary contributions to ethnography, as primary data collectors, were at a high point, and the developing study of anthropology drew heavily on missionary sources for its data.[37] The Report also points in a particular direction, encouraging ongoing study, greater empathy and constructive interaction, all on the basis of clear convictions about the nature of religious truth.

Harold W. Turner's six-feature analysis of primal religions

For a more recent assessment of the primal imagination, we have chosen Harold W. Turner.[38] We do so with respect for the depth of his scholarship, and in recognition of the respect given this New Zealand missionary theologian, and trailblazer of the study of primal religions as a university subject in West Africa and Great Britain, by leading African scholars, such as the late Kwame Bediako. Bediako uses the same article we have chosen by Turner, as the foundation for his own summary of primal religion, in his influential, *Christianity in Africa: The Renewal of a Non-Western Religion.*[39]

In his 1977 article, 'The Primal Religions of the World & Their Study',[40] Turner first explains his preferred terminology. On the grounds that 'One of the first principles in religious studies is that the terms used should, if at all possible, be acceptable to the people described by them', Turner shows that many terms for describing this kind of religion, like 'tribal', 'animist',

---

[36] See, for example the then Reader in Social Anthropology at Oxford University, R.R. Marrett's chapter, 'Anthropology (Social and Religious)', pp. 125-132, which includes coverage of Animism, in one of the first publications to come out of the Edinburgh 1910 follow-up process: H.U. Weitbrecht, (ed.) *A Bibliography for Missionary Students* (London: Board of Study for Preparation of Missionaries, and Oliphant, Anderson & Ferrier, 1913).

[37] See, John M. Hitchen, 'Relations between Missiology and Anthropology Then and Now – Insights from the Contribution to Ethnography and Anthropology by Nineteenth Century Missionaries in the South Pacific', *Missiology*, Vol. 30(4), October 2002, 455-478.

[38] For biographical details on H.W. Turner, see, J.M.Hitchen, 'Harold W. Turner Remembered', *International Bulletin of Missionary Research,* Vol. 26(3), July 2002, 112-3.

[39] Kwame Bediako, *Christianity in Africa: The Renewal of a Non-Western Religion* (Edinburgh & Maryknoll, NY: Edinburgh University Press & Orbis Books, 1995), 93-96. One should also confess, that as a fellow post-graduate student with Kwame studying under Andrew Walls and Harold Turner at the University of Aberdeen in the late 1970s and early 1980s I share Kwame's deep admiration for Turner's work which deserves to be better known in contemporary mission circles.

[40] Harold W. Turner, 'The Primal Religions of the World & Their Study', Victor C.Hayes (ed.) *Australian Essays in World Religions* (AASR: Bedford Park, South Australia, 1977), 27-37.

'ethnic', 'pre-literate', or 'traditional', have become unacceptable, inaccurate, and not universally applicable. He, therefore, proposes 'primal' as the preferred term as the most satisfactory:

> Here [the term primal] conveys two ideas: that these religious systems are in fact the most basic or fundamental religious forms in the overall religious history of mankind, and that they have preceded and contributed to the other great religious systems, ... they are both primary and prior; they represent a common religious heritage of humanity. [41]

We use 'primal' as our preferred term. Turner next offers 'a six-feature framework to assist in the analysis and understanding of these religions.'[42]

Primal religions acknowledge kinship with nature

In primal thought, there is 'a profound sense … that [a human] is akin to nature, a child of Mother Earth and brother to the plants and animals which have their own spiritual existence and place in the universe.' This 'ecological aspect' means plants and animals may have a totemic relationship with humans, they may become tutelary or guardian spirits, and thus the whole environment is to be 'used realistically and unsentimentally, but with profound respect and reverence and without exploitation.'[43]

Primal religions accept human weakness

'There is the deep sense that [a human] is finite, weak and impure or sinful and stands in need of a power not his own. … This sense in primal peoples is no mere reflection of their lack of technological, economic and political power, which was painfully real; rather it is an authentic religious sensibility coupled with a realistic assessment of [a hu]man's condition.'[44]

Primal religions recognize humans are not alone

Humans are 'not alone in the universe for there is a spiritual world of powers or beings more powerful and ultimate' than themselves. 'Primal peoples live in a personalized universe, where there is a will behind

---

[41] Turner, Primal Religions, 28. We note that the term does not make a judgement on the historic pattern of development of religions. It does not assume either an evolutionary development from polytheistic to monotheistic religions, nor a degeneration moving in the opposite direction, the term leaves that set of issues to be addressed on other grounds. It simply is making the statement that in the historic interaction of religious systems the other major world religions each came to, or arose in, a setting where primal systems were in fact already present.

[42] Turner, Primal Religions, 28.

[43] Turner, Primal Religions, 30.

[44] Turner, Primal Religions, 31.

events…' These unpredictable powers belong to another, transcendent dimension surpassing the human realm, and some form a benevolent hierarchy of ancestors, spirits, divinities and high gods. But there is also a variety of evil spirits, demons, malevolent divinities and, 'lesser more earth-born occult powers of wizards and witches.' Even the benevolent divinities are ambivalent and 'may prove hostile'. 'But behind all the terrors of the evil spirit world, there is the still greater comfort that men [sic] are not left alone in this mysterious universe and without direction, for there is the world of the gods and these provide the meaning and the model for all human needs and activities.'[45]

Primal religions expect relations with transcendent powers

Humans 'can enter into relationship with this benevolent spirit world and so share in its powers and blessings and receive protection from evil forces by these more-than-human helpers.' Thus, they look for a more than merely human religion. There is a yearning for the true quality of life that comes from the spirit world and transcends merely human experience. The gods have given religious specialists, powerful rituals, correct sacrifices and proper customs to lead toward this better life. Primal religions are not merely 'mechanistic and ritualistic'. The 'profound emphasis on the transcendent source of true life and practical salvation' is basic.[46]

Primal religions believe in human afterlife – the 'living dead'

The human relationship with the gods extends beyond human death, 'which is not the end.' The 'shaman figure … has seen into the invisible world and the realm of the dead and brought back word of what lies beyond death. In the majority of these religions, the ancestors, the 'living dead', remain united in affection and in mutual obligations with the 'living living.' Concern for proper relations with recently departed ancestors often becomes so absorbing that other divinities appear to fade into insignificance, and the ancestors' mediatorial role overlooked. The hope continues that the living and dead 'will be reunited and both will share in the immortality of the gods.'[47]

Primal religions respect the physical as sacramental of the spiritual

For primal peoples the 'physical' is the vehicle for 'spiritual' power. The universe is sacramental, in the sense that 'there is no sharp dichotomy between the physical and the spiritual.' This accounts for the carefully

---

[45] Turner, Primal Religions, 31.
[46] Turner, Primal Religions, 31-2.
[47] Turner, Primal Religions, 32.

observed ritual, the sacred objects, fetishes and charms used in divining, healings, magic and witchcraft. Moreover, the physical realm is meant to be patterned on the spiritual – the one is the microcosm, the other the macrocosm. With a common 'set of powers, principles and patterns' running through and unifying earth and heaven into a single cosmic, monistic, system, qualified only by an ethical dualism of good and evil. Primal thought sees the cosmos, then, as a unified and essentially spiritual system.[48]

Turner is careful to highlight the diversity within the range of primal religions sharing these six common features. The balance of emphasis put on the different features also varies considerably, with one or more particular feature apparently or well-nigh absent in some cases. He also notes these are living religions, changing and adapting to external pressures and internal circumstances.[49]

Kwame Bediako's 1995 development of Turner's analysis

Bediako, in his chapter, 'The Primal Imagination and the Opportunity for a New Theological Idiom',[50] develops Turner's analysis in significant ways. He uses Turner's analysis, not only to illustrate the features of primal religions, but also as a summary of the pervasive primal world-view found 'across a wide front from worshippers in a continuing primal religious system to Christian believers,' and, which Bediako, therefore, calls the 'primal imagination'.[51]

Bediako also picks up on Turner's later point that primal religions have a 'special relationship' with Christianity since, 'in the history of the spread of the Christian faith … its major extensions have been solely into the societies with primal religious systems.' Turner had suggested:

> There seems to be affinities between the Christian and the primal traditions, an affinity that perhaps appears in the common reactions when Christian missions first arrive ('this is what we have been waiting for') and that is

---

[48] Turner, Primal Religions, 32.

[49] Turner, Primal Religions, 33-34. One of his summary statements is worth noting: "There is nothing so strange about these developments if we pause to recognize the contemporary Western replacement of religion by magic and the occult or its central activity of material acquisition. It is more understandable in the case of primal societies which live so much on the margins of survival than it is in our modern affluent societies. What is remarkable is the sheer spirituality of the religion of so many primal peoples who might have been expected to have little thought for anything but the next meal." p33

[50] In, Kwame Bediako, *Christianity in Africa: The Renewal of a Non-Western Religion* (Edinburgh & Maryknoll, NY: Edinburgh University Press & Orbis Books, 1995), 91-108.

[51] Bediako, *Christianity in Africa*, 1995, 93.

further evident in the vast range of new religious movements born from the interaction between the primal religions and Christianity...[52]

Bediako expresses surprise Turner did not go further and ask, 'how the primal imagination might bring its own peculiar gifts to the shaping of Christian affirmation?' For Bediako, the clue is found in Turner's final feature – the way primal religions see the physical as sacramental of the spiritual, or, as Bediako frames it – the insight that the cosmos is a unified and essentially spiritual system.[53]

For Bediako, both African and Western Christian scholars have struggled with the primal concept of the multiplicity of spiritual beings inhabiting the cosmos, and have sought a resolution by emphasizing the transcendence of God – and thereby downplaying the multiplicity of other divinities of the primal imagination. But Bediako proposes another approach, building on ideas raised by John V. Taylor, and elaborated by African Francophone theologians, Alexis Kagame and Mulago. Whereas many before him had stressed the African Transcendent God concept as the key to meeting the needs of the primal world, Taylor noted the primal world was much more concerned about *this* life, *this* existence and its cares, and joys. For Bediako, 'both views were correct: only ... there was no dialogue between them.' He then quotes Kagame and Bulago approvingly, when they show that the primal imagination 'has as its two fundamental notions and vital centres, God and man.'[54] Bediako sees in their insight a crucial link with Turner's sixth feature of primal religions:

> ...namely that the primal understanding discloses a universe conceived as a unified cosmic system, essentially spiritual, in which the 'physical' acts as sacrament for 'spiritual' power. In such a universe ... the Transcendent is not a so-called 'spiritual' world separate from the realm of regular human existence, since human existence itself participates in the constant interplay of the divine-human encounter. Consequently, the conclusion of Kagame and Mulago that at the heart of the universe and of religion is a divine-human relationship for the fulfillment of man's divine destiny, constitutes a real advance and lies at the heart of the contribution which African theology from a primal perspective can make to a fresh Christian account of the Transcendent.[55]

Or, again, in the 1977 words of the Ecumenical Association of African Theologians at Accra:

---

[52] Bediako, *Christianity in Africa*, 95-6, citing Turner, Primal Religions, 37.
[53] Bediako, *Christianity in Africa*, 96.
[54] Bediako, *Christianity in Africa*, 97-101, citing John V. Taylor, *The Primal Vision: Christian Presence and African Religion* (London: SCM Press, 1963); Alexis Kagame, 'La place de Dieu et de l'homme dans la religion des Bantu,' *Cahiers des Religions Africaines*, Vol. 3(5), January 1969, 1; and Gwa Cikala M. Mulago, *La Religion Traditionelle des Bantu et leur vision du monde*, Kinshasa: Faculte de Theologie Catholique, 1980, 166.
[55] Bediako, *Christianity in Africa*, 101.

> For Africans there is unity and continuity between the destiny of human persons and the destiny of the cosmos ... The victory of life in the human person is also the victory of life in the cosmos. The salvation of the human person in African theology is the salvation of the universe. In the mystery of the incarnation, Christ assumes the totality of the human and the totality of the cosmos.[56]

For Bediako, then, 'the revelation of God in Christ is the revelation of transcendence'. The incarnation, for the primal imagination, is the unveiling of the nature of the whole universe as 'instinct with the divine presence'. The divine destiny of humans is seen as 'an abiding divine-human relationship'. Although the consummation awaits the end time, 'its reality in present existence must also be allowed,' so we should expect outbreaks of transcendence here and now in visions, prophecies and healings.[57] Thus the primal imagination's contribution to theology includes restoring spirituality to its proper place:

> Because primal world-views are fundamentally religious, the primal imagination restores to theology the crucial dimension of living religiously, for which the theologian needs make no apology. The primal imagination may help us restore the ancient unity of theology and spirituality.[58]

Implications for our postmodern context

Let us briefly note some of the conceptual overlaps between these historic snapshots of the primal imagination and features of our contemporary postmodern intellectual climate:

Our last points from Bediako, as with their roots through Turner, back to Edinburgh 1910, suggest a congruence between the pervasive place of spirituality in the primal imagination and postmodernity's call to reclaim the spirituality lost during modernity's over-weaning dependence on rationality.

Primal religions' concern for experience of transcendence and spiritual power in daily human affairs resonates with postmodernity's call for pragmatic experiential realism;

The primal imagination's unwillingness to separate the sacred and secular parallels postmodernity's wholistic emphases;

As Turner noted, in 1977, the primal 'ecological aspect' links with the ecology movements in the West in postmodernity.

Even a bare list like this highlights the potential for mutually beneficial interaction between those upholding the primal imagination and new generations of thinkers immersed in a postmodern mindset. As Bediako has

---

[56] Bediako, *Christianity in Africa*, 102, quoted in, K.Appiah-Kubi and Sergo Torres (eds.), *African Theology en route* (Maryknoll, NY: Orbis, 1970), 193.
[57] Bediako, *Christianity in Africa*, 102-3.
[58] Bediako, *Christianity in Africa*, 105.

shown, we can expect significant initiatives from the primal religious world into creative thinking on these issues in a postmodern climate.

Towards a Missiological Approach to the Primal Imagination in a Context of Postmodernity

To this point, we have explored aspects of postmodern thought and the primal imagination and their inter-relationship. But we must go further. For comparison, mutual understanding, respect and appreciation are not yet missional involvement, necessary as they may be as preparation and to cultivate ongoing attitudes. We propose two further, more directly missional, steps.

A necessary bridge

We shall turn again to Harold Turner for two components to form a bridge between the analysis, thus far, and the biblical and missiological comments, which conclude our paper.

Turner's call for deep-level mission

Harold Turner made a brief contribution, 'The Three Levels of Mission in New Zealand,' to a 1993 conference, evaluating the evangelistic readiness of the church in his homeland.[59] His paper explained how missionaries relating to a new culture interact with the culture's 'Level l' – surface customs and living habits; the 'Level 2' – social structures and institutions; and the deep 'Level 3' – basic axioms, presuppositions and convictions which drive the culture. Turner called for an approach to mission in Western culture that embraces all three levels of the host culture – in this case, New Zealand culture. He challenged the conferees to realise that until the deep level culture – the worldview and presupposition level – comes under the transforming and renewing impact of the Gospel, the task of mission is still incomplete. In considering mission to primal societies, in a postmodern context, in the twenty-first century, we face the same challenge. But what does such deep mission look like when addressing the primal imagination? What kinds of worldview level change are necessary?

---

[59] Harold W. Turner, 'The Three Levels of Mission in New Zealand', Bruce Patrick (ed.) *The Vision New Zealand Congress* (Auckland, Vision New Zealand, 1993), 61-68.

Turner's analysis of the worldview level transformations necessary in primal societies for gospel penetration

Turner offers a possible answer to these questions in another of his lesser known articles, contributed, in 1985, to a symposium entitled 'God and Global Justice: Religion and Poverty in an Unequal World.' [60] After introducing, explaining and illustrating the nature and potential for socio-economic change of the new religious movements burgeoning in primal societies at that time, Turner has a section headed, 'Cultural Foundations for economic Change: A New Worldview.' He sets out the worldview level changes primal societies would need to embrace for them to contribute to a new level of economic change and development. As he put it, '...changes that lead to adoption of a whole new worldview'.

It would be easy to label such suggestions as a classic example of a Westerner imposing his hegemonic metanarrative upon another society. But from his African experience and global awareness, Turner knew well what Myk Rynkewich has illustrated and documented convincingly: that in our postmodern, globalized world, even in the apparently most geographically isolated, culturally insulated, and traditionally committed of primal societies, like the Trobriand Islands of Papua New Guinea, ideas, especially worldview level religious ideas from the whole world flow quickly and freely with life- and community-changing impact.[61] Therefore, missiologically-minded people, today, know it is not a matter of whether worldview level challenges and changes will come to primal societies, but which challenges, and in what direction will the changes move those societies? Hence Turner's recommendations, rather than being a post-colonial imposition, are critically important. They represent the mature reflections of a person, who had given his life serving primal peoples by studying how new religious movements transform primal societies. He offers a deep level missional insight into ways the Christian Gospel interfaces with the primal imagination, as it transitions into a globalized postmodern context. Turner suggests the worldview changes:

> ... may conveniently be examined in terms of five transitions: (1) from a cosmos based on necessary internal relations to one revealing contingent relationships; (2) from dealing with power through magic and ritual to dependence on science and faith; (3) by the addition of history to myth as a new category for dealing with time; (4) from a society that is closed, unitary, and sacral, to one that is open, pluralist and secular; (5) by seeing evil as

---

[60] Harold W. Turner, 'The Relationship between Development and New Religious Movements in the Tribal Societies of the Third World,' in, Frederick Ferre and Rita H. Mataragnon, *God and Global Justice: Religion and Poverty in an Unequal World* (New York: Paragon House, 1985), 84-110.

[61] Michael A Rynkiewich, 'The World in My Parish: Rethinking the Standard Missiological Model', *Missiology* Vol. 30(3), 2002, 301-321.

involving moral rather than ritual pollution, and as located internally in the individual as well as externally in evil forces.[62]

Let us briefly outline each of these:

From a closed, unitary, sacralized cosmos, to an open, desacralized system with contingent interrelations. For Turner, the primal religious regard for harmony between the earth, plant and animal creation and humans and the spirit world, reflected, 'a particular view of the cosmos as a closed and unitary system, to be regarded as sacral at all points, with nature, man [sic] and the gods each playing their *necessary* parts in maintaining the harmonious functioning of the whole. The keyword here is *necessary*, and the main concern is conservation of the given structures in their fixed interrelationships, including those of the creator to the creation.' That view contrasts with the Semitic view, where 'the Creator remains free and sovereign over the creation,' not constricted by the materials at hand, and 'not compelled to create or play any necessary and fixed part in the world' whether of nature or humans. The divine – human relations are always '*contingent* upon the free will of the [creator] and the free responses of [humanity].' This view desacralizes the natural world and social structures, removing inherent fears of spirit powers, so as to open up the universe for scientific exploration and productive use. 'Nature is no longer left in its chaotic or undeveloped state, but is now a gift to be developed, controlled, and enjoyed' by humans as responsible 'stewards to a God who transcends nature.' This does not mean 'desecration or exploitation of nature, but retains the primal religious reverence for nature on a new basis that establishes [human] freedom over against [the] environment.' In matters relating to land usage, travel, and readiness to adopt new forms of agriculture, or industry, 'there is a new element of contingency, openness and responsibility, replacing the fixities and fatalities of the old cosmology…'[63]

Access to power through science and religious faith instead of magic and religious ritual. Traditional primal societies control the powers of nature and the spirit world by magic or appropriate religious ritual. Magic seeks to 'manipulate power through occult knowledge or skills, or potent objects.' Ritual 'relies on ceremonies, sacrifices, words of power,' the skills of sacred specialists, or 'spirit powers present at sacred places.' The two processes 'tend to coalesce and gravitate toward the magical.' For innovative use or development of tribal resources, a worldview change is needed, involving not just new scientific and technological information, but new moral and social views as well. Likewise, in the spiritual realm, the move will be away from magic and ritual to embrace prayer and faith

[62] Turner, Development & NERMs, 1985: 92

[63] Turner, Development & NERMs, 92-3.

coupled with a new attitude to hard work which takes on religious value as 'vocation'.[64]

The addition of history to myth in dealing with time. Primal societies are 'essentially conservative.' Respect for ancestors means the past regulates and legitimizes the present:

> As for the future, although there might be great changes at one level through wars, conquests, fission, natural disasters, or migrations, at the deeper levels of worldviews and basic social forms and sanctions no changes were desired, much less deliberately planned and worked for.' Security was assured by conserving resources and maintaining past norms, not in planning or working for a better, ampler future on a new model. 'Religion was concerned with the regular renewal of the vitalities of man and nature, but not with their radical extension or transformation.'[65]

> Any eschatology, if present, focussed on a return to origins, or repetition of the patterns of culture heroes and 'maintaining reciprocity with the ancestors' – '"more of the same" rather than any real innovation.' Christian teaching and conversion potentially brings a genuine turn around in this primal view of time. It re-orientates a previously past-focussed community to see the possibilities of purpose in a future focussed life-style. Celebrations take on a new historic rather than merely ritualistic orientation. 'The myth form is still needed to deal with the boundaries of time, but it neither dominates the dealing with history nor is confined to the images of the past – eschatology has a new freedom to deal with the future, ' offering hope and ultimate consummation.[66]

From the closed, unitary, sacral society to the open, plural, secular society. Turner points out that 'in most traditional societies in Africa, the tribe, its rulers, and institutions were set within a sacred cosmic order that formed part of the traditional worldview.' The cosmic order prescribed the social structures and its regulating sanctions, and the leaders 'were important channels through which cosmic spiritual forces operated for [the society's] welfare.' The religious and political leadership were normally closely related in these societies, which could be called 'unitary and sacral or "ontocratic."'[67] Turner shows that while the churches in Africa – both mission and independent – have often continued to entertain, at least for a time, the integration of religious and political leadership by church alignment with particular political parties, the trend, especially in the independent churches, is towards: 'passage from a closed, sacral, and unitary society to a modern secular state and religiously plural society capable of reaching beyond the limitations of clan, tribe and language toward new national entities and new international relationships.' These new social structures, often offer unheard-of opportunities for leadership

---

[64] Turner, Development & NERMs, 94-6.
[65] Turner, Development & NERMs, 96.
[66] Turner, Development & NERMs, 96-7.
[67] Turner, Development & NERMs, 98.

both by women and the young along with a radically different voluntary social form.[68]

Evil involves moral rather than ritual pollution and is located internally as well as externally. Cultures vary considerably in how they understand and where their societies locate responsibility for evil. Turner discusses these issues, particularly as they relate to socio-economic development, but their application is much broader.[69] Primal societies locate the cause of misfortune, sickness or disasters in ritual pollution through breaking taboos or neglecting required sacrifices or ritual obligations. Or they may be attributed to witchcraft or sorcery as retribution for failure in obligations to others or to spirit powers. The source is located in an external process or power – seldom if ever is the person held responsible, and natural or physical causes are not accepted as sufficient explanation. While neither downplaying nor ignoring the reality and influence of evil forces and spiritual powers, a worldview level transformation is needed to recognise personal responsibility – whether at a basic physical level, as in not taking practical hygiene measures, or at the level of moral choice and decision-making. Accepting personal accountability – rather than attributing blame to witchcraft or sorcery or to some spirit power – requires a new understanding of a range of theological and social realities – from the nature of sin and accountability of creatures to their Creator, to relationship with a loving and merciful Heavenly Father. But the witchcraft and sorcery which persists, or even increases, in long-evangelized parts of the primal world highlights the importance of this worldview-level change.

Turner has indicated five crucial worldview changes in direction, each with fundamentally religious factors at their centre, and each needing an appropriate missiological response, to enable the primal imagination adequately to address the contemporary postmodern challenges.

A Biblical Platform for Mission to Primal Religious People in a Postmodern Context

Two particular letters of the Apostle Paul offer a basis for the kind of mission our study has shown is necessary amongst primal religious people, in our postmodern context. The first, the Letter to the Galatians, outlines essential emphases of the Gospel message, as it relates to a primal society. The second, 1 Thessalonians, offers models both for delivering and receiving that Gospel message and for appropriate worldview transformations. We offer these as a tentative, evangelical example of what Gorman calls the "missional hermeneutic" needed in exegesis today – "… a

[68] Turner, Development & NERMs, 99.
[69] Turner, Development & NERMs, 99-101.

decidedly post-colonial approach and for Western practitioners, a post-Christendom approach to mission and biblical interpretation." [70]

Galatians: essential contours of the Gospel message for mission to primal religious people in a postmodern context

Working on the basis that the Galatian churches included, along with many Jewish converts, significant numbers of converts from a primal religious background,[71] the major themes, addressed in this letter, offer an agenda contouring the essential features of the Gospel, as it applies to peoples from such backgrounds. These themes provide the theological foundations for the kind of worldview level transformations we have been considering. These foundations are more secure than those inherent in the postmodern de-constructionists' doubts. The special relevance of the themes of the Galatian letter arises from the letter's central concern to counter the imposition of the rites and requirements of the dominant religious culture of Judaism on the now Christian converts, in the different cultural settings of Galatia. For the Apostle Paul, evidently all the themes addressed are essential for dealing properly with the issues at stake, in such situations of assumed religio-cultural hegemony.

Keeping Loyal to the Apostolic Gospel as Universally Applicable for All Cultures. 1:1-2:10. The first section of the letter upholds the apostolic teaching of the Gospel, as the unique and unchanging standard for every cultural setting. Heeding a distortion of the Gospel too quickly becomes turning away from God's free grace given in Christ. To put some other religious formality, such as circumcision, above gratitude for the love and forgiveness offered in Christ, is a culpable betrayal of Christ's love, and turns a vital personal relationship into a merely formal ritual – an ever-present danger in both primal religious and postmodern contexts. Upholding the apostolic Gospel, as the one and only standard for teaching in every culture, directly challenges postmodern assumptions that meta-narratives are necessarily exploitative. The Apostle insists that imposing a

---

[70] See Michael J. Gorman's chapter, 'Theological Interpretation of Scripture,'(pp.139-166), *Elements of Biblical Exegesis,* Rev. and expanded ed. (Peabody, MA: Hendrickson, 2008), 155.

[71] This section assumes the most likely addressees of the Galatian letter were the young churches of the Roman province of Galatia, the churches established during Paul's first missionary journey as recorded in Acts 13-14, we also take for granted that, as the internal evidence suggests (with its references to ritual, ceremonial and the *stoicheia tou kosmou* [elemental powers of the universe]) a substantial proportion of each of these Galatian churches was from a primal religious background as made explicit in the case of the church at Lystra in Acts 14: 8-20. See the standard commentaries, e.g., F.F. Bruce, *The Epistle to the Galatians : a Commentary on the Greek text* (Exeter; Grand Rapids: Paternoster; Eerdmans, 1982).

single culture's religious rituals is hegemonic and exploitative, not the Gospel meta-narrative. By insisting on the global applicability of the one and only Gospel message, Paul claims that this particular meta-narrative, far from being exploitative, is actually liberating and enriching for every culture, as the themes of the letter will explain progressively.

Welcoming the Justified of all cultures as equally accepted by God & socially welcome in church, 2:11-21. The Judaizing delegation from Jerusalem polarized the Syrian Antioch church ethnically. Even Peter and Barnabas opted to keep the peace and withdrew from fellowshipping with non-Jews, with whom they had previously gladly shared hospitality (2:11-13).[72] For Paul, this threatened Gospel truth (2:14). Refusing to sit at table with another believer because of culturally-based religious rules totally contradicted the message and work of Christ. Only faith in Christ Jesus justified anyone before God (2:15-16). Religious ritual and rule-keeping cannot make us acceptable to God. Therefore, it must be the same for acceptability with each other. We will welcome gladly anyone Christ welcomes. Our social behaviour is a clear test of how adequately we have grasped the essence of the Gospel. This gives dignity and honour to every culture, for peoples of each culture are justified before God in the same way – on the basis of faith alone. The Gospel also provides a unique basis for respecting cultural diversity without hegemonic domination. This is Good News, indeed, for both the global resurgences of indigenous identity and the longings of postmodernity for integrity in communal relationships.

Maintaining through faith both ongoing dependence on the Spirit and sharing in our adoptive heritage, 3:1-18. Having clarified the way justification works through faith and results in the believers' dynamic union with the Living Christ (2:20), Paul goes straight into a strong rebuke lest the Galatians forget or underestimate the role of the Holy Spirit in bringing them to faith and equipping them in every aspect of life and service as Christ's followers (3:1-5). Moreover, one purpose of justification through Christ's redemptive work is that we enjoy the reality of the Holy Spirit sharing in our daily lives (3:10-14). The Galatians' previous primal dependence on capricious and unpredictable spirit powers is transformed into continuing reliance, not on a ritualistic or legalistic self-competence, but on an ongoing relationship with the Holy Spirit of God actively working in response to vital faith in the message of the Gospel (3:1-5). This rich spirituality also answers the postmodern yearning for something more than rational self-competence. Christian spirituality focused on the Holy Spirit is also deeply rooted in human history. The Gospel gives us new faith-ancestors and a new cultural inheritance. By sharing in the faith principle by which Abraham lived, we become his descendants and he our

[72] Andrew Walls sets out the issues succinctly in Andrew F. Walls, *The Cross-Cultural Process in Christian History: Studies in the Transmission and Appropriation of Faith* (Maryknoll, NY: Orbis Books, 2002), 77-78.

'father'. Believers receive roots and rights making us heirs of the Christian-Jewish-Hebrew past, and we also share in and anticipate the blessings and culmination of the promises God made to Abraham and confirmed repeatedly through the salvation history of his heirs.[73] The fulfilment of true spirituality, found in the Holy Spirit, is sustained by the depth of historical adoptive roots and identity together with a reorientation towards a forward looking and hope-filled future.

Respecting the local cultural and religious heritage, 3:19-4:11. The Gospel created a major problem for Jews by offering a way to be true children of Abraham that was not based on the Mosaic Law they were meticulously observing. 'What, then, was the purpose of the Law?'(v19). How should they regard this central aspect of their cultural heritage? Paul replied: the Law defines the depth and seriousness of our sin-problem as an instructor, and prepares God's people for their Messiah as a protective custodian. These instructive and protective roles were vital, though limited: Jews knew all too well that Law cannot, in itself, give new life. But what about those of other cultures in the Galatian churches? Their religious heritage and philosophy focused on elemental spirit beliefs about unseen forces active in every realm of daily life – the feared elemental spirit powers of wind, fire, earth and water. Paul ascribes to these traditional religious beliefs the same kind of protective and preparatory role for non-Jews as the Law fulfilled for the Jews. For their followers, primal religions restrain evil, confirm human sinfulness and show how much a divine initiative is needed for ultimate human welfare (4:1-3). In these respects, at least, the Apostle recognises a positive role for pre-Christian cultural values. We are to understand, appreciate and respect the preparatory role of, and recognise the quest inherent within, the traditional religion even as we present Christ as the Fulfiller of the 'desires of the nations'. As Kenneth Cragg puts it: 'Christianity cannot address men [sic] and ignore their gods: it may not act in the present and disown the past ... in seeking men for Christ's sake, it is committed to the significance of all they are in their birth and tradition, both for good or ill. To obey a world-relevance is to incur a multi-religious world...' [74] Andrew Walls speaks of the need to redeem the history of each new cultural group as they respond to Christ.[75] Re-valuing cultural heritage, in the light of Christ's fulfilment, is a vital aspect of

---

[73] See Andrew F. Walls, *The Missionary Movement in Christian History: Studies in the Transmission of the Faith* (Maryknoll, NY: Orbis, 1996), 9ff. on this concept of the "adoptive heritage" of Christians.

[74] Kenneth Cragg, *Christianity in World Perspective* (London : Lutterworth Press, 1968) 65, cited by Kwame Bediako, 'The Holy Spirit, the Christian Gospel and Religious Change: The African Evidence for a Christian Theology of Religious Pluralism", James Thrower (ed.) *Essays in Religious Studies for Andrew Walls* (Aberdeen: Department of Religious Studies, University of Aberdeen, 1986), 45.

[75] In his August 2000 Burns Lectures at Otago University, N.Z.

mission in response to the religious quest of primal societies in our postmodern context.

Living up to our dignity as Christ's family and not reverting to previous cultural norms, 3:25 – 4:31.Christ offers what no other religion can achieve and he accomplishes what all the protective and preparatory Law and elemental spirits could not do. His work transcends social and cultural barriers, which normally keep us apart. Every Christian has equal access to the new family entitlements regardless of race, socio-economic standing or gender. Clothed in Christ and his own life-qualities, we become joint-heirs in his new, united, multiethnic family (3:26-29). He rescues us from our own estrangement and condemnation before God and comes to share God's life with us through the indwelling of the Spirit. He adopts us as full members of his intimate family circle, imparting the privileges of mature children, including direct access to the Father through prayer and a guaranteed share in the family inheritance. In sacral primal societies, personal and communal identities are closely related to the shared religious beliefs of the community – to convert calls their identity into question. The Gospel offers a new identity as family of God in Christ (4:4-7). Christ also frees us from a fearful slave-like relationship with religious systems or powers. He enables us to see their weakness, in comparison to Christ's love-based, relationship-enhancing power, recognizing that any actual strength elemental spirit powers have, like that of a beggar, is merely ascribed by the worshipper and not inherent, nor derived from, a genuinely divine nature. Grasping this, breaks the shackles of subservience to such powers and their associated formal rituals and ceremonialism, motivating us not to revert to a merely traditional, ritualistic level of interaction with God. Proper respect for traditional religion is quite different from going back into its bondages and limitations (4:8-12). Rather, we are to live up to our position as children of God, letting Christ be formed in us, with all that means for a process of ongoing growth into him (4:12-20). Here is the balance to the last section. Proper relationships across cultural boundaries will foster both an exclusive loyalty to Christ and a proper respect for cultural traditions.

Sustaining our vital, cruciform redemptive encounter with Christ through the Spirit, 1:4; 2:15-21; 3:10-14, 26-29; 4:4-7, 9, 19. Running through Galatians chapters 1-4 is a series of Trinitarian, Christological, theological statements we have only mentioned in passing. These form the substance and heart of the theological and experiential thrust of the message, centring on each believer's dynamic life-transforming encounter and ongoing relationship with God in Christ through the Holy Spirit. In Galatians, the believers' relationship with Christ is redemptive. From the announcement in the opening greeting of Christ's self-giving to rescue us from the present corrupt age to fulfil God's will, Paul uses both forensic, 'justification', and commercial, 'redemption' explanatory metaphors to unpack the impact of Christ's death for us. The objective, historical realities of pardon, restored relationship with God, and release from servitude, on the one hand, and, on the other, the richly subjective, personal and communal union with and incorporation into Christ Jesus the Risen living Lord, receive due emphasis (2:15-16, 20-21; 3:10-13, 26-29; 4:4-7). Galatians particularly stresses being crucified with Christ to share a cruciform self-denial of the patterns and values of self and the world (2:20-21; 5:13-18, 24; 6:14, 17). The vital reality of this encounter and continuing faith relationship forms the evangelical heart of the message for people, whose previous lives have been dominated by other spirit powers, and who, in a postmodern context, seek wholeness of life.

We express our freedom in Christ, across the whole culture, allowing the Spirit to transform our personal, social and communal lifestyles, 5:1-6:10. The Apostle, in the rest of the letter, addresses what for the postmodern mindset is rejected a priori – that a metanarrative (other than their own postmodern one) can be universally applicable and, at the same time, genuinely liberating. But this is the Galatian message: the one universal Gospel frees people of every culture in the fullest possible sense. This Gospel, first, frees believers from the bondage of hegemonic cultural expectations (5:1-6). There is no single universal cultural requirement or experience, which other cultures must adopt to live as true Christians. Circumcision, the unique indicator of membership amongst God's people under the old arrangements, or any other such cultural particular, is no longer necessary under the Gospel. In Christ, all we need to enjoy God's acceptance and pleasure is freely accessible, through faith alone, directly from each of our own cultural backgrounds. Regardless of the pressures the dominant religious culture may apply to conform us to its customs and expectations, in Christ we can be ourselves and know Christ accepts us just as we are: '...in Christ Jesus neither circumcision nor uncircumcision has any value. The only thing that counts is faith expressing itself in love' (5:6). Christians are still adept at tripping up their fellow runners by a wrong teaching on such cultural matters. Galatians calls us to pick ourselves up, stand tall in our own cultural integrity, and rejoin the race (5:7ff).

Gospel freedom is also distinctive in its understanding of freedom, not as being to indulge self-centred desires, but being free from them to become free for serving others. Knowing who we are culturally, and how fully we are accepted in Christ, frees us to live beyond the petty confines of cultural bigotry and to serve each other without back-biting or character assassination. God looks for Christ-like love that breaks out of our cultural norms to serve those who do not think or act like us. Accepting our ethnic identity in Christ, frees us for such service (5:13-18).

Gospel freedom and inter-cultural relationships, in the church, develop within a wider spiritual context of conflict between the ways of the Holy Spirit of God and the ways of selfish humanity (5:19-26). The church is called, in each culture, to live by the Spirit, not by the attitudes, values and life-styles of the 'flesh' – our personal, ingrained self-centred choices and habits. Here is a worldview-transforming understanding, enabling us to face the awful depths of evil and depravity in our societies and, instead of attributing them to external spirit powers or non-personal agency, we can face the evil squarely and acknowledge that along with any real external factors, and more basically, accountable human agency, they are at the root of our social and personal dysfunction, since these evils are properly named 'works of the flesh.' In a primal society, as in the postmodern intellectual climate, this is a radically new analysis and prescription. Our desires, thoughts and choices are the root cause of sexual indiscipline, which dehumanizes. Human jealousies and actions distort worship. Our human attitudes and actions, not spirits of ancestors or place, continue and renew subservience to sorcery and idolatry, even where the Gospel has done away with them, at earlier stages of Christian growth, in primal societies. The ethnocentric and narrow, proud attitudes, which divide and disrupt attempts at inter-cultural partnership, arise in the hearts of humans. To blame other spirit powers, or neuroses, or other societally imposed deprivations for these 'works of the flesh,' contradicts this biblical description of their nature. Only the overflow of the fruit of the Holy Spirit in our lives is sufficient to transform these basic attitudes, ingrained within each of us personally from our own ethnic backgrounds. Christ's love, his joy, and his self-control are unnatural to the basic bias of every human society and culture. The productive activity of the Holy Spirit, sourced through dynamic dependence on him through faith, is essential for this depth of lifestyle liberation. This choice between 'works of the flesh' and bearing 'fruit of the Spirit' places moral responsibility firmly on us, as human beings. The Gospel calls is to freedom in the Spirit, whereby we 'keep in step with the Spirit,' within our own cultural context. God's own life, released through our redeemed personalities as we unite across our ethnic divisions, is the pattern (5:22-25). As he concludes the main teaching of the letter, Paul emphasizes further particulars essential, both negatively, for a community threatened by cultural conflict, and positively, for healthy multiethnic co-operation in a congregation impacting its society (6:1-10).

Summary: Exalting in our new, but crucified life as the people of God, not trusting the dominant culture's religious rituals, 6:11-18. Paul takes up the pen from his secretary to sign the letter. He cannot resist a summary paragraph. He pointedly labels the colonizing intention of the circumcision party as cowardice. They attempt to impose their own cultural norms upon others because they cannot face the costly demands of making Christ's crucifixion the pattern for their own lifestyles. To really grasp what Christ did for us, in his death, means dying to our own pride of person, of possessions and of culture; laying down all our boasting at the foot of the cross. Then, as the undeserved grace of God overwhelms and re-creates us, we rise as full members of our own culture, to take our place alongside every other new creature within the true "Israel of God" – a title no longer restricted to one ethnic or cultural group, but now rightly attributed to the 'one new humanity" God is creating from both Jews and peoples of other cultures.[76] To glorify Christ crucified and to share with others as the multiethnic people of God – these are the true goals of the Gospel message for primal peoples grappling with our contemporary postmodern context.

In these inter-dependent Galatians themes, we suggest, the Holy Spirit has set out key contours of the Gospel, with special relevance for believers living within or from a primal religious background. They also address many of the areas of overlap between postmodern and primal perspectives, and, thus, have special significance for mission today.

First Thessalonians: Biblical models for receiving the Gospel and worldview transformations amongst primal religious people in a postmodern context

If Galatians draws the contours of theological emphases appropriate for mission in primal societies, then 1 Thessalonians turns our attention to our methodologies and goals in mission. We focus on three aspects of the models presented in this letter:

The vulnerable, cruciform, whole-lifestyle example of the missionaries, 1 Thessalonians 1:5b; 2:1-12; 2:17-3:6. As Paul reminds the Thessalonians of the beginnings of the mission amongst them, he unself-consciously reveals his own approach as their pioneer missionary, calling on the Thessalonians repeatedly as witnesses to the truth of his testimony. He speaks of how he, literally, 'became among them, for them', 1:5b, indicating the depth of identification and relationship he developed 'incarnationally' with them. His persistence and integrity characterise his expanded summary of that initial claim, as he recounts his movements from facing insults and suffering at Philippi, to courageously telling the News in Thessalonica. Reviewing his motives, he claims he was not people-pleasing. He guarded carefully against error, impurity and deceit in his communications. He did so because of his deeper level motivation, to always be God-pleasing. What he really valued were the humbling, responsible assurances that he was approved, entrusted and attested by God himself (2:1-4). In similar vein, in 2:5-12, Paul reminds the Thessalonians his method was not "image"-making, he did not rely on flattery, and could not be accused of greed. He was no mere popularity-seeker, and as became his regular missionary approach, he did not demand even his basic rights from those he served. He did not just objectively pass on a message, but was selflessly committed to them personally: caring, loving, and sharing as a nursing mother with her

[76] As explained most fully in Ephesians 2:14-18, and expounded eloquently by Andrew Walls, 'The Ephesian Moment,' *The Cross-Cultural Process in Christian History: Studies in the Transmission and Appropriation of Faith* (Maryknoll, NY: Orbis, 2002), 72-81.

children. In his work patterns, he was never merely clock-watching and made it a point of honour not to financially burden those he served. In personal relationships, he could conscientiously claim, expecting both God and the Thessalonians to confirm, he had been pure, upright and blameless. In pastoral relationships, which he accepted as an inherent aspect of his missionary task, he adopted a pattern of parenting believers to equip them for a worthy lifestyle, fitting them for the new kingdom, in which they were now citizens. His sudden departure left him feeling bereft and orphaned from these, with whom he had developed such warm relationships so quickly. He felt very vulnerable, anxiously awaiting news of how they had fared in the pressures associated with his eviction from the city (2:17-3:6). This open, unself-conscious testimony reveals an understanding of mission as primarily a people-forming exercise. For Paul, effectiveness in serving the Gospel was measured by his integrity as the messenger, the resulting lifestyle maturity of the believers being served, plus realistic acceptance of the inherent costs and inter-personal strains of the process.

The Thessalonians' effective reception of the Gospel message, 1:5-8a; 2:13-16. Our Gospel (literally) 'became among you...' wrote Paul (1:5), as he rejoiced in the way it was distinctively received: 'Not only in Word.' It certainly did come in the preaching of the Word – cf., 1:6, 8; 2:13; and the range of verbal communication terms used in Acts 17:2-4. The preached Word was essential – but not sufficient on its own. Three things accompanied their welcoming of the Word: *The Word came ... With power*. Outward evidence, authority, and attestation accompanied the preaching. God was seen working manifestly and effectively among them. They submitted to his Word and he transformed them. The significant proportion of the Thessalonian congregation from a primal religious background knew the importance of this. The primal imagination is all about power: power to control a world of spirit powers, magical formulae, and religious rituals ordering and dominating every aspect of daily life. Into their world had penetrated a new power– the power of another kind of effective word. The word of the Gospel worked in demonstrable ways, in bringing the wholeness and renewal the scriptures call salvation. Their understanding of power changed. Power now related to the Good News that God had broken into their world in person, in Jesus Christ. In love he had given himself to meet their deepest needs. This strange message of love in Christ was 'the power of God for salvation' – the new restorative power, for which they had been searching. Now they linked power, not with magic, witchcraft and sorcery, nor with ritualistic ceremonial, but with the news of the love of Christ. *The Word came ... With the Holy Spirit*. Their conversion involved a personal encounter with God Himself, for the preachers were empowered with Spirit (both are possible readings). The coming of the Word meant coming into living contact with the Spirit of God, meeting, welcoming, and knowing him, in real life encounters. Again, this was good news for primal religionists. Their world had been populated by capricious, unpredictable spirits of ancestors and fearful sacred places. What a difference to now be in a personal relationship with a clean, pure, reliable Spirit, the very Spirit of God himself. The Spirit-endowing word was not disposing of, but renewing and enriching their whole understanding of the spiritual realm, now permeated with the presence of the Living God. *The Word came ...with full conviction*: both of the preachers and of the hearers (i.e. personally relating the Word to their assumptions, presuppositions and worldview beliefs, converting their thought-world and bringing it under the Lordship of Jesus Christ, letting the Word convict attitudes, habits, plans – seeing and owning their selfishness and sinfulness, coming to *plerophoria*, a full assurance, and strong grasp of that Word).

This wholistic Thessalonian reception of the Gospel Word is explained further in 2:13-16. Paul thanks God for the exemplary way the Thessalonians processed the message. They received for themselves as the word heard through the missionary heralds, welcoming the Word for what it is, not a merely human message, but in reality, God's Own Word. What began as an interaction with the messengers in responsive listening and acceptance, became a living encounter, through their message, with God himself, as they heard his voice in the words and message proclaimed. Their faith commitment was the active ingredient enabling this change in reality and perception.

The worldview transformations modelled in the Thessalonians' response. This letter summarizes succinctly the outcomes of effective mission in a primal society. Four key transformations which had become common knowledge in their region (1:7-8):

A personal relationship with the living God in place of a magico-ritualistic subjection to spirit powers, 1:9. They had 'turned to God from Idols to serve the living and true God'. They had converted – changed their minds and lifestyles and discovered the difference between bondage to idols and a vital relationship with the Living and True God. In Thessalonica, religion focused on idols devoted to the powers – whether of the Emperor, or the spiritual powers abounding in local primal beliefs, or the traditional Greek pantheon. Idols, too, devoted to pleasure as in the hedonism and worship of the human body, characteristic of their time. Behind the comment, 'turned from idols', then, lies a depth of insight and awareness that converting to the 'Living God' from that context was a radical, demanding and socially costly turning indeed. But idolatry is the ultimate human frustration, for human meaning is found only in personal 'I-You' relationships – never in 'I-it' relationships. But the latter are all that idols can offer. Add to this the alternative primary concern and past-time of Greek philosophy with its noble, but endless quest for reality, truth, and wisdom, and the turn 'to the Living and True God' also takes on fresh contextual relevance. To personally embrace the One, who with integrity could call himself 'The Truth,' involved a radical realignment of loyalties and devotion – a new kind of service. Again, a significant contrast is implied with the kind of temple service common in their context. Religion was no longer a formal ritual, devoted to capricious spirits, material things, frightening omens or implacable cosmic forces, or their idols and supporting philosophies. Rather, they were pouring out their love and devotion to the Sovereign God, their new Lord, Ruler of the Universe, True and not counterfeit; God Himself, not human substitutes; the God ,who had disclosed himself as the God and Father of our Lord Jesus Christ.

An understanding of time re-oriented to a hope filled expectation of future consummation, and consequent reorienting of personal purpose and moral accountability 1:10; 2:19-20; 3:13; 4:13- 5:11, 23. They had 'turned ... to wait for [God's] Son from heaven whom he raised from the dead – Jesus, who rescues us from the coming wrath' (1:10) Again, this short-hand summary of the Thessalonians' Christology and eschatology speaks of in-depth contextualization in process, right from the start of mission in their midst. Jesus, as Son of God shared his nature and deity, He is coming from heaven – implying his present ascended position and control of history. He had been raised from death – implying awareness of the redemptive nature of his death and victory over the forces of evil, confirmed in resurrection; as well as his presence with and for them as the Living Lord. He rescues from coming wrath – implying a grasp of the justice of God and the human dignity inherent in human accountability; as well as the sense of purpose and destiny such awareness of accountability brings. This implies a new understanding of humanity, as well as human history and God's purposes. Again, it lends depth to Paul's appreciation of their endurance of hope, and his repeated encouragements to moral responsibility in the light of their personal accountability before this returning Judge and Saviour. They now have a new understanding of history – they await the Returning Son of God – time is moving forward to a purposeful goal – not merely repeating itself in endless cycles. Instead of myth and looking backward to past ancestors to control the unknown future, there is now a hope-full expectation and anticipation of a personal consummation and communal re-union as the goal of human history. Mission to the primal imagination involves this depth of worldview transformation.

A practical theology of vulnerable, cruciform suffering in the Spirit, 1:6; 2:2, 9, 14; 3:1-5. Through both his frank auto-biographical transparency in Chapters 1-3 and in his exhortations throughout the letter, Paul conveys a consistent experience and understanding of the centrality of suffering and enduring hardships in Christian life and mission. Empowered by the Holy Spirit to embrace such realities joyfully, enduring suffering becomes an evidence of the integrity and validity of their response to the Gospel. (2:14-15a). In this, the Thessalonians were also imitating the Judean churches, which had suffered persecution (Acts 8:1-4; 11:19). Suffering from fellow-countrymen has been the common lot of God's people through the ages. God utilises suffering both to promote Christian growth in the suffering community and to show the serious culpability of those who continually oppose God's messengers. Pointing for his example to Jews, who consistently opposed the proclamation of the Gospel to peoples of other cultures, Paul notes that such opposition to the mission of God displays ethnic pride, displeases God, multiplies guilt and guarantees God's judgement. Effective mission has always produced both positive and negative reactions, from those in the believers' communities. Therefore, developing an adequate theology to account for hardships in service is a measure of the maturity and stability of new believers, as Paul's open acknowledgement of his own Christ-like vulnerability shows in his reflections in 2:17-3:5. This attitude requires a worldview level thought transformation in societies, where sensual pleasure, prompt self-gratification and hedonistic enjoyment are valued as the norm, as in so many postmodern contexts today.

Epistemological change from dependence on ritual and magic to trust in the Word of God as their practical life-style authority, 1:5; 2:13ff. We explained above the Thessalonians' steps in processing the heralding of the Gospel message. A worldview level epistemological change was implicit in those verses – from formal ritual and magical language appeasing idols and empowering sorcerers, to welcoming, receiving, and responding in faith to the preached and written Word of God through his messengers. This is a massive epistemological re-orientation in a primal society – just as it is a huge epistemological step to trust the Word of God as the living authority for faith and life in a reductionisticly science and reason- dependent Western world.

This warmly biographical, open letter evidences the deep level, at which the Gospel had converted the believers and their assumptions, values and beliefs in Thessalonica. We suggest, in doing so, the letter has modelled patterns of mission methodology and outcomes of special significance for mission in primal societies in our postmodern context.

Combining the contours of missional theology from the letter to the Galatians with these methods and outcomes, exemplified in 1 Thessalonians, gives a strong missiological foundation to address the tensions, issues and insights we have gleaned from our analysis of postmodernity and the primal imagination.

Conclusion

As we face mission at the centennial of Edinburgh 2010, then, our postmodern context presents special challenges for primal societies and the 'primal imagination.' We have traced postmodernity's gift and challenge to primal religious peoples. We have outlined a developing missiological appreciation of the 'primal imagination'. We have suggested steps towards a missiological approach to the primal imagination, concluding with a biblical platform for mission to primal religious people in a postmodern context.

We conclude as we began, with a provocative, Edinburgh 1910 gem, this time from the final sentence of the Commission IV Report's chapter on Animistic Religions. Perhaps it still carries a prescient tone, if we make due allowance for its unabashed paternalism:

> … just as many a parent has re-learned religious lessons by coming into touch with the piety of childhood, so it may well happen that the Christianity of Europe is destined to be recalled, if not to forgotten truths, at least to neglected graces, by the infant Churches that are just beginning to live their lives on the basis of the mercy, the commandments and the promises of God.[77]

Migration patterns and demographic changes in global Christianity, as we enter the twenty-first century, and the argument of this paper, suggest "boomerang challenges," from churches with primal backgrounds, are by no means inappropriate, not only for Europe, but also for Northern Christianity generally in 2010.

---

[77] *Report of Commission IV*, 37.

Multi-Identity of Chinese Christianity in Postmodern China: A Missiological Reflection of Premodernity, Modernity Towards Postmodernity

Jieren Li

Introduction

The 21st century ushers in the postmodern era. The optimism and orderly progressive mentality of the modern era since the industrial revolution has been gradually replaced by the 'unorderly', chaotic and yet interconnected link of the web of life. China is one of the largest developing countries in the world, although the majority of the population (47%) still lives in rural areas, rapid urbanization, industrialization and modernization is turning hundreds and thousands of peasant villages into cities and towns. The migration process also challenges the Chinese people and society, encountering forms of life that range from the premodern, modern to the postmodern. Thus, Chinese postmodernity is not limited to ideological and academic discourse of postmodernists (theorists, writers and artists), but a daily life experience of ordinary people. How does the Chinese church respond to this shifting mood and changing mode of thought in this postmodern era?

This essay will take on the issue of spiritual diversity raised by Chinese Christianity during recent three decades and its significance for the concept of mission in contemporary Chinese society which is shifting from the premodern and modern to the postmodern. The descriptive analysis will focus on three major forms of Christianity, namely institutional, autonomous, and intellectual Christianity. Finally, I will analyze mission obligations of the Chinese church in a society mixing premodernity, modernity and postmodernity.

Understanding Postmodernity in China

Some Western scholars have divided human history into three phases: the premodern, modern and postmodern. Each phase has no precise end but rather each forms a layer, one on top of another, even overlapping to a certain degree. Postmodernity is generally identified by some philosophers and sociologists as the socio-political, socio-economic and cultural condition of contemporary society which exists in new forms of social, cultural, political, and economic states or situations as well as new forms of thinking about modernity. It is also considered as a worldview in the contemporary world. In an academic discourse, postmodernity is also presented as a methodological concept in doing research.

As a universal cultural phenomenon, postmodernity has its roots in the cultural soil of Western post-industrial society. However, according to some Chinese scholars, it is not essentially a Western product, but is also relevant to the Third World and exists in Chinese society.[1] Today, Chinese society has elements of premodern and postmodern in it. Different from the Western postmodern phenomenon, Chinese society, according to some scholars, lacks the conditions for postmodernity. It is arguable that postmodernism is no longer a monolithic phenomenon but rather has generated different forms both in the West and in the East.[2]

In China, there is no exact time when the modern period ended or will end and the postmodern period began or will begin. In other words, the concepts of premodernity, modernity and postmodernity are not rigidly periodized. They are to be found in different places and different periods and all these three can be found existing side-by-side in every corner of society. In most parts of China, especially in rural areas, there are people whose outlook and lifestyle is predominantly premodern, living mainly in a pre-industrial society. Meanwhile, there are people whose outlook and lifestyle is predominantly modern or postmodern living in an industrial even post-industrial society, for example in the metropolis: Beijing, Shanghai, Shenzhen, etc. We may even easily note that premodern, modern and postmodern culture can perhaps be found in the same city, even in the same people.

Therefore, I argue that Chinese postmodernity shall not be simply defined as a periodical notion, as some scholars hold that modernity ended in the 20th century denoted by postmodernity,[3] but rather a cultural phenomenon, a social experience and an ethos or spirit which challenges people and society to explore something new and unknown by an uneven means. In the current context of China, postmodernity should not be understood as a coherent response to the decline of modernity, but rather as a range of responses to all sorts of phenomena of premodernity, modernity and postmodernity.

The modern and contemporary history of Christianity in China has been fascinating with its distinctive experience under Chinese communism.

---

[1] See Wang Ning, 'Postmodernity, Post-coloniality and Globalization: A Chinese Perspective', *Social Semiotics,* Vol. 10, No. 2, 2000.

[2] See Wang Ning, 'The Mapping of Chinese Postmodernity', *Boundary 2*, Vol. 24, No. 3, 1997, 19-40.

[3] For some, postmodernity is defined as a cultural phenomenon in a highly developed Western world periodically in post-industrial society. However, it could also be understood in some developing countries. (See Fredric Jameson, 1984).

When this is put together with the current social, political, and cultural environment, what emerges is a postmodern context for a Christian church. Under the challenge of globalization and the impact of post-coloniality, the Chinese church culturally exists in a postmodern situation.

Modernity propagates the methodology that truth and knowledge should be objective and mathematically precise. Postmodernity, on the contrary, propagates that truth, knowledge, and authority are relatively precise. Chinese Christians of the postmodern era live in a complicated socio-political and socio-economic environment. The basic characteristic of postmodern Christianity in China is its feature of multi-identity. The traditional fundamentalism represented mainly rural Christians and house church goers inherit a premodern theological tradition, governed largely by a worldview centered on God as a defining reality, addressing what is there. It is the issue of ontology. New evangelicalism, mainly new emerging urban churches with modern theological thinking, governed by enlightenment naturalism, addresses how to know and what is there. It is the issue of epistemology. Finally, a small group of cultural or intellectual Christians adopt postmodern thought, governed by pragmatism and existentialism, addressing how Chinese language, culture and experience function to construct theological meaning itself. The new emerging academic school of "Sino-theology" is a typical representation of this.

During the previous three decades (1979-2009), the Chinese church has experienced a great increase in numbers. Typologically speaking, the shift from premodern and modern to postmodern thinking has also emerged in three main types of Christian groups, namely institutional, autonomous and intellectual Christianity. In the following part, I will focus my discussion on how Chinese Christianity has been influenced by what is loosely described as postmodernity, and what impact, if any, that it is having on the Chinese churches' understanding of their mission obligations.

Contemporary Landscape of Chinese Christianity

In mainland China, the Christian church was the fruit and product of Western missions, which stemmed from the revival movements of the 18th and 19th centuries, the student volunteer movement, and the various forms of Pietism. Historically, the Chinese church has been influenced by both theological fundamentalism which is a descendant from Western Puritanism and conservative theology and theological modernism, which is a descendant from enlightenment philosophy and liberal theology. As a result, the Chinese church, in her theological profile, looks far more like the Western church than an Asian Christian community.

After the Cultural Revolution, there has been a rapid growth in the Christian church. The institutional churches of the Three-Self Patriotic Movement (TSPM) are opening and re-opening throughout the entire country with the Communist government's permission. Over fifty million

Bibles have been printed. Hundreds and thousands of autonomous Christian groups[4] have grown very rapidly nationwide outside the control of the authorities. A rise of interest in Christianity among Chinese intellectuals, scholars, and university students has become known as the "fever of Christianity." The lack of strong belief in political ideology and religious faith in post-Mao China has translated into a general interest in religion, particularly Christianity. This spontaneous Christian revival is partially due to the fact of a crisis of belief and widespread dissatisfaction with Marxist communism and Maoist socialism. Economic globalization, marketing materialism, modernization and secularization, have become mainstreams in society, leaving an ideological vacuum that has sparked a renewed interest in issues of spirituality. In this changed environment, there is also great church growth.

Today, when doing academic research on the revival, spread and development of contemporary Christianity in the People's Republic, one must focus on at least these three major groups, namely institutional, autonomous and intellectual Christians.

Institutional Christianity

In this essay, institutional Christianity refers to Protestant churches and meeting points with a clear organizational structure, doctrinal system, and worship pattern, affiliating with the network of the TSPM and China Christian Council (CCC). Often it is termed as "three-self church," "official church," "registered church," or "state recognized church," etc.

According to official statistics from East China Normal University (2008), the Christian population in China is approximately 40 millions.[5] Nearly half of the total Christian population belongs to the TSPM/CCC.[6] Though many autonomous Christian bodies thrive outside the TSPM/CCC structure, it is still the only officially recognized church in current Chinese society.

The TSPM/CCC claims that Chinese Christianity is a post-denominational Protestant body. The CCC is the organizational and ecclesial expression of a post-denominational unity, according to Bishop

---

[4] Different scholars use different terms to describe the Chinese Protestant groups which outside the TSPM/CCC. Some, e.g., Jonathan Chao, use 'house church' or 'underground church;' others, e.g., Alan Hunter and Chan Kim-kwong suggest 'autonomous Christian communities.' In this study, I prefer to use terms 'autonomous Christianity' or 'autonomous church.'

[5] 'Religious believers thrice the estimate' in *China Daily* February 07, 2007 www.chinadaily.com.cn/china/ 2007-02/07/content_802994.htm [August 13, 2009]

[6] In an article 'How Many Sheep Are There In the Chinese Flock?' (*Amity News Service* 2004.11/12.4), the TSPM/CCC claims 18 millions Christians. Many believe that the real numbers are much greater.

Ding Guangxun (K.H. Ting).[7] The paradigm shift from denominationalism to post-denominationalism faces a great ecclesiastical challenge. From the respect of church polity, post-denominationalism is a mixture of polity from three sources, namely Episcopalism, Congregationalism, and Presbyterianism. In 1958, denominations publicly ceased to function, but various traditions, characteristics and expressions of denominational churches still remain. Diversity of spiritual traditions and liturgical expressions became a remarkable feature in China's post-denominationalism.

Bishop Ding's vision is that the CCC would eventually develop into the establishment of a united Church of China as a visible unity of the Christian community. For him, future *ecclesia Sinica* must have five main features as follows: apostolic, episcopal, patriotic, socialistic, and post-denominational.[8] The post-denominational feature might be the most characteristic element in *ecclesia Sinica.* It is also a very postmodern feature. Priority is given to ecclesial unity above denominational identities, the origins of which lie in the Reformation (premodern context) and subsequent development (modern context). It is also true that the government prohibited denominations, and in this sense post-denominationalism is a politically legal requirement. Therefore, it is not a product of postmodernity, but premodernity.

The post-denominational church actually results in a pre-denominational situation. It is apparent that Chinese Christians (in particular there are plenty of people here who are extremely loyal to their denominations, and love the history, tradition and liturgy of their denominations) retain their denominational identity in a post-denominational context. Such a unique religious phenomenon could also be understood as a postmodern reflection of a combination and plurality of the spiritual premodernity (pre-denominationalism), modernity (denominationalism), and postmodernity (post- denominationalism).

The major marks of post-denominationalism also reflect a postmodern feature. First of all, different from a traditional Episcopal polity, which is hierarchical in structure with the chief authority over a local congregation resting on a bishop, *ecclesia Sinica* is an episcopacy, but without a diocesan organization. The position of bishop in the Chinese church has neither authority over the judicatory nor authority to supervise the clergy. The Bishopric is no more than a spiritual symbol. In other words, the hierarchical form of the church structure is deconstructed. Secondly, multi-liturgical practices are expressed in one church, e.g., different practices of baptism and Eucharist. Apparently, diversity is becoming a mainstream in sacramental services. Different from the traditional distinction between

---

[7] Ding Guangxun, *Love Never Ends: Paper by K.H. Ting* (Nanjing: Yiling Press, 2000), 448.

[8] Jieren Li, *In Search of Via Media between Christ and Marx: A Study of Bishop Ding Guangxun's Contextual Theology* (Lund: Lund University, 2008), 304-305.

liturgical and non-liturgical churches, the Chinese church lacks a standardized order of service in the sacrament. Thirdly, a comprehension of ecclesiastical polity becomes the operational and governing structure of a church. Church polity of a post-denomination must be inclusive in character. Though each local congregation has its own characteristic structure because of historical inheritance, the CCC attempts to include three general types of polity, namely Episcopal, Presbyterian, and Congregational polity. All these features are unique from the standpoint of an ecclesiastical perspective of world Christianity, but are also not modern or premodern products.

When postmodernity emphasizes deconstruction, anti-authority, plurality, as well as decentralization, Bishop Ding's vision of *ecclesia Sinica* reflects a typically modern, even premodern, mentality of emphasizing organizational centralization, hierarchical authority, etc. Current decentralization of the post-denominational demonstrates that the Chinese church is struggling in shifting from the modern to a postmodern society.

In postmodern China, the institutional churches are reflecting a feature of diversity rather than unity. Christian councils, on the provincial level, begin to play a more influential role than the CCC headquarters, and the TSPM becomes even more symbolic in its function. There is no longer a super-figure of sorts to lead the church in the post-Ding era. Apart from political support from the authorities, the existence of the TSPM is also losing its legal basis.

As church history reveals, whenever the church becomes over-institutionalized and loses her vigour, there will always be new forms of expression of faith among the ranks of Christians. They are, as a matter of fact, a supplement to institutional Christianity. The rapid emergence of autonomous Christian bodies is a challenge and a supplement to the institutional churches of the TSPM/CCC.

Autonomous Christianity

For some Christians, the institutional church of the TSPM should not be considered as the mainstream of Christianity in China. Today, Evangelicals in both the West and in China consider the majority of Chinese Christians as belonging to the so-called 'house church' which is an autonomous form of Christianity, even though the TSPM/CCC often denies the existence of autonomous churches by claiming that only a limited number of churches are not registered.

In this study, 'autonomous Christianity' refers to independent and unregistered Protestant bodies, which are unaffiliated with the TSPM/CCC in both urban and rural societies. Some scholars, e.g., Edmond Tang, term it as 'grassroots Christianity.'[9]

These Christian bodies do not join the CCC/TSPM because of the following doctrinal and political reasons: (1) The three-self churches accept Communist leadership and governing authority, which is unbiblical and is therefore unacceptable. (2) The TSPM/CCC was initiated by the CCP government and some liberal Christians, and not established on the biblical ground of Christian faith. (3) Pastoral leadership of the institutional church is under the supervision of the RAB. (4) The political unity of the state-church relationship could not be adopted. (5) The mission obligation of the church has been largely limited by the government in the institutional church.[10]

The spread and development of autonomous Christianity has experienced three main waves since Deng Xiaoping's reform and openness at the end of1970s.

The first wave is commonly known as the 'house church' revival movement, which was widespread throughout China in the 1980s. This type of traditional model of 'house church' is well known in the West. During this period, the majority of the house churches spread in both rural and urban areas. However, most churches with limited members (c.a. 30-50 persons/church) have not connected to each other. This type of small house church usually is led by independently self-appointed preachers, and a formal structure and hierarchical leadership are not easily distinguishable. Most of these small groups' preachers are not full-time staff. Since the feature of over-independence, the development of this Christian movement has been slow and has less influence nowadays.

The second wave could be considered as the 'network-church' movement in the 1990s. The so-called 'five network,' namely the China Gospel Fellowship and Fengcheng Church of Heibei province, Lixin and Yinshang Fellowship of Anhui province as well as some autonomous denominations, existed before the liberation, e.g., Little Flock. The True Jesus Church is the major representative of this group. There is a clear distinction between church leaders and believers as well as between different levels of leadership. Usually, a clearer structure and organizational form of leadership, formal structure and hierarchical leadership are clearly visible. There is a full-time staff. These five networks claim more than

[9] See Edmond Tang, 'The Changing Landscape of Chinese Christianity' *China and Christianity* (London: SCM, 2008).

[10] See 'Attitude of Chinese House Churches Toward the Government, Its Religious Policy, and the
Three Self Movement', Aikman, David. *Jesus in Beijing: How Christianity Is Transforming China and*
Changing Global Balance of Power (Washington DC: Regnery Publishing, 2003), 304-305.

eighty million believers in the house church movement.[11] In 1998, several of these large network churches issued a joint appeal to the Chinese government and publically argued why they would not join the TSPM/CCC. They also outlined a joint confession of faith, which is the first doctrinal statement of the Chinese house church. Most of the network church is charismatic and Pentecostal orientated in practice and theology.

The rapid urbanization ,since the later 1990s, has already deconstructed the development of rural churches. It is almost inevitable that most of these rural based networks are in a rapid process of disintegration. Some have built their network as a new type of semi-urban church again in cities. However, as a marginalized group in society, these churches have gradually lost ground for future development.

The third wave is identified as the 'city-church' movement. Different from the first wave, these churches mainly develop in cities in the 21st century, though they share some spiritual similarities with the traditional house-church movement. It is difficult for them to integrate into the house churches due to their background and they cannot join the institutional churches either. Therefore, they have formed a new type of church in the cities, often called 'the Third Church.' Many church members are Chinese from overseas, highly educated professionals, and university students. For them, there is no historical burden, which the traditional house church has inherited, since the 1950s. It also creates a possibility to co-operate with three-self churches. They support public registration of the churches as NGOs in Chinese society. Many young professionals have formed office fellowships holding Bible studies, spiritual gatherings and Sunday worship together in workplaces, hotels, and even in conversion centres.

These three waves are composed of a non-institutionalized Christian movement co-existing in China today. Although most do not pose a threat to Chinese society, autonomous churches in China do pose definite challenges to the TSPM/CCC and the institutional form of Christianity. Another issue is church registration. Most of these unregistered Christian groups are not recognized as legalized non-profitable organizations. They are neither governed by the state legislation on management and administration, nor by an affiliation of the TSPM, therefore, they should be considered as more of an autonomous form of Christianity. In short, the first wave of the traditional type of house church is mainly located in urban societies, but has very limited influence nationwide. The second wave of network type churches is no longer as powerfully influential as in the 1990s, due to rapid modernization and urbanization. The third wave of a city-church movement represents the current and future trend of autonomous Christianity.

---

[11] See A United Appeal of the Various Branches of the Chinese House Church', *Jesus in Beijing*, 293-294.

Intellectual Christianity

Since the late 1980s, intellectuals have shown an unprecedented openness and passion for Christian culture and values. An increasing number have sought to learn about Christianity, but it has not always led them to become baptized as members of the church. From the academic circles to different social sectors, academic and cultural studies on Christianity have become popular, leading to the emergence of an intellectual Christianity.

The emergence of intellectual Christianity or "cultural Christians" reflects a clear postmodern feature of contemporary Chinese society—pluralistic. According to Zhuo Xinping, today, the tendency of pluralism and individualism in the Chinese church becomes visible. The intellectuals try to find some useful elements in Christianity for China's cultural reconstruction in the process of social transformation.[12] Therefore, the purpose of knowing Christianity is not for self-salvation, but for the reconstruction of Chinese cultural values and the significance of Christianity for Chinese society.

Generally, there are three main groups of the so-called "cultural Christians." Firstly, they are those intellectually cultured people who already have a personal conversion to Christianity and are actively involved in church ministry. Secondly, there are those who accept Christian truth and are even baptized, but do not belong to the church. Thirdly, there are those who at least partially agree with Christian teachings, values, and culture but mainly engage in academic research. If to be a Christian means to belong to the church according to St. Cyprian, these scholars studying Christianity should not be considered Christians.

The majority of these intellectuals are not Christians in a traditional sense, and they do not profess a Christian faith personally. Their interest in Christianity mainly comes through cultural and academic research. For them, Christianity is primarily a culture rather than a religion. It is debatable whether or not they could be considered as Christians. Whatever the case, this new phenomenon, which was born in the 1980s and is still a burning issue, has already caught the attention of global Christianity, and it contributes a sense of multi-identity in a postmodern world.

The encounter of Christianity with Chinese intellectuals is a complicated multi- faceted process.[13] Most cultural Christians are perhaps careless of spiritual salvation from an ecclesiastical point of view. However, they are much more careful in the encounter between Christian theology and

---

[12] Zhuo Xinping, 'Discussion on "Cultural Christianity"', *China and Christianity: Burdened Past, Hopeful Future* (Armonk, New York; London: M.E. Sharpe, 2001), 287.

[13] See Stephen Chan, 'Christian Philosophy and the Rise of Cultural Christians in China: An Exploration in the Relationship of Christian Theology and Chinese Culture.'

Chinese culture, and the progress of indigenization and contextualization of Christianity. They have to cultivate the field of Christian theology, Western philosophy, Marxist-Maoism, and Chinese traditional culture and religions.

What is of interest is the relationship between academic studies and spiritual commitment. Related questions are raised: what does this kind of intellectual Christianity mean for salvation if it has no ground for the ultimate concern? Will it be possible to develop authentic Christian theology outside the church?

The phenomenon of intellectual Christianity in mainland China is still in its primitive stage. It is hardly to find out any spiritual contribution. However, the new phenomenon facilitates the indigenization and contextualization of Christianity in Chinese culture. It creates a possibility for mutual understanding and dialogue between China and the West from a perspective of Christian faith.

Chinese Christianity in Postmodern China

Concerning the postmodern challenge to Christianity in China, the following features have been discovered.

First of all, decentralization is becoming a new tendency in the current and future development of Christian movements.

The eighth National Chinese Christian Conference (2008) shows that institutional Christianity, namely the three-self churches, has already entered into the post-Ding period. Bishop Ding's real influence is apparently decreasing, due to the fact of his age and health. Contrary to Ding's hierarchical leadership style, the national TSPM/CCC is facing a challenge of church unity and administrative centralization. Currently, many local congregations and leaders, on the provincial level, seem to favour a policy of decentralization of the church. A further development of post-denominational unity towards a united church of China is also threatened.

Decentralization of *ecclesia Sinica* means that church leaders of the new generation believe that the interdependencies of these local churches cannot be simplified into a hierarchical structure or 'solved' via a 'top-down' approach. The solutions must, on the contrary, be via a 'down-top' and solved at each point from each perspective, and the solutions transmitted to the other points and re-evaluated continuously. This is also due to the fact that the decision makers are shifting away from a fixed centralization or hierarchical structure (e.g., the Old Three Self) to a more democratic orientated leadership.

Secondly, the recent development of indigenization and contextualization also reflects a postmodern impact upon Chinese churches. Contrary to economic globalization and cultural postcoloniality, which somehow promote universalism, postmodernity promotes localization and contextualization. When Chinese Christians are challenged by globalization spiritually, economically and culturally, theological indigenization and contextualization become essential for the Chinese church in finding her own voice against the backdrop of globalization. In other words, the challenge of Western Christianity in the form of globalization have the odd effect of making the Chinese Christians in a defined Chinese culture think more clearly about China as the place in which we do theology.

Several Western Christian scholars interpret the mainstream of this religious phenomenon as a form of Christianity with a Pentecostal and charismatic character. The faith has been expressed in ways that strongly emphasized the miraculous, divine healing in prayer, and speaking in tongues.[14] Apparently such an argument is questionable in terms of their methodology. However, in rural areas, there has been a revival of folk Christianity,[15] which is different from a traditional understanding of Christian belief. To term it as 'folk Christianity' is mainly because of certain parallels between the Christian practices and the practice of traditional folk religions. Other scholars prefer to term it as the 'folk-religionization' of Christianity.[16] This is due to the fact that folk religions have an impact on or have even transformed Christianity to become a common phenomenon in rural villages. Indeed, in many cases, almost all kind of folk religious practices could be found in Pentecostal charismatic groups in China.

It is doubtless there has been a constant religious revival in rural China during recent decades. However, it is unclear whether the so-called 'folk Christianity' could be considered as a Pentecostal and charismatic movement. It is also questionable whether these Chinese 'neo-charismatics'[17] could really be identified as charismatic Christians, in terms of the Western theological notion. In fact, religious phenomena of rural China are very complex and extremely diverse. Luke Wesley argues that 80% of Chinese Christians are charismatic.[18] These interpretations commonly ignore a basic element: how the Chinese traditional folk beliefs

---

[14] See Edmond Tang, 'The Changing Landscape of Chinese Christianity', *China and Christianity* (London: SCM Press, 2008), 17-19.

[15] It is composed of some Christian ideas and practices outside the approval or authority of Roman Catholicism, Protestantism, or others.

[16] Gao Shining, 'Chinese Christianity in the 21st Century', *Christian Theology and Intellectuals in China* (Aarhus: Aarhus University, 2003), 55. Edmond Tang, 'Yellers and Healers: A Study of Pentecostalism and Grassroots Christians in China', *Asian and Pentecostalism: Charismatic Face of Christianity in Asia*, 2005, 484.

[17] The term is used by Daniel Bays to describe those are not affiliated with the historic, classical Pentecostal groups. Usually traditional charismatic Christians believe prophecy, tongues, and healing (1 Cor. 12:8-10) are available to the church today. In addition to the beliefs above, classical Pentecostals believe speaking in tongues is the accompanying sign of baptism in the Holy Spirit.

[18] Luke Wesley, *The Church in China: Persecuted, Pentecostal, and Powerful* (Baguio: AJPS Books, 2004), 225-254.

have strongly re-shaped Christian faith. Although these Chinese believers hold certain Pentecostal beliefs, e.g., speaking in tongues, miraculous healing, visions, dreams, and raptures, all these charismatic expressions of faith can be found in various spiritual practices of folk religions. As Daniel Bays argues, being possessed by a spirit is similar to Taoist tradition, which has influenced the local society, since spirit mediums were also familiar with such concept.[19] Such a kind of Christianity adapted diverse forms of folk religions and served merely as a folk religion. Many people do hold such attitudes, and their spiritual concepts and practices were based on their original religious mentalities.[20]

Theoretically, this is also a matter of religious contextualization and syncretism. Christian teachings and charismatic doctrines have been more or less indigenized into the Chinese religious and cultural soil. A common danger in contextualization occurs when Christianity harmonizes with local social, political, cultural and religious settings to the point where it becomes impossible to discern any distinguishing feature that can be called Christianity. The current development of the charismatic movement in China faces this challenge.

Finally, plurality also becomes a characteristic of postmodern Christianity in China. There are institutional and autonomous Christianity, registered and unregistered church, denominational and post-denominational structure, intellectual and grassroots Christian, etc. A new emerging phenomenon that is very interesting is the city-church, not only filled with urban Christians, but also believers from the villages. With villagers migrating to cities, rural churches also sent their preachers and evangelists to work and pioneer the so-called 'semi-urban church'. These churches usually keep a rural worldview, a religious mentality, as well as a spiritual tradition, which are predominately premodern, though they live in modern, even postmodern, urban society.

During the time from premodern/modern to postmodern, the Chinese church has to re-examine her understanding of the uniqueness of Christian faith. The majority fundamentalists-evangelicals from both institutional and autonomous churches hold to an exclusivist position, based on traditional Protestant doctrine. They assert that salvation is exclusively through the historical manifestation of Jesus Christ's crucifixion on the cross and resurrection. Others take an inclusivist position which is more or less based on Catholic orthodoxy or a Protestant re-interpretation of the gospel. They hold that the historical disclosure in Jesus exhibits God's salvation through the eternal *logos* or cosmic Christ. Christ is *Lux Mundi*, the 'light' of the world that from the beginning has been the life and salvation for human

---

[19] Daniel Bays, 'Christianity and Chinese Sects: Religious Tracts in the Late Nineteenth Century,' *Christianity in China: From Eighteenth Century to the Present* (Stanford: Stanford University Press, 1996), 129.

[20] Leung Ka-lun, *The Rural Churches in China Since 1978* (Hong Kong: Alliance Bible Seminary, 1999), 223.

beings. Hence, while salvation comes only through *logos*, it is unlimited to en explicit knowledge of gospel or religion—Christianity. Bishop Ding and his followers proclaim such a teaching in the institutional church. Thirdly, there is a very small numberof Christian intellectuals from a pluralist position which understands the salvation activity of God even more broadly. In contemporary China, a religiously pluralistic society, it is necessary to build up communication and co-operation among religions. In particular, the Chinese government is atheistic. Pluralism will facilitate the development of religious freedom. For them, God is said to be at work in all religions. Thus all religions can be effective paths to salvation.

The postmodern religious perspective is inherently pluralistic and relativistic. The descriptive discussions above show that the validity of traditional Christian teaching has been challenged. However, the postmodern context celebrates diversity and relativity and advocates a dialogical search for solutions to truth. Actually, it will be also beneficial to the church's survival and development in an atheistic Communist society. Chinese postmodernity is hardly totally broken down within the modern and premodern context. Much of the anxiety that has met the shift into contemporary social relations can be accounted for by examining the continuities with the past.

Implications of Mission in Postmodern China

The theme of this essay is around 'mission and postmodernity in China' dealing with missiological issues raised by the postmodern phenomenon in contemporary Chinese church and society and their significance for mission. The following section, I will describe three major missiological responses from institutional, grassroots, and intellectual Christianity.

Ecclesia Sinica: A response from the institutional church

During the colonial era, Christians presented Western missions in a totally positive light. After the establishment of the People's Republic, from a perspective of anti-imperialism, Communists re-interpret mission as the servanthood of colonialism and the cultural invasion of imperialism in China.

In the 1980s, as a new Western cultural trend, postcolonialism has been introduced in China. Historically, China has never experienced colonialism. Hence, some argue the irrelevance of a postcolonial discourse.[21]

[21] China was never completely colonized by any imperial and colonial power, however, after the Opium War, China sighed numbers of unequal treaties with western countries, and the colonial powers broke the door of China. Therefore, China is commonly understood as a semi-colonized country before the formation of the PRC (1949).

Nevertheless, the importance of postcolonial critics rests on the fact that imperialism and colonialism continues ideologically in everyday culture and values.[22] Therefore, some scholars argue that discussions of postcolonialism seem merely to be a cultural strategy in the struggle against Western cultural hegemonism and linguistic imperialism and against the overall process of moderning China.[23] However, in the framework of academic discourse, postcolonialism could be a powerful analytical method to evaluate the impact of globalization upon the Chinese church in a postmodern context. Especially, in recent decades, theologians and missiologists have begun to understand mission history from a perspective of globalization. It also draws some inspiration from Chinese Christianity today.

The Communist theorists and patriotic church leaders argue that Christianity was introduced to China via imperialism and colonialism. Since 1978, Chinese society has been strongly influenced by the market economy and global capitalism, which challenge the traditional and conservative Communist understanding of Christianity. China's re-opening of an institutional church (1979) and relaxing of religious freedom for Christians, fulfil the demands of modernization by globalization and Western economic power. If globalization is a new form of imperialism, as some scholars interpret, then it might exercise its power through two ways: the economy and culture or ideology.

During the past three decades, every aspect of Chinese society has indeed been re-molded by Western thought, culture, science, and technology. People, culture, economy, intellectuals, politics, in short the whole of China is experiencing a process of transformation from Mao's movements of decolonization, e.g., Cultural Revolution to Deng's acceptance of the modern movement of globalization. Nevertheless, there has always been an anti-West trend within Chinese society, the Communist Party, as well as the patriotic church. The state/party occasionally claims that they will not allow bourgeois and imperial power to gain ground in China again. The 'Old Three Self' patriotic leaders of the institutional church remain as the leadership in the context of China's rapid process of modernization and Westernization, and consistently interpret the missionary movement through a lens of imperialism and colonialism. A recently released anthology, *Remembering the Past as a Lesson for the Future*[24] repeated historical platitudes of imperialistic forces using Christianity to invade China. This work represents a hierarchical response of the institutional church to the missionary movement. Many churchmen question the relevance of this work in times of globalization, and whether it

---

22 See Rey Chow, *Writing Diaspora: Tactics of Intervention in Contemporary Cultural Studies* (Indianapolis: Indiana University Press, 1993).

23 Wang Ning, *The Mapping of China's Modernity*, 1997, 36.

24 Luo Guangzong, ed., *Qianshi buwang huoshi zhishi* (Shanghai: TSPM/CCC, 2004).

is still adequate to publish a book dedicated to missionary history in China and its links to imperialism. Apparently, without repeating the slogan of anti-imperialism, the TSPM would lose its roots and it would be difficult to maintain its hierarchical leadership in the name of patriotism and a spirit of autonomy.

In the religious circle, patriotism has always been a hot issue, since the middle of the 20th century. The formation of the Three-Self movements highlighted that the political patriotism of Christians became the leading theme of the institutional church against imperialism and colonialism in the 1950s. In the new historical period with economic reform and openness, patriotism politically still plays a crucial role in opposing the infiltration of Western neo-colonial powers through the activities of economic and cultural globalization, such as the accession of the WTO and Beijing Olympic Games.

Political patriotism in the TSPM, which is different from Frantz Fanon's nationalism, emphasizes the church's loyalty to the political leadership of the Communist government and institutionally cuts off relations with Western churches and missions. In the name of patriotism, the hierarchy of the institutional church develops its notion of Chinese centrism, namely *ecclesia Sinica,* which is a Christian version of Sino-Centrism. The Chinese church is an independent, post-denominational, and three-self church under the leadership of the CCP. Institutional Christianity and is used to play an important role in the construction of a national consciousness in contemporary society, particularly under the impact of Westernization.

During the period of decolonization in Mao's China, the Communist leadership tended to use Christianity to promote political patriotism against Western imperialism and colonialism. During the period of globalization, once again the institutional church becomes a tool to promote Christian patriotism, which actually supports China-centrism against Western infiltration on the ideological-political arena through its missions.

In this postcolonial discourse, the recent development of institutional Christianity reflects that the Chinese church, in upholding patriotism against the infiltration of Western power, also has became an agent of postcolonial China-centrism.

In the beginning of Hu Jingtao's regime (2003), the government propaganda emphasized building 'scientific development' and a 'harmonious society.' It also lay down a principle for the institutional church in its mission agenda. The mission of the church is a mission to us rather than others. Therefore, in the national seminary, Paul Knitter and John Hick's theologies of religion are highlighted in the classroom. There, all religions and faiths, including atheism, are granted equal status on the assumption that they all strive for the salvation of human beings on earth. Salvation is re-interpreted as a socio-political and socio-economic harmony.

The 'Back to Jerusalem' movement: A fundamentalist Evangelical response

The 'Back to Jerusalem' Movement is a representative case study of a Chinese fundamentalist evangelical mission in the non-institutional church. It is a Christian campaign initiated by Chinese believers of house churches to send Chinese missionaries to the Buddhist, Hindu and Muslim world between China and Israel. It presents a traditional fundamentalist-evangelical understanding of a modern mission movement revival in China.

For this group, the Chinese church should not only be part of, but also lead global missions in the 21st century. Some church leaders present an idea of sending 100,000 missionaries to unreached people of 51 nations in the Middle-East.[25] Gradually, the vision becomes preaching the Christian message to the Muslims in Arabic countries, and bringing the gospel back to Jerusalem before the second coming of Christ. Along the ancient Silk Road, the vision is to share the gospel to 5200 unreached tribes and groups. This is also a vision of Sino-centrism with spiritual orientation.

These Christian leaders consider that the gospel started in Jerusalem, and then spread in a Westward direction into North Africa, Europe, and Latin America in history. It has continued to spread Westward to Asia around the globe. Today, the Christian message is preached in China geographically as its farthest point. The leaders of this movement claim that they see that to fulfil the Great Commission of Jesus Christ is to encircle the whole global world with the gospel until it goes back to Jerusalem where it began 2000 years ago.[26]

This type of mission obligation represents a traditional fundamentalist evangelical missionary calling. Their theology of mission comes from the acceptance of a pre-millennialist vision and literary interpretation of the end times of the Bible. Therefore, these church leaders commonly believe that Christ will return soon and inaugurate an earthly regime of a thousand years, and it will be based at Jerusalem. For them, China is transforming Christianity as much as it transformed Europe and America. China will become God's New Israel and New Jerusalem. Apparently, these Chinese evangelists dream of initiating another Christian Crusade to the Muslim world. An element of nationalistic pride mixing with a spiritual obligation of world mission will facilitate the ignorance of religious conflicts and cultural diversities. The Chinese Christian exclusivist attitude, in respect to other religions in general, and Islam in particular, is decidedly premodern or modern in some of its manifestations. The same is true of the position of Western evangelicalism. It also reminds that the premodern and modern

[25] The origin of this idea was born at the so-called Beijing Forum in February 2002. In the meeting, some American missionaries tried to help the house church leaders to implement their dream of evangelizing the entire world with particular focus on going back to Jerusalem. (See David Aikman, 2003, 194-195)

[26] For details, see Paul Hattaway, *Back to Jerusalem* (2005).

Western missionary movement mixed with colonial attitudes and behaviour for the Chinese people in 19th century. Therefore, for some, it is becoming a new form of Christian heterogeneity.

These criticisms are at least partially true because the recognition of religious plurality, spiritualities, and cultures is the context. It reminds that many of the premodern forms of evangelistic mission will have to change if they are to be accepted in a modern and postmodern society. The plurality of religion suggests that postmodern Christians should consider religious plurality to be God's purpose.[27]

The Sino-theology movement: A response from intellectual Christians

Apparently, intellectual Christianity is a new phenomenon and expression of Christian faith in China. It challenges the traditional and institutional form of Christianity from theological, ecclesiastical, and missiological perspectives. For most of these cultural Christians, a transcendent divinity can be mediated through culture and ethos and no longer necessarily through the ecclesial institution or Christian community alone.

Apparently, the mission obligation for the cultural Christians is far away from the traditional ecclesial body. Mission, for most of these cultural Christians, should not be narrowly understood as a concept of evangelization towards personal conversion from other traditional religions or other faiths, to follow Jesus Christ. All faiths must be respected as a people's way of seeking God. Dialogue between Christianity and other faiths, rather than proclamation of the Christian gospel, is the basis of Christian missions. This is a typical postmodern instrumentalist viewpoint of mission.[28] They purse an ideal state of Christian identity in the pluralistic concepts of values and life.

These scholars criticize an evangelical devaluation of these other religions and cultures and a total identification of the gospel with a Western form of Christianity and Western culture. Contextualization becomes an important theological issue for their consideration. They point out that there was not an adequate idea of the transcendence of the gospel over religions and cultures, and ,therefore, the idea of the Church of Christ as a ferment transforming all religions and cultures and taking new incarnations within them did not find enough expression in contemporary Christian practice of both institutional and non-institutional Christianity. As a theological as well as cultural response, therefore, many of these cultural Christians attempt to promote a Sino-theology, which is loaded with the traditional cultural and the existential experience of the Chinese people. Different from traditional

---

[27] WCC An Ecumenical Consultation in Geneva Switzerland (1982).

[28] According to instrumentalist epistemology, all faiths are seen as autonomous, incommensurable paradigms, and because people have no privileged position from which to judge them. Therefore, they must be affirmed as subjectively true. (See Paul G. Hiebert, *Missiological Implications of Epistemological Shift*, 1999, 60).

Chinese theology, Sino-theology has a concern with the humanistic rather than ecclesial approach. It is questionable whether it is possible to develop an authentic Christian theology outside the church.

The research dimensions of Sino-theology contain almost all fields of Christianity, e.g., patristics, medieval thought, Reformation, etc. However, the most valuable part is the encounter and dialogue between Christianity and Chinese culture. Contextualization and indignation become the most important work for building Sino-theology by these Chinese intellectuals. It is significant because Sino-theology is generating the possibility of a *Sinica*-style, not Western-style Christianity that the world has never really known before.

They insist on the use of the Chinese language in reading, thinking and writing theology, so that Chinese intellectuals do not have to submit to the language hegemony of the West, like in English or German. Otherwise, there is no way for the Chinese to formulate a Chinese Christian theology by using Western languages.

Intellectual Christianity encourages Chinese scholars to formulate their own agenda of Christian theology in Chinese according to Chinese tradition, cultural sources and socio-political contexts, instead of imposing the agenda of Western theology on theological discourse in China. Apparently, such a force for Christian studies promotes not only theological diversity and religious plurality. Especially, the resources of Chinese culture are compatible and pluralistic, which include traditional religious culture, namely Confucianism, Taoism, and Buddhism, as well as the contemporary orthodox ideology of the country, namely, Marxism, Maoism.

Different from the traditional Chinese church which is very Bible-oriented, cultural Christians try to provide a holistic tradition of Christianity in theological discourse. It means that Judeo-Christianity, Catholicism, and the Eastern and Greek Orthodoxy are included, in addition to the Protestant tradition. In this academic circle, there is more dialogue and co-operation between Chinese scholars and Western theologians than any other Christian groups. Such mutual academic communication in Christian theology, which is still in the primitive stage, could enhance the theological weakness of institutional and non-institutional Christianity. It also enables Chinese theology to become a component part of ecumenical theology.

Through various academic and cultural endeavours, cultural Christians try to transplant the Western -oriented Christian thoughts, religious values and theological ideas into cultural, religious, ideological systems of contemporary China. Although most churchmen consider this form of Christian thinking more culturally than religiously dominated, promoting Christian research and religious studies is beneficial to the Chinese intellectuals, who are gradually moving from atheism to theism. Meanwhile, many Chinese scholars, in the process of doing Christian studies, gradually shift their understanding of Christian faith from objective and theoretical analysis to subjective and spiritual experience. In other words, Christianity is no longer interpreted as knowledge or culture, but life and spirit.

BITTER AND SWEET TEARS: EXPLORING THE SPIRITUALITY OF THE EASTERN CHURCH FATHERS IN THE LIGHT OF POSTMODERN 'ENTHUSIASTIC CHRISTIANITY' IN RUSSIA

Olga Zaprometova

The challenges of postmodern pluralism have produced insecurity and made room for doubts and hesitations that go beyond the issue of faithfulness to Scripture. We have more knowledge about God but less knowledge of God, less experiences of His presence and personal encounters with His love. Postmodernity does not trust abstract ideas. Everything is tested through a personal relationship. The crisis of self-identity in contemporary society is often considered to be a result of secularization and many Christians are trying to find a solution in the 'fellowship of the Holy Spirit.' In Russia there is a growing interest in 'enthusiastic Christianity'[1], which some scholars characterize as an extra dimension of emotionalism that sometimes reaches exaltation. Is it possible however to see this phenomenon as a new manifestation of the open emotional expression which was both recognized by Eastern Christianity and formed an integral part of its tradition many centuries ago? Or is it a response to the advent of postmodern symptoms in Russian society?

We have to accept the fact that, as elsewhere in the world, many Russian Christians nowadays feel themselves 'homeless', moving from one church to another as religious institutions become marketing agencies and religious traditions become consumer commodities. Feeling and being 'at home' in this sense, is a gift and a call from God. We are immersed in a postmodern[2] identity crisis. The postmodern self is de-centered, disoriented, fragmented and tossed by the wind of every impinging image and context. Will this new movement of 'enthusiastic Christianity' be able and ready to envisage

---

[1]The author is using this term to include Pentecostals, Charismatics and Neocharismatics. See: Stanley M. Burgess & Eduard M. van der Maas (eds.) *The New International Pentecostal and Charismatic Movements* (Grand Rapids, Michigan: Zondervan, 2003), xix-xxii.

[2]In this paper the author is referring to post-modernity and post-modernism as the terms generally used to describe the aspects of contemporary culture that are the result of the unique features of late 20th century and early 21st century life.

its mission calling in such a context? This study is an attempt to do three things:

1) To find answers to many questions posed by those who are taking Christian living as an ongoing drama. Who in Russia today is truly postmodern? To what extent is this so, and in what ways?

2) To show the role of emotions in the development of the practice, as well as the doctrine, of spiritual life by analyzing the teachings of representatives of the Eastern Church (Gregory the Theologian, Isaac of Nineveh and Simeon the New Theologian).

3) To make a link with today's preferences by pointing to the success of "enthusiastic Christianity" in contemporary Russia. Can this be regarded as a direct response to the advent of postmodern symptoms in Russian society? How does 'rejoicing Christianity' envisage its mission calling in this context?

The First World War witnessed the end of the modern era including its hope to achieve all kinds of progress in society. According to Boris Pasternak, 1913 was the last year during which it was easier to love than to hate. Anna Akhmatova defined 1914 as the beginning of the 20th century. Although the early years of the 20th century seemed promising both for the Orthodox and for Evangelical Protestants in Russia, the declaration that followed the revolution (1918) regarding the separation of the churches from the state and of the schools from the churches, removed the legal basis of all religious institutions, which was not restored till 1989[3]. After the two World Wars the European countries were disillusioned with the idea of the ongoing progress of civilization towards a better future. Eurasia was swept by waves of different enthusiastic movements much more than the rest of the world. The utopian ideas required more and more sacrifices, as a kind of 'game', for the sake of 'happiness' promised by all kinds of leaders. As a result, the youth became apathetic toward the enthusiasm of previous generations and did not want to make sacrifices for the sake of a better life. 'Better to take life as it is, to enjoy it for your own good, there is no absolute truth to dedicate your life to totally and so, .. there is no meaning to this life.'

In the late '70s and early '80s of the last century, Russian scholars noticed the historical shift that had been taking place in the former Soviet Union, defined by them as a crisis of civilization. It was considered to be the response to the social and cultural changes that the society had undergone, and the formation of new stereotypes. It was already noticed that postmodernity allowed for plural interpretations. Nowadays, the inner man is fragile and facing problems as never before. The Russian Christian analysts report on the decline of the first wave of religious enthusiasm, which appeared on post-Soviet territory and of the aspiration for the second

[3]Walter Sawatsky, 'Orthodox-Evangelical Protestant Dialogue on Mission-Challenges and Shifting Options', *Acta Missiologiae 1* (2008), 11-31.

one to come[4]. Religion, however, does not disappear from the social stage. Religious experience reflects the multiplicity of transformations and a human being's way of life. The godless way of life, implanted by mass media does not leave us without a perspective on what concerns secularism and religion. Quite the opposite! The deconstruction of traditional dispositions and beliefs, which is now taking place, gives a chance for a new social search for religious truth[5].

Russian secular philosophers of today envisage the future of mankind to be the acquisition of religious meaning. They are expecting the renaissance of a set of religious beliefs. G. Kiselev, in his paper 'Postmodernity and Christianity', reminds us that the traditional self-identity in Eastern Christianity is fellowship between a human being and God. This mystical encounter is a process. According to this modern Russian scholar, the very first Ecumenical task of contemporary Christianity is to understand its true position and place in world history. Kiselev stresses that Russian religious philosophy has been waiting for the new birth of Christianity since the end of the 19th century. This religious philosophy claimed as well that a true spiritual renaissance of the world might be expected only through the intervention of the Holy Spirit[6]. It definitely seems that the pendulum never stops swinging back and forth, and the ongoing search for truth, for meaning and for experiencing the Absolute (God) is essential for postmodernity as never before. The paradigm of love in contemporary Trinitarian thought might be taken as an example of a synthesis of Western and Eastern Christian thought, that is turning out to be of special interest for the growing 'enthusiastic' Christians[7].

It is assumed that most Western readers have little experience with the Orthodox tradition, its richness and variety that so greatly influenced the formation of the 'Russian soul'. The priority given to emotional values over material ones by the Russian character is a well known fact[8]. Emotions are one of the mightiest powers in history and culture. The academic world is going through a process of analyzing the 'emotional revolution' in the humanities and sees it as a new paradigm shift. In 2007 an international conference on 'Emotions in Russian History and Culture' was held in

---

[4]Pavel Levushkan, 'The Church proved to be unprepared for the coming of the Google world,' *Mirt* 1 (2009), 12-13 (in Russian).

[5]Alexander S. Vatoropin, Konstantin M. Olkhovikov, 'The Perspectives of Secularism and Religion in the Post-modern Era', *Social Sciences and Modernity* 3 (2003), 136-145 (in Russian).

[6]Grigory S. Kiselev, 'Post-modernity and Christianity', *Questions of Philosophy* 12 (2001), 3-15 (in Russian).

[7]See the doctoral dissertation of Mikhail Aksenov-Meerson – *The Love Paradigm and the Retrieval of Western Medieval Love Mysticism in Modern Russian Trinitarian Thought* (1996).

[8]Alla Sergeyeva, *The Russians: Behavior Stereotypes, Traditions, Mentality* (Moscow: 'Science', 2005), 136 (in Russian).

Moscow. Among the problems raised at this forum were inter alia: emotional responses to the texts that represent culture, emotions as a discipline, and the role of emotions and historical memory.

The growing Pentecostal and Charismatic congregations that are often referred to in some circles as 'enthusiastic Christianity', differ from evangelical fundamentalists in their search for truth. This truth can be found, according to them, not only in the sphere of the mind (teaching, doctrine), but also in spiritual experiences. These experiences are followed by a change of attitude and conduct, which is the essential part of true conversion. The Pentecostal worldview is characterized primarily by the emphasis put on the importance of communion with God, and by the claim that love is an emotional experience[9].

First, let me remind the reader what is the difference between a Western and an Eastern understanding of 'doing' theology. The very term 'theology' is often misunderstood. It is commonly agreed that theology deals with the knowledge of God which man strives to acquire. It is also often accepted that theology seeks to explain the relations between God and man (God and the created world) and aims at explaining current social problems in the light of the Gospel and the Scriptures. Theology is seen as a contemplative discipline, which helps human beings to have better understaning of God and the world He created. For the East, theology starts with the *ortho-doxy*, understood as proper worship. According to James Stamoolis, theology is something in which believers must participate: 'For the Orthodox, all theology is worship; all worship is theology'[10]. For the West *ortho-doxy* is related more to the correct understanding of doctrinal statements (taking a different meaning of the Greek word *doxa* which underlies the second element of the word 'orthodoxy'). It is a rational way of thinking. In other words, the difference is in the emphasis put on the experiential versus the rational way of doing theology. The experiential way is related to the prayer life of a believer and is inseparable from the spirituality of a Christian. However, it does not mean that Western theology excludes the spiritual life of the believer, nor that Eastern theology excludes a correct understanding of doctrine.

Let us turn now to the writings of the Eastern Church Fathers in order to see whether there is any place for emotions that may be relevant to our postmodern era. One of the most famous Jewish exegetes of pre-Christian times, Philo of Alexandria, wrote about *drunkenness, sober ecstasy* and *intellectual rage/fury* when trying to describe his own spiritual/intellectual experience[11]. His approach to biblical exegesis is in accord both with the

---

[9]Jackie D. Johns, 'Pentecostalism and the Postmodern Worldview', *Journal of Pentecostal Theology* 7 (1995), 73-96.

[10]James Stamoolis, *Eastern Orthodox Mission Theology Today.* (New York: Orbis Books, 1986), 10.

[11]For Philo it is still more the intellectual experience. See: Kenneth Schenk, *A Brief Guide to Philo* (Moscow: St. Andrew's Biblical-Theological Institute, 2007), 23.

earlier Jewish tradition (1 Sam 1:13-16) and with that later developed in the New Testament (Acts 2:12-15; Eph 5:18). In the Bible, such an emotional state of praying is compared to drunkenness (1 Sam1:13-16; Acts 2:12-15; Eph 5:18). Tertullian, the 3rd century North African theologian, talked about the marriage of a believer's soul to the Holy Spirit, followed by the physical body. This is his way of explaining how a soul is able to feel God, and to witness His mighty deeds through prophecies and feelings/emotions[12]. Gregory the Theologian (4th century) is considered to be one of the creators of the Theology of Light in the Christian tradition, which later was further developed by the Hesychast movement. His teaching on the vision of God is inseparable from his teaching on the knowledge of God. Gregory the Theologian points out that a person can see God only by feeling His mystical presence. The pinnacle of the whole Christian life, according to him, is *deification* or *theosis* (unification of a human being with God)[13]. The term *deification* appears to be a Latinate calque of *theosis* rather than an accurate translation of its meaning, and this serves to obscure rather than illuminate the dialogue between the Eastern and the Western Christianity. *Theosis* includes two complementary stages of deification: the process towards deification and the state of deification. Gregory the Theologian affirms that the first 'stage of theosis' takes place in our current life, and the second one will be accomplished in the age to come; now we only foretaste theosis, but there is the eschatological theosis that is waiting for us at the 'fulfilment of times', the one we will be able to enjoy fully[14] The way leading to deification is a human being's love for God, as expressed in prayer and mystical experience as well as in the fulfilment of the New Testament commandments. Although God still remains unknowable, inexpressible, unreachable, and invisible, prayer is primarily a meeting with the living God. A human being is seeking God and is in need of fellowship with Him, and God is seeking those who are *thirsty after Him, continually and abundantly outpouring* (Himself) *upon*

---

[12]Quintus Tertullianus, *On the Soul.* (St.Petersburg: Oleg Abushko's Publishing House, 2004), 139 (in Russian); www.krotov.info/ (in Russian)

[13]*Deification* is the ancient theological word used to describe the process by which a Christian becomes more like God through His grace (2 Pet 1:3-4). Because of the incarnation of the Son of God, because the fullness of God has inhabited human flesh, being joined to Christ means that it is again possible to experience *deification,* the fulfillment of our human destiny. According to the Orthodox tradition, nourished by the Body and Blood of Christ, we are partaking in the grace of God, in His strength, in His righteousness, in His love, and are therefore enabled to serve Him and glorify Him. Thus, while remaining human, we are being *deified.*

[14] Alfeyev, *The Life and Teaching of St. Gregory the Theologian,* (Moscow: Lovers of Church History Society's Press, 1998), 391, citing Gregory's *Oration* 38, 11, 22-24 (in Russian).

them[15]. Praying to Christ was an integral part of Gregory's spiritual life. His prayers were filled with a deep personal love for Christ[16].

According to Archimandrite George, "Theosis is the acquisition of the Holy Spirit, whereby through God's grace Christians become participants in the Kingdom of God. ... Theosis begins here in time and space, but it is not static or complete, it is an open-ended progression uninterrupted through all eternity"[17]. This process of deification is fairly close description of the process that Protestant theology describes as *sanctification* and might be considered as one of the possible themes for the future dialogue between Pentecostal and Orthodox communities.

Bitter and Sweet Tears

The experiences of a person on his journey towards God appear also in the Syrian Christian literature. One of the outstanding representatives of the Syrian tradition in the Eastern Church is Isaac the Syrian (7th century), for whom spiritual life starts with the turning of the soul to God and the rejection of the ways of this world. According to him, the world is the sum of a human's passions. Like Gregory the Theologian, for whom prayer was an encounter with the living God, Isaac the Syrian claimed that *life in God was a sensation or feeling of His presence.* When for some reason this presence is lost, the believer is unable to find peace until he/she feels His presence again[18].

Here one has to take into consideration that in our postmodern world the word 'passion(s)' has three different meanings: (1) etymologically, the word does mean suffering, but in modern language, this meaning is pretty well restricted to a theological context, speaking about the passion fo Christ; (2a) in common usage, the word is often synonym for emotion, but is rather stronger, meaning an overwhelming enthusiasm for something[19]; (2b) in tabloid style usage, it has strongly sexual overtones, and, for a lot of people, this may even have become the primary meaning. There are several interpretations of the concept of passions in Patristic literature, including

---

[15]Alfeyev, *The Life and Teaching of St. Gregory the Theologian*, 360 (in Russian).

[16]According to Origen, one has to pray only to God the Father *through Christ,* because Christ Himself did this and taught it to His disciples – Matt 6:9; 26:39; Lk 11:2; John 12:27; 17:11 et al. All the known Early Church liturgies are addressed to God the Father. Liturgies addressed to God the Son appeared not earlier than in the fifth century, in the era of the Christological controversies.

[17]George, Archimandrite. *Theosis: The True Purpose of Human Life*. (Mount Athos: Holy monastery of St. Gregorios, 2006), 86.

[18]Alfeyev, *The World of Isaac the Syrian* (Moscow: Lovers of Church History Society's Press, 1998), 109 (in Russian).

[19]See Land, Steven J. *Pentecostal Spirituality: A Passion for the Kingdom* (Sheffield, Sheffield Academic Press, 1997). Here is the example that a passion can be a fixed attitude, not just a temporary enthusiasm.

two major ones: passion as a sinful inclination and passion as an inherited ability of a soul which might be turned to (for) good as to evil[20].

According to Isaac the Syrian, there are three stages along the way to a human's unification with God: repentance, purification and perfection or in other words: change of will, freedom from passions, and the acquisition of perfect love and the fullness of God's grace. Repentance[21] starts when one feels sinful, due to the intervention of God's grace[22]. Teaching on repentance and on the encounter of a human soul with God is closely related to Isaac's teaching on tears. When referring to the Saviour's words: *Blessed are they that mourn* (Matt 5:4), Isaac adds that *the one who is in the love of God will never lack the grace of tears because he/she is never lacking the source that is feeding him/her: the remembrance of God. That is why even when he/she is sleeping he/she is talking to God*[23]. Isaac distinguishes between bitter and sweet tears, tears of repentance and tears of affection (*slezy umilenia* – Slavic) given to a person when he or she reaches purity of heart. The last type of tears means 'tenderness' ('tender-hearted'), 'mildness' or 'meekness'. Tears in prayer testify that a prayer is accepted by God. According to Isaac, endless crying may start for any of the following three reasons:

> ... from awe and wonder occasioned by the mystery of revelation that is revealed to the
> mind only rarely – tears begin to pour unbidden and without the will of a person and
> without forcing ... ;
> ... from the love to God that inflames the soul to such an extent that a person cannot bear
> this love without continuous crying from pleasure because of its sweetness ...;
> ... from great humbleness of hear.t[24]

Unification with God is impossible without prayer because prayer is a personal encounter with God. Isaac underlines how one has to pray: attentively, with deep feeling and with tears (because *the grace of tears is the fullness of prayer*[25]), with fervour and faith. This *amazement, wonder, and rapture* of the mind under the influence of the Holy Spirit, and seeing the Divine Light in a state of *silence* and *peace* is sometimes called ecstasy. When realizing that one does not belong to oneself but rather to God, one is

---

[20]Ware K.T. *The Meaning of "Pathos" in Abba Isaias and Theodoret of Cyrus (*Studia Patristica: XX. Louvain, 1989), 315-322.

[21]Greek – *μετανοια*, means "change of thoughts, change of mind".

[22]Augustine, Wesley and many others wrote about the same, while Pentecostals preach about this as well.

[23]Quoted according to Alfeyev, *The World of Isaac the Syrian*, 145.

[24]Quoted according to Alfeyev, *The World of Isaac the Syrian*, 147. At the same time, according to Alfeyev, Isaac does not always define the line between the two types of tears: they are more likely two aspects of the same experience – 148.

[25] Alfeyev. *The World of Isaac the Syrian*, 153.

going out of oneself and can no longer tell whether one exists in present time or in eternity[26]. *When the control and supervision of the Spirit rules over the mind ... then freedom is taken from nature and the mind is led instead of leading*[27]. An intense personal fellowship between a human being and God is taking place. What a *soul is praying for is no longer represented by the words of the prayer itself, but rather by feeling and experiencing the spiritual realities of the world yet to come.* These realities are *beyond human understanding, except by the power of the Holy Spirit. ... From this experience of prayer the Holy Spirit lifts the soul up to meditation that is called spiritual vision*[28].

The image of drunkenness caused by wine helps Isaac describe the experience of a mystical encounter, which is in itself the introduction to the heavenly joy and pleasure of the Kingdom of Heaven.

> ... Quite often it happens that a person bows his knees in prayer, his hands are lifted up to heaven, his face is turned to the Cross of Christ and all his thoughts are brought together in prayer to God, and at the same time, as a human being is praying to God with tears and affections, suddenly a spring starts to spurt in his heart, pouring out pleasure; then parts of his body are weakened, his eyes close, the face bent over to the earth, his thoughts are changing in such a way that he cannot bow down from the joy that is exciting his whole body[29].
>
> ... From time to time however the mind is taken from the prayer and carried to heaven as a captive and involuntary tears like springs of water pour over the face and water it. At the same time the person himself feels at peace, is speechless and filled with amazing vision and truly this is a ceasing of prayer; it is a state that is above prayer – a state of constant amazement in the face of every one of God's creatures, like those who have lost their senses because of wine[30].
>
> When the soul is drunk with the joy of hope and the joyfulness of God, the body does not feel sorrows. ... This happens when the soul enters into the joy of the Spirit.[31]

Such experience is frequently associated by Isaac with the Eucharist, in which the true love of God is revealed to a human being.

Simeon the New Theologian (10th-11th centuries) is regarded in the West as the most outstanding of the medieval mystics for his charismatic approach to Christian life. Like Gregory the Theologian, Simeon speaks

---

[26]Vladimir Lossky, *Essays on the Mystical Theology of the Eastern Church,* (Moscow: SEI Center's Press, 1991), 156-257 (in Russian).
[27]Quoted according to Alfeyev. *The World of Isaac the Syrian,* 230.
[28]Quoted according to Alfeyev. *The World of Isaac the Syrian,* 23-33.
[29]Quoted according to Alfeyev. *St. Simeon the New Theologian and the Orthodox Tradition,* (Moscow: Lovers of Church History Society's Press, 1998), 396-397 (in Russian).
[30]Quoted according to Alfeyev. *The World of Isaac the Syrian,* 259.
[31]Quoted according to Alfeyev. *The World of Isaac the Syrian,* 262.

about his experiences of the Divine Light and mentions it in all his writings. Besides these experiences, Gregory mentions as well prayer *in other tongues* and how much his *soul suffers* and *cries*[32]. Tears, as a theme in Simeon's writings, are associated with the themes of love for God and vision, as in Isaac's writings. Simeon gives testimony regarding the process of a person's transformation, which takes place in turning to God in prayer, and in shedding bitter tears of repentance and grief. Once the state of a clean heart and the vision of the Divine are reached, there is a consolation, and the person experiencing it sheds sweet tears (Matt. 5:8). When envisaging God and listening to His revelations, the person becomes a light. All of Simeon's personal experiences, which form the basis of his theology, are not just an individual search for God, but rather the very revelation of God Himself to a human being. He perceives this experience as a feeling of light and a flood of tears – a reaction to God's presence unseen by his earthly sight[33].

It is often argued that deep Christian affections are at the core of Pentecostal spirituality and they are considered by many as essential for understanding theology. For one of the most widely recognized Pentecostal authors of today, Steve Land, deep Christian affections are different from mere feelings or moods. Pentecostal prayer shapes and expresses the affections that Land is interpreting as 'a passion for the Kingdom'[34]. This passion is different from temporary feelings or shallow emotions. Love as such, including the love for God, is a passion. We do not love principles, we love the Person. As defined by Jürgen Moltmann, these differences can be 'noticed when praying to the Father, to Christ and to the Spirit, and are reflected in the different forms of intercession, invocation and adoration'[35].

One can compare the three components of the Eastern Church Fathers' mystical encounter with the Holy Spirit which have been discussed in this paper with the three major characteristics of Pentecostal theology: orthodoxy, orthopathy and orthopraxy. The first concerns prayer, in which an encounter with a living God is taking place. Its goal is a vision of God, knowing His will and accepting it freely. The second corresponds to experiencing the presence of God, as expressed in various ways (tears, ecstasy, etc.). The third is the transformation of a believer's way of life (*deification*) as described by the Eastern Fathers'[36].

---

[32]Alfeyev, *St. Simeon the New Theologian and the Orthodox Tradition,* (Moscow: Lovers of Church History Society's Press, 1998), 601.

[33]Alfeyev, *St. Simeon the New Theologian and the Orthodox Tradition,* 340 –350

[34]Steven J. Land, *Pentecostal Spirituality: A Passion for the Kingdom* (Sheffield: Sheffield Academic Press, 1997).

[35]Jürgen Moltmann, *The Spirit of Life: A Universal Affirmation* (Minneapolis: Fortress Press, 1994), 12.

[36]Olga M. Zaprometova, 'Experience of the Holy Spirit in the Context of Patristic Tradition. The Pentecostal's Reading', *Pages* 13/1 (2008/2009): 63-90 (in Russian).

Literally, spirituality means life in God's Spirit, and a living relationship with Him. As we can see, experiencing the Holy Spirit is inseparable from the Spirituality of the Eastern Church tradition. Bitter and sweet tears, as well as joy and love, were a vital part of the transformation process going on in a Christian, which was embraced by the teaching on *deification.* The writings of the Eastern Fathers give us valuable evidence of the variety and richness of the ancient Church's spiritual life, and its ability to incorporate reflections of spiritual experience into its doctrine.

In sum, one may see the important place of emotional experience, not just in the practice of praying, but also in the development of doctrine. This experience was always an integral part of Eastern Christian spirituality.

Theology begins when one first prays, since praying is a deeper mode of understanding than knowing by means of reason alone[37]. Although the term "deification" is unknown to Pentecostals, most of them speak about the importance of the fellowship of a Christian with the living God. The Pentecostal movement stresses the value of religious experience, which may transform the postmodern fragmentation. Experiencing the Holy Spirit is inseparable from a Pentecostal spirituality, and it is on these grounds that Pentecostals are often accused of being emotional at the expense of being rational[38].

Pentecostalism is fundamentally experiential and culturally constructed (formed by the culture). However, it is this experiential and inter-cultural approach which allows for greater possibilities. M. Cartledge defines Pentecostalism as a worshipful experience and a crisis experience (that must be understood in a Christian context). It is also a social context which theologically may be accounted for in a broad sacramental sense[39]. Prayer is the centre of Pentecostal spirituality. Since prayer is communion and a dialogue, which involves a relationship in passion between those who pray and God, it is the place where the encounter between a human being and the living God occurs. The Pentecostal worldview is characterized primarily by the emphasis it puts on the importance of communion with God, and by claiming constantly that love is an emotional experience. Salvation, when conceived of as a communion, involves a response of freely given love, and a sincere turning of the human will towards God and His ways. This makes communion with God deeper and deeper.

As R. Roberts has observed, all the peculiarly Christian emotions are founded on a passionate interest in the Kingdom of God[40]. Some contemporary Pentecostals define their own personal experiences as

---

[37]Don E. Saliers *The Soul in Paraphrase: Prayer and the Religious Affections* (Akron: OSL Publications, 2003), 70.

[38]Land, *Pentecostal Spirituality,* 132.

[39]Mark J. Cartledge, 'Pentecostal Experience: An Example of Practical-Theological Rescripting', *JEPTA* 28/1 (2008), 21-33.

[40]Robert C. Roberts, *Spiritual Emotion: A Psychology of Christian Virtues* (Grand Rapids: Eerdmans, 2007), 196.

charismatic manifestations or deeds of the Holy Spirit, which result in the decision to follow Him. Love for God and neighbour is the basis for the mission calling of the new 'enthusiasts': to spread the Kingdom of God through witnessing, preaching and ministering as well as through different forms of social work. T. Richie underlines the importance of the Pentecostal heritage of ecumenicalism and inclusivism, as an answer to the religious diversity and the pluralistic opinions in our contemporary world[41]. 'Rejoicing Christianity' must envisage its mission calling and consider carefully the distinctiveness of its own worldview in the context of the postmodern era[42]. Nowadays Pentecostals (including the Charismatic movement which some Russian authors call Neo-Pentecostalism) are growing in number in Russia, and have become a visible phenomenon in both the religious and the social spheres, attracting the attention of the media and provoking considerable controversy[43]. Still, due to the secularization of society and to the new phenomenon of postmodernity, unlike in their early years, Pentecostals are no longer regarded as a sect. In general, the crisis of postmodernity in Russia results in longing for a restoration of the supernatural, a strengthening intercultural relations, an attraction to mystery and an affirmation of the more figurative and symbolic forms of communication. 'Enthusiastic Christianity' has a lot to offer to the unhappy ones in society, who are thirsty and in search of a new spirituality. However, one should not disregard the importance and richness of the spiritual heritage of Estern Spirituality, now embedded in a way in the 'Russian soul'.

This paper has attempted to show that in a sense the new movement of 'rejoicing Christianity' is a direct response to the advent of postmodern symptoms in Russian society. In view of our culture's orientation to success, to production and prestige and to all the requirements that follow such an orientation, our inner being is longing for deeper spirituality, quiet and peace. It is reflected in the search for religious experience, for deeper affections and for meaning in a committed Christian life. The encounter with God's Spirit, i.e. the experiencing of the *Ruakh* of God is first and foremost a stirring one[44]. The intention of this paper has been to create a

---

[41]Tony Richie, '"The Unity of the Spirit": are Pentecostals inherently ecumenists and inclusivists?' *JEPTA* 26.1 (2006), 21-35.

[42]Jackie D. Johns, 'Pentecostalism and the Postmodern Worldview', *JPT* 7 (1995), 73-96.

[43]It is a surprise that the denomination, whose history in Russia can be traced to the beginning of the 20th century and which experienced all the difficulties of religious persecution, equally with the representatives of the Orthodox Church and other confessions, though recognized all over the world, in Russia is still sometimes considered to be a cult.

[44]Anton Houptepen, *God: the Open Question. Theological Perspectives of the Modern Culture* (Moscow: St. Andrew's Biblical-Theological Institute, 2008), 330 (in Russian).

link to the past, this includes both to find the roots of postmodern Pentecostalism's experiential theology and of its rich emotional outpouring in experiences presented in the Patristic tradition as part of a process of seeking self-identity, and at the same time to strengthen awareness of the inter-cultural relationship between the two eras.

The search for a more solid and constructive dialogue between followers of Eastern and Western Christian traditions is one of mankind's most urgent tasks, especially in the light of globalization. Let us keep the 'windows of theology open', since this may be the proper answer to both the scepticism and the fundamentalism of our times. Without overlooking the experiential component of conversion, which plays a role in the process of reaching salvation and full communion with God, 'enthusiastic Christianity' has begun to seek its roots in Holy Scriptures and in Church tradition. Will the 'enthusiasts', together with some contemporary Orthodox theologians, choose to follow the way of Neo-Patristic synthesis, or will they claim that this represents only an escape from the problems imposed by postmodernity, an escape which can be no more than a slavish imitation of tradition, one which rejects any theological development? Will also the Orthodox Church, the most prominent religious power in contemporary Russia, be ready to recognize the reality of the encounter with Christ, which 'enthusiastic Christianity' advocates and testifies to? Let us remember that, so far, these are open questions, and that the secular analysts are waiting for a response from the Church, not just in the form of official ecclesiological-political acts or documents, but rather in reflections, conjectures or insights from its individual members.

Exploring the spirituality of the early Church Fathers can serve as a helpful way for Pentecostal and Charismatic believers in Russia to overcome the postmodern crisis of self-identity. It may help find in Church history answers relevant to the contemporary Russian context. This will enrich mission activity in Europe both East and West, and even in Asia, due to the spread of Russian Orthodoxy by emigration, and in view of globalization and the postmodern identity crisis. The emphasis put on 'enthusiastic Christianity' is not a doctrinal question. Instead of logical/rational theological *Regula fidei* formulations/concepts, it suggests rather an experiential side as the basis of Christian faith. This is a much more promising approach to mission in postmodern Russia. In the postmodern world, one has not just to see with one's own eyes but also to feel with one's own heart, to experience in one's whole being the presence of God and His love. Mission must follow worship/doxology. Thus, we may see in what sense an understanding of the role of emotions in the Eastern Christian tradition might become a bridge to understanding the growth of 'enthusiastic' Christianity in contemporary Russia. The experience of closeness of God and His intimate presence is greater than theological proofs of God's existence for secularized society. Love is more than an attribute of God! It is His essence. The Christian East with its rich religious experiences, described by the Early Church Fathers, seems to be more attractive to disappointed postmodernists, especially the younger generation. Will its theological treasure be embraced by contemporary 'enthusiasts'?

INTERROGATING *MISSIO DEI*: FROM THE MISSION OF GOD TOWARDS APPRECIATING OUR MISSION TO GOD IN INDIA TODAY

J. Jayakiran Sebastian

Problematizing *Missio Dei*

> '... Listen, my darling, if you're going to be religious, you must be either a Hindu, a Christian or a Muslim. ...'
> 'I don't see why I can't be all three. Mamaji has two passports. He's Indian and French. Why can't I be a Hindu, a Christian and a Muslim?'
> That's different. France and India are nations on earth.'
> How many nations are there in the sky?'
> She thought for a second. 'One. That's the point. One nation, one passport.'
> 'One nation in the sky?'
> 'Yes. Or none. There's that option too, you know. These are terribly old-fashioned things you've taken to.'
> If there's only one nation in the sky, shouldn't all passports be valid for it?'
> A cloud of uncertainty came over her face.
> 'Bapu Gandhi said –'.
> 'Yes. I know what Bapu Gandhi said.' She brought a hand to her forehead. She had a weary look, Mother did. 'Good grief,' she said.[1]

Faced as we are, in the first decade of the twenty-first century, with a plethora of mission theologies, combined with major efforts to think about the need of mission in a globalized context, the question regarding the relevance and understanding of the term 'mission' is a pressing one. A recent issue of the *International Review of Mission* is devoted to the theme 'Missio Dei Revisited Willingen 1952-2002.'[2] This issue contains a wide range of articles looking at the concept from historical and contextual perspectives. Writing from a contemporary Korean perspective, one of the writers points out that the concept has 'broken down barriers but it has also created new ones: barriers between conservatives and progressives, between evangelism and humanization, between saving souls and social involvement,' and goes on to say that such barriers are only 'gradually disappearing.' This article raises two important questions as a conclusion:

---

[1] Yann Martel, *Life of Pi: A Novel* (New Delhi: Penguin Books, 2002), 73-74.
[2] *International Review of Mission*, Vol. XCII, No. 367 (October 2003).

first, the relationship between *missio Dei* and money; and second, the relationship between *missio Dei* and other religions.[3]

This paradigm, that of understanding mission as *missio Dei*, has dominated missiological thinking for the last fifty years at least,[4] and has been enormously influential and has generated a rich assortment of theological, ecclesiological and missiological thinking.[5] However, for various reasons, not least connected with my engagement with the issues and themes raised by a pluralistic and post-colonial approach to the missiological questions of our time, I have increasingly become uneasy with the concept of *missio Dei*. It is not that I believe that the concept has not made a significant contribution to our understanding of mission and missiology, but I have come to believe that we need to interrogate this

---

[3] Soo-il Chai, 'Missio Dei – Its Development and Limitations in Korea,' *IRM* (October 2003), 548- 549.

[4] David Bosch, in his magisterial *Transforming Mission: Paradigm Shifts in Theology of Mission* (Maryknoll, NY: Orbis, 1991), explores the background of the emergence of this term, pointing out as to how the idea emerged at the Willingen Conference of the International Missionary Council in 1952, where the the influence of Karl Barth 'on missionary thinking reached a peak' and where the 'classical doctrine on the *missio Dei* as God the Father sending the Son, and God the Father and the Son sending the Spirit was expanded to include yet another 'movement': Father, Son and Holy Spirit sending the church into the world.' (p. 390). Bosch goes on to explore how this term has had important implications for the *missiones ecclesiae* and indicates the processes by which nearly all Christian denominations have welcomed and used this term. (pp. 389-393).

[5] See, for example, the contribution of Arthur F. Glasser, in *Announcing the Kingdom: The Story of God's Mission in the Bible* (Grand Rapids, MI: Baker Academic, 2003), who interprets the goal of *missio Dei* as that of incorporating 'people into the Kingdom of God and to involve them in his mission.' He also deplores the 'non-involvement in mission on the part of the church' because involvement is necessitated by the reality that 'the Father is the Sender, Jesus Christ the One who is sent, and the Holy Spirit the Revealer ....' (p. 245) This is to be read within the conviction of the writer that 'at every level of the biblical evidence conversion demands commitment to conduct that is reflective of the coming Kingdom of God.' He goes on to ask: 'Is it not also true that persons who are not born again may on the day of judgment wish that they had never been born at all?' (p. 358).

The influential Indian Jesuit thinker, Michael Amaladoss, in his article, 'The Trinity on Mission,'Frans Wijsen and Peter Nissen, eds., '*Mission is a Must': Intercultural Theology and the Mission of the Church* (Amsterdam: Rodopi, 2002), 99-106, writes that 'To contemplate the Trinity, our mission in the world is a freeing experience, so that we can carry on our own mission without aggression and anxiety, conscious that we are making a real contribution to the realization of God's plan for the world. We learn to be sensitive to what God is doing in the world and to co-ordinate our own mission with God's mission' (p. 106). As a supplement to this from a different context, see Darrell L. Guder, 'From Mission and Theology to Missional Theology,' *The Princeton Seminary Bulletin*, Vol. XXIV, No. 1, New Series (2003), 36-54.

concept and offer a theological critique of how this concept has played out in empirical terms, in order to provoke and stimulate other, possibly more productive and more relevant, ways of thinking and acting in this religiously plural and culturally globalized world.[6] This discontent resulted in the following proposal that I made during an international consultation sponsored by the World Council of Churches. (The theme of the consultation itself is symptomatic of the wider concern with the issue of missiology and relevance, missiology and credibility.) At this meeting[7] I suggested that:

> [a] re-examination of the missio Dei paradigm is necessary, because what is needed today is a mission paradigm that affirms our mission to God. Having gone through the consequences of theological thinking regarding the mission of God, and having explored human responsibility in this task, a reversal of the direction in trying to take seriously the human experience of both variety and difference in God/divinity, and what this means for the question as to whether there can ever be an understanding of a common mission of humankind, becomes an urgent theological task.[8]

Naturally, such an affirmation provoked concern, a desire on the part of the participants to probe into the source of such discontent, and a genuine bewilderment that such a mode of questioning had even been thought necessary. If Nirmal was right in his famous assertion that God does not read or write theology and that 'theology has nothing to do with God,'[9] can we 'transpose' this theological point to the field of missiology and ask in what sense we can make the claim that mission is *of* God? If mission is not *of* God, then what mission are we talking about? We have not been afraid of coming to terms with the reality that mission as a human enterprise has

---

[6] The directions in which I have been thinking can be found in my articles, 'Issues of Conversion and Baptism in relation to Mission,' P. Victor Premasagar, ed., *New Horizons in Christian Mission: A_Theological Exploration*, Gurukul Summer Institute 1999 (Chennai: Gurukul, 2000), 375-393; 'Conversion and its Discontents,' *Bangalore Theological Forum*, Vol. XXXII, No. 1 (June 2000), 165-172; and 'A Strange Mission Among Strangers: The Joy of Conversion,' Andrea Schultze, Rudolf v. Sinner, Wolfram Stierle (Hg.), *Vom Geheimnis des Unterschieds: Die Wahrnehmung des Fremden in Ökumene-, Missions- und Religionswissenschaft* (Münster: LIT Verlag, 2002), 200-210.

[7] *Believing without Belonging: In Search of New Paradigms of Church and Mission in Secularized and Postmodern Contexts*, Northelbian Centre for World Mission/ Christian Jensen Kolleg, Breklum, Germany, 26th June-2nd July, 2002.

[8] Now published in J. Jayakiran Sebastian, 'Believing and Belonging: Secularism and Religion in India,' *International Review of Mission*, Vol. XCII, No. 365 (April 2003), 204-211, quotation on 211.

[9] See the provocative questions and incisive probing in Arvind P. Nirmal, 'Theological Research: Its Implications for the Nature and Scope of the Theological Task of the Church in India,' Gnana Robinson, ed. *For the Sake of the Gospel: Essays in Honour of Samuel Amirtham* (Madurai: T.T.S. Publications, 1980), 73-82.

been flawed and problematic,[10] where it has been asserted that '[a]long with gunboats, opium, slaves and treaties, the Christian Bible became a defining symbol of European expansion.'[11] Have we then tried to cover up the harsh realities of how mission was organized, and how mission was experienced, by talking about something which could be indicated to have a divine origin?[12] If mission is both a divine and a human enterprise, then what? Why use binaries?[13] Can binaries become so intertwined that disentanglement is not only impossible, but also unnecessary? Why not talk about mission as 'theandric' – not as the 'result' of binaries being intertwined, but as the very nature of the being of the divine?[14]

---

[10] Reflecting on the biblical models of mission, Bosch writes that our missionary ministry 'is never performed in unbroken continuity with the biblical witness; it remains, always, an altogether ambivalent and flawed enterprise. Still we may, with due humility, look back on the witness of Jesus and our first forebears in the faith and seek to emulate them.' David J. Bosch, 'Reflections on Biblical Models of Mission,' James M. Phillips, and Robert T. Coote, eds. *Towards the Twenty-first Century in Christian Mission: Essays in honor of Gerald H. Anderson* (Grand Rapids, MI: Eerdmans, 1993), 190. The idea of mission as emulating Jesus is expressed by Lucien Legrand, when he writes: 'Many are the paths of mission. Ultimately, they all follow the way of Jesus: emerging, going elsewhere (Mark 1:38), they return to Jerusalem (Mark 10:32; cf. Luke 9:51), and from there, by death and the Resurrection, lead to the glory and the oneness of God.' In Lucien Legrand, *Unity and Plurality: Mission in the Bible*, trans. Robert R. Barr (Maryknoll, NY: Orbis Books, 1990), 163.

[11] R.S. Sugirtharajah, *The Bible and the Third World: Precolonial, Colonial and Postcolonial Encounters* (Cambridge: Cambridge University Press, 2001), 1.

[12] Paul G. Hiebert, in his *Missiological Implications of Epistemological Shifts: Affirming Truth in a Modern/Postmodern World* (Harrisburg, PA: Trinity Press International, 1999) concludes by saying that 'In mission, our central task is not to communicate a message but to introduce people to that person, Jesus Christ' (p. 116). However, several questions remain: How do we 'introduce' anyone? Can there be an introduction without interpretation? Why and how are we motivated to introduce someone to 'people'?

[13] Sugirtharajah writes: 'Colonialists often discursively constructed contrastive paradigms such as Christian/savage, civilized/barbaric and orderly/disorderly in order to define themselves, and also to explain the dominance and acceleration of colonial rule. Such contrastive pairings helped to condemn the other as inferior and also helped to determine the nature of their hold over the people they subjugated. The early missionary hermeneutics which abetted in this enterprise extrapolated this binary view to inject its own biblical values into the private and public lives of the colonized, and for the good of nations which were still living in a 'savage' state. In his *The Bible and the Third World*, 62-63.

[14] Slavoj Žižek, the 'wild man of theory' and provocative culture critic, writes in his *The Puppet and the_Dwarf: The Perverse Core of Christianity* (Cambridge, MA: MIT Press, 2003), 138: 'Insofar as the ultimate Other is God Himself, I should risk the claim that *it is the epochal achievement of Christianity to reduce its Otherness to Sameness*: God Himself is Man, "one of us." ... The ultimate horizon of Christianity is thus not respect for the neighbor, for the abyss of its impenetrable

If 'life is always *on the way* to narrative, but it does not arrive there until someone hears and tells this life as a story,'[15] then has the *missio Dei* concept reversed the direction and tried to shape a story out of its own understanding of the narrative, a narrative not weaved on the way, but offered ready-made, one-size-fits-all, to those on the way? The recent prophetic and provocative 'Princeton Proposal for Christian Unity' notes that the 'life of the church ... calls for continuous critical sifting and reconstruction of human identity. Elements that constitute our differences must be questioned, judged, reconciled, and reconfigured within the unity of the body of Christ ....'[16]

In one sense, this concern was also the concern of the one who did more than anything else to put the concept of *missio Dei* at the forefront of ecumenical thinking: Georg F. Vicedom. It was dissatisfaction with the way in which mission had been sought to be justified on the basis of 'missionary thought in the Bible,' or as being 'possible and necessary among the nations,' or as 'being derived from the church as a secondary assignment,' or as part of the spreading of 'Christian culture.' For Vicedom, the *missio Dei* derives from the reality that 'the Bible in its totality ascribes only one intention to God: to save [hu]mankind.'[17] One is justified in asking whether Vicedom is right in ascribing the desire to save as being the only intention exhibited by God in the Biblical testimony. Nevertheless what emerges is the sense of dissatisfaction with what passes for mission in his context and his desire to remind the church that 'God Himself does mission work.'[18] It is interesting that Vicedom concludes his

---

Otherness; it is possible to go beyond – not, of course, to penetrate the Other directly, to experience the Other as it is "in itself," but to become aware that there is no mystery, no hidden true content, behind the mask (deceptive surface) of the Other.'

[15] Richard Kearney, *On Stories* (London: Routledge, 2002), 133. Italics in original.

[16] Carl E. Braaten and Robert W. Jenson, eds. *In One Body Through the Cross: The Princeton Proposal for Christian Unity* (Grand Rapids, MI: Eerdmans, 2003), section 23, 28. The document goes on to note that 'our churchly identities lack the winnowing and transformative power of the gospel. Our missions in a particular place all too easily enter into complex collusions with divisions of class, culture, ethnicity, or status already present there. Rather than reconciling the divided, the gathering of men and women into churches may reinforce their divisions.' Sections 33, 34.

[17] Georg F. Vicedom, *The Mission of God: An Introduction to a Theology of Mission*, trans. Gilbert A. Thiele and Dennis Hilgendorf (Saint Louis: Concordia Publishing House, 1965), 4.

[18] Vicedom, *The Mission of God*, 51. This affirmation leads Vicedom to an explicit and heavy Christological concentration when he writes: 'The special *missio Dei* begins with Jesus Christ, for in Him God is both the Sender and the One who is sent, both the Revealer and the Revelation, both the Holy One who punishes and the One who redeems. Through His Son in the incarnation and enthronement God makes Himself the very content of the sending. ... The work of providing the

work with a section on the 'church of suffering' and writes that the 'suffering of the congregation culminates in the redemption, which is bestowed when Jesus Christ ushers in His Kingdom. With this God concludes His *missio*.'[19] What happens when the *missio Dei* is trumpeted and reinforced by churches and structures, which have moved a long way away from 'suffering,' however suffering is defined?[20]

Of interest, at this point, is the Princeton Theological Seminary doctoral dissertation by Ken Miyamoto. Miyamoto, in his impressive work, which offers a nuanced and critical reading of the emergence and use of this idea in the ecumenical movement and in the Asian setting, reminds us that the Trinitarian understanding of *missio Dei* quickly moved to an exploration of how this matters and has consequences when one affirms the reality of this world as the arena of God's activity and God's mission.[21] Miyamoto has revised and summarized part of his thinking in his contribution to the noteworthy new book, edited by Lalsangkima Pachuau, *Ecumenical*

---

content of the sending is completed in Jesus, and thus meaning and goal have been given to every sending. Beyond Jesus there is no further revelation of God. Even the Holy Ghost derives His message from the things of Jesus and in this way leads all men into all truth. Since Jesus died and rose for the salvation of men, any redemption apart from Him is impossible, even though men ever and again strive to classify Christ among many figures who try to indicate a way of salvation. Whoever places Christ's 'once-for-all-ness' in question also places the one God who has sent Him in question. ... Apart from this *missio Dei* in Jesus Christ there can be no further sendings today.' (pp. 52-54)

[19] Vicedom, *The Mission of God*, 142.

[20] One must also note the suspicion that postmodern thinking has generated among some missiologists. Much of it is based on a stereotypical, narrow and caricatured understanding of the promise and attraction of postmodern thinking to those who see in its varieties stimulating new ways of orientation and thinking. An example of this suspicion is found in the book by Paul Avis, *A Church Drawing Near: Spirituality and Mission in a Post-Christian Culture* (London: T & T Clark International, 2003), where he writes: 'The mission of the Christian Church cannot collude with the acids of post-modernity. We used to use the expression 'the acids of modernity', but modernity now looks comparatively benign. Christian theology can recognize common ground and common interests with modernity, even in the absence of a common framework of beliefs and values .... Above all, Christianity cannot baptize the post-modernistic dissolution of the self, of community and of reason. ... Post-modernity knows no accountability. Individual or group self-expression is self-authenticating. The rainbow of spiritualities invites no boundaries or bonds. But these constraints are indispensable, nevertheless' (p. 94). It is ironic that modernity is upheld as some kind of benign bulwark against the permeating 'acids'! In addition, all talk about 'constraints' is problematic, especially when seen from the point of view of those who have been constrained in various ways, not least, theologically.

[21] Ken Christoph Miyamoto, *God's Mission in Asia: A Comparative and Contextual Study of This-Worldly Holiness and the Theology of Missio Dei in M..M.. Thomas and C.S. Song* (Ph.D. diss., Princeton Theological Seminary, 1999).

Missiology.[22] Here he writes that 'ecumenical Asian theologians have almost always used "*missio Dei*" with a world-centric connotation. They have appropriated this Western term as the symbol that provides a focus around which this-worldly holiness in the Asian churches is given a coherent expression.'[23] Questions abound: how does one link 'this-worldly holiness' and the commitment to justice and social transformation? The respected ethicist, James Gustafson, offers us sharply-pointed questions regarding our understanding of God's 'preferential option' for the poor and oppressed:

> If God prefers the poor, why am I, my family, and countless others so fortunate? If God prefers the poor, is the destitution, the pain and suffering of those millions whose plight draws our compassion due only to the human fault – sin? Or is much of it the outcome of historical and natural conflicts and forces beyond the capacity of any individual human, or any government, or any nongovernmental organization, to alleviate, not to mention eliminate? If God prefers the poor, is God impotent to fulfill that preference? Or is it up to Christians, and non-Christians who often better marshal their powers, to actualize God's preference for the poor? … It is clearly the Christian mission to prefer the poor and oppressed. But if that is a purpose of the Almighty, the Almighty is not Almighty.[24]

---

[22] Ken Christoph Miyamoto, 'This-Worldly Holiness and the *Missio Dei* Concept in Asian Ecumenical Thinking' Lalsangkima Pachuau, *Ecumenical Missiology: Contemporary Trends, Issues and Themes* (Bangalore: United Theological College, 2002), 9-28. The various articles in this book raise a variety of questions, and probe a range of issues.

[23] ibid., 118. Miyamoto goes on to point out that the understanding of the *missio Dei* 'has not been limited to this function,' and that several Asian theologians have used this concept to contribute creatively 'to the emergence of contextual theology in Asia'

[24] James M. Gustafson, *An Examined Faith: The Grace of Self-Doubt* (Minneapolis: Fortress Press, 2004), 105.

An evocative poem, written in the North American context of consumerism and charity, resonates with this: *Beatitudes*

Blessed is the Eritrean child,
flies rooting at his eyes for moisture. Blessed
the remote control with which I flipped on past.
Blessed the flies whose thirst is satisfied.
Blessed the parents, too weak to brush away
the vibrant flies. …
Blessed
my silence and my wife's as we chewed our hot
three-cheese lasagna.
Blessed the comedies
we watched that night, the bed we slept in, the work
we rose to and completed before we sat
once more to supper before the television,
a day during which the one child died

These poignant questions serve to raise more questions. Is *missio Dei* the only authentic way of valorising mission? Must we 'regress' into the infinite depths of the heart of God in order to find a 'source' for mission? In other words, as Richebächer asks, is *missio Dei* the 'basis of mission theology or a wrong path?'[25]

At first glance, the formulation of the phrase 'mission to God' appears almost comical. We are so used to the other phrase, 'mission of God', which runs off our lips and emerges almost full-blown from the mind,[26] that any 'tampering' with such a time-honoured formulation seems sacrilegious. While it is true that it has certainly been a powerful concept, which has generated reams of theological reflection and informed missiological praxis, nevertheless, a shifting of the point of view is desirable, in order to interrogate this concept and respond from a perspective, which has been *impacted* by this concept, but has not been given sufficient opportunity to *inform* it. What I am saying is that, in order to stimulate and generate divergent viewpoints, one needs to interrogate our understanding of the *missio Dei* concept, which seems to have achieved a paradigmatic status on par with *homoousios* in contemporary theological and missiological discourse.

These ideas resonate with what Thomas Thangaraj fears, when, drawing upon his experiences of dialoging in intercultural and inter-religious contexts, he writes that using *missio Dei* as a starting point results in opening 'the discussion with well-developed Christian theological

---

and many like him. Blessed is the small check
we wrote and mailed. Blessed is our horror.

(Andrew Hudgins, *Ecstatic in the Poison: New Poems* [Woodstock, NY: Overlook Press, 2003], 56.)

[25] Wilhelm Richebächer, '*Missio Dei*: The Basis of Mission Theology or a Wrong Path?' in *IRM* (October 2003), 588-605. Richebächer concludes by pleading 'for a more precisely defined formulation based on the original meaning and function, viz. that of *missio Dei Triunius*, for the sake of the invitation to believe and the dignity of all religions' (p. 599). Jacques Matthey, in his article 'God's Mission Today: Summary and Conclusions' (*IRM* [October 2003], 579-587), reflecting critically on the conference commemmorating the 50th anniversary of Willingen where the papers in the special issue of *IRM* were presented, asks whether one can continue to use the *missio Dei*, or do we need a different paradigm?' He cautions us against trying to go 'deeper into any analytical description of inner-trinitarian *processiones'*, and asks: 'Who are we to know the inner life of God? We could easily fall into the temptation of transferring to God our vision of the ideal community or society.' He also reminds us that 'If we were to lose the reference to *missio Dei*, we would again put the sole responsibility for mission on human shoulders and thereby risk, missiologically speaking, believing that salvation is gained by our own achievements"' (p. 582).

[26] Here is just one example: '*God is the main and the most important protagonist of all missionary activity*. Mission is initiated, developed, and completed by God.' In Carlos F. Cardoza-Orlandi, *Mission: An Essential Guide* (Nashville: Abingdon Press, 2002), 47 (italics in original).

assertions about God's nature and character [which] already close the doors on conversation before it begins.'[27] One may ask what is wrong with 'well-developed' theological assertions. Thangaraj does an admirable job of tracing the appearance of the concept in ecumenical discussions, situating it in the emergence of the ecumenical movement, and presenting its meaningfulness, or otherwise, in contemporary religious and social realities. Drawing from his own experiences in India, along with a deep sense of gratitude to the missionaries, whose labour among his forebears led to 'liberation, the flourishing of their human potential, and a regaining of their dignity and pride,'[28] Thangaraj discusses problems associated with the uncritical use of the *missio Dei* terminology and goes on to investigate the concepts of *missio humanitatis* (defined as '*an act of taking responsibility, in a mode of solidarity, shot through with a spirit of mutuality*')[29] and, in terms of a Christian theology of mission, *missio ecclesiae*, where he develops the understanding of the mission of 'ecclesial communities' as '*cruciform responsibility, liberative solidarity, and eschatological mutuality*.'[30] Thangaraj is aware that an uncritical use of terms like 'human' and 'church' can lead to the charge of essentialism, and notes that even though there is 'a multiplicity of understandings of the human, we can recognize the interconnectedness of these differing views at the level of self-consciousness, historicity, and ecological interdependence.'[31]

Coming to a specifically Christian theology of mission, Thangaraj picks up the metaphor of a journey and asks:

> Is God indeed in mission? If so, what does it mean to speak of God's being in mission? If we go back to our earlier definition of mission as going-forthness, one can see how the Christian theological tradition can rightly claim God to be in mission. This claim is sustained by two specific beliefs about God. First, at the very heart of the inner self of God there is a journeying or going forth. The doctrine of the Trinity is a significant way in which the Christian faith has celebrated this idea. ...
>
> Second, God is also portrayed as One who is going forth toward all creation. The doctrine of the Incarnation is concerned precisely with the explication of the idea of God's going forth toward the world. ...
>
> ... the picture of God that emerges in the Christian theological tradition is a God who is in mission – going forth in God's own self, and going forth toward the world for its redemption and fulfillment. Therefore, what we are

---

[27] Thomas Thangaraj, *The Common Task: A Theology of Christian Mission* (Nashville: Abingdon Press, 1999), 38.
[28] Thangaraj, *The Common Task*, 28.
[29] Thangaraj, *The Common Task*, 58, italics in original.
[30] Thangaraj, *The Common Task*, 64, italics in original. The concepts are elaborated upon in the following pages, 64-76.
[31] Thangaraj, *The Common Task*, 45.

> attempting is to reconstruct the three leading concepts – responsibility, solidarity, and mutuality – in light of this 'missionary' God.[32]

Thus, for Thangaraj, one needs to take seriously the question of the *movement*, the movement of God, the movement by God, which raises the question if 'God takes time in his time for us,'[33] then how do we use our time for God? How do we 'use' our time in a meaningful and authentic manner, when time has to be measured against eternity? What I want to reiterate here is that we need to recognize that our inter-relationship with each other and with God involves our 'movement' to God, a God who is on a pilgrimage to us. Avoiding the charge of disguised Pelagianism, I want to use a modified version of the title of one of the most important works by the Franciscan saint Bonaventure (1221-1274),[34] through which one can talk about the journey of humanity to God: *humanitatis itinerarium in deum*. While this particular phrase may echo the many efforts that have been made to talk about the pilgrimage or quest of human beings to know or to seek God,[35] what we need to do is to add the word 'mission' and see how it unfolds: *missio humanitatis qua itinerarium in deum*.

---

[32] Thangaraj, *The Common Task*, 63. Also see the questions he raises in M. Thomas Thangaraj, 'Evangelism sans Proselytism: A Possibility?' in John Witte Jr. and Richard C. Martin, eds. *Sharing the Book: Religious Perspectives on the Rights and Wrongs of Proselytism* (Maryknoll, NY: Orbis, 1999), 335-352, notes 408-409.

[33] Robert W. Jenson, *Systematic Theology Volume 2: The Works of God* (Oxford: Oxford University Press, 1999), 35. Jenson also writes that the 'envelopment of our time by God is itself accomplished in the course of our time' (p. 27). For more on how Jenson uses and understands the concept of 'time' see Douglas Knight, 'Jenson on Time'" in Colin E. Gunton, ed. *Trinity, Time, and Church: A Response to the Theology of Robert W. Jenson* (Grand Rapids, MI: Eerdmans, 2000), 71-79.

[34] Saint Bonaventure, *Itinerarium Mentis In Deum, Works of Saint Bonaventure, II*, intro., trans., comm. Philotheus Boehner (Saint Bonaventure, NY: The Franciscan Institute, Saint Bonaventure University, 1956). The title is translated as 'The Itinerary of the Mind into God"' (p. 51).

[35] I am aware of the particular way in which the understanding of *itinerarium* emerges in the context of Franciscan spirituality and mystical practice in Bonaventure, where the mendicant life forms the background to his thinking and praxis. K.R. Sundararajan (Professor of Theology at St. Bonaventure University, St. Bonaventure, NY) writing on Ramanuja and Bonaventure, notes that for Bonaventure, the 'spiritual journey … is a meditative process. First, one reflects on the vestiges of God in creation, then one contemplates humans as reflecting the power, wisdom, and goodness of God. Then one meditates on the Trinity, and through the divine, leaps into the final mystical experience of unity. This is indeed the proper ending of the spiritual journey, the state of salvation.' K.R. Sundararajan, 'The Spiritual Journey: A Comparative Study of Bonaventure and Ramanuja' in Steven L. Chase, ed. *Doors of Understanding: Conversations in Global Spirituality in Honor of Ewert Cousins* (Quincy, IL: Franciscan Press, 1997), 269. In his 'Preface' to this volume, Raimondo Panikkar, when talking about identity and difference, draws our attention to the 'ground on which the differences rest' (p. xiv). Panikkar, in reflecting on his experiences as a pilgrim who travelled on foot to

Given the fact that the heading of this section has used a lot of Latin, one is justified in raising the issue regarding the 'Latin captivity' of mission. Must mission be conceptualized in neat Latin phrases in order to generate discussion, not least about what things "really" mean?! In moving away from the Latin phrase *missio Dei*, why are we talking in Latin about another way of looking at things? Is there a subtle attempt here to display intellectual and philological sophistication and erudition, in order to make a point? At the same time, we have to ask about how the concept of 'missio' itself functions. If one does not deal with this then one is in danger of playing 'language games' and trivializing the importance of this investigation.

At this point, let me recollect a story from the writings of India's Nobel-Prize winning author Rabindranath Tagore. In one sense it is an incomplete story:

> Once after school I saw a most amazing spectacle from our western verandah. A donkey – not one of those donkeys manufactured by British imperial policy but the animal that has always belonged to our society and has not changed in its ways from the beginning of time – one such donkey had come up from the washerman's quarters and was grazing on the grass while a cow fondly licked its body. …[36]

What's the purpose of this you may well ask? I am not trying to draw a connection between the *missio Dei* as traditionally understood and the donkey 'manufactured by British imperial policy,' nor am I trying to link my attempt to define 'our 'mission *to* God' as something that 'has not changed in its ways from the beginning of time'. Nevertheless, I think that Tagore has made an interesting point. The same (or at least a similar) thing can appear differently when

- the ideological basis of how an issue or concept has been presented in discourse is probed and explored;
- the location of the one doing the interrogation becomes a matter not just of information, but is acknowledged and problematized; and
- the taken-for-granted nature of something that has won a well-deserved place not only in the history of literature, but in the imagination of thinking people, is now held up for investigation.

Mount Kailash in the Himalayas, has also pointed out that the 'awareness that the pilgrimage is possibly a way without return leads the pilgrim to the insight that all of his[her] worldly accomplishments are not that important. Thinking that they are is one of the main causes of despair on the part of so many of our contemporaries.' Quoted by James Wiseman in a homily, 'Pilgrimage Beyond Competitiveness,' *Newsletter of St. Anselm's Abbey*, (Winter 2003), 13.

[36] Translated in the 'Appendix: Historicality in Literature', by Ranajit Guha, *History at the Limit of World-History* (New Delhi: Oxford University Press, 2003 [orig. Columbia, 2002], 97.

Probing into Alternate Ways of Thinking and Acting Missiologically

There has been a great deal of thought expended on the understanding of mission as *missio Dei.* It is not my intention to discount this. At the same time we need to recognize and take into account the reality that dissatisfaction with this term already exists.[37] Bosch writes that:

> It cannot be denied that the missio Dei notion has helped to articulate the conviction that neither the church nor any other human agent can ever be considered the author or bearer of mission. Mission is, primarily and ultimately, the work of the Triune God, Creator, Redeemer, and Sanctifier, for the sake of the world, a ministry in which the church is privileged to participate .... Mission has its origin in the heart of God. God is a fountain of sending love. This is the deepest source of mission. It is impossible to penetrate deeper still; there is mission because God loves people.[38]

Given this, I believe that my own exploration are an attempt to honestly and creatively explore how a shift from the overbearing emphasis on *missio Dei* (with all the epicycles that it generates) to understanding *our* mission *to* God can contribute to our discussion.[39]

Bert Hoedemaker has pointed out that mission thinking:

> was domesticated by an ecumenical paradigm that was characterized by the rediscovery of the church as the essential unit of witness and by a concept of global salvation history with the reigning Christ as its center. The concept of missio Dei served to express the coherence of these elements, and a continuing discussion on the relation between mission and unity became necessary. Against the background of serious challenges to the missionary movement ... the whole paradigm became a powerful tool to create a broad

---

[37] Bosch, in *Transforming Mission* refers to an article (in Dutch) by Bert Hoedemaker (p. 392). Bosch comments that Hoedemaker may be right to some extent in his critique that the concept can 'be used by people who subscribe to mutually exclusive theological positions.'

[38] Bosch, *Transforming Mission*, 392.

[39] One is reminded of a comment made by the Dutch Reformed theologian, Arnold A van Ruler, who in one of his essays first published in Dutch in 1953, and then in German in 1954, talking about 'Theologie van het Apostolaat' – rendered as 'A Theology of Mission' – writes about the danger of identifying God with 'the missionary enterprise of christianization, with the progress of his Word. ... God deals with us, also when he uses us as his instruments, as human beings – that is, in our freedom and independence. God even seems to place the entire matter of his mission in our hands.' In Arnold A. van Ruler, *Calvinist Trinitarianism and Theocentric Politics: Essays Toward a Public Theology*, trans. John Bolt, Toronto Studies in Theology, Vol. 38 (Lewiston: Edwin Mellen Press, 1989), 209. Interestingly, van Ruler makes a distinction between mission in Europe and Asia, talking about mission in 'de-Christianized' Europe as being mission in a context of 'repudiated Christianity', and mission with 'respect to paganism' as 'bringing of the truth to those who live in a complex of lies' (p. 224). In this sense he has not moved very far from Kraemer!

> and strong ecumenical movement. At the same time, it can be observed in hindsight that the vagueness and pliability of the missio Dei concept, as well as the unsolvability of the mission-unity question, signalled the incompleteness of the learning process.[40]

The theologian of inter-religious dialogue and inter-religious relationships, Paul Knitter, has examined the question of mission in a dialogical context in great depth in his many writings. Exploring the idea of the reality that within 'God's very being there is communication, communication that is not one-sided but *relational*,' he writes:

> This same dialogical nature of God is carried out in God's missio ad extra – the divine going forth in self-communication to finite creatures. It is a communication that is never imposed on the recipients. Rather, creatures are affirmed, respected. They, too, must speak. And God's communication, in a real sense, is dependent on that speaking and response (otherwise free will would not be real). Creatures may not have the power to break off the conversation for good, but they certainly are part of determining its content, direction, and outcome. Therefore, in the self-communicating mission of God, the Divine not only speaks, but listens, waits, values, challenges, and – some Jewish and process theologians would add – learns from the response of creation. The missio Dei is therefore the dialogus Dei.[41]

Given this reality, we need to ask:

What is the relationship between mission and the church? If the church can only be defined in relation to its self-understanding of the mandate which it claims to have inherited, then has the experience and reality of mission in the twentieth century been sufficiently and soberly investigated? Can one claim to need some more 'distance' before such an undertaking is carried out, or, given the urgency of the situation at the beginning of the twenty-first century, especially in the current Indian scenario, can we be complacent and watch things as they are and allow our theological thinking and our missiological praxis to drift, and claim that this is because of the 'blowing of the Spirit'?

How do we come to terms with the 'deep ambivalence'[42] with which those of us who are the recipients of the *missio*, whether of God or not,

---

40 Bert Hoedemaker, *Secularization and Mission: A Theological Essay* (Harrisburg: Trinity Press International, 1998), 33-34.

41 Paul F. Knitter, *Jesus and the Other Names: Christian Mission and Global Responsibility* (Maryknoll, NY: Orbis Books, 1996), 145.

42 I used these words in my doctoral work, J. Jayakiran Sebastian, '... *baptisma unum in sancta ecclesia...': A Theological Appraisal of the Baptismal Controversy in the Work and Writings of Cyprian of Carthage* (Delhi: ISPCK, 1997), 176, to characterize my analysis of Enlightenment ideology, 'whose ideals regarding progress, emancipation, maturity, the power of knowledge and the role of reason, were, in many ways, used to justify the 'necessity' of imperialism and colonialism.' I went on to argue that this 'ambiguity has to be recognized by those of us who come from the churches which grew out of the European missionary expansionist program, a program which was deeply informed by pietistically undergirded and

have to reckon with in our attempts to come to terms with what such a missiological encounter has led us to be today? Asking, along with Samartha, as to why the words 'mission and conversion' are 'received with such dread in countries in Asia and Africa even to this day,'[43] it is necessary to face up to the reality that mission *as experienced* hardly meets the criterion spelt out in the theological understanding of the *missio Dei*. One may argue that it is precisely because of this difference that the need and necessity of the *missio Dei* corrective is necessary – in order that such issues can be put in perspective. However, is this not like offering soap made by multi-national companies to poor children in Indian villages to make them wash their hands to prevent diarrhoea and dysentery, and then making them pay for the fact that rural sanitation has deliberately been a low priority for national economic planning and for the globalized practitioners of local forms of self-reliance?

Recently, seemingly informed and comprehensive, detailed and elaborate Biblical exegesis led to a conclusion that 'the role of the church of the ages' is to acknowledge that the 'disciples' mission is to be characterized by an obedient relationship to their sender, Jesus, by a separation from the world, and by an inaugurated eschatological outlook. This perspective is to inspire the church's ingathering of believers into the Messianic community.'[44] In this context, where one is not able to get away from Biblically-inspired traditional language and imagery, then should we not acknowledge that the usage of *missio Dei* has only served to reinforce such traditional concepts and understandings of mission and missiology and has hardly played a role in offering alternate and more nuanced and sensitive ways of thinking?

In India there is an extensive discussion going on regarding the nation, identity, religion and tolerance.[45] How have we succeeded in integrating

---

biblically clarified and interpreted "Enlightenment perspectives", which were mainly, but not exclusively, transmitted through the medium of hymns.' Also see David J. Bosch, *Believing in the Future: Toward a Missiology of Western Culture* (Harrisburg: Trinity Press International, 1995), 5-13, for his comments on the 'legacy of the Enlightenment.' In addition, Andrew Louth, *Discerning the Mystery: An Essay on the Na'ure of Theology* (Oxford: Clarendon Press, 1983) has a chapter on 'The Legacy of the Enlightenment," (pp. 17-44), where, protesting against the one-sided manner in which 'all concern with truth has been relinquished to the sciences,' he wrestles with the reality that this legacy is 'no simple, uncomplicated heritage.'

[43] S.J. Samartha, *One Christ – Many Religions: Toward a Revised Christology*, third Indian ed. (Maryknoll, NY, Orbis; Bangalore: South Asia Theological Research Institute, 2000), 169.

[44] Andreas J. Köstenberger, *The Missions of Jesus and the Disciples According to the Fourth Gospel – With Implications for the Fourth Gospel's Purpose and the Mission of the Contemporary Church* (Grand Rapids, MI: Eerdmans, 1998), 220.

[45] For example, see the range and variety of articles in K.N. Panikkar, ed. *The Concerned Indian's Guide to Communalism* (New Delhi: Viking/Penguin Books

such analysis into our discourse on mission? How has missiological praxis been impacted and how have the wide variety of the practioners of mission responded to such discourse? Since postcolonialism has enabled one 'to throw off the victim syndrome' and prevents 'interpretation from being too nativistic or nationalistic,'[46] how have we imbibed such modes and ways of thinking into our understanding of ourselves and of our mission?

Another important point, that needs to be taken up here, is that regarding the link between the understanding of 'our' mission to God and terrorism.[47] This is an important and, as all of us are aware, a painful reality as we move, chastened and uncertain, into the 21st century.[48] The issue becomes even more pressing as we are confronted with two realities:

the reality that many acts of terror *in the present* are motivated and informed by an understanding that such actions are part of an important and even soteriologically significant accomplishment of the individual (or group) to and for God.

the reality that many acts of terror *in the past* were motivated and informed by an understanding that such actions were part of an important and even soteriologically significant accomplishment of the individual (or group) to and for God.

It is precisely because of this history that I believe we need to explore how an understanding of our mission to God has functioned and *ought* to function in contemporary theological discourse and action in India today.

Prioritizing our Mission to God

Am I not being rather naïve in all this? Is not any attempt to move the discourse from talking about the mission *of* God to *our* mission to God

---

India, 1999), and S.L. Sharma and T.K. Oommen, eds. *Nation and National Identity in South Asia* (Hyderabad: Orient Longman, 2000).

46 R.S. Sugirtharajah, *Postcolonial Criticism and Biblical Interpretation* (Oxford: Oxford University Press, 2002), 39.

47 Regarding violence, Andrew J. Kirk, in *What is Mission? Theological Explorations* (London: Darton, Longman and Todd, 1999) notes that overcoming violence and building peace 'is rarely, if ever, mentioned in any of the major works on mission.' (p. 143). Kirk concludes his explorations with the affirmation that 'Mission is traveling. It is being on a journey. It is a restless moving towards the time when God will be all in all in creation and salvation (1 Cor. 15:28). Christians are in transit. They have never landed at their final destination in this life. There is no vacation from the Gospel calling. The only thing that 'cannot be shaken' is the Kingdom of God (Heb. 12:28)' (p. 232). It is interesting that the word 'landed' is used. Without trying to be specific, one can ask whether those who 'landed' on the two gigantic structures, which perhaps symbolized for them that which 'cannot be shaken,' were not motivated by a similar ideological orientation cloaked in the symbolism of another religion?

48 See the moving and disturbing reflections in Rowan Williams, *Writing in the Dust: After September 11* (Grand Rapids, Michigan: Eerdmans, 2002).

dangerously simplistic? At least in talking about the *missio Dei,* we had a reference point beyond ourselves and an orienting centre beyond ourselves. Who is this 'our' – who are the 'we'? Is this not sinking into the sands of relativity and subjectivity, and is such an attempt doomed, not even to leave footprints on these sinking and shifting sands, which all too quickly will regain their original texture, undisturbed by the struggles played upon them, benignly waiting for the next theological debate to fall into them? Even if this 'we' encompasses the church, '[i]n this time of unparalleled threat to all of existence, the idea of a solely church-centered approach to mission seems parochial and self-defeating. The *missio Dei* proves greater than the limits of vision and resources of Christ's church.'[49] So – does not the affirmation of the *missio Dei* help to serve as a corrective to our quick, and perhaps futile, attempt to locate missiological activity in the church or in ourselves?

What are the contours of talking about the implications of a missiological understanding of *our* mission to God? For those of us, who have a deep and abiding commitment to the exploration of theological issues and themes that we believe are crucial in the present context of pluralism and disparity, religious and economic, the question regarding our mission to God holds both promise and frustration. Promise, because we can now own responsibility for our actions and truly attempt to translate our commitment to both inter-religious understanding and missiological praxis in a world of competing claims and counter-claims regarding how the divine is conceived and understood; frustration, because such an endeavour is fraught with the possibility of motivations being misunderstood and propositions and proposals being misattributed, with motives being implied.

Yet, in this postcolonial context, it is necessary to straddle the world of promise and frustration, because our mission to God speaks of responsibility and not just of grace. 'In postcolonial memory it is the memory of present predicaments that recalls the dislocations of the past.'[50] Such memories demand that we go in search of not just new meanings but new epistemologies – even those that have to be arrived at by rejecting the existing ones. It is only then that what we do belies the fear expressed in the following words:

> On one hand, it is critical to question authoritative Eurocentric imaginings, to interrogate the aggressive self-representations of post-Enlightenment traditions and Western modernities. After all, epistemic violence is very much part of our here-and-now, defining the murky worlds we inhabit. On the other hand, we also need to guard against adopting and reproducing the

---

[49] Donald E. Messer, *A Conspiracy of Goodness: Contemporary Images of Christian Mission* (Nashville: Abingdon Press, 1992), 71.

[50] Barnor Hesse, 'Forgotten Like a Bad Dream: Atlantic Slavery and the Ethics of Postcolonial Memory,' David Theo Goldberg and Ato Quayson, eds. *Relocating Postcolonialism* (Oxford: Blackwell Publishers, 2002), 165.

several facile strains of anti-Enlightenment rhetoric that are on offer today. To reify and romanticize traditions or communities is not only to construct a new nativism – it is also to mock the subjects we study, to pillory the peoples who form the basis of our interventions, to stage other forms of epistemic violence.[51]

Thus, what one is engaged in is not the 'dissolution of differences but about re-negotiating the structure of power built on differences.'[52]

Our mission to God is not afraid to affirm new knowledge forms that come from the so-called margins. It will find a way of questioning received ideas of mission and yet create a notion of mission that is not simply built on any form of nativism. Those, for whom the violence of mission in various overt and subtle forms has contributed directly and indirectly to what it is that defines their identity in the India of today, are not prepared to run away from the processes necessary for the re-signification of what it means to talk about our mission to God. The 'our' seeks to reclaim space, reach out in order to seek partnerships across ancient enmities, explore traditions and experiences from the past, valorise and interrogate the complexities of the present, and foster any inquiry that seeks to understand rather than explain, in a spirit of honest listening and learning.

How far have we really got? Talking about our *mission* is not just talking about us. We are very good at that and can go on indefinitely on this track. We need to talk about our mission to *God*. Is this a long and convoluted way round to come back to our starting point about the *missio Dei*? While we continue to debate this, let me affirm that this displaced (misplaced?) way of interrogation forces us to re-examine the manner in which we begin and the way in which the beginning is shaped, not by a referent outside ourselves, but by an appeal to indicate, as unambiguously as possible, how we understand ourselves and our mission to God in this world of religious variety and economic disparity.

In India, in the first decade of the twenty-first century, as we attempt to articulate the way in which we understand and define our mission to God, we need to affirm that we:

have to look beyond the traditional hermeneutical arenas, such as in the Christian West. What these new readings in foreign contexts do is to relativize the Christian text and invite and force Christian interpreters to keep their eyes open to disruptive, even uncomfortable, readings. This means constantly rethinking Christian hermeneutical conclusions, accepting them as only provisional, and acknowledging their methods as tentative. Anything

---

[51] Saurabh Dube, 'Travelling Light: Missionary Musings, Colonial Cultures and Anthropological Anxieties,' Raminder Kaur and John Hutnyk, eds. *Travel Worlds: Journeys in Contemporary Cultural Politics* (London: Zed Books, 1999), 46-47.

[52] R.S. Sugirtharajah, *Postcolonial Reconfigurations: An Alternative Way of Reading the Bible and Doing Theology* (St. Louis, MO: Chalice Press, 2003), 126. The quotation comes from a chapter entitled 'Postcolonialism and Indian Christian Theology.'

> other than this will be a return to the exegetical imperialism that has often marked and marred Christian scholarship.[53]

Herein lies the challenge that we should not be afraid of accepting. Our mission to God forces us to try and articulate – and contemplate – who this God really is. This attempt comes about because we are forced to look into ourselves, our fears and frustrations, our prejudices and our value-systems, our happiness and our use of pleasure, in order that we may be ready and willing to give expression to the hope that is within us, a hope that engages our very being in our mission to God through our mission to our neighbour, whoever this neighbour may be, and whatever 'mission' this neighbour may have to us, in the gloriously frightening and exhilarating multiplicity of the pilgrimage of life in India today.

Conclusion: On the Way to Mission

Donkeys have become quite a rare sight in urban India today. But as a child, growing up in Bangalore, I remember feeling sorry for the dhobi's donkeys, plodding patiently along, with an immense burden of either dirty or freshly-washed clothes on their backs. My grandmother pacified me by saying that donkeys have a very strong backbone and that what looked like a terribly heavy load was actually quite manageable! Well, if Jesus deigned to ride on a donkey's back, symbolizing the *missio humanitatis qua itinerarium in deum*, there must be something in it ....[54]

---

[53] R.S. Sugirtharajah, 'Son(s) Behaving Badly: The Prodigal in Foreign Hands,' A.K.M. Adam, ed. *Postmodern Interpretations of the Bible: A Reader* (St. Louis, Missouri: Chalice Press, 2001), 204-205. This essay is now a chapter in R.S. Sugirtharajah, *Postcolonial Reconfigurations*, 37-50.

[54] This essay has benefitted from comments by Peter Casarella, Sathianathan Clarke, John Flett, O.V. Jathanna, Robert Jenson, Christoffel Lombard, David C. Scott, Mrinalini Sebastian, Max Stackhouse, and John C.B. Webster. My thanks to all of them. It was originally published in Max L. Stackhouse and Lalsangkima Pachuau, eds. *News of Boundless Riches: Interrogating, Comparing, and Reconstructing Mission in a Global Era*, Vol. I (Delhi: ISPCK/UTC/CTI, 2007), 2-4. I thank the editors for granting me permission to republish this.

Responses from the Edinburgh 2010 Conference

Presentation from the Perspective of Peace and Reconciliation

Sebastian C.H. Kim

I should like to begin by expressing my appreciation for the papers presented on the topic of mission and postmodernities, and for the work of the study group who have written such a helpful report.

I fully agree with what has been said, but there is one thing I would like to point out. The definition of postmodernity used in the report seems to assume a linear historical development of postmodernity in the West, and then a spreading out to the rest of the world. But I would like to say that postmodernity arises simultaneously in different contexts. It is not only a product of the West, but of everywhere. For example, if we look at young people, their shared culture everywhere is similar regardless of context, and not only in the West, and yet, in each place, it can be regarded as arising out of local historical development. Furthermore, this development does not always follow the same trajectory as in the West, as we see from the way mobile phones have bypassed landlines altogether in some places.

Among the nine themes of 2010, Mission and Postmodernities stands out compared to 1910 because it is a fundamentally new topic and highlights what has changed in the last one hundred years. Therefore, we need to make a particular effort to have a new approach to mission in the postmodern context.

My role, in this short presentation, is to reflect on the theme from peace and reconciliation perspectives. York St John University, where I teach, is involved in an ongoing peace and reconciliation project. We have held three International Conferences on Peace and Reconciliation. This series was established, in 2006, to provide a platform for both scholars and practitioners in the fields of peace and reconciliation. The nature of the conference is interdisciplinary but perspectives from theology and religious studies are particularly to the fore. It is held in partnership with Youngnak Presbyterian Church, Seoul, South Korea, and has a particular interest in peace and reconciliation on the Korean peninsula. The first conference at York St John University, in 2006, took the theme 'In Search of Shared Identity: The Korean Peninsula and Other Contexts'. The second at University of California, Los Angeles, in 2009, was concerned with 'Embracing the Displaced: Shaping Theories and Practices for a Sustainable Peace'. In 2010, Youngnak Presbyterian Church is marking the tenth anniversary of the passing of its founder pastor, Rev. Kyung-Chik Han. Youngnak Presbyterian Church currently has over 60,000 members and 500 sister churches world-wide, and Rev. Han was one of the most respected religious leaders in South Korea. He was awarded the Templeton Prize in 1992, and made a significant contribution to the relationship between the people in North and South Korea. In his honour, the third conference will be a major event co-hosted with Youngnak Church in Seoul, to which 140 theologians and church leaders from 70 countries are being specially invited to attend and discuss the theme, to make 350 participants in all. The plenary papers of all these conferences are being published to encourage wider interaction among the scholars, peace activists, policy makers and religious communities.

One distinctive feature of our approach is to collect stories, poems and visual images from people around the world engaged in peacemaking. These are being added to a database to make them more widely available. This is in keeping with one of the characteristics of postmodernity. Rather than following systematic or logical argument on the basis of facts and knowledge, postmodern thinking tends to emphasise personal experiences. I would like to give three examples here of the kind of material that is included. All of these are from the Korean context.

First, a story. One of the most telling aspects of despair and hope in the Korean situation is the experience of divided families and relatives, and the story of Kim Haksoo, a prominent artist and an elder of a Methodist Church in Seoul, is not an unusual one. He was married with four children and lived in Pyongyang, just before the war broke out. After the short occupation of Pyongyang by the UN, when the UN troops had to withdraw from the city, he was advised to escape to the South with them, leaving the rest of the family behind. This was because of the fear of Communist retaliation and the fear that, as a Korean man, he would be forced to join the Communist army, and also on the understanding that the UN troops would soon return to recapture the city. Just before the time to leave, his wife went out to borrow money for his journey to the South. Because he could not hold the last vehicle any longer, he had to say good-bye to his children only, and left to come to Seoul. When the war ended, he could not go back and could not get any news about the family. For nearly forty years, he was living with the guilt feeling of not having said good-bye to his wife and, though many, who fled from the North re-married in the South, he remained single. In 1989, he unexpectedly received news from his close friend, who had visited North Korea, that his wife and family were still alive and that his wife had also remained single. He had very mixed emotions – on the one hand, he rejoiced that they were still alive and well, but he very well knew that they could not yet be united. He continues to hold *han* (or anguish) deep inside his heart but he is able to deal with it through his faith in Christ and by his dedication to painting. Perhaps, as C.S. Song suggests, Elder Kim longs that this *han* may be a seed in the womb for reconciliation, and that he will one day be united with his family.[1]

Second, a poem: 'Rice is heaven'. This poem is a powerful tool written by Kim Chi Ha, a Catholic activist, who was imprisoned many times for his stance on behalf of the economically and politically oppressed.

Food is heaven
As you can't go to heaven by yourself
Food is to be shared
Food is heaven
As you see the stars in heaven together
Food is to be shared by everybody
When the food goes into a mouth
Heaven is worshipped in the mind
Food is heaven
Ah, ah, food is
To be shared by everybody.[2]

This poem has been used to encourage the people to see the importance of sharing food with poor people in the South as well as the North.

Third, a picture: *Minjung* (liberation) theologians in Korea use pictures to communicate their theology to the general public. For example, one picture shows the figure of a Korean Christ wearing traditional women's clothing and staggering under the weight of a cross. Attached to the cross is a large bulky package, which is in the shape of the Korean peninsula, and tied in the middle by a piece of string. It illustrates how Jesus Christ bears the burden and pain of the divided Korea and identifies with the *Minjung,* the masses, female as well as male. Pictures such as this have been powerful media for people to get to grips with the reality of poverty and injustice, and the call for peacemaking between North and South Korea.

For mission, in the twenty-first century, understanding the new culture of postmodernity is of central importance. Experience is a key word for postmodernity. People with a postmodern outlook do not want to be persuaded by argument, but respond to experiences conveyed in stories, poems and images. Unless the church touches people's hearts and enters their experience, mission will be ineffective. Utilising varied approaches of conveying and creating experience, such as those outlined above, is vital, along with the traditional approaches of theologising and strategising. Let us use creative ways and means to carry out our work!

---

[1] Sebastian C.H. Kim, 'Reconciliation Possible? The Churches' Efforts Toward Peace and Reunification of North and South Korea', in Sebastian C.H. Kim, Pauline Kollontai & Greg Hoyland (eds.) *Peace and Reconciliation: In Search of Shared Identity* (Aldershot, UK: Ashgate, 2008), 161-184, see 176.

[2] Kim Chi Ha, *The Gold-Crowned Jesus and Other Writings* (Maryknoll, NY: Orbis Books, 1978), 30.

POSTMODERNITIES, MISSION AND ECOLOGY

Ernst M. Conradie

What on earth does ecology have to do with postmodernity and mission? The report of the study process, leading to the Edinburgh 2010 conference, rightly picks up three important themes, where these concepts intersect, namely, that of hope for the future, the postmodern critique of the ideology of mastery and control and the call for priestly duties, described here in terms of the rather controversial notion of 'stewardship'.[1]

Does this mean that ecological issues are addresses satisfactorily in the report? In my view it is not so strange that the report associates modernity with ecological destruction. This critique of the logic of mastery and control is indeed a standard one in literature in the field of environmental ethics. However, it is somewhat odd that postmodernity is described as being 'more in tune with ecological concerns'.[2] The question is, whether such a discontinuity with modernity, can be so readily identified in this case.

The report rightly observes that postmodernity hardly has the appeal in impoverished countries of the global 'South' that it has in the affluent and, perhaps, somewhat leisured countries of the global 'North'.[3] Here, one may need to consider the term 'sub-modernity', suggested, amongst others, by Jürgen Moltmann.[4] This term indicates the impact of modernity on those that are marginalised by the current neo-liberal global economy. One would also need to consider neo-Marxist critiques on whether the economic systems, underlying modernity, have actually changed. Thus, it becomes a question of what has actually changed and what has remained the same.

It is fairly clear that something has indeed changed and this may well be expressed in terms such as an 'incredulity towards meta-narratives', scepticism about the dream of progress, a disbelief in universality of human rationality (but perhaps not of human dignity) and prevailing uncertainty. I find the analyses by Zygmunt Bauman on 'liquid modernity' and the shift

---

[1] On this controversy, see Chapter 4 of my *An ecological Christian anthropology: At home on earth?* (Aldershot: Ashgate, 2005).

[2] See Daryl Balia & Kirsteen Kim, *Edinburgh 2010 Volume II: Witnessing to Christ today* (Oxford: Regnum Books, 2010), 81.

[3] Balia & Kim, 69.

[4] Jürgen Moltmann, *God for a secular society: The public relevance of theology* (Minneapolis: Fortress Press, 1999), 11-17.

towards a consumer society plausible. The contrast may then be sketched, in terms of a shift from an economy oriented towards production to one focusing on consumption, the shift from rationality to consumer choice, taste and feeling, from the Protestant work ethic to the aesthetic of pleasure, from activism to (passive) reception.[5]

This emphasis on the consumer society may help us to understand one of the aspects, where a cultural shift from modernity to postmodernity is less obvious than is often assumed. This relates to the celebration of diversity that is typically associated with postmodernism. This suggests an openness to radical diversity compared to the hegemony of mastery, inclusion and control associated with modernity. There is a downside to such diversity, namely, the prevailing experience that everything is in flux. Heisenberg's uncertainty principle, therefore, occupies an iconic position in postmodern societies. Over everything hovers a question mark. For Christians, this prompts concerns over criteria in searching for truth but also in the quest for justice and for human rights and the resistance against evil. How can evil be identified, named and resisted in a climate of diversity and uncertainty?

What is far more worrying though is the way, in which new constellations of unity rush in to fill the ideological gap left by the demise of modern security. Admittedly, unity is no longer provided by the nation state, or the tribe, or the dream of progress. Here, one may also consider the impact of Christian and other forms of fundamentalism that offer simplified constructions of such unity.

However, far more significant than that, especially in terms of ecological concerns, is the impact of the consumer society. The celebration of diversity can easily be reduced to nothing more than consumer choice. Then, one may also wish to emphasise the homogeneity and, indeed, the hegemony of consumerist culture[6] – a Coca-Cola advertisement in every town in Africa, the same shopping malls everywhere, the same products offered by the same companies to offer us pleasure and healing, if not salvation.

It is this consumer lifestyle, easily associated with societies, where postmodernism is celebrated, and the economic production processes required that have led to ecological destruction, most notably to climate change. Not surprisingly, the lifestyle of the so-called consumer class[7] has been easily exported from North America to other Western countries, to South East Asia and to every corner of the globe. Tragically, the whole

---

[5] See Zygmunt Bauman, *Work, consumerism and the new poor* (Philadelphia: Open University Press, 1988), *Liquid modernity* (Oxford: Blackwells, 20000, *Consuming life* (Cambridge: Polity Press, 2007).

[6] See Colin Gunton, *The One, the Three and the Many: God, creation and the culture of modernity* (Cambridge: Cambridge University Press, 1993), 13.

[7] For this term, see especially the Worldwatch Institute's report on the *State of the world 2004* edited by L. Starke (2004).

'global village' has come under the spell of the 'American dream' of the pursuit of happiness, here and now. Consumerism has been described as the most successful and fastest growing religion of all times.[8] Since the lifestyles of the consumer class are so visibly demonstrated, paraded and advertised, it should come as no surprise that consumerism also describes the hope and aspiration of the global middle class and, indeed, of the poor, if not the destitute.

Indeed, the dream of everyone is to have their own car and suburban home and to be able to relax with a drink and a barbeque next to a swimming pool, at a spa or resort in the company of friends and influential people. That is indeed portrayed as a form of 'salvation', as heaven on earth. In religious terms, this advocacy for a consumer lifestyle is most obviously expressed through the preaching of the prosperity gospel. This has a particularly strong appeal amongst the emerging middle class, for example, in South Africa. The impact of consumerism in the South African context was notably recognised in a speech by the former president, Thabo Mbeki:

> Thus, everyday, and during every hour of our time beyond sleep, the demons embedded in our society, that stalk us at every minute, seem always to beckon each one of us towards a realisable dream and nightmare. With every passing second, they advise, with rhythmic and hypnotic regularity – get rich! get rich! get rich! And thus has it come about that many of us accept that our common natural instinct to escape from poverty is but the other side of the same coin on whose reverse side are written the words – at all costs, get rich! In these circumstances, personal wealth, and the public communication of the message that we are people of wealth, becomes, at the same time, the means by which we communicate the message that we are worthy citizens of our community, the very exemplars of what defines the product of a liberated South Africa.[9]

Indeed, the hope and yearning of the world's poor is to achieve an equally affluent standard of living. The hope of the poor is typically based on what money can buy. They dream of winning the lotto. They desire the affluence, which they do not have and probably have little hope in obtaining. As William Gibson observes, from within the USA, this has far-reaching psychological consequences: 'The unhappiness often felt by persons of limited income is their sense that they have failed to meet the standards of success held by society and by themselves. They are not affluent but they wish they were. They want far more of the abundance displayed in the television commercials. They are saddled with debt because they have succumbed too frequently to the lure of the ads.'[10]

---

[8] See David Loy, 'The religion of the market', *Journal of the American Academy of Religion* 65/2, 275-290.

[9] Thabo Mbeki, Nelson Mandel Memorial lecture (2006), widely published on the internet at that time.

[10] See William E. Gibson, 'The lifestyle of Christian faithfulness' in M. Schut (ed.)

The ecological problem is that the consumerist lifestyles of the world's affluent centre are in themselves not sustainable. Such lifestyles cannot be replicated by the planet's entire human population, currently estimated at 6.8 billion. The impact of such levels of consumption on fresh water supplies, air quality, forests, the climate, biological diversity and human health would be severe. The consumer culture enjoyed by the affluent, therefore, can be maintained only at the expense of the majority on the economic periphery. This also raises question marks about the notion of 'sustainable development'. Insofar as development discourse assumes growth in biophysical economic output, such development cannot be sustainable. Of course, the recognition of the limits to economic growth raises serious questions about economic justice. Since so-called 'developing' nations demand the right to strive towards the economic prosperity maintained by industrialised countries, it is extraordinarily difficult to come to global consensus on how to address ecological problems, such as climate change.[11]

What, then, are the implications of the interface between postmodernity and ecological destruction for an understanding of Christian mission? Two brief observations would have to suffice here.

Firstly, in a consumer society, any form of Christian mission can easily be reduced to the providing of more consumer products, in this case, religious goods and services, delivered to religious consumers, who select for themselves a product that they feel they may need. They select a church, where they may feel at home, and where their needs may be met. Where religious affiliation is a matter of choice, churches become vendors of religious services and goods. A commodity-orientated church is in competition with other churches to deliver the best goods and to deliver that in a more digestible form than its competitors.[12]

Secondly, the need for an appropriate vision for the future is crucial. Without such a vision people perish. In the context of environmental destruction and climate change, this is crucial because the future is, indeed, unattractive. As a result, people return to the default position, namely, the ennui, relaxation, therapy and boredom of the consumer society. They put their trust and their faith in their personal survival skills, in their education, the capital in their bank accounts, in their pensions. Since this is evidently foolish, Christians may need to be bold in proclaiming and embodying a

---

Simpler living compassionate life: A Christian perspective (Denver: The Morehouse Group,1999), 133-134.

[11] For a more detailed survey, see my *Christianity and a critique of consumerism: A survey of six points of entry* (Wellington: Bible Media, 2009). For a discussion of the ecological impact of consumerism, for example on climate change, see my *The church and climate change: Signs of the Times Series Volume 1* (Pietermaritzburg: Cluster Publications, 2008).

[12] See my *Christianity and a critique of consumerism* for a more detailed discussion.

different vision, namely, a vision of a renewed earth, in which God is coming to dwell, a vision of justice, peace and God's sustained love for God's own creation.[13] Such a compelling vision may not be typical of postmodernity – probably because of the hegemony of the dream of progress, development and a consumerist lifestyle for all. Since such a vision is widely recognised not to be sustainable, this often gives birth to despair. Such despair is not conducive to an environmental ethos, praxis and spirituality either. Here the proclamation of the Christian message of hope may, indeed, become crucial for an understanding of Christian mission in a postmodern context.

[13] See, for example, the document *Climate Change – A Challenge to the Churches in South Africa,* produced by the Climate Change Committee of the South African Council of Churches (SACC, Marshalltown, 2009), where such a vision is explored in some depth.

MISSION AND POSTMODERNITIES

Claudia Währisch-Oblau

Speaking here as a representative of the 2009 United Evangelical Mission Theological Consultation on Mission, I would like to briefly raise three topics that I feel are missing from the study paper we have received.

The very basic question that is underlying everything, I want to say here, is this: How can the Gospel of Christ be lived and preached in the marketplace without becoming a commodity? How can we make sure that evangelism does not become marketing?

Following Christ and preaching the Gospel always moves in the tension between contextualization and counter-culture – the Word has become flesh, God became human in Jesus Christ, but this human person, nevertheless, was different from all other humans, in ways that we need to always understand anew.

The first topic I would like to raise is: How we can phrase our Gospel message,so that it speaks to the burning questions of our time? I very much doubt that 'How do I find a graceful God?' is what keeps people awake today. The questions are rather 'How can I find a good life?' or 'Who / what can protect me from evil powers bent to destroy life?' Consequently, in my country, Germany, there is now a lively discussion on whether we should give up (or at least tone down) the interpretation of the cross of Christ as a sacrifice for the salvation of sinners and rather stress that Christ's death was a consequence of his message of unconditional love for everyone and his challenge of the powers that be. In the African and Asian churches of the UEM community, the question of protection from evil powers is paramount.

And that brings me to my second issue: One of the big trends of postmodernity is the return of the irrational. Whether it is esotericism in the West, or the resurgence of witchcraft and magical practices in Africa and Asia, rationalistic critique has lost its power. The issue, here, is not deconstruction, but rather protection. I believe that Pentecostal and charismatic churches are growing because they have found an answer to this need: Rituals of deliverance from demons, protective prayers and a theology that names threatening powers. While I know plenty of social science research into this phenomenon, I really miss a well-grounded theological debate. We are beginning to engage in this now within the UEM community.

And then the third issue: Mission is no longer a movement from the North to the South, but coming from everywhere going everywhere in the globe. The Edinburgh study process does mention this phenomenon in several instances. But one question has not been asked explicitly: Are churches only those who are sent into mission, or are they also recipients of mission? Concretely: African, Asian and Latin American Christians are moving to Europe and tell us that they want to bring revival to our dead or dying churches. If their mission is, indeed, driven by the Holy Spirit, what does this mean for the churches in the North? How can we properly receive this mission?

Could it be that mission today is, first and foremost, neither winning souls for Christ, nor identifying the Spirit at work in world events, but rather trying to live as the body of Christ, a community, which overcomes borders and limits (racial, social, economic, cultural) in an increasingly fragmented world? If that is the case, we would have to seriously critique any ecclesiological or missionary concepts that allow the church to break into ever smaller and more homogeneous groups – even if these seem to be successful, in terms of winning new members.

PRESENTATION OF POSTMODERNITY

Gianni Colzani

I am a Catholic priest and I belong to the diocese of Milan, but, for these past ten years, I have been teaching theology of mission at the Pontifical Urbaniana University. As agreed with Prof. Kirk, I have been entrusted the task of illustrating the Catholic position. From the beginning, I must say that I have no other title than my competence; I do not belong to the magisterium, and in the Catholic world, theology offers its reflections to the Christian community, but then it is up to the Episcopal or pontifical magisterium to agree with them or not.

The theme of postmodernity is a recent one. However, in 1950, R. Guardini had already predicted the birth of a new conception of life and of the world, [1] and it is JLyotard – in 1979 – who speaks about the "postmodern condition".[2] Postmodernity is understood in opposition to modernity. However ,not everybody agrees about its precise meaning and about the relationship between the two epochs. I understand modernity on the basis of the unlimited perfectibility of the person, on a conception of history as continuous progress and happiness as its ethical instance; the failure of this plan is evident to everybody, and drives Habermas to think modernity as an unaccomplished plan and to perceive postmodernity as a critical re-commencement of the failed objectives.[3] Today, the most common idea perceives postmodernity as a new epoch: the fragmentation of identity, existential uncertainty and instability of life make it impossible to use the same categories, which were formerly used.

Postmodernity: Which? What Meaning?

A lot depends on what one intends with postmodernity. I will recall two interpretations linking the first to the thought of Vattimo and Rorty and the second to the vision of Baumann and of Taylor. Vattimo abandons the

[1] Guardini, R. *La fine dell'epoca moderna. Il potere* [1950], Morcelliana, Brescia 1993. About his thought see Kobylinski, A. *"Modernità e postmodernità". L'interpretazione cristiana dell'esistenza al tramonto dei tempi moderni nel pensiero di Romano Guardini*, Pontificia Università Gregoriana, Roma 1998.

[2] Lyotard, J.F. *La condizione postmoderna. Rapporto sul sapere* [1979], Feltrinelli, Milano 2002.

[3] Habermas, J. *Il discorso filosofico della modernità*, Laterza, Roma-Bari 1987.

traditional Christian vision of rationality as a way to truth about God and man and, in postmodernity, he perceives the attitude of whoever welcomes precariousness, multiplicity and the contradictory of an ephemeras reality; [4] according to him, in the weak thought he perceives the key for the decrease of violence and the democratisation of society with the spreading of pluralistic and tolerant attitudes. Rorty, instead, proposes an agreement with the community, which the individual lives in.[5] In this logic, postmodernity is a post-metaphysical epoch, which does not feel regret for the truths of the past, nor desire for new certainties; postmodern man is a person who is alone, who does not feel the need for the reassurance offered by God: 'half-truths' which enable him to live with himself and with his own lack of foundations, are enough for him. If there is something that he needs, this is lay ethics and not a faith. In this way, postmodernity is a revolution of the West's spiritual world, a re-organisation of its cultural universe, a different mental coherence, with the aim of a new social cohesion. A similar perspective cannot but question faith: it is a question of redefining the social and cultural meaning of its presence in history.

The position of Baumann and of Taylor is different, for they try to re-think Christian faith in a postmodern epoch. In 1993, Baumann published *Postmodern ethics*[6], a text, in which he maintains that morality does not depend on society as both the above authors propose, but on the contrary, morality is the foundation of social life. According to Baumann, ethical judgement belongs to the person as such, and cannot be delegated to others; going back to Lévinas, he maintains that in countenance with the 'other', an unconditional responsibility is inherent, an original ethical instance that is in opposition with relativism. The meeting with the other is an experience that challenges the authority and the freedom of the individualistic I; putting into question the spontaneity of the person, the meeting with the other's countenance becomes the foundation of an original, ethical relationship with reality.

---

[4] Vattimo's journey starts with Vattimo G. & P.A. Rovatti. *Il pensiero debole*, Feltrinelli, Milano 1983; also by him, Vattimo, G. *Opere complete*. I/1-2: *Ermeneutica*, Meltemi, Roma 2007-2008; Id., *Addio alla verità*, Meltemi, Roma 2009; Id., *Oltre l'interpretazione. Il significato dell'ermeneutica per la filosofia*, Laterza, Roma-Bari 1994.

[5] Rorty, R. *La filosofia e lo specchio della natura* [1979], Bompiani, Milano 1986; Id., *Verità e progresso. Scritti filosofici*, Feltrinelli, Milano 2003; Id., *La filosofia dopo la filosofia*, Laterza, Roma – Bari 2008. Su Rorty si veda. Hottois, G. & M. Weyemberg (ed.) *Richard Rorty. Ambuigüités et limites du postmodernisme*, Vrin, Paris 1994.

[6] Baumann, Z. *Postmodern ethics*, Blackwell, Oxford (UK) – Malden (MA) 1993 (tr. it. *Sfide dell'etica*, Feltrinelli, Milano 1996). Altri lavori: Id., *Il disagio della postmodernità* [1997], Mondadori, Milano 2002; Id., *La società dell'incertezza*, Il Mulino, Bologna 1999; Id., *La solitudine del cittadino globale* [1999], Feltrinelli, Milano 2000; Id., *Una nuova condizione umana* [2003], Vita e Pensiero, Milano 2003.

For his part, Taylor[7] has deeply analysed the history of secularisation, where he pointed out the presence of an anthropological constant, which had substituted the preceding spiritual order centred on God with two immanent realities: the rational control of nature and the authentic and uninhibited expression of one's own subjectivity. According to his point of view, not only have these two anthropological constants acquired an absoluteness, which, historically, is on a par with the Hebrew-Christian theism, but they have made people put the question of *fullness* in a new way, that is a kind of interior richness and fullness which are symbolic place of people's integral way of being-in-the-world. This humanism has maintained the dignity of the person but, instead of founding it on God, it is described according to an immanent conception, which is, moreover, at the basis of the kind of fragility, which accompanies our life today.[8]

These are the *unquiet Frontiers of Modernity,*[9] which are continually challenged by existential fragility, by the futility of everyday and by the mediocrity of our real life. Whilst Vattimo and Rorty totally adhere to this, and Baumann appeals to social ethics, Taylor maintains that Christianity should not express an antagonistic conception that proclaims the truths of the faith and their metaphysic and natural foundation, but needs to accept to take its place in this pluralism, as one of the possible choices, which the person could make. It is an indication that can make sense under the social and public profile, but never below the personal one; a political order that accepts human finiteness, knows that this produces a plurality of positions rather than untouchable truth. In this pluralistic context, Taylor puts the question of *fullness*: this term refers to a kind of fullness of life, to an interior richness, to a deep reconciliation, which believers relate to the meeting with God, while non-believers associate it with a sort of authentic humanity. If faith can cultivate the dream of a rebirth, of a 'born-again', it is in this challenge that it needs to enter.

The Challenges of Postmodernity

More than to make list of problems, I would like to go to the core of the problem. One can say that postmodernity invests above all anthropology; it touches, even more, the whole of Christian soteriology and puts Christology and the role of the church in question. In this immanent vision of salvation, our time pursues salvation without a Saviour, reconciliation without a Reconciliator. Is it possible to formulate such a perspective? Can a Christian love this world positively or must he go back to the Johannine

[7] Taylor, Ch. *A Secular Age*, The Belknap Press of Harvard University Press, Cambridge (MA) – London 2007 (ed. it: *L'età secolare*, Feltrinelli, Milano 2009). Sul tema si veda l'ampio dibattito di area italiana: *The s* Taylor, Ch. *A Secular Age*, in "Euntes Docete" 62 (2009/2), 5-123.

[8] Taylor, Ch. *A Secular Age*, 531.

[9] Taylor, Ch. *A Secular Age*, 711-727.

warning, where one must be in the world but not of the world?[10] Is the being-in-the-world a value or a hard necessity? Since, in this way, the discussion goes back to the revelation and to the event that confesses a God, who 'so loved the world that He gave His only born Son'[11]. The soteriological problem is widened to include the mission of the Risen one and of his community.[12]

To face this problem, one can start from Taylor's critique that indicated the *turning point* in a 'theism characterised by providential traits'; in his point of view, this has led to an 'organic but impersonal conception of reality'. There, where God is seen as an omnipotent Being and supreme Creator, the access to the design of God takes place through the world, so that, in an immanent perspective, a road is open for a conception of the world and its truth, which can do without God. Thus, this poses the problem of relationships between the theological understanding of reality and the intellectual vision of the cosmos; the theological conception of the cosmos is de-structured, to be then re-composed around reason and human freedom as the centre of history. Still left to be known is the sense and value of the human search for truth in itself, as well as an order of democracy and of the rights of persons. Political theology and the theology of liberation cannot be set aside.

Without mentioning historians of thought, like K. Löwith [13] and H. Blumenberg,[14] and sociologists,[15] like P. Berger and A. Seligman, we find many questions here. There is an epistemological diminution that reduces knowledge to scientific knowledge, and, in this way, forgetting that at the core of knowledge we do not find the 'experiment' but the totality of the human experience.[16] Besides the separation between politics and religion, to which the West aspire be now consolidated, it is, in reality, more fragile than what is normally thought; after the fall of the wall of Berlin and the explosion of fundamentalism, the reflection on the public role of religions is once again an arduous point and it oscillates between the private conception of the West, that looks upon religions as a person's right, and the Arabic-Asian conception, which makes of it a criterion of people's

---

[10] Jn 17,11. 14-18.

[11] Gv 3,16.

[12] Mt 28,10-20; Mc 16,15.

[13] Löwith, K. *Significato e fine della storia. I presupposti teologici della filosofia della storia* [1953], Comunità, Milano 1963.

[14] Blumenberg, H. *La legittimità dell'età moderna* [1966], Marietti, Genova 1992.

[15] On sociology refer to the general reconstruction made by Lübbe, H. *La secolarizzazione. Storia e analisi di un concetto*, Il Mulino, Bologna 1970; U. Ruh, *Säkularisierung als Interpretationskategorie. Zur Bedeutung des christlichen Erbes in der modernen Geistesgeschichte*, Herder, Freiburg-Basel-Wien 1974. Together with them refer to Nijk, A.J. *Secolarizzazione*, Queriniana, Brescia 1973.

[16] Siegwalt, G. *Dogmatique pour la catholicité évangélique. Système mystagogique de la foi chrétienne*. III: *L'affirmation de la foi*. I: *Cosmologie théologique: sciences et philosophie de la nature*, Labor et Fides – Cerf, Genève – Paris 1996, 137-146.

unification and an orientation for custom.[17] One can say that Christology and Soteriology, rationality and its anthropological importance, sociability supported by the civil and democratic organisation, are invested by this problem.

A Working Hypothesis

The first problem is ontological and gnosiological reductionism, which expresses 'a widespread distrust of universal and absolute statements, especially among those, who think that truth is born of consensus and not of a consonance between intellect and objective reality'.[18] Here, we find a decline in absolute certainties, where precariousness and what is provisional occupy a central position, a renunciation of the totality of sense and its fragmentation, which lead to a life characterised by what is provisional and fleeting; the human and the humanising sense of faith is under discussion as well as the meaning of reason in the sphere of the act of faith. Without entering into the question, I would only like to say that the kind of reason that concerns revelation is that, which is capable of understanding how revelation is a historic person, that is, a reality which is not subduable as an object but which, as an experience, questions intelligence and freedom. The background of faith and the theological reflection spring forth from here, from a gift that comes to us and urges us to assume our responsibility.

According to my point of view, this revelation is agapic-kenotic: therefore, its content is found in the divine agape and in the *kénosis* its form at the height of the content. Vibrant with the love of Christ and sent in service of this love, mission has its heart within the agape, in the openness towards the other and in its donation to the other. And this other, is primarily the non-Christian, above all the one who can also refuse the faith. Being a living and personal crystallization of this love, the believer and the church are at the service of a love, which is addressed towards everybody. As Paul arrives to offer himself, 'anathema, separate from Christ, to the advantage of his brothers',[19] therefore, love belongs to Her on account of the reality, which postmodernity understands as finiteness and multiplicity, and it is possible for Her to accept the challenge, which Taylor indicated as the aspiration to *fullness* and to the experience of fragilization.

In accompanying the pathway of this concrete humanity, the church cannot but call upon the dignity, the foundation on which lies 'only in the mystery of the Word made flesh' and cannot but proclaim that, on the basis of the universal love of Christ, the holy Spirit gives everyone the possibility

---

[17] Ferrari, S. (ed.) *Introduzione al diritto comparato delle religioni. Ebraismo, islam e induismo*, Il Mulino, Bologna 2008.

[18] *Fides et Ratio* 56.

[19] Rm 9,3.

of coming into contact with the paschal mystery, in the way that God knows.[20] Mission needs to be understood from this background.

In this sense, John Paul II speaks about faith as a 'convinced advocate and convincing in reason'[21] and Benedict XVI asks for 'a faith ally of intelligence' and sustains that 'not acting according to reason, is contrary to the nature of God'[22] It goes without saying that the kind of reason, which is invoked here, is not any kind of knowledge, but one, which is capable of establishing a relationship with God. In his comment about Pope Ratzinger's speech in Regensburg, J. Habermas[23] asks for an alliance between 'the illuminated conscience of modernity' and the 'theological conscience of world religions', in view of a commitment that goes against the defeatism of reason, which the author sees being carried out by the 'positivistic scientism,' as well as by the 'tendencies of a derailed modernisation that seem to obstruct more than favour the imperatives of its morals of justice'. This position is not acceptable because Habermas realizes the separation between the Hellenistic heritage, that is reason, and the Jewish inheritance, that is soteriology.

According to Christian Duquoc, this is the time for a theology, where the solidity of faith does not match with the capacity of organic and global synthesis: for the postmodern theologian, the exchange with this culture functions as an opening for a search for truth, which represents a further peculiar motive of faithfulness to the revelation.[24] According to Christoph Theobald, we instead need to re-understand, in terms of wisdom, the work of reason in the bosom of this culture.[25] If there can be a theology, it needs to be a theology of this kind. Postmodern theology appears to be a theology without global and definite solutions, but capable of understanding the providential sense of this difficult time, which solicits the development of the prophetic role of the church as a school of humanity, and to transform the deep sense of the limit in a need for spirituality and for transcendence.

---

[20] *Gaudium et Spes* 22.

[21] Ivi.

[22] A cross reference to the famous speech held by J. Ratzinger at the university of Regensburg on12th September 2006. In this passage Benedetto XVI cites a passage of the «Controverse VII 3b» (in Khoury, A.Th. *Manuel II Paléologue. Entretiens avec un Mussulman. 7 ͤ Controverse*, Cerf, Paris 1966, 144-145); it is the VII Controvery which the BysantineEmperor Manuele II Paleologo had with a Persian expert of Christianity and Islam. These two meetings probably go back to winter of 1391 and their drafting in the form of a diary could be the work of the same emperor.

[23] Habermas, J. *Contro il disfattismo della ragione moderna. Per un nuovo patto tra fede e ragione*, in «Teoria politica» 23(2007), n. 1, 5-10. The original text appeared on the edition of 10th February, 2007 of *Neue Zürcher Zeitung*.

[24] Duquoc, Ch. *La teologia in esilio. La sfida della sua sopravvivenza nella cultura contemporanea* [2002], Queriniana, Brescia 2004, 95.

[25] Theobald, Ch. *Il cristianesimo come stile. Un modo di fare teologia nella postmodernità*. II, Dehoniane, Bologna 2009, 147.

The multi-culture of Western societies should, and must, make use of the dialogue with the relational vitalism of the African world[26] and with the religious and spiritual sense of the Asian world. Perhaps, it is not by chance, that in a prophetic text, at the end of his long pontificate, John Paul II spoke about the relationship with this world indicating an 'enormously rich body of teaching and *the striking new tone* in the way it presented this content constitute as it were a proclamation of new times'.[27] For mission, this is a time of sowing, rather than one of fruits, a sowing, in which the love of God has become the essence of an attentive and responsible love for human destiny.

---

[26] Nkafu Nkemkia, M. *Il pensare africano come "vitalogia"*, Città Nuova, Roma 1995. See also the conception of P. Tempels who places 'vital energy' as foundation of African philosophy: Tempels, P. *Filosofia bantu* [1946], Medusa, Milano 2005.

[27] John Paul II, *Tertio millennio adveniente* 20.

North American Pentecostal Reflections on Postmodernity

Harold D. Hunter

I must say that reading the Edinburgh 2010 Commission III document on postmodernity was an authentic postmodern encounter. The framers of this document concede that their report is not 'structured' but rather 'flashes and glimpses of the issues,' which is not simply a commentary on their process but their version of postmodernities. Speaking metaphorically, my first reaction was how would this team manage the cross-cultural dimensions of Noah's Ark? However, I read later in the document that they are theoretically capable of rebuilding a Bosnian Mosque.[1]

Please note that while the Edinburgh 2010 Commission III report may often be quite fluid, it yet firmly rejects Christian mission that is not 'holistic,' a requirement if it is to be 'valid and relevant'. 'It is always proclamation, dialogue and action in service for justice; it is always word and deed.' This is more apparent, where we are told that the Bible is 'no longer seen as an infallible guide' since 'oppression is not only due to abuse of the biblical texts, but is inherent in the texts themselves.'[2]

I, for one, would be cautious about suggesting that oppression is part of the theological intent of scripture. I noticed that male language is used of God in the Edinburgh 2010 document.[3] I was one of the architects of the 2000 WARC – Pentecostal dialogue report entitled 'Word and Spirit, Church and World' that insisted on inclusive language for God. Do the framers of the Commission III report not view such language as oppressive?

There is also irony, here, in that the framers call for both 'word and deed,' which is actually a hallmark of Pentecostal spirituality. Notice the warning about abuse of scripture, when pitting John 3:16 for the Lausanne Movement over against the WCC attraction to Luke 14:18-19.[4] This is of interest, in part, because Pentecostals have been quite literal about bringing

[1] 'Mission and Postmodernities,' Section 7, *Edinburgh 2010: Witnesses to Christ Today*, Volume 2, edited by Daryl Balia and Kirsteen Kim (Oxford: Regnum Books, 2010), 82.

[2] 'Mission and Postmodernities,' 5:4, 79, 6:4, 81.

[3] 'Mission and Postmodernities,' 5:2, 77.

[4] 'Mission and Postmodernities,' 5:4, 79.

in the 'poor, the crippled, the blind and the lame' (Luke 14:21, NRSV) as well as going 'out into the roads and the country lanes and compelling people to come in, so that my house may be filled' (Luke 14:23, NRSV).

The Edinburgh 2010 Commission III report has this to say about Pentecostals:

> Pentecostalism … although having strong pre-modern characteristics, might be said to be in part a postmodern phenomenon, insofar as it has existed on the fringe of modernity, frowned upon by the established church as well as secular society. Nevertheless, it proved adaptable, not the least due to its fluid or plastic nature, antedating the whole discussion around postmodernities. It may, therefore, be more successful than most churches in addressing postmodern concerns.[5]

I should say that, in the sense that Classical Pentecostalism has been ridiculed, marginalized and suppressed by colonizers from Magisterial Christianity and in the USA by particular Evangelicals, that there is some merit to the concept that we seek liberation. It was no small challenge for me to do a Ph.D. on Pentecostal pneumatology in the 1970s. When I tried to start a Pentecostal group at the American Academy of Religion in 1984, I was told that we were not allowed to have our own voice but others could speak for us. My early ecumenical work in the 1980s was drowned out by voices from outside the Pentecostal Movement.

Perhaps this idea in the Edinburgh 2010 report is like trying to square a circle because, on the one hand, the Pentecostal church of my youth broke new ground in breaking Jim Crow Laws, yet we very much lived in a sub-culture given many names like Victorian, Puritanical, pre-Chalecedonian, sub-modern, etc. The label varied according to the outside 'expert'. However, in terms of technology, we were quick to adapt to loudspeakers on the top of cars, radio, and television and even distributed tracts by throwing them out of little airplanes. And, today, during a Sunday morning worship service, some are e-mailing, texting, tweeting, and facebooking, even if they are not watching a hologram, making their own virtual church or viewing a cyberchurch on an iPhone or iPad. I am quite sure that the latter is not being true to our heritage from Azusa St., the Welsh Revival, Pandita Ramabai in India, and our other fathers and mothers.

Pentecostalism and the charismatic movement have unwittingly been radically influenced by Gutenberg's invention, making possible the world-wide parade of Bibles, along with the proliferation of defiant commentators, spawned, in part, by Luther's idea of direct access to God. Thus, this group helps define the expression from 'Gutenberg to Google' that explores concepts like cyberchurch and even cyber-Eucharist, which prompts the question of whether we would be well served by a compassionate version of 'China's Great Firewall'.

---

[5] 'Mission and Postmodernities,' 5:2, 77.

I appear to some as a living dinosaur. My father's generation knew about brush arbors and graduated to the sawdust trials with tent revivals. They faced threats by people with guns, knives, fire, hangings, poison, whips, brute force, etc., although this does not compare to what is still going on with Pentecostals around the world, as we still have martyrs. It is possible that the first Pentecostal martyr in the U.S.A. was killed by police in 1918, due to his commitment to pacifism.[6]

Have you ever met someone raised in Pentecostal revival services, where 'everything was moving but the pews'? Well, sometimes I saw the pews move. *The Live Coals of Fire* started in 1899 shows that B.H. Irwin appointed African-American W.E. Fuller a ruling elder. In 1904 Fuller wrote to J.H. King's *Live Coals* praising God for 'the blood that cleans up, the Holy Ghost that fills up, the fire that burns up, and the dynamite that blows up.' By 1905, Fuller, age 30, was one of three assistant general overseers to FBHC General Overseer J.H. King.

The 'radical' Pentecostal church, in which I was raised, kept us in church all the time from early in the morning and past midnight. We prayed, sang, preached, testified of miracles, etc. In terms of evangelism, we evangelized our own families and people, who came to our churches, which was true if they had already been baptized even by us.

My early years were spent witnessing on the streets, going house to house, handing out tracts at any opportunity, preaching revival services night after night, and so on, that was not for the faint of heart. We were told that this was a sign of the empowering presence of the Holy Spirit and were driven with a sense of urgency so that the 'world may believe'. But not 'believe' like the Edinburgh 2010 Commission III report 5:2, where one can be exclusivist, inclusivist, pluralist or whatever yet 'earnestly desire all to be saved and come to a knowledge of the truth (1 Tim 2:4)'.[7]

Did we get support from my other Christian brothers and sisters? Usually, no. What I heard was 'They are illiterate'. Well, we memorized more Bible verses than many of them had ever read. I guess they never heard of a 'sword drill'. Did they not go to the funeral of the likes of Bishop B.E. Underwood and see the worn out Bible in the casket? I heard them say, 'They don't have cathedrals'. Okay, so we had brush arbors and hit the sawdust trail, but this means only that we have something in common with the 'tree-churches' of Africa or the house churches of China, none of which it has been argued were foreign to churches of the 1st century. 'They're weird!' Yes, we were taught that it was okay to be 'peculiar' and that was worn as a badge of honour. Now, even my Orthodox friend, from Crete, said we are really in post-postmodernity, where people are returning to what has been proven true through the ages.

---

6 See Paul Alexander, *Peace to War: Shifting Allegiances in the Assemblies of God* (Telford, PA: Cascadia Publishing House, 2009), 136-137.

7 'Mission and Postmodernities,' 5:2, 77.

David Carter's study of Edinburgh, 'The Edinburgh Missionary Conference Centenary' in *Ecumenical Trends* 39:3, concludes that 'In the end unity and mission are one.' This UK Roman Catholic says unity based on the John 17:21 should move to 'so they may believe'. Would this not be a compelling argument for Pentecostals, who claim that evangelism is a top priority and perhaps even the fifth mark of the Church? Carter is captivated with Christian Churches Together in England (CTE) even making flattering parallels to the intent of Edinburgh 2010 (p. 4).[8]

Here is a proposal from my paper to the August 2010 Pentecostal World Conference in Sweden. It is one thing for IPHC founder G.F. Taylor to say the Azusa message is a truth worth dividing the church, but are current members of the Pentecostal World Conference willing to say they are global churches then shy away from their responsibility in pursuing various avenues of unity? For example, in the USA, is it sufficient to participate in PFNA now PCCNA and NAE then PWF and various specialist groups of interest? Is CCT a substitute for NCCCUSA or another avenue? Is the Global Christian Forum an alternative or replacement for the World Council of Churches?[9]

The Edinburgh 2010 Commission III paper suggests that, for some, 9/11 may have destroyed much of the stuff of postmodernity. This seems unlikely, as the USA, in particular, is a mixture of so many different contexts, although many are not well represented in our media. Notice the move of Harvey Cox from *The Secular City* (1965) to *Fire from Heaven* (1994), once he realized Pentecostals ignored the thesis of his famous book. Of course, now we have *The Future of Faith* (2009) where Cox portrays the Age of the Spirit as where Christians ignore dogma and embrace spirituality, which advances his advocacy of major world religions and is quite compatible with the primary version of postmodernity advocated in the Edinburgh 2010 Commission III report.

'In many ways, although limited to affluent society, postmodernity represents the voice of marginalized people insisting on equal treatment, on their angle of approach and point of view being as valid as those traditionally favoured'.[10] Concerning the notion that the report's version of postmodernity is particularly linked to the affluent, I would say that is true in terms of the working poor church, in which I was raised and which I have visited on five continents. In other words, social location is an issue in this discussion.

On the other hand, I cannot endorse the concept represented in the report that appears to reduce Pentecostalism to what I have elsewhere called Enthusiastic Pneumatomania. These phenomena are not unique to

---

[8] David Carter, 'The Edinburgh Missionary Conference Centenary,' *Ecumenical Trends* 39:3 (March 2010), 4-5.

[9] Harold D. Hunter, 'The Nature and Mission of the Postmodern Church,' paper read to the Pentecostal World Conference, August 26, 2010 in Stockholm, Sweden.

[10] 'Mission and Postmodernities,' 2:2, 65.

Pentecostals and absolutely not true of many Pentecostals around the world. I will concede, however, that there is a strand of the Pentecostal Movement, of which this is true and much like the Edinburgh 2010 Commission III report play down the 'doctrinal'. There is no concern here that Buddha will supplant Jesus even though Dr. Yonggi Cho, founding pastor of Yoido Full Gospel Church, spoke at a Buddhist University some eight years ago. Also, when the report tries to blur traditional lines that have defined salvation, remember that for some Pentecostals their call for unity is really one of uniformity built on the foundational concept that we are talking about Christians in the first place, who will in time become Pentecostals.[11]

Anyway, beware what you hope for when you supplant Christian theology with a nebulous concept of 'authentic spirituality,' as clearly there are forms of this search that would be rejected by the framers of the Edinburgh 2010 Commission III report. But have Pentecostals spawned more abberations than German universities that I had to study as a seminary student in the 1970s? Do you really want more 'tele-evangelists'? Apparently not, as they quickly condemn 'allegedly divinely appointed charismatic leader(s) of faith fellowships'.[12]

Brighton '91

I have reviewed the Edinburgh 2010 Commission III report from many different angles, but in an attempt to be faithful to the assignment, I would like to try and locate part of the discussion from a Pentecostal perspective. This can be illustrated by commenting on the first global conference for Pentecostal scholars known as Brighton '91. It may be possible to consider this something of a Pentecostal narrative linked to 'the Spirit blows where it wills' (John 3:8).

The Theology Track of Brighton '91 was organized by Monsignor Peter Hocken and me. This concept cemented in my mind, during a five year span, where I traveled to 35 countries, spread across five continents. In the late 1980s, I went to Geneva, Switzerland and spoke directly to Emilio Castro, then General Secretary of the WCC, asking to bring together

---

[11] 'Mission and Postmodernities,' Section 3, 71, 5:1, 75, 5:2, 76; Amos Yong, 'From Azusa Street to the Bo Tree and Back: Strange Babblings and Interreligious Interpretations in the Pentecostal Encounter with Buddhism,' in *The Spirit in the World: Emerging Pentecostal Theologies in Global Contexts*, edited by Veli-Matti Kärkkäinen (Grand Rapids: Eerdmans, 2009), 203-226; Harold D. Hunter, 'Global Pentecostalism and Ecumenism: Two Movements of the Holy Spirit'? in *Pentecostalism and Christian Unity: Ecumenical Documents and Critical Assessments*, edited by Wolfgang Vondey (Eugene, OR: Pickwick Publications, 2010), 20-33.

[12] 'Mission and Postmodernities,' 6:2, 80, 6:1, 80.

Pentecostal scholars in conjunction with the upcoming WCC General Assembly known as Canberra '91 with the theme 'Come, Holy Spirit'.

When it became apparent that Canberra '91 was not going to co-operate with me, months later I went to the UK and met with Michael Harper and others to explain my vision and desire to link with their projected conference to be held at Brighton. They reluctantly agreed and eventually asked Peter Hocken to assist me with the programme.

What we accomplished at Brighton '91 was unique, in that it was the first such meeting for Pentecostal scholars brought together from six continents. In an effort to seek a balance between the Global North and Global South, the conference was invitation only. We also provided simultaneous translation in four languages. Our presenters were Roman Catholic, Orthodox, Protestant, Pentecostal, AICs and other Christian groups like 'house-churches'.

Although Peter Hocken vetoed my invitation to speakers like the legendary Frank Chikane and others, we managed to tackle a wide range of topics such as the following:

1. Other Living Faiths
2. Liberation Theology
3. Social justice
4. Gender Equality
5. Apartheid
6. Salvation of all Creation
7. Physical Challenges
8. Martyrdom

The framers of the Edinburgh 2010 Commission III report identify the Church's prophetic role as struggling for peace and the integrity of creation and combating injustice. The framers also complain that some churches will not care about the environment because the earth will eventually perish. How does one explain that the founder of the original Earth Day was a Pentecostal?[13]

In the immediate aftermath of Brighton '91, I made these comments in an article published shortly after Brighton '91. This was part of my response to the *BEM* document that was published in the *Journal of Ecumenical Studies*:

> Pentecostal ecclesiarchs should have some fears allayed by the healthy respect for Scripture evident in BEM and the absence of any trace of an arid academic enterprise of disaffected intellectuals. Confessing The One Faith's depiction of Nicene thought as 'doxological' and 'confessional' fits well in categorizing pentecostals over against the 'historical-critical' preoccupation of Modernity. Tension between Pentecostalism and Modernity has given rise to labels such as 'precritical' and 'submodern'. The theological orientation of

---

[13] 'Mission and Postmodernities,' 5:3, 78, 6:5, 82. See Harold D. Hunter, 'Pentecostal Social Engagement: Excerpts From Around the World,' Edinburgh 2010 Commission VII.

> Pentecostal scholars unveiled at Brighton '91 may constitute a constructive theological proposal on equal footing with more widely publicized perspectives. A descriptive account of such would give voice to new insights for handling racism, sexism, socio-economic oppression, the environment, etc. Judging by "Postmodern Theology: Christian Faith in a Pluralist World," the Brighton scholars may model a legitimate postmodern agenda. Primary dissenters will be sympathizers of Altizer's ethnocentric scheme narrowly defining postmodern culture as marked by a noticeable absence of God. Part of the rationale for utilizing this descriptive category is because postmodernity is a polyglot term that admits determinism, scientific hegemony, etc., have given way to contingency and relativism. It is not difficult to support Robert Bellah's multilingualism over against the metalanguage of science. The Brighton '91 model figures in because it is not unrelated to Peter Hodgson's material norm identified as liberation.[14]

Looking back on Brighton '91 and like conferences, where I have participated or organized, I can say that I feel justified in applying postmodernity to this work. This is not simply a matter of the subjects that were addressed, but the way that they were handled. We did not use speakers from the Global North to speak for the Global South and tried to engender cross fertilization on any topic at hand, while deliberating cultivating the considerable diversity of the Pentecostal Movement that is often unknown by observers.

Not every session met our lofty goals and that is apparent in the published papers, yet this was the first event of its kind, which meant to provide a model for others to follow. As it turns out, more often than not, I ended up being an organizer or presenter in many such international events that would follow. In other words, Brighton '91 established a model that has been followed, not only in terms of events, but also in ongoing organizations that have taken shape in various continents. Contrast this with the admission of the Edinburgh 2010 Commission III report that they fell well short in this regard.[15]

Abandon All Hope Ye Who Enter Here?

Is hope irreconcilable with postmodernity? When one goes to the Edinburgh 2010 Commission III report 4:1, one has to reckon with the possibility that postmodernity may surrender hope. I, for one, am not willing to do this and was glad to see a course, later in the document, where hope was invoked as necessary for transformation. However, earlier in the document, they dismiss the related comments by David Kettle as modern not postmodern.[16]

---

[14] Harold D. Hunter, 'Reflections by a Pentecostalist on Aspects of BEM,' Journal of Ecumenical Studies 29:3/4 (Summer/Fall 1992), 323-324.

[15] 'Missoin and Postmodernities,' Section 7, 83.

[16] 'Mission and Postmodernities,' 4:1, 72, Section 3, 71.

The Edinburgh 2010 paper says that postmoderns, who wrote this paper, give up such a notion and are more aligned with the New Testament.

> As is natural with emerging movements, the organisational structure of the church in New Testament times is still fluid; there is not even yet a clearly defined borderline between Jews and Christians. Perhaps postmodernity, with its emphasis on life and experience rather than on structures and membership, is in many ways closer to New Testament ecclesiology than what can be said of some of the more traditional Christian positions? [17]

This is not a convincing argument for me, when this logic then is taken to mean salvation outside the church. Whatever happened to theological discussions of election? Postmoderns have little tolerance for theological discussions. Yet, I cannot resolve such a critical issue simply by something like a phenomological perspective. Here is the way I put it in my 'Two Movements' article for Wolfgang Vondey's 2010 book on Pentecostal ecumenism: 'In whatever ways Pentecostals conceive of the Spirit outside the church, and however they might rightly engage in inter-faith conversations, they have generally not affirmed a ubiquitous salvific presence'.[18]

Also, it seems that the writers of the Edinburgh 2010 paper believe in some truths, whether absolute or not, because they talk about trying to improve the world and not simply accepting things as they are. They obviously do not want to give up on hope or ignore those in poverty. In light of this paper, how does one categorize things like helping the poor, equal treatment of women, fighting racial discrimination, and so on? By the way, the firm position toward the end of the paper about their version of postmodernity I found at odds with the opening that seemed more receptive to other postmodernities.

Conclusion

My ecumenical journey has been one of a simple pilgrim seeking truth. I have no illusions about what John 17:21 means in this context, but rather know that the wider the circle, the more whole I am as a person. Although it may disappoint some, I will say, without apology, that I remain a Pentecostal Christian. However, allow me to define what this means as my journey continues to be enriched by my engagement of other Christians, other religions, and the whole of Creation.

---

[17] 'Mission and Postmodernities,' 5:2, 76.

[18] Hunter, 'Global Pentecostalism and Ecumenism,' 31. See Amos Yong, *Hospitality & The Other: Pentecost, Christian Practices, and the Neighbor* (Maryknoll: Orbis Books, 2008).

RESPONSES AND REFLECTIONS

Rolv Olsen

The Core Group, in its statement submitted to the Edinburgh 2010 Conference, identified some key questions concerning mission in relation to postmodernities, such as: whether there is room for hope in postmodernity, whether conversion necessarily is legitimate, and whether Christians can witness to absolute standards of right and wrong in a society losing its belief in ethical absolutes. At the conference the consequences for mission in a postmodern context were discussed in relation to truth and evangelism in an environment where claims to universal truth are viewed with suspicion, in relation to the church in an age of individualistic spirituality and privatized faith, in relation to salvation versus the allegedly many paths to God, and in relation to evangelism and witness, since being and doing are much more important than saying. In other words, how to find the proper balance between word and deed, combining bold proclamation with humility. Areas especially recommended for further consideration were the exercise of leadership, spiritual formation and of theological education, the Bible and hermeneutics, ecology and the environmental crisis, and reconciliation and healing.

After the responses from representatives of the transversal themes and regional/confessional perspectives that were part of the Edinburgh 2010 project, the delegates were divided into small groups along geographical and cultural lines, in order to enable the groups to address more seriously the multifaceted nature of postmodernities by letting each group focus on the particular contextual challenges. Each group was asked in the first group session to identify three issues relating to postmodernities, and in the second to outline three main issues to be addressed by the church in its continuing mission. In what follows, a brief survey of the key issues and priorities addressed by the different regional groups is given.

The *Northern and Continental European* group, although probably having the smallest population base, was by far the largest, probably reflecting variations in the perceived urgency of the topic as well as the proportionally higher number of participants from the region in the conference as a whole. Thus, the group members decided to from two sub-groups. The first sub-group identified as the three main issues: consumerism and market ideology, mistrust of grand narratives, truth claims, authorities and institutions, and individualism. Issues addressed were authenticity, especially in communicating one's faith; the need for a narrative rather than an argumentative approach in witness, and the Church as a social network in response to consumerism. The second sub-group perceived the main issues relating to postmodernities to be consumerism, community without commitment, and plurality and relativism. The most urgent issues recognized by the group were, a thirst for authentic, committed community, the challenge to live out the meaning of the good news in daily life, addressing the whole of creation, acknowledging the brokenness, limitedness and vulnerability of all human endeavors, emphasizing that the church is the work of the Holy Spirit through weak vessels.

The group from *Central and Southern Europe* listed the issues it addressed as life in community, focus on personal relations, creating new ministries for lay people, encouraging ways to reveal and discover beauty, openness to transcendence and silence, and the need for a prophetic voice offering alternatives to current social pressures.

The main issues perceived by the group from *Africa and of African Descent* were uncertainty, facing a liquid future, the ideological load of postmodernities, and the alienation caused by individualism. Emphasis was given to the questions of neo-liberal capitalism and post-colonial reality, stressing the need to carve out opportunities for new generations, the building of a capacity to resist the new empires, modernity, colonialism and cultural hegemonies. The issues they addressed were a need for a prophetic vision, imagination and leadership to confront the structures and agendas of the dominant neo-liberalism, neo-colonialism, patriarchy and consumerism, a need to foster communities of character and discipleship, based on mutual recognition, respect and reciprocity, and a need for discernment of God's presence and the art of participatory theological reflection.

The group from *East Asia and Oceania* perceived the main issues as disenchantment with progress and westernization, combined with the pursuit of consumerism, fragmentation of society, and search for meaning, common roots and cohesiveness in society. Issues the group addressed were the challenge of modernization and westernization, the need to counter the overwhelming thrust of consumerism, and the emphasis on growth and numbers in some churches, endangering their credibility. The group envisioned a rediscovery of a liturgical worship addressing the emotional needs of worshipers, overcoming the disenchantment with rationalism and modernism, Christians developing new forms of spiritual interaction, being relevant to the context without falling into the temptation of letting fashionable trends or new technology set the agenda, new opportunities for Christian voices to be heard, and the Christian church relearning how to speak prophetically in ways that address social concerns of society in general in a relevant and acceptable manner, expressed in a vocabulary that resonates with ordinary people.

In the group representing the *Asian Continent and the Middle East*, the discussion was influenced by the fact that postmodernity is scarcely a new phenomenon to the continent, but is an inherent part of the context. Asia may be regarded as already having been postmodern for thousands of years. Thus, the issues perceived were, just how 'modern' is postmodernity, why one has to identify oneself in categories defined by the West, and a suspicion toward all so-called meta-narratives. Issues addressed were recognizing the context, realizing that in Asia truth is regarded as experience rather than proposition, the need for a community that is an alternative to consumerism, and a proper balance between stability and change.

The *Latin American and Spanish* group identified as main issues a 'melting pot' globalization and a consequent search for identities, the growing concern about loneliness, individualism and depression, resulting in a loss of the notion of what is real and what is a simulacrum, and a relativization of truth. The group maintained that issues to be addressed included finding a synthesis between rational and emotional approaches to human beings in an integral and contextual way, the avoidance of a 'market' or 'consumerist' mentality in the church, the building of communities of faith that make sense in people's lives and integrate all kinds of people, and addressing with a prophetic voice the challenges presented by postmodernity.

The *Anglo Saxon Commonwealth* group perceived the main issues concerning postmodernities as the search for significance, diversity and pluralism, consumerism and choice, the dialectic between experience and truth – on both the virtual level and that of reality, and a practice of authority based on fluidity and relationship. The issues it addressed were expressed as, living an authentic Christian life as a community, addressing fragmentation and being committed to a visible demonstration of fullness of life and hospitality, developing an aesthetics of truth, and the dynamic tension between the global and the local.

The *Anglo Saxon North American* group saw as issues to address how to enable people to experience church as community and to establish authentic community, making it possible to move from experience to commitment, how to express the role of Christ in order to convey the full meaning and extent of the freedom that he has promised to give, expanding the meaning of the good news in a context where the forensic understanding of atonement alone may be perceived as too narrow, and showing a radical love and hope that counters the fragmentation of relationships.

What does all this signify for the church in its mission in a postmodern environment? It might be tempting and fitting to merely let the above plethora of voices and viewpoints speak for themselves, imitating postmodernity in giving space to all viewpoints without giving any indications of preference or try to reconcile the tensions within. However, some key issues and priorities do emerge. The recommendations from the Core Group, as expressed in their submission to the Edinburgh 2010 Common Call, emphasise crucial issues and give food for further reflection:

> We see the present era called 'postmodern' characterized by fragmentation, relativism and consumerism as a surrogate of sense. At the same time, it is marked by a new search for authentic life in fullness, fluidity, choice and freedom of expression, and by more interconnectedness than ever.
>
> For your mission,
>
> ...we envision authentic communities of compassion, not boasting in the possession of the truth, but depending on the God's Holy Spirit of Christ for witness and dialogue. These will be able minister to, and to integrate, diverse people, and to live with the contraditions this implies. Young people are given a space, and empowerment. Women and men share power and responsibilies fairly.
>
> ...we feel compelled to develop a new zeal for justice, peace and the protection of creation, listening to the voices from abroad, and even at the cost of inevitable conflict in and about our own churches.
>
> ...we will be more bold and creative than ever in developing aesthetics of liturgy reflecting the beauties of creator and creation. We will celebrate with new songs, with movement or in silence, using significant symbols, rediscovered from our own or borrowed from other traditions.

Bibliography

Abromeit, Hans-Jürgen. ‚Wahrnehmungen aus dem Bischofsamt in Ostdeutschland". *LVK-Forum* 3/2002, 26-30.

Ahdar, Rex,.'Indigenous Spiritual Concerns and the Secular State: Some New Zealand Developments,' *Oxford Journal of Legal Studies*, 23(4), 2003: 611-637.

Aikman, David. *Jesus in Beijing: How Christianity Is Transforming China and Changing Global Balance of Power*. Washington DC: Regnery Publishing, 2003.

Alexander, Paul. *Peace to War: Shifting Allegiances in the Assemblies of God.* Telford, PA: Cascadia Publishing House, 2009.

Alfeyev (Hieromonk Illarion). *The Life and Teaching of St. Gregory the Theologian.* Moscow: Lovers of Church History Society's Press, 1998. (In Russian)

______. *The World of Isaac the Syrian.* Moscow: Lovers of Church History Society's Press, 1998. (In Russian)

______. *St. Simeon the New Theologian and the Orthodox Tradition.* Moscow: Lovers of Church Society's Press, 1998. (In Russian)

Amaladoss, Michael. 'The Trinity on Mission." Frans Wijsen and Peter Nissen (eds.) *'Mission is a Must': Intercultural Theology and the Mission of the Church.* Amsterdam: Rodopi (2002), 99-106.

Anderson, A. 'Pentecostalism, the Enlightenment and Christian Mission in Europe." *International Review of Mission* 95 July/October (2006), 276-281.

Appiah-Kubi, K. and Sergo Torres (eds.). *African Theology en route,* Maryknoll, NY: Orbis, 1970

Aspekte der Mission und Evangelisation im heutigen Europa. Auf dem Weg zu einer gemeinsamen Mission." *Ökumenisches Forum* 18 (1995), 327-331.

Avis, Paul. *A Church Drawing Near: Spirituality and Mission in a Post-Christian Culture.* (London: T & T Clark International, 2003.

Bärend, Hartmut. *Kirche mit Zukunft. Impulse für eine missionarische Volkskirche.* Gießen, 2006.

Bauman, Z. *Postmodern ethics.* Oxford /Malden (MA): Blackwell, 1993.

_____. *Il disagio della postmodernità.* Milano: Mondadori, 1997/2002.

_____. *La società dell'incertezza.* Bologna: Il Mulino, 1999.

_____. *La solitudine del cittadino globale.* Milano: Feltrinelli, 1999/2000.

_____. *Una nuova condizione umana.* Milano, Vita e Pensiero, 2003.

Bays Daniel H. ed. *Christianity in China: From Eighteenth Century to the Present*. Stanford: Stanford University Press, 1996.

Bediako, Kwame. *Christianity in Africa: The Renewal of a Non-Western Religion,*

Edinburgh & Maryknoll, NY: Edinburgh University Press & Orbis Books, 1995.

_____. 'The Holy Spirit, the Christian Gospel and Religious Change: The African

Evidence for a Christian Theology of Religious Pluralism", in James Thrower (ed.) *Essays in Religious Studies for Andrew Walls*, Aberdeen, Department of Religious Studies, University of Aberdeen, 1986, 44-56.

Bellow, Saul. 'The Distracted Public." The Romanes Lecture, Oxford University, 10 May 1990.

_____. *It All Adds Up: From the Dim Past to the Uncertain*

_____. *Future: A Non-fiction Collection.* New York: Viking (1994), 153–69.

_____. *Believing without Belonging: In Search of New Paradigms of Church and Mission in*

_____. *Secularized and Postmodern Contexts.* Northelbian Centre for World Mission/ Christian Jensen Kolleg, Breklum, Germany, 26th June-2nd July, 2002.

Berger, Peter. *Heretical Imperative: Contemporary Possibilities of Religious Affirmation.* London: Collins, 1980.

Bergunder, M. 'Mission und Pfingstbewegung." Dahling-Sander (ed.) *Leitfaden Ökumenische Missionstheologie.* Gütersloh: Kaiser, 214ff.'Bevans, Stephen and Richard Schroeder. *Constants in Context: A Theology of Mission for Today.* Maryknoll, NY: Orbis, 2004.

Blocher, Gene. 'An Explanation of Postmodernism." Castell (*et al.* eds.) *An Introduction to Modern Philosophy: Examining the Human Condition.* New York: Macmillan College Publishing House, 1994.

Bloom, Alan. *The Closing of the American Mind.* New York: Simon & Schuster, 1987.

Blumenberg, H. *La legittimità dell'età moderna* Genova: Marietti, 1966/1992.

Böhlemann, Peter. *Wie die Kirche wachsen kann und was sie davon abhält.* Neukirchen-Vluyn, 2006.

Bonaventure. *Itinerarium Mentis In Deum, Works of Saint Bonaventure, II,* intro., trans., comm. Philotheus Boehner (Saint Bonaventure, NY: The Franciscan Institute, Saint Bonaventure University, 1956.

Bosch, David J. *Believing in the Future: Toward a Missiology of Western Culture.* Harrisburg: Trinity Press International, 1995.

______. "Reflections on Biblical Models of Mission." in Phillips, James M.and Robert T. Coote eds. *Towards the Twenty First Century in Christian Mission: Essays in Honor of*

Gerald H. Anderson. Grand Rapids, MI: Eerdmans(1993),190 ff.

_____. *Transforming Mission: Paradigm Shifts in Theology of Mission.* Maryknoll, NY: Orbis, 1991.

Bouman, J. ‚Ethik und Kultur in einer multikulturellen Gesellschaft." *European Journal of Theology* 4 (1), 79-87.

Braaten, Carl E. and Robert W. Jenson (eds.) *In One Body through the Cross: The Princeton Proposal for Christian Unity.* Grand Rapids, MI: Eerdmans, 2003.

Budapest Perspectives: Towards an Agenda of Hope for Europe. www.hfe.org.

'Can Europe be saved? A Review Essay." *International Bulletin of Missionary Research* 31 (3/2007), 121-125.

Cardoza-Orlandi, Carlos F. *Mission: An Essential Guide.* Nashville: Abingdon Press, 2002.

Carter, David. 'The Edinburgh Missionary Conference Centenary." *Ecumenical Trends* 39:3 (March 2010), 4ff.

Cartledge, Mark J. 'Pentecostal Experience: An Example of Practical-Theological Rescripting." *JEPTA 28/1* (2008), 21-33.

Chai, Soo-il. 'Missio Dei – Its Development and Limitations in Korea." *IRM* (October 2003), 548- 549.

Chesterton, G. K. *Orthodoxy.* London: John Lane, 1909.

______. 'Reflections on a Rotten Apple." Chesterton, *The Well and the Shallows.* London: Sheed & Ward, 1935.

Chidester, David. 'Credo Mutwa, Zulu Shaman: The Invention and Appropriation of Indigenous Authenticity in African Folk Religion,' in Chidester, David, Abdulkader Tayob and Wolfram Weisse (eds.) *Religion, Politics and Identity in a Changing South Africa*, [Religion and Society in Transition, v.6] Munster: Waxmann, 2004, 69-88.

Chow, Rey. *Writing Diaspora: Tactics of Intervention in Contemporary Cultural Studies.* Indianapolis: Indiana University Press, 1993.

Clausen, Matthias, Ulf Harder and Michael Herbst. *Emmaus – Auf dem Weg des Glaubens. Basiskurs 2.0.* Neukirchen-Vluyn 2008.

Cohen, A.P. *The Symbolic Construction of Community*, London: Tavistock, 1985

Conference on World Mission and Evangelism. *A Letter from Athens to the Churches,networks and communities*, 2005, http://www2.wcccoe.org/pressreleasesen.nsf/index/pu-05-16.html.

Conradie, Ernst M. *An ecological Christian anthropology: At home on earth.* Aldershot: Ashgate, 2005.

_____. *Christianity and a critique of consumerism: A survey of six points of entry.* Wellington: Bible Media, 2009.

_____. *The church and climate change: Signs of the Times Series Volume 1.* Pietermaritzburg: Cluster Publications, 2008.

Cragg, Kenneth. *Christianity in World Perspective*, London: Lutterworth Press, 1968.

Danaher, James P. *Postmodern Christianity and the Reconstruction of the Christian Mind*. Bethesda/Dublin/London: Academic Press, 2001.

Davie, Grace.'Is Europe an exceptional case?' *International Review of Mission* 95 July/October (2006), 247-258.

____. *Religion in Modern Europe: a Memory Mutates*. Oxford: OUP, 2000.

Ding, Guangxun. *Love Never Ends: Paper by K.H. Ting*. Edited by Janice Wickeri. Nanjing: Yiling Press, 2000.

Dube, Saurabh.. 'Travelling Light: Missionary Musings, Colonial Cultures and Anthropological Anxieties." Kaur, Raminder and John Hutnyk, eds. *Travel Worlds: Journeys in Contemporary Cultural Politics*. London: Zed Books (1999), 46-47.

Duquoc, Ch.. *La teologia in esilio. La sfida della sua sopravvivenza nella cultura contemporanea*. Brescia: Queriniana, 2002/2004.

EKD-Text 68: *Das Evangelium unter die Leute bringen. Zum missionarischen Dienst der Kirche in unserem Land*. Hannover, 2000.

Farley, Edward. Transforming a Lukewarm Church." *The Christian Century,* August 27-Sept 3 (1997), 754-757.

Feldtkeller, A. 'Verlangt der gesellschaftliche Pluralismus nach einer ‚pluralistischen Religionstheologie'?" *EvTheol* 58 (6/1998), 445-460.

Ferrari, S. (ed.) *Introduzione al diritto comparato delle religioni. Ebraismo, islam e induismo*. Bologna: Il Mulino, 2008.

Feyerabend, Paul. *Against Method. Outline of an anarchistic Theory of Knowledge*. London: Verso, 1975.

Forsyth, P.T. 'A Rallying Ground for the free Churches: The Reality of Grace." *Hibbert Journal*, IV (1906), 828.

Friesen, J. Stanley. *Missionary Responses to Tribal Religions at Edinburgh, 1910*, New York: Peter Lang, 1996.

Fuchs, O. ‚Was ist Neuevangelisierung?" *Stimmen der Zeit* 210 (1992), 465-471.

Gallagher, Michael Paul. 'The Tone of Culture: from Prometheus to Narcissus." Gallagher, *Struggles of Faith*. Eire: Columba Press (1990), 84–93. Displayed online at www.gospel-culture.org.uk/Gallagher.htm

Gao Shining. 'Chinese Christianity in the 21st Century." *Christian Theology and Intellectuals in China*. Aarhus: Aarhus University, 2003.

Gabriel, Karl. e.a. *Religion und Kirchen in Ost(Mittel)Europa: Deutschland-Ost*. Gott Nach dem Kommunismus: Ostfildern, 2003.

Geller, Helmut, Karl Gabriel e.a. ‚Die Kirchen in der DDR vor und nach der Wende". Karl Gabriel e.a.. *Religion und Kirchen in*

Ost(Mittel)Europa: Deutschland- Ost. (P. M. Zulehner e.a. (eds.) Gott nach dem Kommunismus: Ostfildern, (2003), 325-336.

George, Archimandrite. *Theosis: The True Purpose of Human Life.* Mount Athos: Holy Monastery of St. Gregorios, 2006.

Gibbs, Eddie and Ryan Bolger. *Emerging Churches: Creating Christian Community in postmodern cultures.* Grand Rapids: Baker, 2005.

Gibson, William E. 'The lifestyle of Christian faithfulness." M. Schut (ed.) *Simpler living compassionate life: A Christian perspective.* Denver: Morehouse Group (1999), 133-134.

Glasser, Arthur F. *Announcing the Kingdom: The Story of God's Mission in the Bible.* Grand Rapids, MI: Baker Academic, 2003.

Graham, Elaine and Walton Heather. 'Walk on the Wild Side: A Critique of *The Gospel and Our Culture.*" *Modern Churchman* 33, no. 1 (1991), 5-7.

Grenz, Stanley. *A Primer on Postmodernism*, Grand Rapids, MI: Eerdmans, 1996.

Guardini, R. *La fine dell'epoca moderna. Il potere.* Brescia: Morcelliana, Brescia 1950/1993.

Guder, Darrell L. 'From Mission and Theology to Missional Theology." *The Princeton Seminary Bulletin*, Vol. XXIV, No. 1, New Series (2003), 36-54.

_____. (ed.) *Missional church: A Vision for the Sending of the Church in North America. The People of God Sent on a Mission.* The Gospel and our culture series: Grand Rapids, Mich.: Eerdmans, 1998.

Guha, Ranajit. *History at the Limit of World-History.* New Delhi: Oxford University Press, 2003 [orig. Columbia, 2002].

Gunton, Colin. *The One, the Three and the Many: God, creation and the culture of modernity.* Cambridge: Cambridge University Press, 1993.

Gustafson, James M. *An Examined Faith: The Grace of Self-Doubt.* Minneapolis: Fortress Press, 2004.

Habermas, Jürgen.*Time of Transitions.* New York: Polity Press, 2006.

_____. 'Contro il disfattismo della ragione moderna. Per un nuovo patto tra fede e ragione." *Teoria politica*, 23(2007), 1, 5-10.

_____. *Il discorso filosofico della modernità.* Roma/Bari: Laterza, 1987.

Halík, Tomás. 'The Soul of Europe: An Altar to the Unknown God." *International Review of Mission* 95 July/October (2006), 265-270.

Hanson, A.,'The Making of the Maori: Culture Invention and its Logic,' *American Anthropologist,* Vol 91(1989): 890-902

Harrison, Simon. 'Cultural Boundaries', *Anthropology Today*, Vol. 15(5), Oct 1999, 10-13

Harvey, David. *The Condition of Postmodernity: An Inquiry into the Origins of Cultural Change.* Oxford: Blackwell, 1990.

Hattaway, Paul. *Back to Jerusalem.* Waynesboro: Gabriel Publishing, 2005.

Hay, David and Kate Hunt. *Understanding the Spirituality of People who don't go to Church.* Nottingham: Centre for the Study of Human Relations, University of Nottingham (2000), 38.

Herbst, Michael. ‚Ach, Sie sind also der Missionar!? Kontext, Enstehungsgeschichte und Aufgaben des Greifswalder Instituts.“ Herbst, M., Ohlemacher, J., Zimmermann, J. (ed.) *Missionarische Perspektiven für die Kirche der Zukunft.*Beiträge zur Evangelisation und Gemeindeentwicklung 1, Neukirchen: Neukirchener Verlagsgesellschaft (2005), 30-46.

_____. (ed.) *Emmaus – Auf dem Weg des Glaubens. Handbuch.* Neukirchen-Vluyn ²2006.

_____. , Johannes Zimmermann und Jörg Ohlemacher (eds.) *Missionarische Perspektiven für die Kirche der Zukunft.*Beiträge zur Evangelisation und Gemeindeentwicklung 1, Neukirchen: Neukirchener Verlagsgesellschaft, 2005.

Hermelink, J., R. Kähler, B. Weyel. ‚In der Vielfalt liegt die Stärke. Konsequente Mission oder interessierte Kommunikation – wie soll sich die Kirche orientieren?“ *Zeitzeichen* 1 (2001), 38-40.

Hesse, Barnor. ‘Forgotten Like a Bad Dream: Atlantic Slavery and the Ethics of Postcolonial Memory.” Goldberg, David Theo and Ato Quayson (eds.) *Relocating Postcolonialism.* Oxford: Blackwell Publishers (2002), 65.

Hiebert, Paul. *Missiological Implications of Epistemological Shifts: Affirming Truth in a Modern/Postmodern World.* Christian Mission and Modern Culture: Harrisburg: Trinity, 1999.

_____. ‘The Category *Christian* in the Mission Task’ in *Anthropological Reflections on Missiological Issues*, Grand Rapids, MI: Baker Books, 1994,107-136.

Hitchen, John M. ‘Relations between Missiology and Anthropology Then and Now – Insights from the Contribution to Ethnography and Anthropology by

Nineteenth Century Missionaries in the South Pacific, *Missiology*, Vol 30(4) October 2002:455-478

_____. ‘Harold W. Turner Remembered’, *International Bulletin of Missionary Research,* Vol 26(3): July 2002, 112-3.

Hoedemaker, Bert. *Secularization and Mission: A Theological Essay.* Harrisburg: Trinity Press International, 1998.

Hottois, G. and M. Weyemberg (ed.). *Richard Rorty. Ambuigüités et limites du postmodernisme*. Paris: Vrin, 1994.

Houtepen, Anton.. *God: the Open Question. Theological Perspectives of the Modern Culture.* Moscow: St. Andrew's Biblical-Theological Institute, 2008. (In Russian)

Huber, W. ‚Auf dem Weg zu einer missionarischen Kirche.” Feldtkeller, A., T. Sundermeier (ed.) *Mission in pluralistischer Gesellschaft.* Frankfurt: Lembeck (1999), 107-135.

Hudgins, Andrew. *Ecstatic in the Poison: New Poems.* Woodstock, NY: Overlook Press, 2003.

Hunter, Harold D. 'Global Pentecostalism and Ecumenism: Two Movements of the Holy Spirit?" *Pentecostalism and Christian Unity: Ecumenical Documents and Critical Assessments.*Vondey, Wolfgang (ed.) Eugene, OR: Pickwick Publications (2010), 20-33.

_____. 'Reflections by a Pentecostalist on Aspects of BEM," *Journal of Ecumenical Studies* 29:3/4 (Summer/Fall 1992), 323ff.

Illustrated London News, quoted in Jaki, Stanley L. *The Purpose of it all.* Washington: Regnery Gateway, 1990.

International Review of Mission Vol. XCII, No. 364 and 365, (Jan and Apr 2003).

International Review of Mission, Vol. XCII, No. 367, (October 2003).

'Introduction to the Programme of the Conference." *International Review of Mission* 95 (July/October 2006), 232-235.

Ivereigh, Austen. 'Europe of the Heart." *The Tablet*, 13.05.2004, http://www.thetablet.co.uk/articles/2469

Jackson, Darrell. ‚Von Lausanne nach Athen: Europäische Mission in ökumenisch- evangelikaler Begegnung." *Europa: Christen, Kirchen und Missionen, Jahrbuch Mission 2006.* Hamburg: Missionshilfe (2006), 253-265.

Jenson, Robert W. *Systematic Theology Volume 2: The Works of God.* Oxford: Oxford University Press, 1999.

Johansson, Lars. 'New Age – a synthesis of premodern, modern and postmodern." Sampson, V. Samuel, C. Sugden (eds.) *Faith and Modernity*, Oxford: Regnum (1994), 208-251.

John Paul II. *Tertio millennio adveniente* 20.

Johns, Jackie D. 'Pentecostalism and the Postmodern Worldview." *Journal of Pentecostal Theology* 7 (1995), 73-96.

Kagame, Alexis. ' La place de Dieu et de l'homme dans la religion des Bantu.' *Cahiers des Religions Africaines*, Vol 3(5), January 1969,1-11

Kasdorf, Hans und Friedemann Walldorf (ed.) *Werdet meine Zeugen: Weltmission im Horizont von Theologie und Geschichte.* Neuhausen: Hänssler, 1996.

Kasper, W. *On The 'New Evangelisation of Europe'*.. http://www.mwi-aachen.org

Kearney,Richard. *On Stories* London: Routledge, 2002.

Keifert, Patrick. *We are here now.* Idaho: Eagle, 2006.

Keskitalo, Jukka. *Kristillinen usko ja moderni kulttuuri: Lesslie Newbigin käsitys kirkon missiosta modernissa länsimaisessa kulttuurissa* [The Christian Faith and Modern Culture: Lesslie Newbigin's View of the Church's Mission in Modern Western Culture] Suomalaisen Teologisen Kirjallisuusseuran Julkaisuja 218. Helsinki: Suomalainen Teologinen Kirjallisuusseura, 1999.

Khoury, A. Th. *Manuel II Paléologue. Entretiens avec un Mussulman. 7 e Controverse.* Paris: Cerf, 1966.

Kim, Kirsteen. 'Post-Modern Mission: A Paradigm Shift in David Bosch's Theology of Mission?" *IRM* 89 No. 353 (1999), 172-179.

Kippenberg, Hans and Tilman Seidensticker (ed.) *The 9/11 Handbook: Annotated Translation and Interpretation of the Attackers' Spiritual Manual.* London/Oakville: Equinox, 2006.

Kirchenamt der EKD (ed.) *Reden von Gott in der Welt. Der missionarische Auftrag Der Kirche an der Schwelle zum 3. Jahrtausend.* Frankfurt/M., 2001.

_____. *Kirche der Freiheit. Perspektiven für die evangelische Kirche im 21. Jahrhundert. Ein Impulspapier des Rates der EKD.* Hannover, 2006.

Kirk, J. Andrew. ' "A Secular Age" in a Mission Perspective: A Review Article.' *Transformation,* Vol. 28, No. 3, July 2011, 172-181.

_____. 'Postmodernity." J. Corrie (ed.) *Dictionary of Mission Theology: Evangelical Foundations.* Nottingham: IVP (2007), 298-303.

_____. 'Religious pluralism as an epiphenomenon of Postmodern Perspecitivism." Mortensen, Viggo (ed.) *Theology and the Religions: A Dialogue.* Grand Rapids: Eerdmans (2003), 430-442.

_____. *The Future of Reason, Science and Faith: Following Modernity and Postmodernity.* Aldershot: Ashgate Publishing, 2007.

_____. *What is Mission? Theological Explorations.* London: Darton, Longman and Todd, 1999.

Kiselev, Grigory S. 'Post-modernity and Christianity." *Questions of Philosophy 12* (2001), 3-15. (In Russian)

Knight, Douglas. 'Jenson on Time." Gunton, Colin E. ed. *Trinity, Time, and Church: A Response to the Theology of Robert W. Jenson.* Grand Rapids, MI: Eerdmans, (2000), 71-79.

Knitter, Paul F. *Jesus and the Other Names: Christian Mission and Global Responsibility.* Maryknoll, NY: Orbis Books, 1996.

Kolig, Erich, 'From a "madonna in a condom" to "claiming the airwaves": The Maori cultural renaissance and biculturalism in New Zealand,' in Meijl, Toon van, and Jelle Miedema (Eds) *Shifting Images of Identity in the Pacific,* Leiden: KITLV Press, 2004:135-157

_____. 'Legitimising Belief: Identity Politics, Utility, Strategies of Concealment, and

Rationalisation in Australian Aboriginal Religion,' *Australian Journal of Anthropology,* Vol. 14 (2), 2003,209-228.

Kobylinski, A. *"Modernità e postmodernità". L'interpretazione cristiana dell'esistenza al tramonto dei tempi moderni nel pensiero di Romano Guardini.* Roma: Pontificia Università Gregoriana, 1998.

Kohut, Heinz. *The Analysis of the Self: A Systematic Approach to the Psychoanalytic Treatment of Narcissistic Personality Disorders.* New York: International Universities Press, 1971.

Köstenberger, Andreas J. *The Missions of Jesus and the Disciples According to the Fourth Gospel – With Implications for the Fourth Gospel's Purpose and the Mission of the Contemporary Church.* Grand Rapids, MI: Eerdmans, 1998.

Kraus, C. Norman. *Christian Mission in the Postmodern World: An Intrusive Gospel?* Downers Grove: IVP Press, 1998.

Kretzschmar, G. ‚Wahrnehmung statt Mission. Alternative Sichtweisen zum EKD-Papier, Das Evangelium unter die Leute bringen." *Praktische Theologie* 91 (2002), 328-343.

Kuhn, Thomas. *The Structure of Scientific Revolutions.* Chicago: University of Chicago Press, 1970.

Land, Steven J. *Pentecostal Spirituality: A Passion for the Kingdom.* Sheffield: Sheffield Academic Press, 1997.

Lasch, Christopher. *The Culture of Narcissism.* New York: Norton, 1979.

_____. *The Minimal Self: Psychic Survival in Troubled Times.* New York: Norton, 1984.

_____. *The True and Only Heaven: Progress and Its Critics.* New York: Norton, 1991.

'Lausanne Occasional Paper 45: Religious and non-religious Spirituality in a Postmodern [Western] World." Clayton, David (ed.) *A New Vision, A new Heart, A Renewed Call: Lausanne Occasional Papers from the 2004 Forum of World Evangelization in Pattaya, Thailand.* Pasadena: William CareyLibrary, 2005, Vol. 2, 171-242.

Legrand, Lucien. *Unity and Plurality: Mission in the Bible.* Trans. Robert R. Barr. Maryknoll, NY: Orbis Books, 1990.

Leithart,Peter J. 'Jane Austen, Public Theologian." *First Things*, 139 (January 2004), 28-38.

Leung, Ka-lun. *The Rural Churches in China Since 1978.* Hong Kong: Alliance Bible Seminary, 1999.

Levushkan, Pavel. 'The Church proved to be Unprepared for the Coming of the Google World." *Mirt 1* (2009), 12-13. (In Russian)

Li, Jieren. *In Search of Via Media between Christ and Marx: A Study of Bishop Ding Guangxun's Contextual Theology.* Lund: Lund University, 2008.

Lienemann-Perrin, Christine, Hendrik Vroom, Michael Weinrich (ed.) *Contextuality in Reformed Europe: The Mission of the Church in the Transformation of European Culture.* Amsterdam, 2004.

Long, J. 'Generating Hope: A Strategy for Reaching the Postmodern Generation." Carson, D.A. (ed.) *Telling the Truth: Evangelizing Postmoderns.* Grand Rapids, Mich.: Baker (2000), 322-335.

Lossky, Vladimir. *Essays on the Mystical Theology of the Eastern Church.* Moscow: Center's Press, 1991. (In Russian)

Löwith, K. *Significato e fine della storia. I presupposti teologici della filosofia della storia.* Milano: Comunità, 1953/1963.

Loy, David (ed.) *Healing Deconstruction: Postmodern Thought in Buddhism and Christianity*. Atlanta: Scholars Press, 1996.

_____. 'The religion of the market." *Journal of the American Academy of Religion* 65/2, 275-290.

Louth, Andrew. *Discerning the Mystery: An Essay on the Nature of Theology*. Oxford: Clarendon Press, 1983.

Lübbe, H. *La secolarizzazione. Storia e analisi di un concetto*. Bologna: Il Mulino, 1970.

Luhmann, Niklas. *Inklusion und Exklusion*. Soziologische Aufklärung. Bd.6: Opladen (1995), 237-264.

Luibl, Hans-Jürgen. ‚A-3024: Auf der Suche nach Europas Seele." *Hermeneutische Blätter* 1-2/2005. www.leuenberg.net , 17.8.2009.

Luo, Guangzong, ed. *Qianshi buwang huoshi zhishi*. Shanghai: TSPM/CCC, 2004.

Lutheran World Federation. *Episcopal Ministry within the Apostolicity of theChurch. The Lund Statement by the Lutheran World Federation – A Communion of Churches.*Lund, 2007.

Luz, Ulrich. 'Canonical Exegesis and Hermeneutics of "effective history"." *Studies in Matthew*. Grand Rapids: Eerdmans (2005) 333-348.

Lyotard, Jean-François. *La Condition Postmoderne: Rapport sur le Savoir*. Les Editions de Minuit, 1979.

MacIntyre, Alasdair. *After Virtue: A Study in Moral Theory*. London: Duckworth, 1981.

Maddock, Kenneth. 'Revival, renaissance and the meaning of modern constructions in Australia,' Erich Kolig and Hermann Muckler (eds.) *Politics of Indigeneity in the South Pacific: Recent Problems of Identity in the Pacific* [Novara Bd 1],Munster: LIT, 2002:25-46.

Marcel, Gabriel. 'Some Thoughts on Faith." Marcel, *Being and Having*. London: Dacre Press (1949), 203-216.

Martel, Yann. *Life of Pi: A Novel*. New Delhi: Penguin Books, 2002.

Matthews, Melvyn. *Delighting in God*. London: Collins, 1987.

Matthey, Jacques. 'God's Mission Today: Summary and Conclusions." *IRM* (October 2003), 579-587.

Merkel, Angela. Speech to the European Parliament in Strasbourg on Wednesday, 17 January 2007.

http://www.eu2007.de/en/News/Speeches_Interviews/January/Rede_Bundeskanzlerin2.html

Messer, Donald E. *A Conspiracy of Goodness: Contemporary Images of Christian Mission*. Nashville: Abingdon Press, 1992.

Meštrović, Stjepan. *Postemotional Society*. London: Sage, 1997.

Miyamoto, Ken Christoph. *God's Mission in Asia: A Comparative and Contextual Study of This-Worldly Holiness and the Theology of Missio Dei in M. M. Thomas and C. S. Song*. Ph. D. diss.Princeton Theological Seminary, 1999.

_____. 'This-Worldly Holiness and the *Missio Dei* Concept in Asian Ecumenical Thinking." Lalsangkima Pachuau. *Ecumenical Missiology: Contemporary Trends, Issues and Themes.* Bangalore: United Theological College (2002), 99-128.

Moltmann, Jürgen. *God for a secular society: The public relevance of theology.* Minneapolis: Fortress Press, 1999.

_____. *The Spirit of Life: A Universal Affirmation.* Minneapolis: Fortress Press, 1994.

_____. *Theology of Hope.* London: SCM, 1967.

Moore, Peter. *Disarming the Secular Gods.* New York: IVP, 1989.

Morgan, Diane. 'Postmodernity and Architecture." Stuart Sim (ed.) *The Icon Dictionary of Post modern Thought.* Cambridge: Icon Books (1998), 79ff.

Movements and Christian Communities 'Together for Europe', http://www.miteinander-wie-sonst.de/_en/home.html

Mulago, Gwa Cikala M. *La Religion Traditionelle des Bantu et leur vision du monde.* Kinshasa: Faculte de Theologie Catholique, 1980.

'Multifaceted Christianity and the Postmodern Religious Condition: Reflections on its Challenges to Churches in the Northern Hemisphere.'

NDR-Nordreportage. *Herr der 13 Türme - Der Landpfarrer vom Randowtal.* 25th Februar 2008, 18.15h North German Broadcast Station (NDR).

Netland, H. *Encountering Religious Pluralism.* Downers Grove, Ill.: IVP, 2001.

Neubert, Ehrhart. Konfessionslose in Ostdeutschland. Folgen verinnerlichter Unterdrückung". *PTh* 87 (1998), 368-379.

Newbigin, Lesslie. *A Word in Season: Perspectives on Christian World Mission*, Eleanor Jackson (ed.) Grand Rapids, Mich.: Eerdmans/Edinburgh: Saint Andrews Press, 1994.

_____. 'Can the West be Converted?" *International Bulletin of Missionary Research* 11, no. 1 (1987), 2-7.

_____. *Foolishness to the Greeks: The Gospel and Western Culture* (Grand Rapids, Mich.: Eerdmans, 1986.

_____. ‚Modernity in Context." *Postmodern and Christians.* Reid, John, Lesslie Newbigin, and David Pullinger (eds.) Carberry: Handsell Press, 1996, 8ff.

_____. *Proper Confidence: Faith, Doubt & Certainty in Christian Discipleship* Grand Rapids, Mich.: Eerdmans, 1995.

_____. 'Religious Pluralism: A Missiological Approach." *Studia Missionalia* 42 (1993), 231ff.

_____. Religious Pluralism and the Uniqueness of Jesus Christ." *International Bulletin of Missionary Research* 13, no. 2 (1989), 50ff.

_____. ‚The Enduring Validity of Cross-Cultural Mission," *International Bulletin of Missionary Research* 12 (1988), 50ff.

_____. *The Gospel in a Pluralist Society.* Grand Rapids, Mich.: Eerdmans, 1989/Geneva: WCC Publications, 1989.

_____. *The Open Secret: An Introduction to the Theology of Mission.* Rev. ed. Grand Rapids, Mich.: Eerdmans, 1995, orig. 1978.

_____. *The Other Side of 1986: Questions to the Churches.* Geneva: WCC Publications, 1984, 1-6.

_____. 'The Secular Myth." *Faith and Power: Christianity and Islam in 'Secular' Britain.* Newbigin, Lesslie, Lamin Sanneh, and Jenny Taylor (eds.) London: SPCK, 1998, 13ff.

_____. *Truth and Authority in Modernity,* Christian Mission and Modern Culture Series Valley Forge, Penn.: Trinity Press International, 1996.

_____. *Truth to Tell: The Gospel as Public Truth.* Grand Rapids, Mich.: Eerdmans, 1991.

Nijk, A.J. *Secolarizzazione*. Brescia: Queriniana, 1973.

Nirmal, Arvind P. 'Theological Research: Its Implications for the Nature and Scope of the Theological Task of the Church in India." Gnana Robinson, ed. *For the Sake of the Gospel: Essays in Honour of Samuel Amirtham.* Madurai: T. T. S. Publications, 1980, 73-82.

Nkemnkia, M. Nkafu.. *Il pensare africano come "vitalogia"*. Roma: Città Nuova, 1995.

O'Donovan, Oliver. *The Ways of Judgement.* Grand Rapids, Mich.: Eerdmans, 2005.

Panikkar, K. N. ed., *The Concerned Indian's Guide to Communalism.* New Delhi: Viking/Penguin Books India, 1999.

Pascal, Blaise. *Pensees, No. 414.* Harmondsworth: Penguin, 1966.

_____. *Pensees,* VIII: Diversion (nos. 132-139), 37- 43.

Pattison, Stephen. 'The Shadow Side of Jesus." *Studies in Christian Ethics* 8 (2/1995), 54-67.

Payne, Michael W. 'Mission and Global Ethnic Violence.' *Transformation*, Vol. 19(3), July 2002:206-216.

Péguy,Charles. 'L'Espérance." Peguy, *Basic Verities.* Pantheon Books, (eng. 1943), 232-249.

*Perspektiven für die Kirche der Zukunft.*Beiträge zur Evangelisation und Gemeindeentwicklung 1, Neukirchen: Neukirchener Verlagsgesellschaft (2005), 17-29.

Philipps, T.R., D.L. Okholm. *Christian Apologetics in the Postmodern World.* Downers Grove: InterVarsity, 1995.

Pittkowski, Wolfgang. ‚Konfessionslose in Deutschland". W. Huber e.a. (eds.) *Kirche in der Vielfalt der Lebensbezüge. Die vierte EKD-Erhebung über Kirchenmitgliedschaft.* Gütersloh (2006), 89-110.

Polanyi, Michael. *Personal Knowledge: Towards a Post-Critical Philosophy.* Chicago: University of Chicago Press, 1958.

_____. 'Why did we destroy Europe?" P. Weiss (ed.) *Knowledge in Search of Understanding: The Frensham Papers.* New York: Future Publications, 1975, 1-8.

Pommersche Evangelische Kirche. *Leben in Gottes Gegenwart. Perspektiven für die Pommersche Evangelische Kirche. Ergebnisse des Leitbildprozesses von 2002 bis 2005.* Greifswald, 2005.

Postman, Niel. *Amusing Ourselves to Death: Public Discourse in the Age of Show Business.* London: Methuen, 1987.

Raschke, Carl. *GloboChrist: The Great Commission Takes a Postmodern Turn.* Grand Rapids, Mich.: Baker Academic, 2008.

Ratzinger, Joseph/ Benedikt XVI. *Jesus von Nazareth. Erster Teil: Von der Taufe im Jordan bis zur Verklärung*, Freiburg: Herder, 2007.

_____. *Salz der Erde: Christentum und katholische Kirche im neuen Jahrtausend. Ein Gespräch mit Peter Seewald.* Stuttgart: DVA, 1996. http://www.ewtn.com/vnews/getstory.asp?number=19347, 17.8.2009.

Reimer, J. "They come with a message: The gospel of missionaries from the Two- Thirds World in old Europe." *Missionalia* 35 (2/2007), 3-17.

Richebächer, Wilhelm. '*Missio Dei*: The Basis of Mission Theology or a Wrong Path?" *IRM* (October 2003), 588-605.

Richie, Tony. "'The Unity of the Spirit": are Pentecostals inherently Ecumenists and Inclusivists?' *JEPTA 26.1* (2006), 21-35.

Riggs, John W. *Postmodern Christianity: Doing Theology in the Contemporary World.* Harrisburg/London/New York: Trinity Press, 2003.

Rinn, Maren. *Die religiöse und kirchliche Ansprechbarkeit von Konfessionslosen in Ostdeutschland. Eine Analyse auf Grundlage empirischer Untersuchungen in derEvangelisch-Lutherischen Landeskirche Mecklenburgs und Evangelischen Landeskirche Anhalts.* Hannover (2006), 50-52. Found at http://www.ekd.de/si-download/SI-Konfessionsloe_Ostdeutschland-korr2.pdf on Feb 20th, 2007.

Roberts, Robert C. *Spiritual Emotion: A Psychology of Christian Virtues.* Grand Rapids, Mich.: Eerdmans, 2007.

Rorty, R. *La filosofia dopo la filosofia.* Roma/Bari:Laterza, 2008.

_____. *La filosofia e lo specchio della natura.* Milano: Bompiani, 1974/1986.

_____. *Verità e progresso. Scritti filosofici.* Milano: Feltrinelli, 2003.

Ruh, U. *Säkularisierung als Interpretationskategorie. Zur Bedeutung des christlichen Erbes in der modernen Geistesgeschichte.* Freiburg/Basel/Wien: Herder, 1974.

Rynkiewich, Michael A. 'The World in My Parish: Rethinking the Standard Missiological Model.' *Missiology* Vol. 30(3), 2002:301-321.

Saliers, Don E. *The Soul in Paraphrase: Prayer and the Religious Affections.* Akron: OSL Publications, 2003.

Samartha, S. J. *One Christ – Many Religions: Toward a Revised Christology* 3rd Indian ed. Maryknoll, NY, Orbis/ Bangalore: South Asia Theological Research Institute, 2000.

Sampson, P. 'The Rise of Postmodernity." Sampson, V. Samuel, C. Sugden (eds.) *Faith and Modernity*, Oxford: Regnum (1994), 29–57.

Sampson, V. Samuel, C. Sugden (eds.) *Faith and Modernity.* Oxford: Regnum, 1994.

Sanneh, Lamin. *Translating the Message: The Missionary Impact on Culture.* Maryknoll, NY: Orbis Books, 1989.

Sawatsky, Walter. 'Orthodox-Evangelical Protestant Dialogue on Mission Challenges and Shifting Options." *Acta Missiologiae 1* (2008), 11-31.

Sayers, Dorothy. *Creed or Chaos: and other Essays in Popular Theology.* London: Methuen, 1947.

Schäfer, Klaus. 'Mission in Secular and Postmodern Societies: The Example of Germany." *International Review of Mission* XCII No. 364 (2003), 40-44.

Schenk, Kenneth. *A Brief Guide to Philo.* Moscow: St. Andrew's Biblical Theological Institute, 2007. (In Russian)

Schönborn, Christoph Cardinal. ‚Der Papst auf der Agora. Über einen Anspruch, den allein Gott stellen kann." *"Jesus von Nazareth" kontrovers: Rückfragen an Joseph Ratzinger.* Theologie aktuell 1: Berlin-Hamburg-Münster: LIT (2007), 9-17.

Schreiter, Robert J. *The New Catholicity: Theology between the Global and the Local.* Maryknoll, NY: Orbis, 1997.

Schweitzer, Friedrich L. *The Postmodern Life Cycle: Challenges for Church and Theology.* St. Louis: Chalice Press, 2004.

Sebastian, J. Jayakiran. '... *baptisma unum in sancta ecclesia...': A Theological Appraisal of the Baptismal Controversy in the Work and Writings of Cyprian of Carthage.* Delhi: ISPCK, 1997.

_____. 'Believing and Belonging: Secularism and Religion in India." *International Review of Mission*, Vol. XCII, No. 365, (April 2003), 204-211.

_____. 'Issues of Conversion and Baptism in relation to Mission." P. Victor Premasagar ed. *New Horizons in Christian Mission: A Theological Exploration.* Gurukul Summer Institute 1999. Chennai: Gurukul (2000), 375- 393.

_____. 'Conversion and its Discontents." *Bangalore Theological Forum*, Vol. XXXII, No. 1 (June 2000), 165-172.

_____. 'A Strange Mission among Strangers: The Joy of Conversion." Schulze, Andrea, Rudolf v. Sinner, Wolfram Stierle (Hg.) *Vom Geheimnis des Unterschieds: Die Wahrnehmung des Fremden in Ökumene-, Missions- und Religionswissenschaft.* Münster: LIT Verlag (2002), 200-210.

Sennett, Richard. *The Fall of Public Man.* New York: Knopf, 1977.

Sergeyeva, Alla. *The Russians: Behavior Stereotypes, Tradition, Mentality.* Moscow: *Science*, 2005. (in Russian).

Sharma, S. L. and T. K. Oommen, eds. *Nation and National Identity in South Asia.* Hyderabad: Orient Longman, 2000.

Siegwalt, G. *Dogmatique pour la catholicité évangélique. Système mystagogique de la foi chrétienne.* III: *L'affirmation de la foi.* I: *Cosmologie théologique: sciences et philosophie de la nature.* Genève/Paris: Labor et Fides – Cerf, 1996.

Sire, James W. 'Why should anyone believe anything at all." Carson, D. A. (ed.) *Telling the Truth: Evangelizing Postmoderns.* Grand Rapids, Mich.: Baker, 93-101.

Smith, James K.A. *Who's Afraid of Postmodernism? Taking Derrida, Lotard, and Foucault to Church.* Grand Rapids: Baker Academic, 2006.

Squire, Aelred. *Asking the Fathers.* London: SPCK, 1973.

Stackhouse, Max L. and Lalsangkima Pachuau, eds. *News of Boundless Riches: Interrogating, Comparing, and Reconstructing Mission in a Global Era,* Vol. I. Delhi: ISPCK/UTC/CTI (2007), 26–44.

Stamoolis, James. *Eastern Orthodox Mission Theology Today.* Maryknoll, NY: Orbis Books, 1986.

Stanley, B. 'Defining the Boundaries of Christendom: The Two Worlds of the World Missionary Conference, 1910.' *IBMR* 30 (4/2006), 171-176.

_____. *The World Missionary Conference*, Edinburgh 1910, [Studies in the History of Christian Missions] Grand Rapids, MI: Eerdmans, 2009.

Starke, L. (ed.) *State of the world 2004. Worldwatch Institute Report.* 2004.

Stott, John R. *Making Christ Known Historic Documents of the Lausanne Movement.* Carlisle: Paternoster, 1996, 99-100.

Stuhlmacher, Peter. *Biblische Theologie und Evangelium. Gesammelte Aufsätze.* WUNT 146: Tübingen: Mohr-Siebeck, 2002.

Sugirtharajah, R. S. *The Bible and the Third World: Precolonial, Colonial and Postcolonial Encounters.* Cambridge: Cambridge University Press, 2001.

_____. *Postcolonial Criticism and Biblical Interpretation.* Oxford: Oxford University Press, 2002.

_____. *Postcolonial Reconfigurations: An Alternative Way of Reading the Bible and Doing Theology.* St. Louis, MO: Chalice Press, 2003.

_____. 'Son(s) Behaving Badly: The Prodigal in Foreign Hands." A. K. M. Adam ed. *Postmodern Interpretations of the Bible: A Reader.* St. Louis: Chalice Press (2001), 204-218.

Sundararajan, K. R. 'The Spiritual Journey: A Comparative Study of Bonaventure and Ramanuja." Chase, Steven L. ed. *Doors of Understanding: Conversations in Global Spirituality in Honor of Ewert Cousins.* Quincy, IL: Franciscan Press, 1997, 269ff.

Sundermeier, Theo. *Was ist Religion? Religionswissenschaft im theologischen Kontext. Ein Studienbuch.* Gütersloh, 1999.

Taylor, Charles. *A Secular Age.* Cambridge, MA: Belknap Press of Harvard University Press, 2007.

Taylor, John V. *The Primal Vision: Christian Presence and African Religion.* London: SCM Press, 1963.

Tempels, P. *Filosofia bantu.* Milano: Medusa,1946/2005.

Tertullianus, Quintus. *On the Soul.* St. Petersburg: Oleg Abushko's Publishing House, 2004.

Thangaraj, Thomas. 'Evangelism sans Proselytism: A Possibility?" Witte, John Jr. and Richard C. Martin eds. *Sharing the Book: Religious Perspectives on the Rights and Wrongs of Proselytism.* Maryknoll, NY: Orbis Books 1999, 335-352.

_____. *The Common Task: A Theology of Christian Mission.* Nashville: Abingdon Press, 1999.

'The Berlin Conference 2004'. www.asoulforeurope.eu/what/berlin-conference/2004, 18.8.2009.

The Climate Change Committee of the South African Council of Churches. *Climate Change – A challenge to the churches in South Africa.* SACC, Marshalltown, 2009.

Theobald, Ch. *Il cristianesimo come stile. Un modo di fare teologia nella postmodernità.* II. Bologna: Dehoniane, 2009.

The Postmodern Condition: A Report on Knowledge. Minneapolis: University of Minnesota Press, 1984.

Thomas, N. *Classic Texts in Mission and World Christianity.* Maryknoll, NY: Orbis Books, 1996.

Tiefensee, Eberhard. ‚Chancen und Grenzen von "Mission" – im Hinblick auf die konfessionelle Situation in den neuen Bundesländern". M. Bartels und M. Reppenhagen (eds.). *Gemeindepflanzung – ein Modell für die Kirche der Zukunft?* BEG 4: Neukirchen-Vluyn (2006), 68-85.

Turner, Harold W. 'New Religious Movements in Primal Societies.' John R. Hinnells (ed.).*A New Handbook of Living Religions.* London: Penguin, 1997, 581-593.

_____. 'The Three Levels of Mission in New Zealand.' Bruce Patrick (ed.) *The Vision New Zealand Congress.* Auckland: Vision New Zealand 1993, 61-68.

______. 'The Relationship Between Development and New Religious Movements in the Tribal Societies of the Third World.' Frederick Ferre and Rita H. Mataragnon, *God and Global Justice: Religion and Poverty in an Unequal World.* New York: Paragon House, 1985, 84-110.

______. 'The Primal Religions of the World & Their Study.' Victor C.Hayes (ed)., *Australian Essays in World Religions.* Bedford Park, South Australia: AASR (1977), 27-37.

Tylor, Edward Burnett. *Primitive Culture: Researches into the Development of Mythology, Philosophy, Religion, Language, Art and Custom.* 2 Vols., London: John Murray, 1871.

Uhalley, Stephen Jr. and Xiaoxin Wu, eds. *China and Christianity: Burdened Past, Hopeful Future*. Armonk, New York : M.E. Sharpe, 2001.

Ustorf, Werner. *Christianized Africa – De-Christianized Europe? Missionary Inquiries into the Polycentric Epoch of Christian History: Perspektiven der Weltmimssion,* Wissenschaftliche Beiträge Band 14. Herausgegeben von der Missionsakademie an der Universität Hamburg .Ammersbek bei Hamburg: Lottbeck Jensen, 1992.

______. 'The Emerging Christ of Post-Christian Europe." Foust, T. et al (eds.) *A Scandalous Prophet: The Way of Mission after Newbigin.* Grand Rapids, Mich.: Eerdmans, 128-144.

van Engen, Charles. 'Specialization and Integration in Mission Education." Woddberry, J.D. et al (eds.) *Missiological Education for the 21st Century: The Book, the Circle and the Sandals.* Maryknoll: Orbis Books 1996, 208-228.

______. 'Theology of Mission." Moreau, A.S. et al (eds.) *Evangelical Dictionary of World Mission.* Grand Rapids, Mich.: Baker, 949-951.

van Ruler, Arnold A. *Calvinist Trinitarianism and Theocentric Politics: Essays Toward a Public Theology*, trans. John Bolt, Toronto Studies in Theology, Vol. 38, Lewiston: Edwin Mellen Press, 1989, 209ff.

Vatoropin, Alexander S., Konstantin M. Olkhovikov. 'The Perspectives of Secularism and Religion in the Post-modern Era." *Social Sciences and Modernity 3* (2003), 136-145. (In Russian)

Vattimo, G. *Addio alla verità.* Roma: Meltemi, 2009.

______. *Oltre l'interpretazione. Il significato dell'ermeneutica per la filosofia.* Roma/Bari: Laterza, 1994.

______. *Opere complete*. I/1-2: *Ermeneutica.* Roma: Meltemi, 2007-2008.

______. Vattimo, G. and P.A: Rovatti. *Il pensiero debole*. Milano: Feltrinelli, 1983.

Vicedom, Georg F. *The Mission of God: An Introduction to a Theology of Mission* trans. Gilbert A. Thiele and Dennis Hilgendorf. Saint Louis: Concordia Publishing House, 1965.

Volf, Miroslav. *Exclusion and Embrace. A Theological Exploration of Identity, Otherness and Reconciliation.* Nashville, 1996.

Wake, Joachim.. ‚Missionarische Herausforderungen im gesellschaftlichen Kontext Deutschlands – Perspektive Ostdeutschland". EMW e.a. (ed.) *Aufbruch zu einer missionarischen Ökumene.* Hamburg, 1999, 138.

Walldorf, Friedemann. *Die Neuevangelisierung Europas. Missionstheologien im europäischen Kontext.* Systematisch-theologische Monographien 8. Gießen/Basel: Brunnen TVG, 2002.

_____. "Mission in Partnerschaft: Zum Aufbruch der evangelikalen Missionsbewegung in Afrika, Asien und Lateinamerika." Kasdorf, Hans und Friedemann Walldorf (eds.) *Werdet meine Zeugen. Weltmission im Horizont von Theologie und Geschichte*, Neuhausen: Hänssler, 1996, 221-248.

_____. "Missionarische Bemühungen im Kontext gesellschaftlicher Veränderungen in Deutschland von 1945 bis 2000. Teil 1: Umkehr und Neubeginn (1945-1968)" Evangelikale Missiologie (1/2007), 2-15.

_____. "Missionarische Bemühungen im Kontext gesellschaftlicher Veränderungen in Deutschland von 1945 bis 2000. Teil 2: Von der 68er Revolution bis zum vereinten Deutschland." Evangelikale Missiologie (2/2007), 38-53.

Walls, Andrew F. 'Commission One and the Church's Transforming Century.' David A. Kerr and Kenneth R. Ross (eds.) *Edinburgh 2010: Mission Then and Now*. Oxford: Regnum, 2009.

_____. *The Cross-Cultural Process in Christian History: Studies in the Transmission and Appropriation of Faith.* Maryknoll, NY: Orbis Books, 2002.

_____. *The Missionary Movement in Christian History: Studies in the Transmission of the Faith.* Maryknoll, NY: Orbis, 1996

Wang, Ning. 'The Mapping of Chinese Postmodernity." *Boundary 2*, Vol. 24, No. 3 (1997), 19-40.

_____. 'Postmodernity, Post-coloniality and Globalization: A Chinese Perspective." *Social Semiotics,* Vol. 10, No. 2 (2000), 221-233.

Ware K.T. *The Meaning of 'Pathos' in Abba Isaias and Theodoret of Cyrus.* Studia Patristica. XX. Louvain, 1989.

'Was will eigentlich die Emerging Church?" ('What does the Emerging Church want?'), *Idea-Spektrum* 46, November 12 (2008), 15-18.

Webster, Steven. 'Postmodernist Theory and the Sublimation of Maori Culture.' *Oceania* Vol 63 (3), 1993, 222-239.

Weitbrecht, H.U. (ed.) *A Bibliography for Missionary Students.* London: Oliphant, Anderson & Ferrier, 1913.

Wenzel, Knut. 'Radical Subjectivity." *International Review of Mission* 95 July/October (2006), 259-264.

Werdet meine Zeugen: Weltmission im Horizont von Theologie und Geschichte. Neuhausen: Hänssler (1996), 221-248.

Wesley, Luke. *The Church in China: Persecuted, Pentecostal, and Powerful.* Baguio: AJPS Books, 2004.

Weston, Paul. 'Lesslie Newbigin: A Postmodern Missiologist?" *Mission Studies* 21, no. 2 (2004), 229.

Wilfred, Felix, Edmond Tang, and George Evers eds. *China and Christianity.* London: SCM Press, 2008.

_____. 'Yellers and Healers: A Study of Pentecostalism and Grassroots Christians in China." *Asian and Pentecostalism: Charismatic Face of Christianity in Asia*, 2005.

Williams, Rowan. *Mission-shaped church: church planting and fresh expressions of church in a changing context.* London: Church House Publishing, 2004.

_____. *Writing in the Dust: After September 11.* Grand Rapids, Mich.: Eerdmans, 2002.

Wisdom, John. *Paradox and Discovery.* Oxford: Basil Blackwell, 1965.

Wiseman, James. 'Pilgrimage beyond Competitiveness." *Newsletter of St. Anselm's Abbey.* (Winter 2003), 13.

Wittenberg, H. *Die Lage der ländlichen Arbeiter in Neuvorpommern und auf Rügen.* Leipzig, 1894.

World Missionary Conference, 1910. *Report of Commission IV: The Missionary Message in relation to Non-Christian Religions.* Edinburgh: Oliphant, Anderson & Ferrier, 1910.

Wrogemann, H. ‚Theologie und Wissenschaft der Mission." Dahling-Sander, C. et al. (eds.) *Leitfaden Ökumenische Missionstheologie.* Gütersloh: Kaiser (2003), 17- 31.

Yong, Amos. 'From Azusa Street to the Bo Tree and Back: Strange Babblings and Interreligious Interpretations in the Pentecostal Encounter with Buddhism." *The Spirit in the World: Emerging Pentecostal Theologies in Global Contexts.* Kärkkäinen, Veli-Matti (ed.) Grand Rapids, Mich.: Eerdmans, 2009, 203-226.

_____. *Hospitality & The Other: Pentecost, Christian Practices, and the Neighbor.* Maryknoll: Orbis Books, 2008.

Yu, Carver T. 'Truth and Authentic Humanity." Plenary address at The Gospel and Our Culture Consultation, Swanwick, 1992. Displayed online at www.gospel-culture.org.uk/yu.htm

Zahrnt, Heinz. *Die Sache mit Gott.* München, 1980.

Zaprometova, Olga M. 'Experience of the Holy Spirit in the Context of Patristic Tradition. The Pentecostal's Reading." *Pages 13/1* (2008/2009), 63-90. (In Russian)

Zeh, Juli. *Schilf.* Frankfurt/M. 2007.

Žižek, Slavoj. *The Puppet and the_Dwarf: The Perverse Core of Christianity*. Cambridge, MA: MIT Press, 2003.

Zulehner, Paul M. „Aufbrechen oder untergehen. Wie können unsere Gemeinden zukunftsfähig werden?" Herbst, M., Ohlemacher, J., Zimmermann, J. (ed.) *Missionarische Missionarische Perspektiven für die Kirche der Zukunft*. Beiträge zur Evangelisation und Gemeindeentwicklung 1, Neukirchen: Neukirchener Verlagsgesellschaft, 2005, 17-29.

_____. e.a. (eds.). *Gott nach dem Kommunismus*. Ostfildern, 2003.

Biographies

Contributors

Gianni Colzani is a Catholic priest of the Diocese of Milan and professor in the Faculty of Mission Sciences at the Pontifical Urbaniana University, Rome.

Ernst M. Conradie teaches Systematic Theology and Ethics in the Department of Religion and Theology at the University of the Western Cape in South Africa, He is the author of several books in the field of ecotheology and is the convenor of a major research project on "Christian Faith and the Earth". He may be contacted at econradie@uwc.ac.za

Marco Fibbi has 16 years of experience and practice as a minister in several realities of the Catholic Church in Italy. In addition to his position as responsible for Social Communication in the Diocese of Rome (1992-), he is currently assistant for junior girl and boy scout groups (2005-2007) and was responsible for a group of teenagers (2002-2005), and in the past acted as assistant for youngsters participating in Catholic Action (i.e., the major Italian lay Christian association, 1992-2002).

Jan-Olav Henriksen is professor of systematic theology and philosophy of religion at (MF) Norwegian School of Theology, Oslo, and professor in religious studies, with emphasis on contemporary religion, in the University of Agder, Kristiansand, Norway. Henriksen is trained as both a philosopher and as a theologian and holds doctorates in both subjects. He has published widely in the field of systematic theology, including studies on theological anthropology, empirical studies of religion, moral philosophy and philosophical critique of religion. His most recent books in English are *Desire, Gift and Recognition: Christology and Postmodern Philosophy* (Eerdmans, Grand Rapids 2009), and *Finitude and Theological Anthropology* (Peeters, Leuven, 2010)

Michael Herbst published a doctoral thesis on the topic: "Missionarischer Gemeindeaufbau in der Volkskirche" ("Missional Church Development in the German Institutionalized Church") which is still widely referred to. He served as pastor in a parish and as a healthcare chaplain from 1985-1996 before he was appointed to the chair of Practical Theology at the Ernst Moritz Arndt University of Greifswald. He is founding director of the German "Research Institute for Evangelism and Church Development" with currently 9 researchers on staff, co-editor of the learned journal

"Theologische Beiträge" ("Theological Inquiries"), and the series "Beiträge zur Evangelisation und Gemeindeentwicklung" ("Contributions to Evangelization and Church Development"). He was elected dean of the Faculty of Theology in Greifswald from 2003-2006 and from 2008-2009 before he was elected as vice-principal of Greifswald University. He preaches regularly and is leader of a church plant in Greifswald. His wife and his four grown children share his enthusiasm for soccer, movies and long hikes into the Scandinavian wilderness.

John M. Hitchen, BA, BD, PhD, a New Zealander, is currently Senior Lecturer in Mission Studies, Laidlaw College and Laidlaw-Carey Graduate School, Auckland, New Zealand. John served with his wife, Ann, from 1965-1979 as Dean and Principal of the Christian Leaders' Training College, in Papua New Guinea. His 1984 University of Aberdeen, Scotland, PhD focused on 19th Century mission in the Pacific. On the faculty of Laidlaw College (formerly the Bible College of New Zealand) since 1987, he served as National Principal from 1990-1998.

Harold D. Hunter is currently Director of the IPHC Archives & Research Center. Denominational executive positions, seminary teaching and ecumenical dialogues have taken him to more than 60 countries. Hunter co-edited with Peter Hocken *All Together In One Place* (Sheffield, 1993), co-edited with Cecil M. Robeck Jr., *The Suffering Body* (Paternoster, 2006) in addition to *The Azusa Street Revival and Its Legacy* (Pathway, 2006), and released *Spirit Baptism: A Pentecostal Alternative* (Wipf & Stock, 2009). His articles have appeared in international journals, dictionaries and encyclopedia. Dr. Hunter engages the World Council of Churches, the World Alliance of Reformed Churches (WARC), the NCCCUSA Faith and Order Commission, and the International Charismatic Consultation (ICC).

Veli-Matti Kärkkäinen (Dr.Theol.Habil., University of Helsinki) is Professor of Systematic Theology at Fuller Theological Seminary, Pasadena, CA and Docent of Ecumenics at the University of Helsinki. Native of Finland, he has also lived and taught theology in Thailand. Author of 200 articles and more than ten books, including *Trinity and Religious Pluralism* (Ashgate) and *The Trinity. Global Perspectives* (WJKP), he is also the co-editor of *The Global Dictionary of Theology* (IVP). Dr. Kärkkäinen has participated widely in the ecumenical, theological, and interreligious work of the World Council of Churches, Faith and Order, as well as two international bi-lateral dialogues.

David Kettle was an Anglican priest and Co-ordinator of the Gospel and Our Culture Network in Great Britain (www.gospel-culture.org.uk). He has ministered in England and New Zealand. He is author of *Western Culture in Gospel Context* (Wipf & Stock, forthcoming), the Grove Booklet *Beyond*

Tragic Spirituality: Victimhood and Christian Hope (2005), and a number of published papers in journals and books. He was married to Anne, a General Medical Practitioner, and they have four adult children. Sadly David Kettle passed away on 11th March 2011.

Sebastian Cho Kim is Professor of Theology and Public Life in the Faculty of Education and Theology of York St John University, UK. He is a Fellow of the Royal Asiatic Society and the author of *In Search of Identity: Debates on Religious Conversion in India* (OUP, 2003) and co-author of *Christianity as a World Religion* (Continuum, 2008, with Kirsteen Kim). He was formerly Director of the Christianity in Asia Project and taught World Christianity at the Faculty of Divinity of the University of Cambridge. He is founding and current Editor of the *International Journal of Public Theology.*

J. Andrew Kirk, *see Core Group.*

Jieren Li, Dr. Theol. in Missiology with Ecumenism, Lund University, is Senior Pastor of International Mandarin Service at Beijing international church. He is now an adjunct Professor of Malaysia Baptist Theological Seminary, as well as a theological consultant of the WCC-ETE for Chinese churches. He has authored dozens of articles and the monograph *In Search of the Via Media between Christ and Marx: A Study of Bishop Ding Guangxun's Contextual Theology* (2008). He also studied and worked in Finland and Sweden.

J. Jayakiran Sebastian, *see Core Group.*

Friedemann Walldorf, D.Th., University of South Africa, is lecturer and Head of Department of Mission Studies (Missionswissenschaft) at the Freie Theologische Hochschule Gießen (FTH) in Germany (Gießen School of Theology). He and his wife were missionaries with the German Missionary Fellowship (Deutsche Missionsgemeinschaft) in Madrid, Spain. His research centers on the history and theology of mission in western pluralist and migrant contexts and the cultural interaction of mission, arts and music. His publications include *Die Neuevangelisierung Europas* (2002) and *Mission und Reflexion im Kontext* (2010).

Claudia Währisch-Oblau is an ordained minister of the Evangelical Church in the Rhineland/Germany, and holds a doctorate in theology from Heidelberg University. From 1985-1997, she worked for the Amity Foundation (a development organization closely connected to the China Christian Council) in Nanjing and Hongkong. From 1998-2006 she coordinated the Program for Cooperation between Migrant and Indigenous Churches of the German Region of the United Evangelical Mission (UEM), a communion of 35 churches on three continents. Since 2007, she has been serving as Executive Secretary for Evangelism of UEM. She is a founding member of GloPent, the European Research Network on Global Pentecostalism.

Olga Zaprometova graduated from the Moscow State University (1977), finished her Ph.D. in Enzymology (Bakh's Institute for Biochemistry, USSR Academy of Sciences, 1986). Completed a Bachelor of Arts (correspondent program of the Christian Life College; Chicago, IL) and M.Div. ("Church of God" Theological Seminary (Cleveland, TN, 2000). Director of the Mission Possible-Moscow (1991-1995), Director of the Correspondent Christian Educational Program (1995-1998). Academic Dean of the Eurasian Theological Seminary (ETS-Moscow, 1998-2008). She lectures at the ETS-Moscow and St. Andrew's Biblical Theological Institute (Moscow, Russia).

Core Group

Kajsa Ahlstrand, b 1959, Teol. Dr. Uppsala, Sweden, 1993. Ordained pastor, Church of Sweden,1980. Parish Pastor and Student Chaplain, 1980-1993. Lecturer in Inter-Religious Encounter and Inter-Confessional Encounter, Linköping University, Sweden, 1993-1994. Researcher, Church of Sweden, Uppsala 1994-2006. Professor, Missiology, Uppsala University 2006-.

J. Andrew Kirk, BD, London; BA, Cambridge; MPhil, London; PhD, Nijmegen. Has spent his life in theological education in South America and the United Kingdom. He retired in 2002 from his teaching position at the University of Birmingham, England. Among his fifteen books is *What Is Mission?: Theological Explorations* (1999) and *The Future of Reason, Science and Faith: Following Modernity and Postmodernity* (2007). His latest book is *Civilisations in Conflict? Islam, The West and Christian Faith* (2011).

Rolv Olsen, b. 1956. Cand.theol., School of Mission and Theology, Stavanger, Norway 1984. Teol.lic., Lund University, 2001, teol.dr., 2007. Missionary pastor, Norwegian Missionary Society (NMS), Taiwan, 1985-90. Student pastor, NMS, Oslo, 1990-92. Missionary pastor, Christian Mission to Buddhists (CMB) (now: Areopagos), superintendent, Tao Fong Shan Christian Centre, Hong Kong, 1992-98. Research Scholarship, CMB, 1998-2000. Director, Egede Institute, 2000-02, 2004-. Lecturer in KRL (Christianity, Religions and Lifestands) in various University Colleges, 2000-. Asia Secretary, Areopagos, 2009-10. Parish pastor, 2010-. Doctoral dissertation: *"Prevailing Winds": An Analysis of the Liturgical Inculturation Efforts of Karl Ludvig Reichelt.*

Tania Petrova, b. 1969. M. Div. 1996, Church of God Theological Seminary, USA. Drs, IBTS, Prague (University of Wales) Academic Dean, Sofia Pentecostal College 1997-2000. Vice-rector for academics, Bulgarian Evangelical Theological Institute 2000-2003. Rector, Bulgarian Evangelical Theological Institute, 2003-present. Convener for the National Research Group on Church Growth in Bulgaria, 2008-present. Standing Committee Member, Societas Oecumenica, 2008-present.

Teresa Francesca Rossi, Associate Director Centro Pro Unione, Rome. Professor of Ecumenical Theology at the Pontifical University of St. Thomas Aquinas, Rome (and Vice-Dean of the Faculty of Theology (2002-2007); at the Pontifical Atheneum St. Anselm, Rome and at the Istituto Filosofico Teologico, Viterbo. Member of the Joint Working Group between the Catholic Church and the World Council of Churches; Member of the Baptist-Catholic International Theological Conversations (II phase) and of the Catholic-Pentecostal International Theological Dialogue (VI phase). Member of the Commission on Ecumenism and Dialogue of the Diocesis of Rome (1992-2009). Responsible of various Ecumenical educational project and author of various contributions particularly in the field of Catholic Theology and Ecumenism, Ecumenical Formation, Pentecostalism. Translator and Editor of the official Italian version of the Material for the Week of Prayer for Christian Unity.

J. Jayakiran Sebastian, Rev. Dr., b. 1958. Dr. Theol. (magna cum laude) University of Hamburg, Germany, 1997. Presbyter of the Church of South India. Has been Professor, United Theological College, Bangalore, India, and served as Chairperson of the Department of Theology and Ethics and Dean of Doctoral Studies. Currently H. George Anderson Professor of Mission and Cultures and Director of the Multicultural Mission Resource Center at The Lutheran Theological Seminary at Philadelphia, PA, USA. Books: *"... baptisma unum in sancta ecclesia...": A Theological Appraisal of the Baptismal Controversy in the Work and Writings of Cyprian of Carthage* (1997), and *Enlivening the Past: An Asian Theologian's Engagement with the Early Teachers of Faith* (Gorgias Press, 2009).

REGNUM EDINBURGH 2010 SERIES
Series Listing

David A. Kerr, Kenneth R. Ross (eds.)
Edinburgh 2010
Mission Then and Now
2009 / 978-1-870345-73-6 / xiv + 343pp (paperback)
2009 / 978-1-870345-76-7 / xiv + 343pp (hardback)

No one can hope to fully understand the modern Christian missionary movement without engaging substantially with the World Missionary Conference, held at Edinburgh in 1910. As the centenary of the Conference approaches, the time is ripe to examine its meaning in light of the past century and the questions facing Christian witness today. This book is the first to systematically examine the eight Commissions which reported to Edinburgh 1910 and gave the conference much of its substance and enduring value. It will deepen and extend the reflection being stimulated by the upcoming centenary and will kindle the missionary imagination for 2010 and beyond.

Daryl M. Balia, Kirsteen Kim (eds.)
Edinburgh 2010
Witnessing to Christ Today
2010 / 978-1-870345-77-4 / xiv +301pp

This volume, the second in the Edinburgh 2010 series, includes reports of the nine main study groups working on different themes for the celebration of the centenary of the World Missionary Conference, Edinburgh 1910. Their collaborative work brings together perspectives that are as inclusive as possible of contemporary world Christianity and helps readers to grasp what it means in different contexts to be 'witnessing to Christ today'.

Claudia Währisch-Oblau, Fidon Mwombeki (eds.)
Mission Continues
Global Impulses for the 21st Century
2010 / 978-1-870345-82-8 / 271pp

In May 2009, 35 theologians from Asia, Africa and Europe met in Wuppertal, Germany, for a consultation on mission theology organized by the United Evangelical Mission: Communion of 35 Churches in Three Continents. The aim was to participate in the 100th anniversary of the Edinburgh conference through a study process and reflect on the challenges for mission in the 21st century. This book brings together these papers written by experienced practitioners from around the world.

Brian Woolnough and Wonsuk Ma (Eds)

Holistic Mission

God's plan for God's people 2010 / 978-1-870345-85-9

Holistic mission, or integral mission, implies God is concerned with the whole person, the whole community, body, mind and spirit. This book discusses the meaning of the holistic gospel, how it has developed, and implications for the the church. . It takes a global, eclectic approach, with 19 writers, all of whom have much experience in, and commitment to, holistic mission. It addresses critically and honestly one of the most exciting, and challenging, issues facing the church today. To be part of God's plan for God's people, the church must take holistic mission to the world.

Kirsteen Kim and Andrew Anderson (Eds)

Mission Today and Tomorrow

2011/978-1-870345-91-0

The centenary of the historic and influential World Missionary Conference held in Edinburgh 1910 presented a unique opportunity for the whole church worldwide to come together in celebration, reflection and recommitment to witnessing to Christ today. Edinburgh 2010 also engaged in serious study and reflection on the current state of world mission and the challenges facing all those who seek to witness Christ today. The results of this research was presented and debated within the context of Christian fellowship and worship at the conference in June 2010. This record of that conference is intended to give the background to that Call, to share the spirit of the conference, and to stimulate informed and focused participation in God's mission in Christ for the world's salvation.

Tormod Engelsviken, Erling Lundeby and Dagfinn Solheim (Eds)

The Church Going Glocal

Mission and Globalisation 2011/978-1-870345-93-4

This book provides thought-provoking and inspiring reading for all concerned with mission in the 21st century. I have been challenged by its contributors to re-think our Gospel ministries in our new local contexts marked by globalisation and migration. With its biblical foundation, its missiological reflection and interaction with contemporary society I warmly recommend this volume for study and pray that it will renew our passion for the Gospel and compassion for people.

REGNUM Studies in Global Christianity

(Previously GLOBAL THEOLOGICAL VOICES series)

Series Listing

David Emmanuuel Singh (ed.)
Jesus and the Cross
Reflections of Christians from Islamic Contexts
2008 / 978-1-870345-65-1 / x + 226pp

The Cross reminds us that the sins of the world are not borne through the exercise of power but through Jesus Christ's submission to the will of the Father. The papers in this volume are organised in three parts: scriptural, contextual and theological. The central question being addressed is: how do Christians living in contexts, where Islam is a majority or minority religion, experience, express or think of the Cross? This is, therefore, an exercise in listening. As the contexts from where these engagements arise are varied, the papers in drawing scriptural, contextual and theological reflections offer a cross-section of Christian thinking about Jesus and the Cross.

David Emmanuuel Singh (ed.)
Jesus and the Incarnation
Reflections of Christians from Islamic Contexts
2011/978-1-870345-90-3

In the dialogue of Christians with Muslims nothing is more fundamental than the Cross, the Incarnation and the Resurrection of Jesus. This book contains voices of Christians living in various 'Islamic contexts' and reflecting on the Incarnation of Jesus. The aim of these reflections is constructive and the hope is that the papers weaved around the notion of 'the Word' will not only promote dialogue among Christians on the roles of the Person and the Book, but, also, create a positive environment for their conversations with Muslim neighbours.

Sung-wook Hong
Naming God in Korea
The Case of Protestant Christianity
2008 / 978-1-870345-66-8 / xiv + 170pp

Since Christianity was introduced to Korea more than a century ago, one of the most controversial issue has been the Korean term for the Christian 'God'. This issue is not merely about naming the Christian God in Korean language, but it relates to the question of theological contextualization—the relationship between the gospel and culture—and the question of Korean Christian identity. This book examines the theological contextualization of the concept of 'God' in the contemporary Korean context and applies the translatability of Christianity to that context. It also demonstrates the nature of the gospel in relation to cultures, i.e., the universality of the gospel expressed in all human cultures.

Hubert van Beek (ed.)
Revisioning Christian Unity
The Global Christian Forum
2009 / 978-1-870345-74-3 / xx + 288pp

This book contains the records of the Global Christian Forum gathering held in Limuru near Nairobi, Kenya, on 6 – 9 November 2007 as well as the papers presented at that historic event. Also included are a summary of the Global Christian Forum process from its inception until the 2007 gathering and the reports of the evaluation of the process that was carried out in 2008.

Paul Hang-Sik Cho
Eschatology and Ecology
Experiences of the Korean Church
2010 / 978-1-870345-75-0/ 260pp (approx)

This book raises the question of why Korean people, and Korean Protestant Christians in particular, pay so little attention (in theory or practice) to ecological issues. The author argues that there is an important connection (or elective affinity) between this lack of attention and the other-worldly eschatology that is so dominant within Korean Protestant Christianity. Dispensational premillennialism, originally imported by American missionaries, resonated with traditional religious beliefs in Korea and soon came to dominate much of Korean Protestantism. This book argues that this, of all forms of millennialism, is the most damaging to ecological concerns.

Dietrich Werner, David Esterline, Namsoon Kang, Joshva Raja (eds.)
The Handbook of Theological Education in World Christianity
Theological Perspectives, Ecumenical Trends, Regional Surveys
2010 / 978-1-870345-80-4/ 759pp

This major reference work is the first ever comprehensive study of Theological Education in Christianity of its kind. With contributions from over 90 international scholars and church leaders, it aims to be easily accessible across denominational, cultural, educational, and geographic boundaries. The Handbook will aid international dialogue and networking among theological educators, institutions, and agencies. The major objectives of the text are (1) to provide introductory surveys on selected issues and themes in global theological education; (2) to provide regional surveys on key developments, achievements, and challenges in theological education; (3) to provide an overview of theological education for each of the major denominational / confessional traditions; and (4) to provide a reference section with an up-to-date list of the regional associations of theological institutions and other resources.

David Emmanuel Singh & Bernard C Farr (eds.)

Christianity and Education

Shaping of Christian Context in Thinking

2010 / 978-1-870345-81-1/ 244pp (approx)

Christianity and Education is a collection of papers published in *Transformation: An International Journal of Holistic Mission Studies* over a period of 15 years. It brings to life some of the papers that lay buried in shelves and in disparate volumes of *Transformation,* under a single volume for theological libraries, students and teachers. The articles here represent a spectrum of Christian thinking addressing issues of institutional development for theological education, theological studies in the context of global mission, contextually aware/informed education, and academies which deliver such education, methodologies and personal reflections.

J.Andrew Kirk

Civilisations in Conflict?

Islam, the West and Christian Faith 2011- 978-1-870345-71-2

Samuel Huntington's thesis, which argues that there appear to be aspects of Islam that could be on a collision course with the politics and values of Western societies, has provoked much controversy. The purpose of this study is to offer a particular response to Huntington's thesis by making a comparison between the origins of Islam and Christianity; the two religions that can be said to have shaped, in contrasting ways, the history of the Western world. The early history of each faith continues to have a profound impact on the way in which their respective followers have interpreted the relationship between faith and political life. The book draws significant, critical and creative conclusions from the analysis for contemporary intercultural understanding, and in particular for the debate about the justification of violence for political and religious ends.

REGNUM STUDIES IN MISSION
Series Listing

Kwame Bediako

Theology and Identity

The Impact of Culture upon Christian Thought
in the Second Century and in Modern Africa

1992 / 1-870345-10-X / xviii + 508pp

The author examines the question of Christian identity in the context of the Graeco–Roman culture of the early Roman Empire. He then addresses the modern African predicament of quests for identity and integration.

Christopher Sugden

Seeking the Asian Face of Jesus

The Practice and Theology of Christian Social Witness
in Indonesia and India 1974–1996

1997 / 1-870345-26-6 / xx + 496pp

This study focuses on contemporary holistic mission with the poor in India and Indonesia combined with the call to transformation of all life in Christ with micro-credit enterprise schemes. 'The literature on contextual theology now has a new standard to rise to' – Lamin Sanneh (Yale University, USA).

Hwa Yung

Mangoes or Bananas?

The Quest for an Authentic Asian Christian Theology

1997 / 1-870345-25-8 / xii + 274pp

Asian Christian thought remains largely captive to Greek dualism and Enlightenment rationalism because of the overwhelming dominance of Western culture. Authentic contextual Christian theologies will emerge within Asian Christianity with a dual recovery of confidence in culture and the gospel.

Keith E. Eitel

Paradigm Wars

The Southern Baptist International Mission Board Faces the Third Millennium

1999 / 1-870345-12-6 / x + 140pp

The International Mission Board of the Southern Baptist Convention is the largest denominational mission agency in North America. This volume chronicles the historic and contemporary forces that led to the IMB's recent extensive reorganization, providing the most comprehensive case study to date of a historic mission agency restructuring to continue its mission purpose into the twenty-first century more effectively.

Samuel Jayakumar

Dalit Consciousness and Christian Conversion

Historical Resources for a Contemporary Debate

1999 / 81-7214-497-0 / xxiv + 434pp

(Published jointly with ISPCK)

The main focus of this historical study is social change and transformation among the Dalit Christian communities in India. Historiography tests the evidence in the light of the conclusions of the modern Dalit liberation theologians.

Vinay Samuel and Christopher Sugden (eds.)

Mission as Transformation

A Theology of the Whole Gospel

1999 / 0870345133/ 522pp

This book brings together in one volume twenty five years of biblical reflection on mission practice with the poor from around the world. The approach of holistic mission, which integrates proclamation, evangelism, church planting and social transformation seamlessly as a whole, has been adopted since 1983 by most evangelical development agencies, most indigenous mission agencies and many Pentecostal churches. This volume helps anyone understand how evangelicals, struggling to unite evangelism and social action, found their way in the last twenty five years to the biblical view of mission in which God calls all human beings to love God and their neighbour; never creating a separation between the two.

Christopher Sugden

Gospel, Culture and Transformation

2000 / 1-870345-32-0 / viii + 152pp

A Reprint, with a New Introduction, of Part Two of Seeking the Asian Face of Jesus

Gospel, Culture and Transformation explores the practice of mission especially in relation to transforming cultures and communities. - 'Transformation is to enable God's vision of society to be actualised in all relationships: social, economic and spiritual, so that God's will may be reflected in human society and his love experienced by all communities, especially the poor.'

Bernhard Ott

Beyond Fragmentation: Integrating Mission and Theological Education

A Critical Assessment of some Recent Developments in Evangelical Theological Education

2001 / 1-870345-14-2 / xxviii + 382pp

Beyond Fragmentation is an enquiry into the development of Mission Studies in evangelical theological education in Germany and German-speaking Switzerland between 1960 and 1995. The author undertakes a detailed examination of the paradigm shifts which have taken place in recent years in both the theology of mission and the understanding of theological education.

Gideon Githiga

The Church as the Bulwark against Authoritarianism

Development of Church and State Relations in Kenya, with Particular Reference to the Years after Political Independence 1963-1992

2002 / 1-870345-38-x / xviii + 218pp

'All who care for love, peace and unity in Kenyan society will want to read this careful history by Bishop Githiga of how Kenyan Christians, drawing on the Bible, have sought to share the love of God, bring his peace and build up the unity of the nation, often in the face of great difficulties and opposition.' Canon Dr Chris Sugden, Oxford Centre for Mission Studies.

Myung Sung-Hoon, Hong Young-Gi (eds.)

Charis and Charisma

David Yonggi Cho and the Growth of Yoido Full Gospel Church

2003 / 1-870345-45-2 / xxii + 218pp

This book discusses the factors responsible for the growth of the world's largest church. It expounds the role of the Holy Spirit, the leadership, prayer, preaching, cell groups and creativity in promoting church growth. It focuses on God's grace (charis) and inspiring leadership (charisma) as the two essential factors and the book's purpose is to present a model for church growth worldwide.

Samuel Jayakumar

Mission Reader

Historical Models for Wholistic Mission in the Indian Context

2003 / 1-870345-42-8 / x + 250pp

(Published jointly with ISPCK)

This book is written from an evangelical point of view revalidating and reaffirming the Christian commitment to wholistic mission. The roots of the 'wholistic mission' combining 'evangelism and social concerns' are to be located in the history and tradition of Christian evangelism in the past; and the civilizing purpose of evangelism is compatible with modernity as an instrument in nation building.

Bob Robinson

Christians Meeting Hindus

An Analysis and Theological Critique of the Hindu-Christian Encounter in India

2004 / 1-870345-39-8 / xviii + 392pp

This book focuses on the Hindu-Christian encounter, especially the intentional meeting called dialogue, mainly during the last four decades of the twentieth century, and specifically in India itself.

Gene Early

Leadership Expectations

How Executive Expectations are Created and Used in a Non-Profit Setting

2005 / 1-870345-30-4 / xxiv + 276pp

The author creates an Expectation Enactment Analysis to study the role of the Chancellor of the University of the Nations-Kona, Hawaii. This study is grounded in the field of managerial work, jobs, and behaviour and draws on symbolic interactionism, role theory, role identity theory and enactment theory. The result is a conceptual framework for developing an understanding of managerial roles.

Tharcisse Gatwa

The Churches and Ethnic Ideology in the Rwandan Crises 1900-1994

2005 / 1-870345-24-X / approx 300pp

Since the early years of the twentieth century Christianity has become a new factor in Rwandan society. This book investigates the role Christian churches played in the formulation and development of the racial ideology that culminated in the 1994 genocide.

Julie Ma

Mission Possible

Biblical Strategies for Reaching the Lost

2005 / 1-870345-37-1 / xvi + 142pp

This is a missiology book for the church which liberates missiology from the specialists for the benefit of every believer. It also serves as a textbook that is simple and friendly, and yet solid in biblical interpretation. This book links the biblical teaching to the actual and contemporary missiological settings with examples, making the Bible come alive to the reader.

Allan Anderson, Edmond Tang (eds.)

Asian and Pentecostal

The Charismatic Face of Christianity in Asia

2005 / 1-870345-43-6 / xiv + 596pp

(Published jointly with APTS Press)

This book provides a thematic discussion and pioneering case studies on the history and development of Pentecostal and Charismatic churches in the countries of South Asia, South East Asia and East Asia.

I. Mark Beaumont
Christology in Dialogue with Muslims
A Critical Analysis of Christian Presentations of Christ for Muslims from the Ninth and Twentieth Centuries
2005 / 1-870345-46-0 / xxvi + 228pp

This book analyses Christian presentations of Christ for Muslims in the most creative periods of Christian-Muslim dialogue, the first half of the ninth century and the second half of the twentieth century. In these two periods, Christians made serious attempts to present their faith in Christ in terms that take into account Muslim perceptions of him, with a view to bridging the gap between Muslim and Christian convictions.

Thomas Czövek,
Three Seasons of Charismatic Leadership
A Literary-Critical and Theological Interpretation of the Narrative of Saul, David and Solomon
2006 / 978-1-870345484 / 272pp

This book investigates the charismatic leadership of Saul, David and Solomon. It suggests that charismatic leaders emerge in crisis situations in order to resolve the crisis by the charisma granted by God. Czovek argues that Saul proved himself as a charismatic leader as long as he acted resolutely and independently from his mentor Samuel. In the author's eyes, Saul's failure to establish himself as a charismatic leader is caused by his inability to step out from Samuel's shadow.

Jemima Atieno Oluoch
The Christian Political Theology of Dr. John Henry Okullu
2006 / 1-870345-51-7 / xx + 137pp

This book reconstructs the Christian political theology of Bishop John Henry Okullu, DD, through establishing what motivated him and the biblical basis for his socio-political activities. It also attempts to reconstruct the socio-political environment that nurtured Dr Okullu's prophetic ministry.

Richard Burgess
Nigeria's Christian Revolution
The Civil War Revival and Its Pentecostal Progeny (1967-2006)
2008 / 978-1-870345-63-7 / xxii + 347pp

This book describes the revival that occurred among the Igbo people of Eastern Nigeria and the new Pentecostal churches it generated, and documents the changes that have occurred as the movement has responded to global flows and local demands. As such, it explores the nature of revivalist and Pentecostal experience, but does so against the backdrop of local socio-political and economic developments, such as decolonisation and civil war, as well as broader processes, such as modernisation and globalisation.

David Emmanuel Singh & Bernard C Farr (eds.)
Christianity and Cultures
Shaping Christian Thinking in Context
2008 / 978-1-870345-69-9 / x + 260pp

This volume marks an important milestone, the 25th anniversary of the Oxford Centre for Mission Studies (OCMS). The papers here have been exclusively sourced from Transformation, a quarterly journal of OCMS, and seek to provide a tripartite view of Christianity's engagement with cultures by focusing on the question: how is Christian thinking being formed or reformed through its interaction with the varied contexts it encounters? The subject matters include different strands of theological-missiological thinking, socio-political engagements and forms of family relationships in interaction with the host cultures.

Tormod Engelsviken, Ernst Harbakk, Rolv Olsen, Thor Strandenæs (eds.)
Mission to the World
Communicating the Gospel in the 21st Century:
Essays in Honour of Knud Jørgensen
2008 / 978-1-870345-64-4 / 472pp

Knud Jørgensen is Director of Areopagos and Associate Professor of Missiology at MF Norwegian School of Theology. This book reflects on the main areas of Jørgensen's commitment to mission. At the same time it focuses on the main frontier of mission, the world, the content of mission, the Gospel, the fact that the Gospel has to be communicated, and the context of contemporary mission in the 21st century.

Al Tizon
Transformation after Lausanne
Radical Evangelical Mission in Global-Local Perspective
2008 / 978-1-870345-68-2 / xx + 281pp

After Lausanne '74, a worldwide network of radical evangelical mission theologians and practitioners use the notion of "Mission as Transformation" to integrate evangelism and social concern together, thus lifting theological voices from the Two Thirds World to places of prominence. This book documents the definitive gatherings, theological tensions, and social forces within and without evangelicalism that led up to Mission as Transformation. And it does so through a global-local grid that points the way toward greater holistic mission in the 21st century.

Bambang Budijanto

Values and Participation

Development in Rural Indonesia

2009 / 978-1-870345-70-5 / x + 237pp

Socio-religious values and socio-economic development are inter-dependant, inter-related and are constantly changing in the context of macro political structures, economic policy, religious organizations and globalization; and micro influences such as local affinities, identity, politics, leadership and beliefs. The three Lopait communities in Central Java, Indonesia provide an excellent model of the rich and complex negotiations and interactions among all the above factors. The book argues that the comprehensive approach in understanding the socio-religious values of each local community is essential to accurately describing their respective identity which will help institutions and agencies, both governmental and non-governmental, to relate to these communities with dignity and respect.

Young-hoon Lee

The Holy Spirit Movement in Korea

Its Historical and Theological Development

2009 / 978-1-870345-67-5 / x + 174pp

This book traces the historical and theological development of the Holy Spirit Movement in Korea through six successive periods (from 1900 to the present time). These periods are characterized by repentance and revival (1900-20), persecution and suffering under Japanese occupation (1920-40), confusion and division (1940-60), explosive revival in which the Pentecostal movement played a major role in the rapid growth of Korean churches (1960-80), the movement reaching out to all denominations (1980-2000), and the new context demanding the Holy Spirit movement to open new horizons in its mission engagement (2000-). The volume also discusses the relationship between this movement and other religions such as shamanism, and looks forward to further engagement with issues of concern in wider society.

Alan R. Johnson

Leadership in a Slum

A Bangkok Case Study

2009 / 978-1-870345-71-2 xx + 238pp

This book looks at leadership in the social context of a slum in Bangkok from an angle different from traditional studies which measure well educated Thais on leadership scales derived in the West. Using both systematic data collection and participant observation, it develops a culturally preferred model as well as a set of models based in Thai concepts that reflect on-the-ground realities. This work challenges the dominance of the patron-client rubric for understanding all forms of Thai leadership and offers a view for understanding leadership rooted in local social systems, contrary to approaches that assume the universal applicability of leadership research findings across all cultural settings. It concludes by looking at the implications of the anthropological approach for those who are involved in leadership training in Thai settings and beyond.

Titre Ande

Leadership and Authority

Bula Matari and Life - Community Ecclesiology in Congo

2010 / 978-1-870345-72-9 xvii + 189pp

This book proposes that Christian theology in Africa can make significant developments if a critical understanding of the socio-political context in contemporary Africa is taken seriously. The Christian leadership in post-colonial Africa has cloned its understanding and use of authority on the Bula Matari model, which was issued from the brutality of colonialism and political absolutism in post-colonial Africa. This model has caused many problems in churches, including dysfunction, conflicts, divisions and a lack of prophetic ministry. Titre proposes a Life-Community ecclesiology for liberating authority, where leadership is a function, not a status, and 'apostolic succession' belongs to all the people of God.

Frank Kwesi Adams

Odwira and the Gospel

A Study of the Asante Odwira Festival and its Significance for Christianity in Ghana

2010 /978-1-870345-59-0

The study of the Odwira festival is the key to the understanding of Asante religious and political life in Ghana. The book explores the nature of the Odwira festival longitudinally - in pre-colonial, colonial and post-independence Ghana - and examines the Odwira ideology and its implications for understanding the Asante self-identity. The book also discusses how some elements of faith portrayed in the Odwira festival could provide a framework for Christianity to engage with Asante culture at a greater depth. Theological themes in Asante belief that have emerged from this study include the theology of sacrament, ecclesiology, eschatology, Christology and a complex concept of time. The author argues that Asante cultural identity lies at the heart of the process by which the Asante Christian faith is carried forward.

Bruce Carlton

Strategy Coordinator

Changing the Course of Southern Baptist Missions

2010 / 978-1-870345-78-1 xvii + 268pp

In 1976, the Southern Baptist Convention adopted its Bold New Thrusts in Foreign Missions with the overarching goal of sharing the gospel with every person in the world by the year 2000. The formation of Cooperative Services International (CSI) in 1985 and the assigning of the first non-residential missionary (NRM) in 1987 demonstrated the Foreign Mission Board's (now International Mission Board) commitment to take the gospel message to countries that restricted traditional missionary presence and to people groups identified as having little or no access to the gospel. Carlton traces the historical development along with an analysis of the key components of the paradigm and its significant impact on Southern Baptists' missiology.

Julie Ma & Wonsuk Ma
Mission in the Spirit:
Towards a Pentecostal/Charismatic Missiology
2010 / 978-1-870345-84-2 xx + 312pp

The book explores the unique contribution of Pentecostal/Charismatic mission from the beginning of the twentieth century. The first part considers the theological basis of Pentecostal/Charismatic mission thinking and practice. Special attention is paid to the Old Testament, which has been regularly overlooked by the modern Pentecostal/Charismatic movements. The second part discusses major mission topics with contributions and challenges unique to Pentecostal/Charismatic mission. The book concludes with a reflection on the future of this powerful missionary movement. As the authors served as Korean missionaries in Asia, often their missionary experiences in Asia are reflected in their discussions.

S. Hun Kim & Wonsuk Ma (eds.)
Korean Diaspora and Christian Mission
2011-978-1-870345-89-7

As a 'divine conspiracy' for Missio Dei, the global phenomenon of people on the move has shown itself to be invaluable. In 2004 two significant documents concerning Diaspora were introduced, one by the Filipino International Network and the other by the Lausanne Committee for World Evangelization. These have created awareness of the importance of people on the move for Christian mission. Since then, Korean Diaspora has conducted similar research among Korean missions, resulting in this book. It is unique as the first volume researching Korean missions in Diasporic contexts, appraising and evaluating these missions with practical illustrations, and drawing on a wide diversity of researchers.

GENERAL REGNUM TITLES

Vinay Samuel, Chris Sugden (eds.)
The Church in Response to Human Need
1987 / 1870345045 / xii+268pp

Philip Sampson, Vinay Samuel, Chris Sugden (eds.)
Faith and Modernity
Essays in modernity and post-modernity
1994 / 1870345177 / 352pp

Klaus Fiedler
The Story of Faith Missions
1994 / 0745926878 / 428pp

Douglas Peterson
Not by Might nor by Power
A Pentecostal Theology of Social Concern in Latin America
1996 / 1870345207 / xvi+260pp

David Gitari
In Season and Out of Season
Sermons to a Nation
1996 / 1870345118 / 155pp

David. W. Virtue
A Vision of Hope
The Story of Samuel Habib
1996 / 1870345169 / xiv+137pp

Everett A Wilson
Strategy of the Spirit
J.Philip Hogan and the Growth of the Assemblies of God Worldwide, 1960 - 1990
1997 /1870345231/214

Murray Dempster, Byron Klaus, Douglas Petersen (eds.)
The Globalization of Pentecostalism
A Religion Made to Travel
1999 / 1870345290 / xvii+406pp

Peter Johnson, Chris Sugden (eds.)
Markets, Fair Trade and the Kingdom of God
Essays to Celebrate Traidcraft's 21st Birthday
2001 / 1870345193 / xii+155pp

Robert Hillman, Coral Chamberlain, Linda Harding
Healing & Wholeness
Reflections on the Healing Ministry
2002 / 978-1- 870345-35- 4 / xvii+283pp

David Bussau, Russell Mask
Christian Microenterprise Development
An Introduction
2003 / 1870345282 / xiii+142pp

David Singh
Sainthood and Revelatory Discourse
An Examination of the Basis for the Authority of Bayan in Mahdawi Islam
2003 / 8172147285 / xxiv+485pp

For the up-to-date listing of the Regnum books see www.ocms.ac.uk/regnum

regnum

Regnum Books International

Regnum is an Imprint of The Oxford Centre for Mission Studies
St. Philip and St. James Church
Woodstock Road
Oxford, OX2 6HR
Web: www.ocms.ac.uk/regnum